بسم الله الرحمن الرحيم

ISLAMIC ART AND ARCHITECTURE

Henri Stierlin

Photographs by Anne and Henri Stierlin

Part I HISTORY AND ART

pp. 1 and 6 Detail of a tile mosaic in the Darb-i Imam Mausoleum, Isfahan.

pp. 2–3 The dome of the Mosque of the Imam, Isfahan.

pp. 4–5 The Hasht Bihisht, or Pavilion of the Eight Paradises, Isfahan.

p. 7 The western *iwan* of the Mosque of the Imam, Isfahan, reflected in the ablutions basin in the courtyard.

First published in the United Kingdom in 2002 by Thames & Hudson Ltd, 181A High Holborn, London WC1V 7QX

First published in hardcover in the United States of America in 2002 by Thames & Hudson Inc., 500 Fifth Avenue, New York, New York 10110

Graphic project
Clara Zanotti

British Library Cataloguing-in-Publication Data
A catalogue record for this book is available from the British Library

Library of Congress Catalog Card Number 2002102346

ISBN 0-500-51100-4

Printed in Italy

Part I HISTORY AND ART

The Spread of the Persian Style from Isfahan to the Taj Mahal

For writers in the 18th and 19th centuries, dazzled by their experience of Isfahan, Iran was a vision of splendour and elegance, refinement and magnificence, and they conflated it with Persia of legendary fame. It was a world apart, poised between the West and China, between the Arab world and Central Asia, bathed in shimmering light, where turquoise-tiled domes glittered beyond the branches of shady trees. And with the thought of Iran comes the thought of cities with names to set one dreaming – Kerman, Yazd, Tabriz, Shiraz, Bam. It was is a world of exoticism, beauty and splendour, whose influence extended over the surrounding regions as far as Uzbekistan and India.

IMAGES OF IRAN

In Iran, the pilgrim in search of beauty finds a land that includes oases set in dazzling white deserts, as well as snow-capped peaks from which life-giving waters flow down to be skilfully managed by industrious people who live in the foothills at the edge of the plains of salt. The traveller intent on discovering the secrets of an art of great splendour gradually becomes aware of the originality of the Persian style, which spread out beyond the borders of present-day Iran and rapidly conquered vast areas, imposing upon them with remarkable consistency the thought, language, and spiritual outlook of Iran. The aesthetic culture of this region is quite distinct from that of its Arab, Armenian, Ottoman and Hindu neighbours. It is both traditional and intensely vital. From pre-Islamic times onward, Iran has been a land of great empires – the Achaemenids, of whom Alexander the Great saw himself as the heir, the Seleucids, the Parthians, and the Sasanians.

The conquest of Iran by Islam came when the country had been disastrously weakened by endless struggles with the Byzantine Empire. A wholly unexpected adversary, from the Arabian peninsula, took advantage of the exhaustion of the two opponents to impose its own rule. After their victory at Nahavand in 642, the Arab tribes occupied the country. With them they brought a new faith, Islam, which had been preached in Mecca and Medina by the Prophet Muhammad, and was based on the Pentateuch, the Five Books of Moses in the Old Testament – which were the basis of Judaism and Christianity too. Islam was introduced into Iran in the second half of the 7th century, and strengthened its hold in the 8th and 9th centuries. Iran became a Muslim country. Following on the Arab conquest, in 685 the Arabic language – vehicle of the Word of the Prophet – was imposed on the administration, the law, and the army. The Persian language, Farsi, now served only for poetry and literature. Between 706 and 715, Arab battalions moved northeast and captured Transoxiana, Khwarazm and Farghana.

Through its national bard, Firdawsi (932–1020), however, Iran began to recover a sense of its own past, and since the 10th century its national consciousness has gone on with increasing strength, combining native traditions with infusions from Islam.

Throughout succeeding centuries, the presence of powerful foreign rulers – Seljuq Turks, Mongols and Timurids – did not affect Iran's distinctive character, since these nomadic or semi-nomadic newcomers were rapidly acculturated. They took over and assimilated the essence of the art and architecture, and also of the spirit, of the Persians, who unlike them spoke an Indo-European language and had lived a permanently settled existence for millennia.

TIME AND PLACE

This overview of the artistic heritage of Iran is concerned with the artistic flowering that followed the Islamization of the people: our story must therefore begin in the 7th century. But evidence is scarce from the first centuries of

Islam, and no clear picture of the arts emerges until the time of Firdawsi, whose Shah-nameh, the 'national' epic, is concerned with the mythical origins of the first rulers, with the religion of Zoroaster, and with the romance of Alexander (Iskandar), before going on to praise the Sasanian dynasty.

The art we shall be looking at falls chiefly between the year 900 and the end of the reign of Nadir Shah in the mid-18th century, with a few excursions into the period of the Qajars, which lasted until 1925. The picture that emerges throughout this long millennium is one of profound vitality.

A problem, when considering Persian art, is to decide on its boundaries. The area within the frontiers of the modern state is the heart and historic centre, but it is no more than the core of a much vaster whole. The same aesthetic is manifest in regions such as present-day Afghanistan and Uzbekistan, which at various times formed part of the Persian world. It is in the northeast that the boundaries are hardest to draw: Khwarazm, Transoxiana, Turkestan and Farghana lie at the outer edge of the world of sedentary life, where it confronts the nomadic tribes of the steppes. But other territories, even farther away, must be considered when one is looking for forms derived from the same inspiration – the Indian subcontinent at the time of the Delhi Sultans and the Mughals.

What are the reasons for such geographical vagueness? How is it that the story of Persian art includes lands so far away? And why is it that capital cities of ancient Persia are now outside the boundaries of Iran? Among outlying cities of Islamic Iran one thinks of Bukhara and Samarqand, and of Herat, Merv and Kabul; among ancient cities, Ctesiphon, on the Tigris River, which was the residence of the Sasanian kings.

SEDENTARY POPULATIONS AND NOMADS

Ever since its beginnings, Iran has been a prey to forces that made it difficult to fix permanent boundaries. These were the nomads, who arrived in recurrent and unpredictable waves to crash against the apparently established 'frontiers'. There they harried the sedentary populations, spreading death and destruction through cultivated areas whose wealth and granaries were a powerful attraction to the horsemen of the steppes in times of famine. The eternal conflict between nomads and sedentary people is a key factor in the history of Iran. From earliest times onward, at the slightest sign of weakness in the central power, Central Asian nomads infiltrated peaceful regions or overwhelmed then with terrible brutality, conquering brilliant cities and laying them waste, destroying everything as they went.

The names of Chinghiz Khan and Timur-i Lang – Genghis Khan and Tamerlane – still resound in these ancient places, and horror is still aroused at the thought of the pyramids of heads and piles of corpses left behind by the wild hordes from the Altai or the borders of Siberia.

The gulf between these very different ways of life is unbridgeable. On one side are the nomads, who follow their flocks across vast pasturelands in response to the changes in climate and rainfall that determine the yield of unirrigated land. On the other side are the farmers, in possession of land that they have improved through constant effort, and who have granaries to tide them over bad harvests. For the nomads, perpetually on the move, power is expressed through the horde as it moves through space. For the farmers, the only conceivable source of power is ownership of land. How can these diametrically opposed concepts, tribe versus land, the source of so many mis-understandings, confrontations and wars, be reconciled? For the sedentary communities, the need to own land, and to protect it with fortresses and walled cities, led to a great appropriation of territory, and tended to protect their stores of food from the envy of the nomads. The nomads, on the other hand, had no resources not provided by their animals, and carried no reserves of food, since these would hamper their mobility. The result was constant antagonism. The split was exacerbated when climatic change caused famines, putting vast numbers of people on the move.

The history of Iran is bound up with the ebb and flow of power. Only a centralized state, a strong kingdom, can defend its borders and sponsor great artistic creations. The centre of gravity may shift. It is to these factors that Persian architecture owes its endless diversity and vitality, of which we shall see many expressions.

THE ZONES OF IRANIAN INFLUENCE

Iran is one of the great world centres of artistic creation. In antiquity, and again during the Islamic period, its position between the West and China helped to make it one of the great sources of art and thought. Iran's originality is such that it ceaselessly invented new forms, and its influence extended over immense regions.

As we have already seen, 'Iran' as a territory has multiple meanings. But broadly one can see it as three regions. First there is modern Iran, within its international frontiers; then there is 'greater Iran', comprising the further areas that formed part of the Persian world at various times in history; and finally there are the areas, often very remote from the core, that show Persian influence.

It is worth looking more closely at these three zones, in order fully to understand the cultural influence of the Persian people under Islam. Modern Iran exists within borders fixed in 1907. It is a vast territory – 1,650,000 square kilometres (637,000 square miles), a little more than five times the surface area of Italy. To the west lie Turkey and Iraq; to the south, the Persian Gulf and the Gulf of Oman; to the east, Pakistan and Afghanistan; to the north, Turkmenistan and Uzbekistan (formerly part of the Soviet Union) and the Caspian Sea; and to the northwest, Azerbaijan and Armenia.

'Greater Iran' is defined as the zone over which Iran long held nominal sway, and on which it impressed the mark of its culture. The territories concerned all belonged at one time or another to a Persian kingdom or empire: examples are Khwarazm, Transoxiana, Farghana and Afghanistan. The Achaemenid and Sasanian dynasties had extended their power over immense areas, from India to Egypt and from Central Asia to Arabia, but 'greater Iran' is not so vast: it is an intermediate area, between the modern state and its farthest historical limits. It extends beyond the modern frontiers to the east as the west and north. Some of the areas concerned were Persian for a long time, such as Afghanistan – which only became independent in the middle of the 18th century – and the irrigated plains of Transoxiana (present-day Turkmenistan and Uzbekistan). Before the advent of Islam, the lands on the banks of the Oxus and Jaxartes (Amu Darya and Syr Darya) Rivers were known as Bactria and Sogdiana; here the presence of nomadic tribes contributed to the creation and disintegration of fluctuating political entities, which sometimes became major centres of Persian civilization. To the southwest, the Mesopotamian plain and the delta of the Karun River, on the Persian Gulf, were for several centuries part of an entity controlled by the rulers of Iran, both during the Sasanian period and at various times in the Islamic period.

Beyond modern Iran and 'greater Iran' lies the area of Persian expansion in the vast plains of the Indian peninsula. Already in prehistoric times tribal peoples had reached the Indus and Ganges basins, finding their way through the mountains of Afghanistan across the Khyber Pass along what were to become established migration routes. They contributed to the settlement of the subcontinent by Indo-Europeans, who pushed the indigenous peoples south as they advanced. The same thing happened again in the Achaemenid period and under the Greek and Sasanian kings. The advent of Islam did not put an end to it. First came the incursions of the Ghurid Sultans, then those of the Ghaznavids, when there were significant population movements; these Turkish and Mongol invaders would sweep down through the valley of Kandahar and capture rich spoils. Eventually they settled in the region of Delhi, founded an independent capital, and imported the thought, religion and arts of Muslim Iran.

With the arrival of the Timurid Babur in the 16th century a great empire arose in India, that of the Mughals. The court spoke Persian (Farsi) and promoted Persian forms in architecture, ornament, manuscript painting, carpets, etc. Here, in this vast area subject to so many diverse influences, the most remarkable qualities of Persian aesthetics and thought took root and flowered – in calligraphy, language, literature, town planning, buildings, plastic arts and decoration. In India the artistic vocabulary of the heartland of Iran and of its outlying regions found perfect expression.

It is important to make clear that while we are concerned to show the spread of Persian forms throughout the Middle East and as far as the Indian subcontinent, we have absolutely no interest in advancing any political/cultural claims. We have no wish to evoke a precedent that would 'justify' some present-day action on the lines of that of Nadir Shah (1739), or of stirring up any kind of 'Pan-Persianism'. What we are concerned to do here is to stress the vitality of a cultural movement and the vigour of a great civilization, to investigate a region poised between Europe and China that occupies a major place in the history of aesthetics and thought – a place that has not always been fully recognized.

THE PERSIAN STYLE

Thus in the Islamic period, between the 10th and the 18th or 19th centuries, there was a vast artistic community in this part of the world that was characterized by a generalized use of the 'Persian style.'

That common aesthetic language is the subject of this book. We shall attempt to trace the unifying features of Persian modes of expression that affected architecture and decoration, manuscript painting, calligraphy, and carpets.

Throughout the vast cultural 'empire' of Iran a form of Islamic art grew up that is extraordinarily unified. It isindependent both of the political orientation and the religious affiliation (Sunni or Shi'ite) of the patrons; and it is also independent of the ethnic origins of the peoples and their leaders who made use of it, be they native Persians or rulers from Turkish or Mongol tribes.

This 'Persian' art finds celebratory expression in mosques, *madrasas*, palaces, fortresses and mausoleums, in masterpieces of poetry, in manuscript painting, in great works of calligraphy, in precious carpets and in sumptuous ceramics. With the originality of its buildings, of their spaces and of their multi-coloured tile decoration, and the refined taste and profound feeling for the natural environment expressed in the 'paradise gardens', the heritage of Iran is a unique treasure. Its creators belong among the world's greatest artists.

An Appendix on 'The Origins of Muslim Iran: History and Culture 622–900' is designed to illuminate the reader's understanding of this complex world where many different cultures came together to form the 'Persian style' that is the subject of this book. There, on pp. 269–96, will be found an overview of the early centuries of Islamic civilization, which sets out the main stages in the expansion of Islam from Arabia, as well as historical and religious turning-points in its development, and also a description of the early buildings constructed under the Umayyad and 'Abbasid dynasties.

SUNNISM AND SHI'ISM

Islam was not long able to enjoy the fine unanimity that its founder hoped would characterize the new faith. Muhammad himself was the victim of intrigues and factionalism; and as doctrine was formalized various currents that were often radically opposed to one another emerged and gathered supporters. There is no end to the sects that arose on the basis of various commentaries on the Qur'an and on the tradition as handed down in the hadith.

The codification of the Sunna (the principles of the Islamic community) was a slow process, marked by the establishment of four ways in the schools of law and theology: the Hanafite, Malikite, Safaite and Hanbalite.

As with the clashes that marked the councils in the early centuries of Christianity, quarrels between theologians did not take long to arise. The Kharijite and Shi'ite movements arose in 656, in connection with the determination of the Prophet's legitimate successor. The choice between Ali (Muhammad's cousin and son-in-law) and Mu'awiya (founder of the Umayyad dynasty) proved irresolvable. The strict, puritanical and egalitarian Kharijites, supporters of Mu'awiya, lost their significance as the power of the Caliphate was progressively diluted under the 'Abbasids; but the the Shi'ites, the partisans of Ali, are still a force today.

The result was a deep schism between the 'orthodox' adherents of Sunnism, who comprised the majority of Muslims, and the Shi'ites, who constituted a 'rebellious' minority. The irreconcilable difference between the two communities concerned the designation of the Caliph, and involved the establishment of principles to govern the handing on of power after the death of the Prophet.

The Sunnis believed that the leader of the Islamic community should be the most able man, and the expatriates from Mecca chose Abu Bakr, thus eliminating the close relatives of Muhammad. To this Ali objected, and he did not change his position when the first caliphs were appointed. He and his supporters, the Shi'ites, refused to recognize the legitimacy of the Umayyads and 'Abbasids. In their opinion, the leader must, of necessity, be a member of the Prophet's family.

Ali was the husband of Muhammad's daughter, Fatima, and it was his role to comment on and interpret the words in the Qur'an. Only the descendants of the Prophet, the Imams, could be legitimate successors and interpreters of the founding texts of Islam. The dramatic death of Ali and the martyrdom of Husayn and many of his descendants were followed by the death or 'occultation' of the twelfth Imam, the 'hidden Imam' (Muhammad al-Muntazar or al-Mahdi al-Hujjah). For Shi'ites, this closed the cycle of the successors and martyrs condemned by the 'Abbasid Caliph al-Mansur (754–775) and brought about the pleroma, the completion of the number of the Imams. Those holy figures – along with their descendents, the Imamzadeh – are the objects of intense veneration by the Shi'ite faithful. Imamite Shi'ism counts twelve Imams, and is known as the 'Twelver' sect, as opposed to the 'Sevener' sect of the Ismailites, for whom there were only seven Imams.

The Shi'ites were persecuted by the Muslim majority and suffered many martyrs. They often had to live in hiding, and to endure the oppression of their opponents, and this led them to surround themselves with mystery, to live a secret life, and to develop an esoteric religion with an emphasis on the arcane that Henri Corbin has termed the 'gnosis of Islam'.

THE POSITION OF TURKEY

The present study ranges from Tabriz to Agra, and includes in addition to Iran proper sites in Uzbekistan, allusions to Afghanistan, the cities of Lahore and Multan in Pakistan, and the India of the Delhi Sultanate, the Mughals and the rulers of of Rajasthan.

This is a vast area, but it does not include Turkey, whether European or Anatolian. That does not mean that Turkey was impervious to the 'Persian style'; on the contrary, its influence can be felt in several areas, particularly in carpets, in Iznik ceramics, in manuscript painting, and in a few buildings that display the courtyard plan with four iwans.

In the 11th and 12th centuries, Seljuq Turkish tribes spent time in Iran before Sultan Alp Arslan resumed his march to the west. But when they reached Asia Minor the Turks came into contact with the Roman-Byzantine world, and that exerted an even stronger influence on their art than that of Iran. This is particularly clear in the case of Turkish mosques: with their forms in which covered spaces

pp. 14–15 Map showing the extent of the influence of Persian art, from present-day Iran to Uzbekistan, Afghanistan, Pakistan, and the provinces of Punjab and Rajasthan in India.

are more important than courtyards, and with their stone rather than brick construction, they clearly owe more to Christian than to Persian sources.

Neither the Suleymaniye in Istanbul nor the Selimiye in Edirne displays any Persian influence except in a few decorative details. Much of Arabic-Persian culture was assimilated by the Seljuqs and later by the Ottomans, but the architectural concept of Islamic Turkey is radically different from that of the peoples more profoundly influenced by Iran.

pp. 16–17 Two openings in the gallery round the courtyard of the Mosque of the Imam in Isfahan: the lovely motifs of the glazed tiles or kashi, which cover the façade with scrolling motifs that are both repetitive and varied, provide permanent vegetation around the ablutions basin.

pp. 18–19 Florid decoration on a wing of the Gulistan or 'Rose Garden' Palace in Tehran, an example of late Persian art created under the Qajar dynasty by Agha Muhammad Shah (1742–97). The two lions, which symbolize the sun, come from the bestiary of the Timurids of Samarkand.

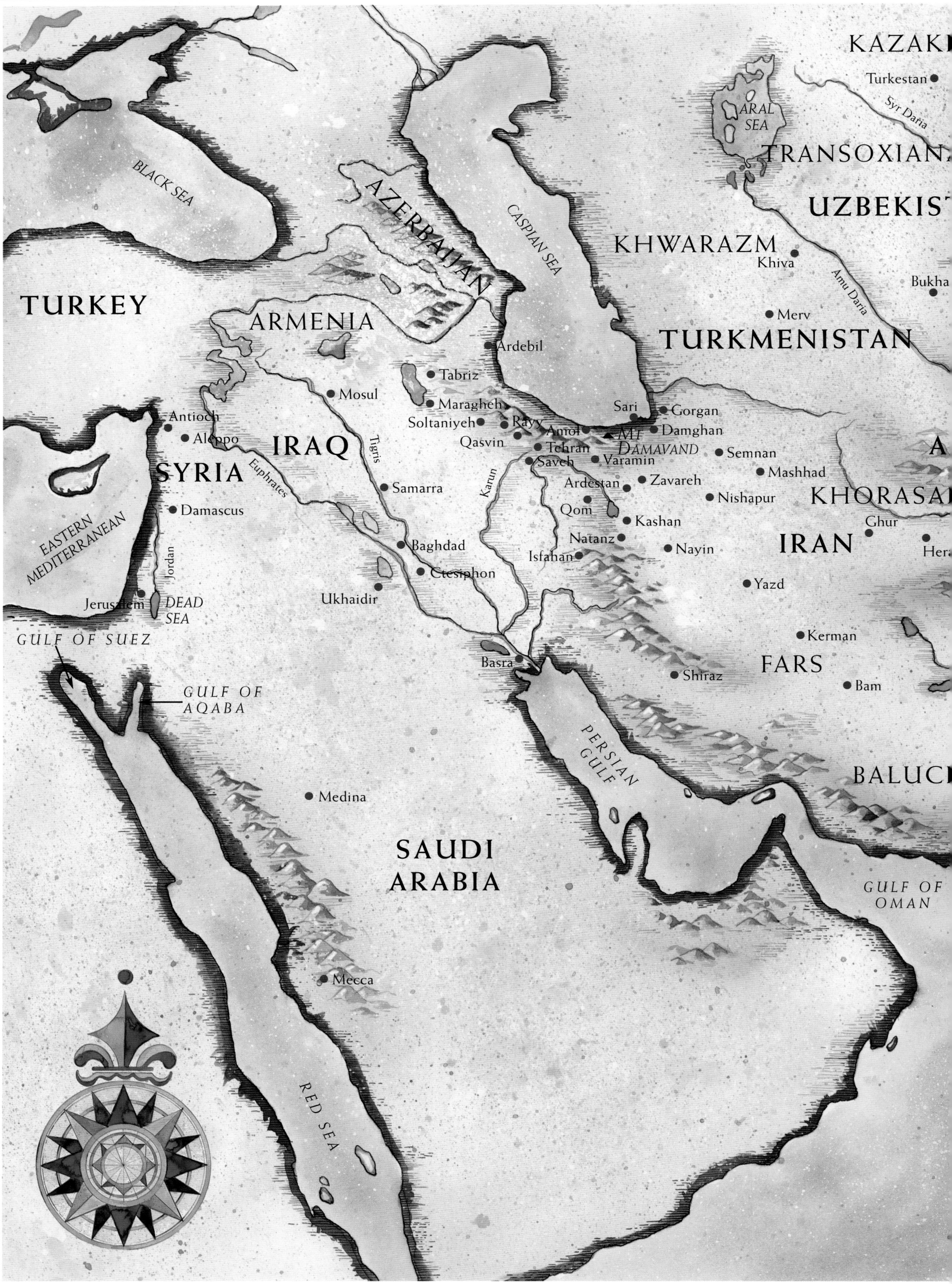

KAZAK
Turkestan
Syr Daria
ARAL SEA
TRANSOXIAN
UZBEKIST
BLACK SEA
AZERBAIJAN
CASPIAN SEA
KHWARAZM
Khiva
Amu Daria
Bukha
TURKEY
ARMENIA
Merv
TURKMENISTAN
Ardebil
Tabriz
Mosul
Maragheh
Sari
Gorgan
Antioch
Soltaniyeh
Rayy
Amol
Damghan
Aleppo
IRAQ
Tigris
Qasvin
MT DAMAVAND
Tehran
Semnan
Saveh
Varamin
SYRIA
Euphrates
Mashhad
Karun
Ardestan
Zavareh
Samarra
Nishapur
KHORASA
Damascus
Qom
Kashan
Ghur
EASTERN MEDITERRANEAN
Natanz
IRAN
Baghdad
Nayin
Jordan
Isfahan
Ctesiphon
Yazd
Jerusalem
DEAD SEA
Ukhaidir
GULF OF SUEZ
Kerman
Basra
FARS
Shiraz
Bam
GULF OF AQABA
PERSIAN GULF
BALUC
Medina
SAUDI ARABIA
GULF OF OMAN
Mecca
RED SEA

TAN
LAKE BALKHASH
Talas
FARGHANA
N
Tashkent
Andizhan
TIAN SHAN
TURFAN DEPRESSION
TARIM BASIN
Samarqand
Shakhrisabz
Balkh
PAMIR
GHANISTAN
HINDU KUSH
CHINA
Kabul
Jam
Ghazna
Kandahar
Indus
HIMALAYA
PAKISTAN
Chenab
Lahore
Multan
Sutlej
Amritsar
Panipat
Delhi
Amber
Jumna
Jaipur
Ganges
Ghaghra
STAN
Sikandra
Agra
Indus
RAJASTHAN
Fatehpur Sikri
Chambal
Gwalior
SIND
Brahmaputra
BENGAL
INDIA
Hyderabad
Gulbarga
ARABIAN SEA
GULF OF BENGAL

1

THE REBIRTH OF IRAN

The defeat of the Sasanians by Arab troops and the occupation of Iran were a supreme humiliation for the Persian people, and that land of ancient civilization and high culture remained in a state of shock for almost two centuries. After the collapse of the Sasanian regime the inhabitants experienced the introduction of a new religion, Islam, which replaced the Zoroastrian cult practiced since the time of the Achaemenid dynasty.

With the spread of the message of the Prophet came the Arabization of the people. Nevertheless, the requirement to speak Arabic, the language of the Qur'an, proved more difficult to impose in Iran than in other territories the Muslims had conquered. In Egypt, Syria and Iraq, and throughout North Africa, there had never been any serious resistance to the Arabic script or the Arabic language. The difference lay in the fact that in the lands conquered by Islam in the Eastern Empire the inhabitants had had their local languages, but they had also had to use Greek or Latin. This was true in the old Hellenized kingdoms of the Near East, where Aramaic existed alongside Greek, and both served to spread the message of Christianity. Latin was the language of the army and the law, especially during the reign of Justinian. But neither Greek nor Latin had been a native language in the regions conquered by the Muslims. In Iran, on the other hand, the language of culture was ancient and well-established: the *Avesta* attributed to Zoroaster, and the Pahlavi literature that began under the Sasanians, had their roots in a very ancient Indo-European past. It is true that not much survives that predates the arrival of Islam: much was lost through invasion and wars, and Zoroastrian writings are extremely rare.

ZOROASTRIANISM AND FIRE-WORSHIP

The dualist religion of pre-Islamic Iran goes back to a period earlier than the Achaemenids. Zoroaster is thought to have reformed this primitive cult, which centred on a fire ritual and animal sacrifices offered to the benevolent god Ahura Mazda (Ormizd), lord of wisdom. The evil divinity, Ahriman, is the adversary against whom man fights when he opposes lies. In Mazdaic eschatology, the judgment of the dead is followed by the destruction of the god of evil and of hell so that Good may triumph. Zoroaster seems to have lived between 628 and551 BCE, and hymns attributed to him are brought together in the *Avesta*, the sacred book codified in the 4th century CE. The Pahlavi script – derived from the script used to write Aramaic, which itself came down from Phoenician – was used from the 2nd century onward, and was later to influence Arabic script. Although the Persians were subjugated by invaders and intensely Arabized, they nevertheless continued to speak their own language and to preserve their own culture.

FIRDAWSI AND THE *SHAHNAMA*

After three centuries of Arab presence, the history and legends of Iran were longing to resurface: this happened through a number of texts. In 976 the poet Daqiqi began a historical work, and not long afterwards the traveller Nasir-i Khusraw (1004–88), who lived in Balkh, wrote an account in Persian of his journey through of the Arab world. Most significant of all for the Persians' rediscovery of their heritage was the great 'national' epic, the *Shahnama* (*Book of Kings*) by the poet Firdawsi (932–1020), born at Tus near Mashhad in Khorasan. In this immensely rich work – which depending on the version has between 60,000 and 80,000 couplets – he looked back to the Iran of antiquity and glorified the mythical and ancient kings, especially the heroes of the Sasanian period. The Persian language, Farsi, was revitalized. There is no question that the *Shahnama* contributed to a profound sense of renewal and to the reawakening of a Persian sense of 'national' consciousness. Its role might be compared to that of Homer's epics for the Greeks.

The growth of literature in Persian can be seen as a gesture of resistance to Iran's conquerors and an affirmation of the nation's special character. Arabic literature in the early years had drawn

p. 20, above Detail of a blue-glazed ceramic bowl from Bamiyan in Afghanistan, early 13th century. (Croisier Collection)

p. 20, below Detail of a decorative motif depicting the mythical *simurgh* bird, on a glazed tile or *kashi* with metallic highlights from Kashan, 13th century. (Cinili Kiosk Museum, Istanbul)

p. 21 Detail of a ceramic vessel from northern Iran, possibly Nishapur, early 13th century. (Foroughi Collection)

opposite, above A Persian horseman, from a manuscript of Firdawsi's *Shahnama* or *Book of Kings*.

opposite, below A stylized character in Pahlavi script, the language of the Sasanians, which was in use before the Arabic script became established in Iran. Surviving examples – this one is on a decorative stucco plaque – are rare. (Iran Bastan Museum, Tehran)

below Miniature from a 16th-century manuscript of the *Shahnama*, showing the ruler Key Kavus, seated under a canopy, ordering the capture of Rustam, the hero of the great Persian epic. (Musée de Chantilly)

on Persian traditions, and Arab scholars had translated works written in Pahlavi, as they had done with Greek in Damascus. The first texts in Persian date from the Tahirid and Saffarid dynasties in the 9th century. Persian, which is derived from the Pahlavi of the Sasanians with additional vocabulary from Arabic, became the language of the people, whereas Arabic was used at court and in the administration.

The creation of poetry in Persian sprang from the desire to express a 'national' identity, in which both the pre-Islamic heritage and the values of the people would be kept alive. It was also an expression of a refusal to take on the language of the foreign occupiers at the expense of local traditions. Rudaki, the official panegyrist of the Samanid court, celebrated the virtues and historic roots of Persian culture. Through the genres of lyric and epic poetry the past and the noble deeds of legend could be brought back to life, and the great ancestors of the Sasanian age glorified.

The poet Daqiqi had begun a 'Book of Kings', but had only written some thousand verses when he died. Firdawsi preserved that work and integrated it into his own *Shahnama*, continuing the epic theme and even retaining Daqiqi's title. Firdawsi himself spent thirty-five years on his vast poem, where thousands of couplets in an epic sweep recount the story of the Persian nation. In it we read of superhuman struggles between the Persians and the Turanis, a mythical people who lived on the frontier of Central Asia in an imaginary location corresponding to Turkestan. The story alludes to the centuries of conflict between Iran and the migrant peoples to the north-east, on the edge of the steppes. In recounting this heroic confrontation Firdawsi writes of landscapes and bloody wars, historic and legendary deeds, love songs and funeral laments, and throughout all he evokes the 'Persian soul'.

Firdawsi gave his audience a vision of man dealing with power, with politics, and with the meaning of life. With its grandiose style and its forceful and melodious language, the epic created the concept of 'Persianness', and it remained a key to the consciousness and life of Persians throughout the entire feudal period and right up to our own time.

Among the characters in the *Shahnama*, it is a surprise to find Alexander the Great featured in the lineage of the great Persian rulers, especially in the Sasanian period. The explanation is that Iran adopted him as the legitimate heir to Darius: Darab, King of Persia, the story goes, had asked Philip II of Macedon for his daughter's hand in marriage, then repudiated her; the princess gave birth to a son, called Alexander, who was to struggle unceasingly to recover his inheritance.

Steps on the Road to Revival

The first signs of Persian influence on the Arab world appeared in the time of the 'Abbasid rulers. They are manifest in the 9th-century architecture of Baghdad and Samarra, which shows knowledge of Sasanian precedent. This movement had as an ever-present aesthetic model the palace of Ctesiphon, which was seen as a paradigm to be equalled if not outdone. But it was also manifest in political events that occurred in Iran from the year 800 onwards. The revolt in Khorasan of al-Ma'mun, son of Harun ar-Rashid and a Persian woman, raised great hopes among the 'Alids or Shi'a – those who supported the Prophet's family and the legitimacy of the caliphate – and when al-Ma'mun became caliph in Baghdad Persians were indeed favoured at court: they held the levers of power in the imperial administration, and imposed the methods of government of the Sasanians.

In 830, al-Ma'mun founded a 'House of Wisdom' or 'House of Science' in Baghdad and brought together scholars and men of letters from all over the Empire. Many Persians were among them, most notably the mathematician al-Khwarizmi (780–850), who made spectacular advances in algebra concerning the solution of linear and quadratic equations and the calculation of square roots, and who introduced the decimal system based on the use of the zero. For him the caliph built an observatory, where he could work out his famous astronomical tables. Al-Ma'mun also set up libraries in Baghdad, where scholars could consult Greek philosophical and scientific works. A flourishing school of translators gave Muslim readers access to ancient sources, especially writings on arithmetic, geometry and astronomy, and medicine and pharma-cology, where developments were based on the work of Hellenistic scholars.

On a political level, al-Ma'mun went so far as to select as his successor a descendant of Husayn, 'Ali ar-Rida, who lived in Medina. The latter was summoned to Merv (in present-day Turkmenistan), where al-Ma'mun had built himself a sumptuous palace, but he was poisoned *en route* by unknown hands, with the aim of preventing reconciliation between the 'Abbasids and 'Alids. The Persian provinces achieved a certain degree of autonomy in 820, however, when Tahir ibn al-Husayn in Khorasan founded the Persian dynasty of the Tahirids, who were to rule over Iran.

The first Shi'ite emirate was established in 864, on the southern shore of the Caspian Sea. Then in 867 the emirate of the Saffarids, of Persian origin, shook off 'Abbasid control and imposed itself in Seistan, Khorasan, Fars and Sind, with its capital at Nishapur. That city flourished between the 9th and 11th centuries, particularly under the Samanids (874–999), and became especially celebrated for the production of remarkable ceramics.

The Samanid dynasty, of Persian origin, took its name from Saman Khuda, a Zoroastrian who converted to Islam in Transoxiana. His grandson overthrew the Saffarids, and founded an empire comprising Transoxiana, Khorasan, Seistan and Tabaristan, with its capital at Bukhara, before

opposite Indian emissaries arrive on elephants at the court of Sultan Mahmud of Ghazna (999–1030). This miniature illustrates a late 14th-century manuscript of the *Jami al-Tawarikh* or *Universal History* of Rashid ad-Din (1247–1318).

succumbing to Mahmud of Ghazna. A first renaissance of Persian language and poetry occurred at the Samanid court with the work of Rudaki (d. 940), the prolific official poet, who came from Samarqand.

An important step in the revival of Iran took place to the east, in what is now Afghanistan. The Turkish dynasty of the Ghaznavids (999–1151), which had sprung from the revolt of a mercenary at the Samanid court, ruled Afghanistan, Iran, the Punjab and Sind. Mahmud of Ghazna, the outstanding figure of the age, after a series of successful campaigns controlled a vast empire that extended from western Iran as far as Delhi in India. This immense territorial unit run by a corps of Turkish warriors prefigured the condition of Iran in the future, under the control of foreign powers – the Seljuqs in the 11th and 12th centuries, the Mongols in the 13th and 14th centuries, and the Timurids from 1370 to 1502. The Ghaznavid empire, where culture played an important role thanks to the contribution of Persians, marked the first time that Turkish tribes had taken possession of the entire country of Iran.

From 833 on Turkish troops had been the strongmen of the 'Abbasids of Baghdad, and the caliph owed his power to them. But the sword was double-edged: in 861 the caliph was assassinated by his army, and power fell into the hands of the 'praetorian guard'. After that the role of the Turks – a nomadic tribal people who traditionally drove their flocks across the unconfined spaces of Central Asia – changed rapidly, and in 956 they crossed the Syr Daria, settled at Bukhara in Transoxiana, and converted *en masse* to Islam. They were to become representatives and champions of a pure, hard Sunnism, spreading orthodoxy through the *madrasas*, Qur'anic schools that fought for the strict observance of the letter of Muslim law. At the same time, the Turks were influenced by Persian thought. Their chiefs, who assumed the rank of sultan, soon became acculturated, and propagated the high culture of the sedentary peoples. Through this subtle combination of military force and artistic refinement, they played a key role in the promotion of Persian forms and ideas. These 'Persianized' Turks created an Islamic commonalty, of which the best example is probably the Seljuq Sultanate (1032–86).

At the same time, the Qarakhanids (999–1212), a Turkish group that were still semi-nomadic but converted to Islam, extended their power over Central Asia from the Tarim desert to Talas, before seizing the province of Farghana. This dynasty soon separated into two groups. The western khanate was forced to submit to the Seljuqs in 1070, while the eastern khanate was invaded in the 12th century by the Kara-Kitay, a Mongol people from China who had migrated to the steppes.

The Ghaznavids fell in 1151, and were succeeded by the Ghurid dynasty from Iran, who were to play an important role in the establishment in India of a Persian-influenced culture. It was Muhammad of Ghur (1173–1206) who founded the Delhi Sultanate.

Architectural Beginnings

Architecture now felt a new impetus. An outstanding example of the new mood is the Tomb of Ismail Samani, built in 907 in Bukhara, in remote Transoxiana, a region where Timurid art was to flourish five centuries later. This rigorously proportioned and geometrical Samanid work, which makes use of brick with remarkable skill and a perfect decorative sense, constitutes a milestone in Islamic architecture. Here we find, for instance, the use of squinches to effect the transition between a square plan and a circular dome – a solution that was to be taken up by the Seljuqs. In Iran proper, the earliest architectural evidence comes from the 'Abbasid period. The old mosque or Tarik Khana at Damghan was partly rebuilt in the Seljuq period, but its oldest elements appear to date from the 8th century. Built of brick, it has a square courtyard surrounded by porticoes, followed by a hypostyle prayer hall divided by cylindrical masonry columns into seven aisles each three bays deep.

The brick minaret of the Tarik Khana, in Seljuq style, with geometrical decoration in relief and Qur'anic inscriptions, was followed by a number of structures that are stylistically similar. Particularly close are the brick minarets that survive in many ancient cities, such as those in Isfahan and Semnan. But there are also funerary structures such as the tower-mausoleum known as the Pir-i Alamdar (1026) at Damghan, with its dome and band of decoration, and the nearby tomb known as Ma'sum Zadeh (1096), which has a door similar to an iwan and walls punctuated by projecting triangular ribs.

One of the most imposing of these tower-tombs of northern Iran is the Gunbad-i Qabus at Gorgan. (*Gunbad* means dome in Persian; from the association of domes with tombs, it came to denote a tomb.) This masterpiece was built for a Shi'ite prince in 1006, under the rule of the Zeyarids of Mazandaran near the Caspian Sea (10th–11th centuries). It is a polygonal tower crowned by a conical roof, related in form to Turkish tombs or *türbes*; entirely constructed of beautiful fired brick, it shoots up to a height of 51 metres from the monotonous landscape of the Turkoman steppes. With its plan which is that of a ten-pointed star, and its great buttresses that narrow slightly at the top, it produces an effect of grandeur and displays an exceptional mastery of brickwork techniques. Two inscriptions in kufic script encircle it, one above the only door and the other below the springing of the roof. This colossal tomb was influential: the star-plan towers at Varamin and Rayy, crowned by rings of *muqarnas*, are its offspring.

At Nayin, to the east of Isfahan, the ancient Friday Mosque, built in 960 but altered many times, has in the area of the *mihrab* a remarkable collection of brick structures of early date. The masonry columns that support the large arches from

opposite The Tomb of Ismail Samani, ruler of Bukhara from 892 to 907, is entirely built of brick (see also *below*). Inside, it displays the earliest example of the highly original structural technique of squinches – arches thrown across the corners of the square cell to support the circular dome. Its decoration consists entirely of bricks, some cut, set in various planes and at various angles.

left The colossal, elegant stellate tower of the Gunbad-i Qabus rises from the plain at Gorgan near the Caspian Sea. It was begun by Sultan Qabus in 1006, under the Zeyarid dynasty, and bears two bands of kufic script as its only decoration.

below The Tomb of Ismail Samani at Bukhara consists of a cubical room covered by a hemispherical dome (*opposite*). Its façades are enlivened by a rich decoration of cut and patterned brickwork.

which the vaults spring are intricately covered with supple interlace and ornamental motifs. This hypostyle building, enlarged several times, displays characteristic Persian four-centred arches, and wooden tie-rods that articulate the space and stiffen the structure.

An early and still timid attempt at an *iwan*, fronting the wider central aisle, was inserted in the courtyard at Nayin, perhaps during the Seljuq period. The great *iwan* of the old mosque of Semnan was introduced in the Timurid period (15th century).

One of the first monuments with a central courtyard and four *iwans* is the Ghaznavid palace at Lashkari Bazar, which dates from the reign of Mahmud (998–1030). This formula was to be much used in Persian mosques and *madrasas* (Sunni Qur'anic schools): we shall be following its evolution up to the Safavid period, and will see its diffusion through all the lands influenced by Iran. The open space of the courtyard is of fundamental importance in Persian architecture, and governs the concept of all types of building – secular structures such as houses, caravanserais and palaces, and religious monuments such as *madrasas* and mosques. This concentration on the courtyard, which often leads to a complete disregard for the treatment of outward-facing as opposed to inward-facing façades, is profoundly Persian. We shall find that brick architecture, too, is characteristic of Iran: there it flowered early, and never went out of fashion.

THE SELJUQS: A VIGOROUS ART

The Seljuqs owe their name to Seljuq, who converted his nomadic Central Asian Turkish tribe to Islam. From the area east of the Caspian Sea they moved west, crossed the Oxus (Amu Daria) in 1025, defeated the Ghaznavids in 1040, and pressed on to take Baghdad in 1055, putting an end to the Buyid Shi'a guardianship over the caliph. Their leader, Toghrïl Beg, the first Seljuq sultan (1038–63), became caliph; like all the Turks, he set out to be a pious defender of Sunni Islam.

The Seljuqs of Iran (1032–1186) are not to be confused with the branch of the tribe led by Alp Arslan, Toghrïl Beg's successor, who conquered the Anatolian plain and, after defeating the Byzantine Emperor Romanus IV Diogenes at Manzikert in 1071, founded the Sultanate of Rum.

The Persian branch captured Nishapur and in 1051 made Isfahan their capital. There Nizam al-Mulk (1018–92), an accomplished man of letters and able politician of Persian origin, served as vizier, first under Alp Arslan and then under Malik Shah (1072–92). Nizam al-Mulk had a great influence on the development of Isfahan as a centre of Persian power. In a treatise entitled Seyasat-nama he set out the principles of the feudal administrative system of the Islamic middle ages in Iran. Under his aegis, the arts and sciences experienced a renaissance: geog-raphers, doctors, musicians and architects developed a high civilization which was encouraged by the Seljuq rulers. And under Malik Shah the Seljuq empire became as vast as Iran had been under the Achaemenids and Sasanians.

left Seljuq tombs at Zavareh, on the edge of the desert, display the technique of building mausolea of brick. Zavareh, a city some 100 kilometres northeast of Isfahan, prospered during the 12th and 13th centuries.

opposite, below, and above
The Friday Mosque at Zavareh was built in a single campaign in 1135. It is a typical Persian structure, with four *iwans* facing a courtyard (*above*), and displays the fine brickwork in use in Iran during the Seljuq period.
The brick dome over the prayer hall (*opposite, below*) is remarkable for its four complex squinches in the corners. The motif came from the Great Mosque of Isfahan, built in 1088 in the time of Nizam al-Mulk, vizier of the Seljuq Sultan Malik Shah.

During the vizierate of Nizam al-Mulk, the architecture of Islamic Iran developed a distinctive form and the full range of its modes of expression, thanks to the technological innovations of the Seljuq period. Key features are vast conch-shaped *iwans* that face each other in pairs across the square courtyard of a mosque or *madrasa*, marking the two axes of the building that meet in the centre of the basin for ritual ablutions. These *iwans* properly consist of a recessed space, which is covered with a pointed or hemispherical vault but open to the courtyard. As in the royal halls of Sasanian architecture, these 'rooms' are neither indoors nor outdoors. Henceforth the *iwan* was to be a characteristic item in the vocabulary of Islamic architecture. The first, still timid, appearance of this arrangement seems to have been in the palace of Ukhaidir in Iraq, built in 778. In Persian mosques, the monumental *iwans* polarize the space of the courtyard. These distinctively Persian structures derive, as has been said, from the Sasanian royal hall (ill. p. 298, which was the setting of court ritual surrounding the cult of the King of Kings. As an emblematic structure, the *iwan* also gave architects the opportunity to display their imagination and their technological skills: in shape and structural nature the vaults are infinitely diverse. The symbolic character of the *iwan* also appears in the fact that only the inner, concave side can be seen: it is as though the back of the niche and its frame did not exist. This is an architecture of show, not to say of façadism. Descended from a building designed as the setting for appearances of the Sasanian ruler in all the radiance of his majesty, the *iwan* is a sort of shrine: transposed to the mosque of the sultan, this setting for the imperial cult of ancient Persia endowed the place of prayer with an emblematic meaning. It is from the *iwan* that the *khutbah*, the Friday sermon that includes the ruler's name, is preached.

The four *iwans* emphasize the axes of the place of worship, and the principal *iwan*, which leads to the hall containing the *mihrab*, is larger and often framed by a pair of minarets; it indicates the direction of prayer, towards the southwest, to the Ka'ba at Mecca. Typically this *iwan* is more richly ornamented, if not structurally more complex and impressive, than the secondary *iwans*.

An Exemplum: The Friday Mosque in Isfahan

In the variety of their decorative treatment, the four *iwans* of the Friday Mosque handsomely illustrate the architectural inventiveness of Isfahani builders at the end of the 11th century. The one to the north has a simple pointed tunnel vault, but the other three have apses covered with *muqarnas*, or honeycombs. Some of these units are small geometrical hollows, while others are large hollow spherical triangles derived from the squinch – a constructional device that was rigorously and rationally formulated under the Seljuks. The Friday Mosque has two domes, one 14 metres and the other 10 metres in diameter, placed on the same axis, which emphasize the ritual orientation. In these domes the squinch technique that had been introduced in the Tomb of Ismail Samani at Bukhara (ill. p. 26) reached perfection, using only geometrical segments of a sphere. (For the Friday Mosque see below, pp. 214–21.)

Thus it was under the Seljuks that the Persian mosque with four *iwans* developed its classic form. Outside Isfahan, early examples can be seen in the old mosque at Ardestan, in the Friday Mosque of Zavareh (ill. pp. 28–29) and in the Friday Mosque of Natanz, which dates from 1307, at the beginning of the Mongol period.

The Friday Mosque in Isfahan, built under the Seljuks in the 11th century

left The western side of the courtyard, reflected in the ablutions basin. The *iwan* on this side has large-scale *muqarnas*. The ceramic decoration was added later.

above The mosque seen from the air. In the centre is the four-*iwan* courtyard; around it, a ripple of small domes covers the hypostyle halls. The nearest large dome is that over the *mihrab*, of 1072; that in the distance, the Gunbad-i Khaki, dates from 1088.

below The extraordinary ribbed structure at the back of the western *iwan*. The technique used in the 11th century to support large honeycomb vaults grew out of an intensive study of the resistance of brick arches carried out in Seljuq Iran.

The Kingdom of Khwarazm

The mid-12th century saw the rise to power in Transoxiana, south of the Aral Sea, of the shahs of Khwarazm, or Khwarazmshahs. They were Turks who had become converted to Islam and settled in the rich irrigated lands along the lower course of the Amu Darya, at the edge of the steppes. Their dynasty (1097–1230) was at first subject to the Seljuks, but eventually they overthrew their masters and extended their rule as far as the Tigris. These powerful rulers established a remarkable Arabic-Persian culture, founded on economic prosperity derived from successful agriculture, where the arts and sciences flourished. It came to an end before the forces of Chinghiz Khan.

Decorative Stucco and Brickwork and Highlighting in Colour

far left and left The Friday Mosque in Nayin, of the 10th century, marked a new departure: in the area in front of the *minbar* and *mihrab* the brick structure was covered with carved stucco. Some of the cylindrical columns display decorative motifs similar to those of the 9th-century 'Abbasid palaces of Samarra in Iraq.

We have seen how at the beginning of the Islamic period Iran took up the use of brick, usually fired, for its religious architecture. In this the buildings of the Persian plateau would appear to have been influenced by the 'Abbasid art of Mesopotamia (Baghdad and Samarra), which was itself dependent on the local customs of the Sasanians and their tradition of palace architecture (Ctesiphon), and perhaps even on structures of the remote past such as the ziggurat of Chogha Zanbil (13th century BCE) in the lower Karun basin.

The use of brick in Iran is in any case a natural outcome of the geology of the country and the great frequency of earthquakes. Buildings with brick vaults proved more resistant to earthquakes than heavy stone column-and-lintel structures, and the 'flexibility' of brick, combined with the greater ease of construction, made this tough, cheap material the obvious choice for everything from a modest house to a sumptuous mosque. The phenomenon is especially interesting in Isfahan, where the availability of stone quarries could have encouraged the development of ashlar masonry.

The early Islamic religious buildings of the 'Abbasid period on the high plateaus have features that recall Mesopotamian architecture: they are built of brick, and important features of prestigious buildings are emphasized by a layer of stucco patterned with ornamental motifs created by moulding or by carving. This can be seen in the old mosque at Nayin, where some of the stucco reliefs recall the decoration of the palaces of Samarra. The motifs even seem to go back to Sasanian prototypes seen in the sculptured ornament of the grotto of Takh-i Bostan. Given the importance of the sacred text of the Qur'an, it is not surprising that inscriptions in kufic script often appear on arches, friezes and mouldings, providing both decoration and special significance: thus the verses of the Qur'an found their way into architectural decoration. Inscriptions may also provide information such as the date, the ruler, or the master builder in charge of construction. Decorative brickwork can already be seen in seemingly thousands of variations in the Tomb of Ismail Samani at Bukhara, of 907 (ill. pp. 26–27): patterns are skilfully composed from rhythms created by the use of bricks in staggered formations, set horizontally or on end, jutting out, laid in herringbone fashion, etc. In this hazarbaf ('thousand wave') technique a very subtle range of geometrical motifs plays across the forms of architecture.

In the time of the Zeyarids, the decoration of the famous Gunbad-i Qabus at Gorgan consists only of two bands of inscriptions that encircle the tomb (ill. p. 27). Under the Seljuqs ornament became more complex, no longer limited to script alone: it assumed an important role, and drew on a range of repeating abstract motifs. As under the Samanids, decoration was created by playing with the bricks of which the structure was built: there are recessed and projecting bricks, bricks set at an angle of 45 degrees, and friezes of bricks in which raised and recessed areas alternate. Inscriptions became stylized, not least because in calligraphy itself Arabic characters were now written only in rectilinear forms. Rhythmical motifs ruled. Through the use of bricks of different sizes, and of whole, half- and quarter-bricks, recessed or projecting, the masons created dynamic patterns. The shafts of minarets, the tops of funerary towers, arches, capitals and entablatures were covered with designs based on squares, lozenges, interlace, complex interweaving patterns, chevron borders, even rows of *muqarnas*.

below and bottom The Tomb of Ma'sum Zadeh at Mehmandust, near Damghan, 1096. The design takes up the protecting triangular buttresses of the Gunbad-i Qabus (ill. p. 27), and originally included a brick dome. The entrance is surrounded by a flat frame derived from the *iwan*. At the top is an ornamental frieze incorporating meanders and stylized inscriptions, resting on a band of *muqarnas* – a characteristic example of Seljuk decoration in relief brickwork.

This was a monochrome system of decoration, which relied on sun and shade to bring it fully to life. Soon, on important buildings, it was enriched by the introduction of coloured elements. At first, the surface of the masonry was punctuated by a few geometric motifs, which were produced by the use of fired bricks whose exposed surface was covered with a monochrome glaze. This is the technique called *haftrangi* or 'seven colours': only one face of the brick is coloured, but through ingenious alternation highly inventive geometrical effects can be achieved. Soon more coloured accents were introduced by increasing the number of glazed bricks, and it became possible with a limited number of identical elements to compose repeating motifs of squares, stars, polygons, lattice work, nets and edgings that stand out against the plain wall. These inclusions of black or blue glazed brick enlivened both flat and concave surfaces, and freed architecture from the monotony of naked brick.

From these timid beginnings polychromy soon spread, and the great panels surrounding *iwans* were covered with decoration based on stylized script. At first there were austere graphic renderings of the names of Allah, Muhammad, and later Ali; these were were soon joined by entire verses of the Qur'an, which spread out across the walls, covered the friezes, surrounded the *iwans*, and articulated the shafts of minarets. These inscriptions acted like a sort of code on the surfaces of the mosque, transforming the religious building into a manifesto of the Islamic faith, displayed for all the faithful to see.

Gradually, under the Mongols, to a far greater extent under the Timurids, and then under the Safavids, colour came to take over all the visible areas in architecture. This trend was accompanied by the introduction of floral motifs – rinceaux, foliage, vases and bouquets of flowers. But before looking at the spread of polychromy in the form of tile mosaic, we need to consider the origins and the technical characteristics of this polychromatic mode of decoration so perfectly suited to brick buildings.

Polychromy and its Origins

Throughout history, architecture has made use of colour, whether we think of Egyptian temples, Babylonian town walls or ziggurats, the palaces of Knossos, or the monuments of classical Greece. The earliest example is perhaps the decoration of the subterranean tomb of Djoser at Saqqara, of *c.* 2700 BCE, with its rooms covered with panels of blue-green glazed frit. At Babylon, the Gate of Ishtar had highlights of vitrified blue glaze. At Susa in the 6th century BCE, the Achaemenids excelled in glazed ceramic friezes portraying the immortals, or members of the imperial guard. At Constantinople, the gold backgrounds of figurative mosaics illuminated apses and domes. Byzantine mosaics appeared in the Islamic world, too, adorning Umayyad structures in Jerusalem and Damascus.

The art of architectural ceramic made its first appearance in the 'Abbasid period. Interesting evidence comes from Arabic authors: al-Masudi, in his *Golden Meadows* of the mid-10th century, mentions a green dome in Baghdad; earlier still, in 903, Ibn Rustah remarked on the fact that the dome of the Great Mosque in Baghdad was entirely covered with lapis-lazuli coloured bricks; again in the 10th century, Abu Yaqubi praised the green minarets of Bukhara; and the geographer Yakut, writing in 1226, mentions a mausoleum dated 1157 of which the dome was blue.

Developments in architectural ceramic were linked to those in pottery. Already before the end of the 1st millennium BCE techniques of firing were being exploited at Rayy, Nishapur and Samarqand, and slightly later at Gorgan and Kashan. The city of Kashan seems to have had an effective monopoly – based on a secret manufacturing technique? – on the production of glazed tiles for architectural cladding. Indeed, the Persian term *kashi* (a contraction of *kashani*, 'from Kashan') came to be the standard word for the coloured tiles that cover the façades of mosques. Evidence of their use goes back to the end of the 13th century. In his accounts of his travels, Ibn Battuta (1304–77) mentions *kashi* in a number of mosques in Mesopotamia, Isfahan, Tabriz and Mashhad, and it is known that Kashan exported its precious tiles over great distances, as far as Damascus and Cairo.

The potters of Kashan, Jean Soustiel tells us in his study of Islamic ceramics, were in the habit of signing and dating both tiles used to cover public buildings and finer pieces: we are thus endebted to them not only for their fine production, but for valuable information about chronology.

The technique of lustreware with a metallic sheen, which became much sought-after for the cladding of *mihrabs*, was developed at the end of the Seljuq period or under the shahs of Khwarazm. Throughout this time Kashan remained the leader in the production of architectural ceramic and was to remain so even after the Mongol period. Tiles with an iridescent lustre, which was caused by the deposit of oxide vapours on the glaze during vitrification, in the technique known as 'closed oven reduction', were much sought after, especially for the mausoleums of imams in Iran: we find them at Qom, in the tomb of Bibi Fatima, as early as 1208, and at Mashad, in the tomb of the Imam Reza of 1215.

Techiques of polychromy involving the use of pieces of ceramic cut out in shapes so as to form tile mosaics became widespread under the Timurids of Transoxiana. We shall look at them in more detail when we come to consider works of that period, in Samarqand and Bukhara as well as in Isfahan and at sites in central Iran.

above and opposite Kashan lustreware lent itself to calligraphic decorations in Arabic script, sometimes modelled in relief. What had begun as an ornament for *mihrabs* and funerary monuments eventually expanded to produce the polychrome architecture of Iran. In the Islamic world, the city of Kashan long retained a monopoly over *kashi*, or glazed tiles. The octagonal star framing the mythical *simurgh* bird here is a symbol of eternal life; this tile would have been fitted into a complex composition made up of a number of tiles. (Cinili Kiosk Museum, Istanbul)

Ceramics and the Art of the Potter

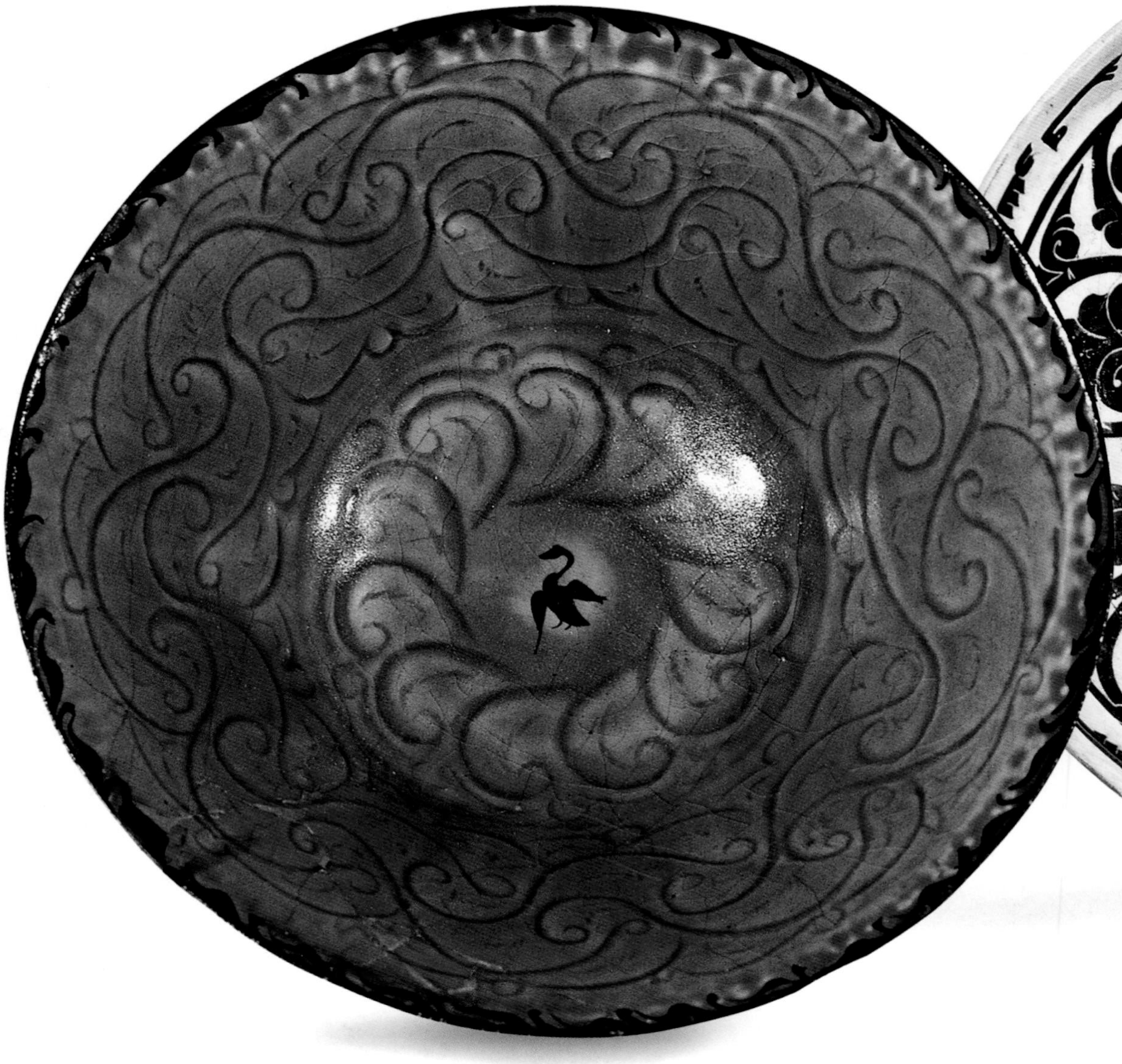

above Bowl decorated with a bird. A transparent turquoise glaze covers shallow wave-like motifs that animate the surface. This piece from northern Iran, Khorasan or Afghanistan is typical of the early 13th century. (Foroughi Collection)

above right Glazed earthenware bowl decorated with black scrolls and palmettes on a white ground, with an inscription round the border. The style is that of Samarqand; the piece probably comes from Nishapur and dates from the 9th–10th century. (Foroughi Collection)

The art of ceramics developed rapidly in the Islamic world. By means of the Silk Road, which was in existence under the Roman empire, Iran and the territories in its orbit early came into contact with China, where the potter's art reached its peak under the T'ang (618–907) and Sung (960–1279) dynasties. Already in the time of the 'Abbasid dynasty, Arab potters and Persian craftsmen of the central plateau had acquired remarkable technical skills – first the development of glazed earthenware, then the use of double firing, and then petit feu or enamel firing in a muffle kiln to obtain multicoloured glazes. They often tried to make pieces that imitated or rivalled Chinese ceramics: such are the famous 'three-colour' bowls which were to make the fame of the potters of Nishapur.

The Persian city of Nishapur in Khorasan, situated on a great international trade route, was one of the principal centres for the production of Islamic ceramics until its destruction by the Mongols in 1221. Other centres were Rayy, Gorgan, Samarqand, Amol and Sari, all in the northern or eastern area of Iran. The prodigious formal invention and endless decorative innovation seen in works produced between the 9th and the early 13th centuries depended on technical experimentation from the 'Abbasid period onwards: the development of tin oxide glazing, of coloured slip under a transparent glaze, and of decoration with variegated glazes resulted in superb pieces. Some of these decorative techniques, which are contemporary with similar developments in China, look astonishly 'modern': we find abstract motifs, dripping, splashing, dappled backgrounds, etc. The rejection of representational imagery results in works that seem to look forward to the trends and spirit of Western art.

Bowls and dishes with a white ground and a glazed inscription in bold black letters round the edge, dating from the 10th century, are among the masterworks of Nishapur and Samarqand. In their sobriety and vigour they recall architectural decorations in which script becomes a major aesthetic and spiritual ingredient. In the late Seljuq period, bowls

above A bowl in *minai* or *haftrangi* technique from Kashan, with highlights of gold leaf on a turquoise glaze, 1186. Figures based on the conventions of Chinese art enact a scene from Firdawsi's *Shahnama*, within an inscription band. (Croisier Collection)

above right A bowl with wavy motifs in the 'three colours' style, from Nishapur or Transoxiana, 10th–11th century. The abstract design is remarkably spare, and given great dynamism by the parallel waves. (Foroughi Collection)

below A dish with an inscription in black on a white ground, from eastern Iran or Transoxiana, 11th century. Calligraphy as a decoration is common in 9th–12th-century ceramics. The texts, which are often difficult to decipher, are usually religious invocations. (Croisier Collection)

and dishes from Rayy and Kashan are increasingly decorated with figures in Chinese style, with broad faces and almond eyes. The designs were produced by the *minai* technique, in which a second *petit feu* or enamel firing fixes the design and the colours. This extremely fine figurative decoration appears to be contemporary with the first illustrated books, and to reflect developments in manuscript painting before the Mongol and Timurid periods.

A relationship grew up between Islamic architecture and ceramics, as polychromy developed in both glazed tiles and ornamental pottery. Similar links grew up between painted ceramics and manuscript illustration, and further similarities can be seen in woven textiles and carpets. What it all shows is the growth of a unitary style in Iran proper and in its spheres of influence between the 10th and 13th centuries, reflecting a great cultural movement. This was unquestionably the golden age of Persian thought and art. Under the Tahirids, the Saffarids, the Buyids, the Ghaznavids, the Samanids, the Seljuqs, and the shahs of Khwarazm, the age was marked by a series of brilliant personalities who fed the Persian renaissance.

The Leading Spirits of the National Revival

The powerful cultural impulse that asserted itself between the 10th and 13th centuries was the product not of one or two individuals but of a wealth of original minds in the arts and sciences, philosophy and poetry, who flourished despite shifts in politics and skirmishes with nomadic tribes to the north-east. Names in this dazzling constellation, some still famous in the West, include Avicenna, al-Farabi, Omar Khayyam, al-Ghazali, Nizami, Sa'di, Nasir ad-Din at-Tusi, and as-Suhrawardi.

Al-Farabi (870–950), a philosopher from Transoxiana, probably a Shi'a, believed that Aristotle and Plato were the source of an eternal truth. He knew both Persian and Turkish, but used Arabic for his commentaries on the Ideal City, seen from a metaphysical, cosmological and political point of view. His thought developed into a theology in which the ultimate goal was happiness, to be found in the Creation. Al-Farabi was the teacher of Avicenna. Avicenna (980–1037) – as Ibn Sina was known in the Western Middle Ages – was both a philosopher and a doctor. A Persian, born near Bukhara, he early mastered the knowledge current in his time; he knew Aristotle through the commentary of al-Farabi, and, building upon the work of Galen, he wrote a *Canon of Medicine* which, translated into Latin, was still used in Europe in the 17th century. He built up a body of philosophy in both Arabic and Persian which centred on the separation of body and soul and the construction of a metaphysics based on a mystical awareness of the Creation and the Self. This characteristically Persian tendency towards mysticism is also seen in the 'Persian Platonist' as-Suhrawardi (1155–91), a 'theosophist' who lived in Isfahan and Baghdad and was condemned to death in Aleppo for his beliefs. He developed a philosophy of light based on the ideas of neo-platonism (especially the 5th-century *Celestial Hierarchy* traditionally attributed to Dionysius the Areopagite), and his theory of mystical illumination underlies many of the theological visions of Shi'ite thought. The Persian theologian al-Ghazali (1058–1111), born at Tus in Khorasan, was made a jurist (*qadi*) at the court of Nizam al-Mulk in Isfahan, and was also a master of Qur'anic sciences in Baghdad. He came to consider theology as a remedy for the disease of unbelief, and, like most Persians, believed in mysticism as a path to knowledge.

Among scientists, the most famous is the Persian mathematician, astronomer and poet Omar Khayyam (1047–1122), celebrated for his *Rubaiyat*, or 'quatrains' with their philosophy of *carpe diem* and their agnostic scepticism free of bitterness or compromise. Born in Nishapur, he lived in Isfahan and Samarqand, where he directed an observatory with the aim of reforming the Persian calendar. In mathematics, he carried on the work in algebra of al-Khwarizmi, and studied the relationships between algebra and geometry, as well as roots and cubic equations. The Persian astronomer and mathematician Nasir ad-Din at-Tusi (1201–74), who was born at Tus and died in Baghdad, supervised the building of the observatory of Maragheh in 1259. He was interested in philosophy and astrology, and translated scientific works of classical antiquity into Arabic and Persian.

Among poets, we have already seen the importance of Firdawsi. Nizami (1140–1209), from Azerbaijan, was a moralist who blended Sufism with popular thought. In *Khusraw and Shirin* he looked to old Sasanian legends and wrote of the love between a Persian king and an Armenian princess, while in his *Romance of Alexander* he developed the legendary image of Alexander the Great or 'Iskandar' into the figure of a bold and wise ruler endowed with prophetic power, as befitted a truly noble king. Sa'di (1213–92) was born in Shiraz and educated in Baghdad. In his *Gulistan* or *Rose Garden*, a collection of lyrical poems in Persian, his inclination towards Sufism shines forth. With the nostalgic atmosphere of his style and its formal perfection classical Farsi became a highly poetic language.

By the beginning of the 13th century, on the eve of the Mongol invasion, Iran had achieved a remarkable revival. The country was truly independent again; it was able to hold its own with 'Abbasid power; Farsi was recognized as an independent language on an equal footing with Arabic, although Arabic script was used; it could boast a powerful and original literature, and, in particular a truly 'national' poetry; it had brought together outstanding scholars in all fields, from astronomy and mathematics to geography and medicine; it had developed a distinctive architectural style that was expressed in buildings throughout Iran and its sphere of influence; it had articulated a mystical theology, contributing both to Sufism and to Shi'ite thought; and in the field of the applied arts, it had managed (by following the model of Chinese ceramics) to create very fine pieces and to work out techniques that were used in the decoration of brick architecture.

THE FOUR-*IWAN* COURTYARD AND THE *MADRASA*: A PERSIAN BEQUEST

Within Iran, the Turkish sultans' zeal for the strict observance of the precepts of the Qur'an, in accordance with Sunni Islam, led to a multiplication of *madrasas*, or Qur'anic schools. Beginning in the Seljuq period, *madrasas* were modelled on the Persian courtyard mosque, with four paired *iwans*. Then, in a missionary push, Sunni theologians established *madrasas* throughout the Islamic world, and the architectural form proved perfectly suited to practical necessity. As we have seen, there were various schools of jurisprudence in the Islamic world, of which the four most important were the Hanafite, Malikite, Safaite and Hanbalite; and the structure of the *madrasa*, with its four *iwans*, lent itself so well to the coexistence of these four currents of classic Islamic thought that it was soon believed to have been designed specifically to meet the needs of the theologians. For this reason, the Persian layout was diffused far and wide; indeed, it was sometimes even used for buildings that had no connection with schools of law.

In Mesopotamia, the al-Mustansir Madrasa in Baghdad, built in 1226 by the caliph al-Mustansir, features a typical four-*iwan* layout around a courtyard with two tiers of arcades; it shows the influence of Iran on the last of the Great 'Abbasids, before the Mongols invaded and sacked Baghdad in 1258 and put the caliph to death. In nearby eastern Turkey, ruled by the Seljuqs of Rum, the *madrasa* known as the Çifte Minare, built at Erzurum in 1253, adopted the 'Persian' layout and the arrangement on two floors around a courtyard, onto which four *iwans* with pointed arches opened. The structure here, however, is in carefully worked ashlar. Only the minarets, with their fluted shafts of brick and their decoration with insertions of blue ceramic, are in the Persian tradition. Under the Mamluks in Cairo, in 1307 Sultan Baybars II el-Gashenkir built a *madrasa/khanaqah*, combining school and monastery, on three levels. Two great *iwans* on the longitudinal axis provide generous shelter under slightly pointed tunnel vaults executed in handsome coursed ashlar. The side *iwans*, on the other hand, have the form of triple arcades, with two piers supporting a lintel, and read as *iwans* only in plan. One of the finest Mamluk examples of the four-*iwan madrasa* overlooking a courtyard came some years later, with the great creation of Sultan Hasan, built in 1356 shortly after a great plague had devastated Cairo. This monumental structure, entirely of ashlar, has four immense 26-metre-high pointed tunnel vaults. The formula was taken up again, on a smaller scale, for the Madrasa of Barquq, built in the main street of Cairo, the Sharia al-Muizz, in 1384.

A final example will show the variety of ways in which this type of layout can be used: the celebrated Court of the Lions in the Alhambra, built under the Nasrids in Granada in 1362. With its domed pavilions at the long ends of the courtyard and its lateral spaces covered with ornate domes – the Hall of the Two Sisters and the Hall of the Abencerrages – it played with the cruciform plan and with the idea of a garden on the model of the Persian *chahar bagh*, and combined this with the system of the courtyard mosque. The original source of that idea, the 10th-century Ghaznavid palace of Lashkari Bazar in Afghanistan, thus found an echo in a palace in Andalusia, away in the distant west.

2

Muslims in India and Mongols in Iran

We now come to one of the most important population movements of the Islamic period in Asia: the expansion into India of the Turkish Ghaznavid Sultans (999–1151/87), followed by the Ghurids who supplanted them. Between 1000 and 1026, Sultan Mahmud of Ghazna launched some seventeen raids towards the Indus plain. He was of Persian origin and had been influenced by the Samanid court, and he was to begin the Islamicization of the kingdoms in the north-west of the Indian peninsula. In this he was carrying on the work of the first Arab caliphs in their great scheme to spread Islam throughout the world.

For several centuries India had seemed, first for the Arabs and then for the tribes of Central Asia, an inaccessible mirage, at the most an area for fruitful raids. The first Muslims had penetrated Sind in 711, but they had failed to cross the Indus delta, and their influence remained marginal. It was left to the Turks to reshape the destiny of the Indian subcontinent. In the 10th century, all of Central Asia was in ferment. Setting off from Ghazna, their capital in Afghanistan, the Sunni Ghaznavids crossed the Khyber Pass in the western Hindu Kush and inflicted terrible raids on the rich cities of the Indus plain. Their leader, Mahmud of Ghazna (999–1030), did not hesitate to confront Hindu armies, which were equipped with war elephants but poorly organized. But he did not not think of occupying the territories that he attacked, year after year, in strikes that gained him immense spoils.

The Ghurids, of Persian origin, succeeded the Ghaznavids and ruled over eastern Iran and Afghanistan, beginning in 1151. After Muhammad of Ghur (1173–1206) had captured Lahore and made it his capital, this new Muslim power established itself in northern India, and began the process of 'Persianization' of the subcontinent. In 1191 the Rajput clans, superior in number, had defeated Muhammad, but he rallied Turkish reinforcements and defeated the Hindus at Taraori in 1192. To strengthen his authority in a precarious situation, he decreed that Delhi, in the Ganges plain, would be the capital of his empire. Thus the end of the 12th century saw the foundation of the first Persian centre of Indo-Muslim art.

THE MARRIAGE OF FIRE AND WATER

The Ghurid presence in India set up a profound rivalry between the two civilizations. The effect of this turbulent Islamic culture irrupting into the ancient world of the Hindus and Jains was like an earthquake. There could be no greater contrast than that between the two indigenous Indian societies and the Persian Turks from Central Asia and Iran. The antagonism was fundamental: Hinduism venerates a thousand gods, whereas the message of the Qur'an is strictly monotheistic, and the façades of Hindu temples are covered with images celebrating the gods of a protean pantheon, while Muslims, inspired by the second of the Ten Commandments, had established an aniconic form of worship that rejected all images.

The contrasts are just as great when it comes to the structural side of buildings: Hindu architecture, with its temples hollowed out of cliffs or built of worked stone, is based on traditional techniques derived from timber construction: piers and lintels are combined with corbelling. Muslim architecture, on the other hand, is based on arches, vaults built up of shaped voussoirs, and domes on squinches. The introduction of these features into India initiated a technological revolution. The dynamic formulas of arcades and vaults used in mosques, *madrasas* and mausoleums provided space for congregational prayer and ritual.

p. 40 above A polychrome detail from the Tomb of Sultan Öljeytu Khudabanda, Soltaniyeh.

p. 40 below The Great Khan Monka, from a 16th-century miniature (the complete image is on p. 49).

p. 41 Detail of the glazed ceramic decorations on the doorway of the Friday Mosque in Natanz, Mongol period, 1304–6.

opposite, above A Mongol encampment: detail of a 15th-century Persian miniature. (Bibliothèque Nationale de France, Paris)

opposite, below The Minaret of Bahram Shah (1118–52) at Ghazna, the capital of the Ghaznavid dynasty in Afghanistan. The eight-pointed star plan and the angled buttresses derive from the Gunbad-i Qabus (ill. p. 27) and look forward to the Qutb Minar in Delhi.

below The Qutb Minar in Delhi, built in 1199 in the new Muslim capital of the Ghurids. It overlooks the Quwwat al-Islam Mosque, founded two years earlier by Muhammad of Ghur's viceroy, Qutb ad-Din Aybak.

ISLAM IN INDIA

The Ghurids were spurred on in their passion for conquest by their desire to spread the word of the Prophet and the message of Islam, with all the zeal of the first Muslims in the 7th and 8th centuries. Behind their proselytizing ardour lay a greed for plunder as well as the believer's duty to fight a holy war or *jihad* against the infidel, and this double motive accounts for the reckless daring of a handful of warriors of Islam in crossing the mountains of Afghanistan to confront the immensity of the Indian subcontinent, determined to found a sultanate there. The Muslims first assumed control of the Indus delta, then rapidly went on to conquer the Ganges plain, and finally occupied a large part of the Deccan. Their ultimate goal was to control all of India – a process that was to take them half a millennium of clashes, bloody wars and destruction.

The Muslim conquerors were no more successful in imposing the Arabic language in India than in Iran and Turkey. Regional languages continued to be used; the Muslim rulers set up Persian, the language of the court, in competition with Hindi; it was later joined by Hindustani and Urdu as important means of communication between different linguistic communities. The Persian contribution was critical in the spheres of culture, literature and technology: in poetry, art and architecture the source is unquestionably Iran.

From Iran and Transoxiana came the forms and spatial organization of buildings, their four-centered arches, symbolism, and the semiology of the court. The same is true for ornament – from arabesques to monumental inscriptions, from interlace to geometrical motifs, from patterns based on stars to flowering branches. There is, however, one fuundamental difference: the materials are no longer the same. Instead of the brick and ceramic of Persian buildings, dictated by Iran's vulnerability to earthquakes, Islamic buildings in India were realized in red sandstone and white marble.

Delhi, the new capital, was founded on an old site which had been occupied by a Rajput clan before it fell into the hands of Muhammad of Ghur. The Indo-Muslim architecture that flourished there grew out of Ghaznavid and Ghurid traditions, which themselves were derived from those that had developed in Iran since the arrival of the Seljuqs in the 11th century, when indigenous architectural traditions were revived and many large mosques were built, notably in Ardestan, Zavareh, Isfahan and Merv. Persian builders, masters of the art of brickwork, made use of four-centered arches and of domes.

The Four-Centered Persian Arch

Monuments built in Iran or in the regions under Persian influence are characterized by arches and vaults with a very distinctive profile. The 'Persian arch' is based on a complex formula. It is neither a semi-circular arch nor a simple pointed arch (like a Gothic arch), although it derives from both: instead, it has a profile that combines tight outer curves at the 'shoulders' with much shallower inner curves that meet in a sharp point. The profile is obtained with the use of a compass, by means of four centres on which the compass point is set: the curve of the 'shoulder' is the segment of an arch of small radius (i.e. with the centre closer to the arch), whereas that of the upper part of the arch has a much longer radius (with the centre far from the arch) – sometimes so long as to make the curvature approach a straight line.

A diagram by the 19th-century French engineer and historian Auguste Choisy shows how the curves of a Persian arch are created in princip[e; other proportions exist as well, depending on date and location.

The advantage of this type of profile over a that of a semi-circular arch is that it exerts less outward thrust for an equal span. The disadvantages are that the component elements or voussoirs are not all identical, and that the shallow angle of the inner, longer arches makes the use of centering necessary.

In purely aesthetic terms, this profile, whether applied to an arch, a vault or a dome, produces a particular effect of elegance and lightness. It is one of the indicators of the influence of the 'Persian style'.

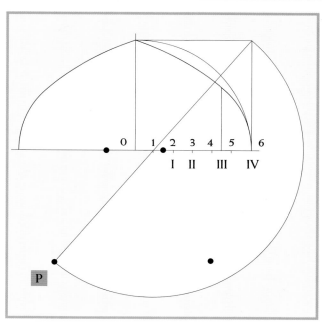

opposite, above The monumental gate or *pishtaq* of the Friday Mosque in Natanz. Built in 1304–6, in the reign of the Il-Khan Öljeytu Khudabanda, it has a polychrome *muqarnas* vault and bands of inscriptions in rigorously geometric kufic script.

opposite, below The honeycomb vault of the dome of the Tomb of Shaikh Abd'as-Samad Isfahani in Natanz, 1308. This structure marks a significant development in the technique of building domes on an octagonal plan. The cruciform shape from which it springs is emphasized by a continuous inscription band.

above Detail of the façade of the Friday Mosque in Natanz, with blue ceramic decoration. The great four-centered arch surmounted by a minaret with geometrical motifs is characteristic of early 14th-century Mongol art in Iran.

right Diagram showing the principle of construction of the Persian four-centered arch. The two lower points (P) mark the centres of circles that determine the shallower upper arcs of the arch, while the two points on the baseline of the arch mark the centres of circles that determine the tighter arcs at the sides. (After Choisy)

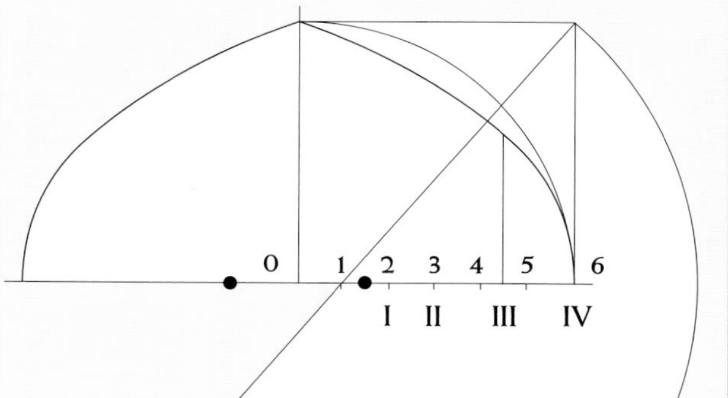

Architecture as a Symbol of Power

The Ghaznavids played a key role in the Persian renaissance, for their court at Ghazna was the home of the celebrated Persian poet Firdawsi (932–1020), author of the *Shahnama*, or *Book of Kings*. They had employed the formula of the courtyard and *iwan* earlier than the Seljuqs, in the palace of Lashkari Bazar. Other notable Ghaznavid architectural achievements include the minaret of Bahram Shah at Ghazna, whose star-shaped plan was to inspire the Qutb Minar in Delhi (ill. pp. 42–43). The Ghaznavids began to decline in the early years of the 12th century, in the reign of Mas'ud III (1099–1115), and the Ghurids took advantage of their weakness to sack Ghazna. It was at this period that the minaret of Jam in Afghanistan – discovered at the beginning of the 20th century in the mountains between Herat and Ghazna – was built; an impressive work no less than 65 metres high, it is another prototype for the Qutb Minar.

An Afghan of Persian origin, heir to the Ghaznavids and Seljuqs, Muhammad of Ghur introduced Persian architectural ideas in his newly founded Delhi Sultanate. The monuments erected by the first Muslim conquerors of India had a powerful semiological and emblematic role. What did architecture mean to these warlords, so recently acculturated?

For these conquerors, some of whom had come from the steppes of Central Asia with no knowledge at all of the art of building, architecture appears to have been a symbol of power. The sultans displayed their power by commissioning great religious monuments and becoming patrons of the arts. They looked to Iran for the best builders of the age, and gave them the task of rendering their reign immortal. More than any other means of expression, architecture has a symbolic character. This quality – which Chinghiz Khan and Timur were to perceive as well – stimulated the creation of monumental works. The Turks and Mongols often confused the magic of construction with that of Creation: to the eyes of a man born in a yurt, the vision of a stone or brick dome seemingly suspended in space must appear miraculous.

The Islamicized Turks set themselves up as defenders of Sunni orthodoxy at a time when the rival Shi'ite and Isma'ili (a Shi'ite sub-sect) doctrines had conquered Egypt and North Africa. For them, the founding of Sunni mosques and *madrasas* had special significance: it expressed the founder's fervour as a believer, and his determination to convert the masses to the faith of the Qur'an. The construction of a monumental and rich building for worship was an achievement as glorious as a victory in battle. Architecture joined the *jihad*, the holy war to extend the Islamic community, in a programme of spiritual conquest. Mosques and *madrasas* were instruments of this diffusion.

In India, the new masters were a tiny minority compared with the masses of their Hindu subjects, and it was important to demonstrate that their strength lay not only in force of arms but in superior technology. By building the largest mosque, the tallest minaret or the most sumptuous sanctuary, a sovereign expressed his religious fervour and demonstrated the excellence of the faith he proclaimed; in India there was an added element, since arches and true domes were unknown. Henceforth these 'marvels' would take on a semiological character, and when no engineers or masons were available to construct them correctly they were imitated.

Monumental architecture played a major role in religious propaganda. Sultans vied with each other, each trying to overshadow the works of his predecessors. Islamic architecture in India is to be seen in this context – the determination to proclaim the glory of Allah and the holiness of his Prophet, Muhammad.

The new Muslim monumental buildings were concentrated in Delhi, the capital founded by Muhammad of Ghur. The sultan was preoccupied by campaigns of conquest in northern India, struggles in Khwarazm, and tribal risings in Afghanistan, and so he placed the city under the control of his general, Qutb ad-Din Aibak, appointing him governor or viceroy around 1192. Qutb ad-Din began construction of a mosque, for which he chose the site of an existing sanctuary that he demolished, and named it Quwwat al-Islam – the Might of Islam. It was intended to be the largest in India, with the tallest minaret. Everything calls for superlatives in this demonstration of the boundless ambition of the Afghan conquerors. In the Quwwat al-Islam Mosque the builders introduced a number of new construction-

opposite, above Detail of the decoration of the *iwan* of the Madrasa of the Imam, Isfahan.

opposite, below The 15th-century winter hall of the Friday Mosque in Isfahan still bears the stamp of the Mongol style. The powerful depressed vaults, whose arches go down to the ground, are lit by small openings glazed with slabs of alabaster.

below An *iwan* in the courtyard of the Madrasa of the Imam, Isfahan, a Qur'anic school built in 1320–40 and dedicated to the theologian Muhammad Baba Kasem al-Isfahani, who died in 1341. The system of large *muqarnas* in the vault is derived from the western *iwan* of the Friday Mosque in Isfahan (*ill.* pp. 218–19).

bottom Carved plaster decoration of the *mihrab* built by the 14th-century Il-Khan ruler Öljeytu Khudabanda, in the northern winter hall of the Friday Mosque in Isfahan. Most of what we see here composes an inscription.

al features: they no longer used bricks, as in the Persian world, but instead chose the fine materials available on the Indian plateau – red-mauve sandstone and white marble, which set up a superb counterpoint – and the master builders gradually taught the local workforce to build arches and vaults.

When Muhammad of Ghur died in 1206, Qutb ad-Din proclaimed himself sultan. The dynasty he founded came to be known as the Slave Dynasty, because Qutb ad-Din was a Mamluk. Career officers of Turkish origin, taken from their families at an early age to become slave-soldiers, the Mamluks through force and cunning eventually became rulers of the empire: they formed the personal guards of the caliph of Baghdad, of the sultans of Cairo, and of other independent kingdoms in the Middle East, and they were ready to act as soon as they sensed a power vacuum or a ruler in decline. From Delhi the Slave Dynasty (1206–90) imposed its authority on the principal regions of India occupied by the Muslims. At the Quwwat al-Islam Mosque, within a century, what had begun experimentally with new techniques had become a vast, sophisticated building project in proportion to the immense size of the country. Its construction was marked by dramatic events, and several of Qutb ad-Din's successors left their mark on it. For an analysis of this grandiose and symbolic building, see pp. 222–29.

The Mongols in Iran

Both India and Iran suffered attacks from various peoples of the steppes, and in the 13th century Central Asia and Iran entered a period of turbulence and chaos that came to a climax with the Mongol invasions. Indeed, the stirrings of the peoples of northern China were felt as far as Western Europe. The age of invasions brought the destruction of crops, the sacking of villages, the ruin of fields and of irrigation methods, the displacement of whole populations, and the deaths of tens of thousands, even hundreds of thousands, of people, in a storm of terror that left pyramids of heads as a memorial. Entire peoples were reduced to slavery, and civilization collapsed.

The attackers were Mongol hordes, who ravaged Asia from China to Anatolia and from Siberia to northern India. Beginning in the 12th century, the nomadic Karakitai on the borders of northern China sought to extend their hold over a vast territory. They headed west, entered Transoxiana north-east of Iran, and defeated the Seljuqs in 1141. Around 1210, however, the conquered territories were taken back from them by the shahs of Khwarazm (see p. 31), who formed a buffer against the peoples from the east. The tribes of Central Asia between Manchuria and Lake Baikal presented a permanent threat; their location and their ethnic origins are still often difficult to determine: some spoke Turkish, some Mongolian, and all led the same pastoral existence, moving throughout vast areas with horses, flocks, yurts and baggage wagons. It was in this 'no man's land' with vague borders that the Mongol hordes rose up; after achieving their own political unity, they prepared to attack the neighbouring sedentary kingdoms.

Their attention first turned to the east, with the aim of breaking down the resistance of China. Temüjin, the future Chinghiz Khan (born some time between 1162 and 1167), attacked the Tartars and subdued them, and in 1188 he managed to unite his own people. In 1206, an assembly of Mongol chiefs – whose religion was shamanism – gave him supreme command of all the tribes. His horsemen invaded north-western China, penetrated the Chin empire in 1211, and took Beijing four years later. After a series of victories on all fronts in Central Asia, Chinghiz Khan reached the frontier of Khwarazm and seized that territory in 1219: the first assault against a Muslim country was completely successful. In 1220, the Mongols took Balkh and Nishapur and invaded Iran, to which the last Shah of Khwarazm, Jalal ad-Din Mingburnu (1220–31), had also laid claim. In 1221 they turned south, moved through the Afghan passes, and penetrated into India, where they encountered resistance from Iltutmish, the Afghan sultan of Delhi. On its western side, Chinghiz Khan's empire now extended from Iran to the Indus basin. His troops launched themselves towards the Caucasus and the Crimea, circled the Caspian Sea and returned to Mongolia in 1225. Two years later, in 1227, the fearsome conqueror died, and his empire was divided among his four sons.

The Il-Khans in Iran

Chinghiz Khan's son Chagatai (1227–42) inherited the former dominions of the Karakitai – the regions near Iran, with the Uigur steppes and the region of Bukhara and Samarqand in Transoxiana. He declared his independence, and his inheritance was divided into two, Transoxiana and Mughalistan. The Mongols knew no boundaries, and the bloody epic of their conquests was now to be played out both on the western front, in Iran and Transoxiana, and in the Indian subcontinent with the Delhi Sultanate. Chagatai conquered Iran in 1235–39, and initiated the dynasty of Mongol sovereigns there known as the Il-Khans, or 'Deputy Khans', of which the first is officially regarded as Hülegü. The Mongols pressed on, reached the Upper Euphrates, and proceeded to take Baghdad, where, to the amazement of the Muslims, they put to death the 'Abbasid Caliph al-Mu'tasim. Thus ended a power than had endured for half a millennium, despite an eclipse towards the last and weakness revealed during

opposite Chinghiz Khan addressing his subjects from the *minbar* of the mosque in Bukhara, from a *History of Chinghiz Khan* by Ahmed Musa of Tabriz, 1397. (British Library, London)

below The Great Khan Monka presiding over festivities in honour of his brother Hülegü, Il-Khan of Iran, from a manuscript of the *Jami al-Tawarikh* or *Universal History* of Rashid ad-Din, late 16th century. (National Library, Tehran)

the period when the caliph, the Head of all Believers, was under the guardianship of the Buyid Emirs. Unlike other regions conquered by the horsemen of the steppes, where civilization collapsed, Iran's experience was positive, and in the most diverse fields. Iran had certainly paid a heavy price, with its cities sacked and part of its population massacred, but under the Il-Khans it experienced real prosperity. The Il-Khan Hülegü (1256–65) had married a Christian woman, and protected his wife's coreligionists. In his capital, Maragheh, in western Iran, he adopted Persian forms of administration, and he summoned to his court all the intellectuals of the period – poets, musicians, manuscript painters, architects, philosophers and scientists; for the scholar Nasir ad-Din at-Tusi he built a famous observatory.

Hülegü's son, Il-Khan Abaqha (1265–81), was a Buddhist, married to a daughter of the Byzantine emperor Michael VIII Palaeologus. His policy was anti-Muslim: he delegated power to his Jewish vizier, Saad al-Dawla, and destroyed the Isma'ilite principality of Assassins at Alamut. He planned an alliance with the Christians, and corresponded with Philip the Fair of France with the aim of organizing a crusade to restore the Latin Kingdom in the Near East, but the plan came to nothing. After the brief interregnum of Ahmad, Arghun came to the throne in 1284 and resumed relations with the European clergy, especially with Pope Honorius IV, favouring the Nestorian Christians.

But then a crucial development occurred in Iran: Il-Khan Mahmud Ghazan (1295–1304), in his new capital of Tabriz, converted to Islam, and the ruling class of the Mongols came to share the religion of the majority. Mahmud Ghazan, a good administrator, applied a policy modelled on the Persian system, with a result that has been called a 'golden age'. He undertook great building campaigns, which employed thousands of local and Armenian workers; he completed the observatory at Maragheh, commissioned a series of public buildings, built bridges, and laid out roads. In short, he renewed the infrastructure, and the country recovered its prosperity.

left and below Ceramic decoration on the interior and exterior of the gallery that runs round the upper storey of the Tomb of Öljeytu Khudabanda at Soltaniyeh. The ornament of the Mongol period favoured geometrical motifs and inscriptions.

Mongol Architecture

Mahmud Ghazan was succeeded by Öljeytu Khudabanda (1304–16), the son of Arghun. Öljeytu wanted to make Twelver Shi'ism the official religion, and to this end in 1307 he began an extraordinary structure at Soltaniyeh, which was to be his new capital, south of Tabriz. This introduced a totally new scale for Shi'ite mausoleums, and had a formal character which, in conjunction with the practice of circumambulation, was intended to respond to the popular wish for ritual. Öljeytu intended that it should contain the relics of the Prophet's descendants, Ali and Husayn, and that it should become the principal centre of Shi'ite pilgrimage. As with many Mongol buildings, such as the Friday Mosque of Tabriz, its vast scale expresses the power of an empire that extended from the Upper Euphrates to the frontiers of India.

The mausoleum at Soltaniyeh covers an area of about 60 x 40 metres and encloses an octagonal space with an interior diameter of 24.5 metres, covered by a dome that reaches to a height of 48 metres above the floor. This inner space has eight *iwan*-like features, on the main axes and the diagonals. The dome is not supported on straightforward squinches, as in Seljuq construction: instead, the transition from the octagonal perimeter wall to its circular base is made by a triple row of stalactites. In its design it marks the appearance of a new technological solution: it is elliptical in section, with a hollowed-out structure, thus prefiguring by more than a century Brunelleschi's dome for Florence Cathedral (though that is much larger, with a diameter of 43 metres).

There is no external buttressing. Instead, on the lower two storeys deep niches are pierced in the walls inside, while on the top storey deep openings face outward, lighting a gallery intended for circumambulation (a gallery perhaps intended for the same purpose also exists in the near-contemporany tomb of Shah Rukn-i 'Alam at Multan: see pp. 54–55). Stretches of solid wall between the triple openings on each side at the top serve to stiffen the structure. This hollowing out of the walls, in a way that recalls Gothic architecture in the West, gives the Soltaniyeh mausoleum a great sense of vertical energy. Finally, eight small minarets surround the egg-shaped dome; they stand on the corners of the octagon, providing a vertical thrust to neutralize the outward forces exerted by the dome, in the manner of Gothic pinnacles.

To be a worthy site for the cult of the Shi'ite imams, the structure was sumptuously decorated, with red, blue, black and white ceramic mosaics forming refined geometrical motifs set into the natural brick. In the end, however, the relics never came to Soltaniyeh. The building became the tomb of its patron, Sultan Öljeitü, and it is as such that it passed into history.

The colossal character of the Mongol architecture of Iran was most apparent in the Friday Mosque of Tabriz, begun around 1310, of which all that survives today is part of the ruined sanctuary with an apsed *mihrab*. In scale the mosque openly competed with the Sasanian palace at Ctesiphon, with its great arch 36 metres high, 27 metres wide and 43 metres deep (ill. p. 298): Taj ad-Din Ali Shah Jilan Tabrizi, one of Öljeitü's ministers, boasted that he had given the Friday Mosque of Tabriz an oblong courtyard that measured 250 x 200 metres and, better still, a brick *iwan* 30 metres in span and 65 metres in depth with a vault that must have been some 40 metres high. The boldness of the scheme can be guessed today by looking at the springing of the arch, on piers 10 metres thick that still rise to a height of 25 metres.

At Natanz, between Kashan and Isfahan, the Friday Mosque, with four classic *iwans*, was built at the beginning of the 14th cen-

tury (ill. pp. 41, 44–45). In addition, it incorporates a mausoleum built in 1308 for Shaikh Abd'as-Samad Isfahani, which has a handsome doorway decorated with polychrome mosaics. (By now, colour was being used on surfaces overall, and play was made with relief, incorporating inscriptions in a very stylized kufic script.) The tomb is covered with a roof in the shape of an eight-sided pyramid, clad with patterns in blue-green ceramic. Inside is a square space with projecting square 'apses' in the centre of each side, producing a cruciform plan which is emphasized at the top of the walls by an inscription band (ill. p. 44 below). Above this, a zone pierced with eight screened windows supports a vault composed of large stalactites. The complex vocabulary is very elaborate and recalls the so-called Tomb of Zubeida in Baghdad, which dates from the 13th century.

Many buildings were erected in the Mongol period, but few survive in good condition. Among those few is a fine building in Varamin with a central dome, erected for Imamzadeh Yahya in a number of campaigns between 1261 and 1307. It has aisles covered with five small domes to buttress the main one, and its interior decoration features carved and undercut stucco work of great refinement, based on logically stylized palmettes and vine-trails. The *mihrab* must have been especially sumptuous: late 19th-century accounts describe it as covered with superb lustreware *kashi*, which have all since disappeared.

Many Mongol buildings were decorated with stucco reliefs of vigorous design (ill. p. 47 below), in which supple floral motifs with plump leaves form arabesques. Their opulent shapes must have been painted in bright colours, but stucco is highly sensitive to humidity and changes in temperature, and the polychromy rarely survives.

above The Tomb of the Il-Khan Öljeytu Khudabanda, Soltaniyeh. The imposing octagonal structure, surmounted by a dome originally flanked by eight minarets, was intended to contain the relics of the first Shi'ite imams, Ali and Husayn.

India under the Tughluqs

Sultan 'Ala ad-Din Khalji was responsible for the final enlargement of the Quwat ul-Islam Mosque in Delhi, and the measures he adopted for reorganizing the country and its economy revived the fortunes of Muslim India, to the point where Muslim troops enjoyed unrivalled supremacy. All of middle India was conquered and annexed between 1297 and 1310, and then general Malik Kafur took possession of the Deccan as far south as Madurai, founding a mosque on the shores of the Indian Ocean facing Sri Lanka to celebrate his triumph. While this expansion was going on, the Khaljis remained alert to the Mongol threat. In 1297 Mongol forces besieged Delhi: there the defenders fended them off, but they went on to sack Lahore. When 'Ala ad-Din died in 1316, Malik Kafur was pitiless in his suppression of any attempt at insurrection. 'Ala ad-Din's son, Qutb ad-Din Mubarak Shah, took advantage of this time of anarchy to seize the throne, but occupied it only for a short time before being murdered by his confidant, Khusraw Khan.

The Khalji dynasty came to an end, and was succeeded in 1320 by the Turkish Tughluq dynasty under Ghiyas ad-Din Tughluq (1320–25). In 1327 a new Mongol expedition was launched against Delhi, but its chief, Termachirin, failed to take the city and converted to Islam. In the realm of art, the Tughluqs fostered a new style notable for its eclecticism. Politically, the beginnings were difficult: the son of Ghiyas ad-Din had his father assassinated, and ascended the throne under the name of Muhammad ibn Tughluq (1325–51). Although he was highly cultured, he pursued incoherent policies, and acted in ways that were unpredictable and unwise. Historians paint contrasting portraits of him. The Arab traveller Ibn Battuta of Tangier (1304–77), who visited India in 1333, noted that the sultan 'loves to give presents and to shed blood'. Muhammad Shah, he added, 'is the most generous and the most bloodythirsty man: at his door you will always find a poor man whom he will enrich and an unfortunate whom he will put to death'; yet he is 'the most humble, fair and just of men. He practices the faith and is very insistent that the faithful observe the times of prayer, and punishes those who do not. He is a king whose happiness is constant and whose fortune is out of the ordinary.'

When Ibn Battuta reached Delhi, he wrote: 'The capital of India is very extensive and populous. It is the largest city in India, if not the largest Islamic city in the East. It now consists of four contiguous cities. The third is Tughluqabad, named after its builder.' Tughluqabad was founded by Ghiyas ad-Din Tughluq in 1321. The city was surrounded by a wall of distinctive profile, with a very marked batter.

The same feature characterizes the tomb that the sultan began to build in 1325 on a small island in the centre of an artificial lake, now drained; it was completed by his son, Muhammad, and its design reflects the period of wars and insurrections in which it was built. It stands within an enclosure that looks like a powerful polygonal bastion, with five massive towers, three of which are squat and broad, with a truncated conical shape, and surmounted by battlements with two levels of arrowslits. A causeway leads to a fortified door, which is overhung on the right by one of the towers, to prevent attackers from using their shields, held on their left side. Within this impressive space, whose irregular shape recalls the prow of a ship, stands the square mausoleum, made of red sandstone, which also has battered walls. The façades are built of immaculately squared ashlar enlivened with details in white marble, and the dome is dazzlingly white. The Tughluq style is powerful and geometric: it combines strongly sloping walls, inspired by defensive architecture, with a strict rationality of form. The hall inside the mausoleum perfectly illustrates this fusion of manners: the lower part of the walls, up to mid-height, is of red sandstone, while the upper part is covered in white marble. The dome rests on smooth squinches that alternate with pointed arches to form an octagon. Throughout, the work of the Indian stonemasons is of superlative quality. Here already, in the first half of the 14th century, Islamic architecture found a fully resolved style that was to influence future dynasties in the Delhi Sultanate.

opposite A miniature from the Demotte *Shahnama*, painted in Tabriz. (Reza Abbassi Museum, Tehran)

below A miniature from the Demotte *Shahnama* portraying the Indian army in flight before the iron horsemen of Iskandar (Alexander). The influence of Chinese manuscript painting is evident, particularly in the shapes of the clouds and of the flames that come from the nostrils of the iron horses mounted on wheels.

Mongol Manuscript Painting

Manuscript painting in Iran experienced its first flowering in the Mongol period. Paper was introduced into Iran from China in 753. In the time of the Il-Khans the first miniatures made their appearance, heralds of an art in which the Persian world was destined to shine with incomparable splendour. The earliest known illustrated Persian manuscript dates from the reign of Ghazan: it was executed in Maragheh, and one can immediately see how much its figurative art owes to Chinese models – which is not surprising, since the culture that produced it had long served as an intermediary between the West and China. It is a bestiary, containing pictures of lions, horses and other animals with some suggestion of their natural setting, including thickets, birds and trees, and dates from 1298.

Some thirty years later, the earliest copies of Firdawsi's *Shahnama* include more sophisticated figures, horsemen, monstrous dragons and horses spitting fire. These were products of the school of Tabriz, which was to be characterized by a perfect rendering of movement, of the composition of crowd scenes, and of the actions of battle. Skies show the influence of Chinese painting, with whorled clouds and brilliant spirals set against intense blue backgrounds. The distinctive Persian vision is most clearly displayed not in landscape but in the rendering of space and of architecture – especially the angled surfaces, walls depicted frontally, and ground portrayed vertically in tiered stages to suggest perspective. Constant development led to the climax of Persian miniature painting in the Timurid period.

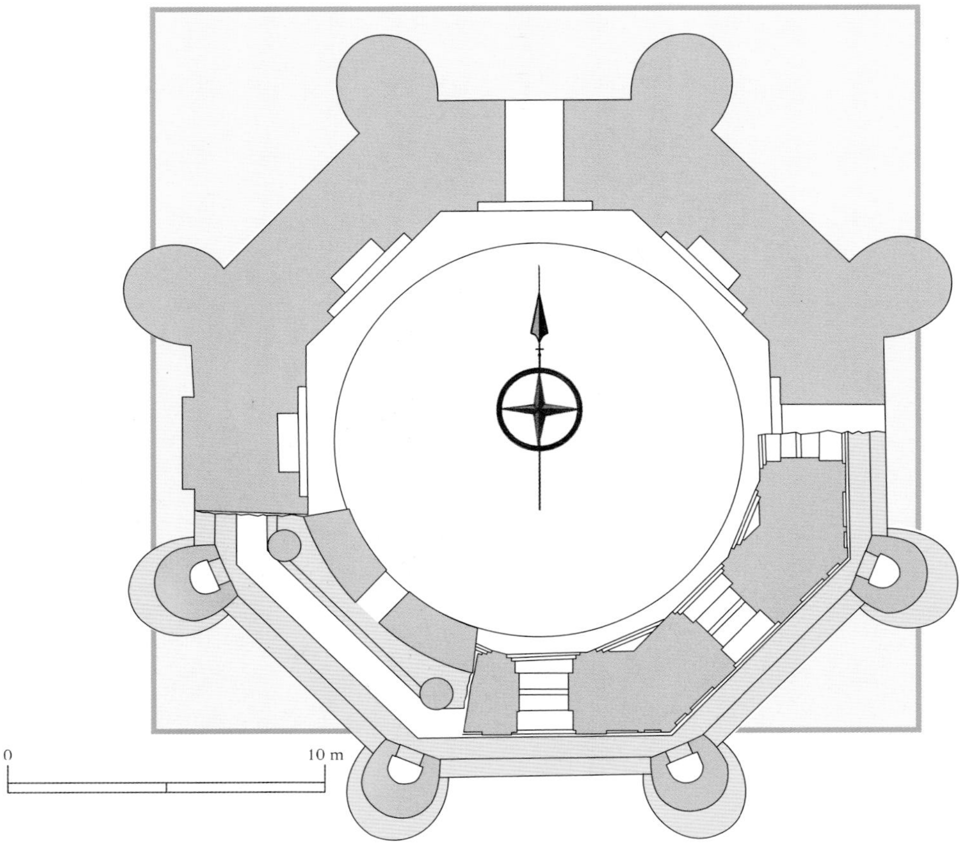

The Tomb of Rukn-i 'Alam at Multan

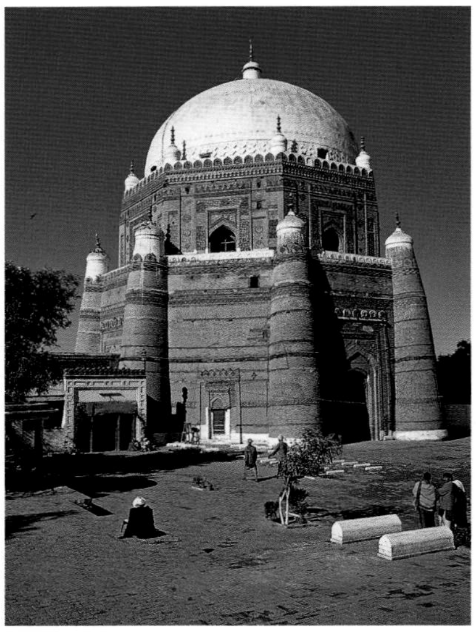

In the 14th century the city of Multan, in the centre of present-day Pakistan, was the capital of the Punjab. A Turkish governor resided there as representative of the sultan in Delhi, Ghiyas ad-Din Tughluq, and there, on his master's orders, he built a magnificent tomb that was destined to hold the remains of a holy man named Rukn-i 'Alam ('Pillar of the World').

The tomb was built in 1320–24 on a height above the city; because of the alluvial nature of the Indus basin, it is of brick and not of stone, as it would have been in Delhi. The design has a strong Persian character, and it is quite different in plan from the tomb that Ghiyas ad-Din built for himself slightly later at Tughluqabad.

The building consists of an octagonal lower storey 27.50 metres in diameter, surmounted by an upper storey and a hemispherical dome. The lower storey, 15 metres high, has a marked batter, like contemporary fortresses, and attached towers at the corners that turn into pinnacles above parapet level. The second storey, also octagonal, is set back, and again has pinnacles at the corners. Its walls rise for 7.5 metres without visible buttressing, despite the thrust from the dome above. The dome internally is 15 metres in diameter and 34.50 metres tall.

The brick fabric of this proud and severe structure is enlivened by decoration in blue ceramic: the framing of the pointed-arched openings of the upper storey, borders, and fictive battlements make play with star motifs, interlace and arabesques. All this ornamentation in blue combines with the dazzling white of the limewashed dome to produce an effect of freshness and lightness. Inside, bands of calligraphy with sacred texts run around the wooden *mihrab* in the tomb chamber.

Consistent with its function as the tomb of a holy man, the building has on the upper level a gallery that could have served for the rite of

circumambulation, permitting the faithful to circle round the tomb chamber, where the venerated cenotaph was located at ground level.

Both the *parti* of this two-storeyed octagonal mausoleum and the brilliant technical skill displayed in its hemispherical brick dome seem to look back to the Iran of the Il-Khans and specifically to Soltaniyeh, where the Mongol Sultan Öljeytu built a grandiose octagonal tomb a few years earlier (see pp. 50–51). Both derive from the octagonal Dome of the Rock in Jerusalem, the oldest Islamic monument, built in 687 (ill. p. 307).

The glazed bricks and tiles that decorate the mausoleum recall the achievements of the Persian artisans of Kashan, Natanz and Tabriz.

opposite, above Composite plan of the ground, gallery and first-floor levels.

opposite, below General view, showing the corner buttresses in the form of attached towers and the hemispherical dome dominating the octagonal structure.

above The decorative motifs in blue-glazed ceramic, combined with the white limewashed surfaces of parapet, pinnacles and the great dome, brighten the bare brick.

3

Samarqand and the Masterworks of the Timurids

After a period of anarchy at the end of the Il-Khan dynasty, the entire region between China and the Mediterranean was again thrown into chaos by the irruption of Timur-i Lang, emir of Transoxiana (1336–1405). Timur the Lame, or Tamerlane, was of Turkish-Mongol stock; his father, Taraghai, belonged to the Barlas tribe and had converted to Islam around 1330. He entered the service of Tughluq Timur, the khan of Mughalistan, and later served Jalal ad-Din in Seistan. He married the daughter of a khan of the family of Chagatai, and through her claimed kinship with Chinghiz Khan.

Timur conquered Transoxiana and proclaimed himself ruler, with a gold crown, in 1370; named Grand Emir by the Mongol 'council', he determined to recreate the empire of Chinghiz Khan. He chose Samarqand as his capital and built a new citadel there, and reorganized the army of Mughalistan so that his troops moved in good order: he was accompanied by cavalry, infantry, transport waggons, treasury and weapons, followed by flocks, horses, camels, and finally the tribe on the march. With these battle-hardened troops he launched a series of military campaigns of unprecedented savagery. In the course of his reign he conquered Khwarazm three times, eastern Iran twice, and western Iran three times. Some historians believe that Timur's troop movements and fearsome expeditions had no clear plan behind them; for others, however, he was motivated by the determination to revive the greatness of Chinghiz Khan. The methods he used were effective, and indeed resembled those of Chinghiz Khan himself. Timur laid waste cities that resisted him, and slaughtered their population. When he took Herat in Khorasan, he sacked the city, sold the inhabitants as slaves, and appointed his son, barely fifteen years old, as governor. He went on to attack Kandahar, besiege Rayy, occupy Soltaniyeh, and take possession of Tabriz in Azerbaijan. Timur wanted to expand his territory in the direction of Iran, where, since the collapse of the Mongols, the Muzaffarids had ruled over Isfahan and Shiraz. According to chroniclers of the time he repressed a revolt in Isfahan at the cost of 70,000 dead, leaving pyramids of heads; and as was his custom, when he quit the city he took withhim a company of architects, artists, scholars, painters and craftsmen.

In 1380, he embarked on a fight to the death against the Golden Horde (a dissident Mongol khanat) and then ravaged the areas of Kipchak, Crimea and Transcaucasus in 1390–95. Turning to India, he overthrew the sultan in Delhi and looted the city for three days; there, too, his warriors erected pyramids of heads, leaving the bodies for the vultures. The plunder was immense: it is said that every soldier took away twenty prisoners as his slaves. The sack of its capital left India weakened and demoralized. Timur returned to Samarqand from India with scores of scholars and thousands of artisans. Khizr Khan was appointed governor of Multan and placed in control of Lahore. The empire of the Delhi Sultans was shattered, and anarchy reigned as power was dispersed among individual cities and provinces; famine and plague were everywhere. India fell into a terrible decline from which it did not recover for half a century. To the west, Timur's armies devastated Aleppo, Damascus and Baghdad. He then decided to attack the Ottomans, and in 1402 defeated Bayazid I near Ankara; the Sultan subsequently died in prison. In 1404 Timur gathered an army of 200,000 men for an invasion of China, but the day after crossing the Syr Darya he fell ill, and then died. His body was carried back to Samarqand.

After much wranging over the succession, Timur's fourth son, Shah Rukh, mounted the throne: born in 1377, he ruled until 1447 and was the founder in 1409 of the Timurid dynasty. At the time of Timur's death the empire he had created was immense: from Anatolia to India, and from the Caspian Sea to the Persian Gulf, he had eliminated all opposition. The 'Scourge of God' who caused Asia and the West to tremble appears in a negative light in the records of contemporary chroniclers, and tales of his destructive power are endlessly repeated. Yet he left a positive legacy as well: thanks to him, Transoxiana saw a remarkable revival of the arts and of culture, and by analogy with the Italian Renaissance, the period between 1405 and 1501 could almost be called a Timurid Quattrocento. A spirit of unprecedented boldness and grandeur diffused the forms and concepts of the 'Persian style' throughout the Middle East and Central Asia.

With the Timurid renaissance the architectural language was revitalized, as new buildings were set within grandiose urban plans. Timur began in Shakhrisabz (also known as Kech), the capital of the Barlas tribe, near his native village: there, from 1379 on, he laid out

p. 56, above and below Details of Timurid tile mosaics on the Great Mosque at Yazd, 15th century.

p. 57 A minaret crowned with *muqarnas*, and the ribbed dome of the Gur-i Emir or Tomb of Timur in Samarqand, 1398–1404.

opposite, above The sultan of Delhi retreating before Timur, from a manuscript of the *Zafarnama*.

opposite, below Timur, depicted in a gouache of 1774. (Bibliothèque Nationale de France, Paris.

above Timur receives the surrender of the Ottoman Sultan Bayazid I (1360–1403). Detail of a miniature from a manuscript of the *Zafarnama*, a history of Timur by Sharaf al-Din 'Ali Yazdi, painted in Shiraz *c.* 1600. (British Library, London.

a huge park with a residence called Ak-Saray, the 'White Palace'. He never lived there, however: he had sprung from a nomad clan, and always refused to settle, preferring to live surrounded by his riches in a tent in one of the ornamental parks that he created around his buildings. At the entrance to Ak-Saray and its green spaces, he erected a formidable gate that even surpassed in scale the colossal Friday Mosque in Tabriz, built by the Il-Khanids. The two enormous piers of masonry survive to a height of 22.5 metres up to the springing of the arch, and the crown of the vault must have been 38 metres high (the building itself was some 50 metres tall) – thus outdoing the famous arch of the Sasanid palace at Ctesiphon (ill. p. 298), which remained a constant challenge for Islamic builders.

In his capital, Samarqand, Timur carried out great works. First of all, for security, in 1370 he built a new citadel, within whose walls were a residence, a guardhouse, and administrative and military buildings. Once that was accomplished, he set about entirely reshaping the plan of the city and placing new structures within it.

The Persianization of Transoxiana

In town planning and architecture, painting and manuscript illustration, astronomy and the sciences, Timur surrounded himself with outstanding figures gathered together from Iran and from regions influenced by Iran, and placed most of the responsibility for development in their hands. He spared no expense, and gave them every opportunity to realize great buildings and to diffuse throughout the empire the ornament and culture that had evolved in Islamic Iran over the last three centuries.

Of the architects and master builders, calligraphers and carpenters who worked on buildings still standing today in Samarqand the names of 108 have been discovered (see Lisa Golombek and Donald Wilber, *The Timurid Architecture of Iran and Turan*, Princeton, 1988), and most of them were of Persian origin. Among those whose patronymics indicate their place of origin (about half), there are no fewer than 6 from Isfahan ('Isfahani'), 6 from Shiraz ('Shirazi'), 7 from Tabriz ('Tabrizi'), and 5 from Yazd ('Yazdi'), as well as others from Amol, Mashhad, Nishapur, Kerman, etc. The list is vivid evidence for the spread of the 'Persian style' in Transoxiana under the Timurids.

Transoxiana, 'the land beyond the Oxus', is an immense region of steppes, where between the Amu Darya and the Syr Darya millions of hectares need only irrigation to be fertile. Here already in antiquity, and especially under the Sasanids, enormous hydrological works were undertaken using the rivers that flowed down to the Aral Sea from the Hindu Kush, Pamir and Tian Shan mountain ranges: the result was to provide now-sedentary farmers with wheat-producing lands that gave rise to flourishing civilizations. After the arrival of Islam, first the Ghaznavids, and then the shahs of Khwarazm in the west, made Transoxiana the centre of great empires.

The growing volume of trade between China and Europe under the Mongols gave new life to the ancient Silk Road, the commercial highway that was already in use under the Romans, and it was on this major artery of international exchange that Timur decided to build his capital. Here, at the end of the 14th century, he made Samarqand the hub of the world, and the lustre of this city from which he reigned over his vast possessions is still perceptible in the unique collection of mosques, mausoleums, *madrasas*, *khanaqahs* (monasteries) and caravanserais and the extraordinary astronomical observatory that survive to this day.

The style of the architecture of Samarqand soon spread throughout the Timurid empire, to Bukhara, Shakhrisabz, Balkh, Herat, Merv, Mashhad, Nishapur, Isfahan, Kashan, Kerman, Natanz, Yadz, and minor centres. This extraordinary flowering, roughly from 1360 to 1510, produced a series of masterpieces: paraphrasing a famous medieval text, one could say that the land was covered with a bright robe of mosques and *madrasas*.

Architecture, with its sumptuous polychrome ceramic decoration, was not the only thing to shine in the Timurid universe: so too did poetry and the arts involved in making books (miniature painting and calligraphy), history, and the sciences. The illustrations of the *Shahnama* produced in Herat and Shiraz are unrivalled in their splendour and virtuosity, even by the manuscript painting of the Safavids.

above Timur captures the city of Herat. This somewhat crude 15th-century Persian miniature conveys the violence of the conflict. (British Library, London)

opposite The splendour of the Timurid court is suggested by this fine 15th-century miniature in the style of Herat. Timur had ascended the throne in 1370 at Balkh in northern Afghanistan, proclaiming himself emir of Transoxiana and the successor of Chinghiz Khan. (British Library, London)

بفرخ ترین ساعت آمد بتخت
خدیو جهانگیر فیروز بخت

The Shah-i Zinda cemetery at Samarqand, ringed by walls and accessible only through an imposing gate built in 1435 by Ulugh Beg (*top*), contains the most notable Timurid tombs, dating from *c.* 1350–1460.

Throughout Transoxiana, Iran (including Khorasan) and Afghanistan some 250 buildings of the Timurid period survive, in restored form or as fragments. To this impressive total one should add all the lost buildings known from chronicles, archives, and historical narratives. Often these buildings are inscribed within a coherent urban plan; mosque, *madrasa*, library, gardens, caravanserai, perhaps even a tomb and associated sanctuary, may be grouped together in an architectural complex.

The Timurid age initiated several town-planning schemes: at Samarqand, for instance, Timur 'made a metropolis out of a village'. He ordered the construction of a bazaar street that crossed the city from end to end, which was vaulted throughout, to provide shade in summer and protection in winter from the icy winds of the steppes. Within it each merchant had an arched bay with a shop facing the street and a storeroom behind. Here you might find every conceivable product from the empire and from distant lands. Timur's new city lay to the south of the ancient citadel, and between the two was the cemetery of Shah-i Zinda. Here the street began. It then passed the immense Mosque of Bibi Khanum (named after Timur's wife), continued towards the complex of the Registan, and finally reached the buildings of the Gur-i Emir, the Tomb of Timur, comprising mausoleum, *madrasa* and *khanaqah*. At intervals along the street there were public fountains, fed by the city's water system.

The residential quarters consisted of a maze of low buildings with flat roofs, usually built of mud brick, each of which had a courtyard in which shade trees grew. There were also vast irrigated public gardens in which people could stroll and relax. Seen from afar, the city of Samarqand appeared covered in greenery.

Ruy González de Clavijo has left an account of the time when he was ambassador to Timur from the court of Spain. The capital then had 150,000 inhabitants within its walls, and more than that number again outside the walls, where incomers were drawn by the thriving economy and its need for manual labour. At its height, the

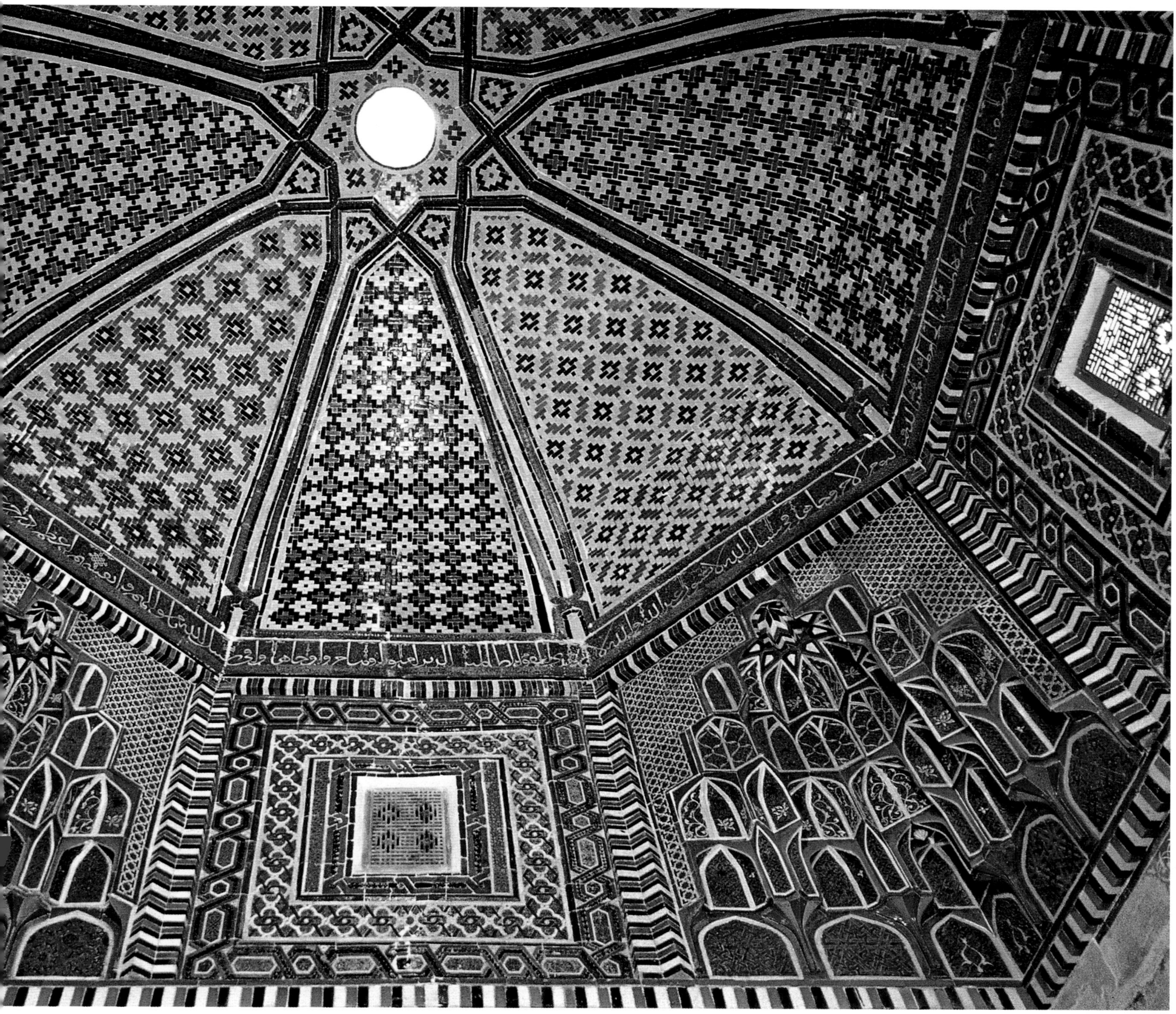

Timurid city must have had a population of 350,000–400,000, a remarkable figure when you think that contemporary Paris, the largest European city after Constantinople, only had 200,000 inhabitants.

This astonishing prosperity can be ascribed in part to the proceeds of sacking and to the tributes paid by conquered cities. But other factors were the substantial expansion of cultivated areas, made possible by the building of further irrigation canals in Transoxiana; the revenue from taxes on trade and on the transport of exotic merchandise such as silk and spices; and the effect of the construction schemes promoted by Timur. These depended on immense injections of funds from subject countries; but those funds, combined with the importation of a multitude of foreign workers, led to fantastic economic growth and to a great increase in the size of the urban population.

opposite, centre The Tomb of Shad-i Mulk Agha, of 1371–83, is lined with very fine polychrome tiles.

opposite, below *Muqarnas* of glazed and relief ceramic on the Tomb of Kutluk Agha, 1361. This building is traditionally believed to be the mausoleum of Timur's wife.

above Inside, the recently restored Tomb of Kutluk Agha has an octagonal dome with squinches filled with *muqarnas*. Its ceramic decoration displays the virtuosity of 14th-century Timurid potters.

Details of tombs in the Shah-i Zinda cemetery: the door of the Tomb of Amir Husayn (*above left*), of 1376, with ceramic decoration in relief; a tile panel on the Tomb of Ustad Alim Nasafi (*above right*), of 1385, with vine scrolls, flowers and geometrical motifs; the Tomb of Khodja Ahmed (*below*), of 1350, with a range of ceramic techniques and a band of dynamic large *thuluth* script; and superb relief *kashi* on the Tomb of Emir Zadeh (*opposite*), of 1386.

South of the old city (which included the old citadel), a cemetery had begun to grow in the 11th century on the site of the burial of an early promoter of the Islamic faith killed at the siege of Samarqand in 677, Kusan ibn 'Abbas, who was a close relative of the Prophet. According to legend he did not die, but was still alive under the city – whence the name of the cemetery: Shah-i Zinda, 'the Living King'. From the mid-14th century onward for a century or so the cemetery was extended in a distinctive way, as a number of rich mausoleums, funerary mosques and commemorative monuments were positioned along the path leading to the shrine. These buildings, inside and out, have ceramic facings in dazzling colours and in all the techniques available at the time. The cemetery became a sort of laboratory for experiments with colour, and even in its ruined state today it provides a display of the most varied shades of blue and turquoise. Mosaics and tiles (*kashis*) glitter, still as bright as when they were first put in position. Developments in architecture were matched by developments in the potter's art, probably under the influence of ceramics from Sung and later Ming China.

As is natural in a cemetery, the buildings themselves are not large. Along the sinuous path there are some thirty small domed structures, which include two mosques that have become the setting for specific rituals. The chief importance of the Shah-i Zinda lies in the early use of polychrome ceramic on both external and internal surfaces, in which a distinctive style emerges, based on formulas from various areas of Iran.

Opposite the cemetery hill a great market grew up, and next to it rose Timur's Friday Mosque, known as the Mosque of Bibi Khanum. There we see the epitome of the new style introduced by the conqueror on his return from India.

Enriched by his victory over the Delhi Sultans, in 1398 Timur decided to build a mosque in Samarqand that would be commensurate with his power. The result was a colossal structure, on the scale of the great entrance portal of the Ak-Saray at Shakhrisabz. Just as Chinghiz

The Mosque of Bibi Khanum, Samarqand, begun in 1398

opposite One of the two secondary domes. Slightly horseshoe-shaped in profile, it has heavy ribs with ceramic decoration and stands on a drum faced with holy inscriptions.

below and bottom The frame of the main *iwan* is flanked by polygonal buttressing towers. Inscriptions and starry motifs of characteristic Timurid splendour cover the entire surface above a high marble plinth decorated with geometrical patterns. With its great height (nearly 40 metres), seen from close to it conceals the dome over the prayer hall.

Khan had delighted in enormous creations, Timur wanted his Friday Mosque to accommodate most of the inhabitants of the capital.

The Mosque of Bibi Khanum stands within a high wall. Its rectangular plan measures 109 x 167 metres, and in typically Persian fashion it has a courtyard (65 x 75 metres) with four *iwans*, one in the centre of each façade. In the middle of the courtyard is a formidable stone lectern, intended for a Qur'an of superhuman dimensions – probably the largest book every made – the better to honour the Word of the Prophet.

At the four corners of the great enclosing wall there were originally four tall cylindrical minarets. Four even taller polygonal minarets, in pairs, flank a monumental *pishtaq* and frame the principal *iwan* that leads to the room containing the *mihrab*. The dome of that room has been rebuilt, but its interior is still in ruinous condition.

The four *iwans* vary in size depending on their function. The one that corresponds to the great entrance portal is of the same width as those on the sides of the court, but deeper. Each of the lateral *iwans* leads into a room with a dome 9 metres in diameter that echoes the main dome. The latter, partly concealed by the great axial *iwan*, has suffered various vicissitudes: it collapsed for the first time in 1404, shortly after its construction, and then again in 1897, when an earthquake destroyed Samarqand. It was rebuilt after 1975 on the basis of a careful study of a surviving fragment by Soviet architects and archaeologists, and now this large, slightly bulbous dome, some 40 metres tall and covered by a superb layer of blue-green ceramic, once again offers its glittering, spherical surface to the rays of the sun, providing a lively contrast to the two secondary domes at the sides, which are lower and which have thirty-six thick ribs enlivened by midnight blue, white and orange tiles.

The courtyard was originally surrounded by three storeys of galleries topped by about four hundred small brickwork domes. While most of the building is of brick, there were also a vast number of monolithic supports: some say 400–480, but, if the reconstructed plan is correct, there would have been 312. These are columns of marble, a stone rare in Transoxiana, which was brought to the site by ninety-five Indian elephants specially trained to transport heavy materials. As in all regions of alluvial soil, there were few local craftsmen capable of working in stone rather than the traditional brick, so two hundred masons were brought from Azerbaijan.

The great entrance *pishtaq* had a colossal archway 35 metres tall: here again, the Timurids were responding to the challenge of the Sasanid *iwan* at Ctesiphon. Sadly its restoration was interrupted by the collapse of the Soviet Union and the independence of Uzbekistan, and it stands filled with metal scaffolding that grows rustier by the day.

Thus Timur spared no expense to give his great mosque an unrivalled splendour. It is unusual in rising from open ground, rather than being fitted into a dense urban fabric like Persian mosques, and it also

has domes of a novel type. Some are smooth and some are ribbed; all stand out high against the sky on a cylindrical drum. This scheme made a double-shell system necessary, since a dome that was tall enough to be effective from outside would be so tall inside that it would produce an uncomfortable space. The Timurid architects therefore built a second, lower shell inside, leaving an empty, windowless space between the two, which had no purpose other than to accommodate the patron's wish for grandeur without and ease of proportion within. Possibly the earliest dome of this type is that of the Gur-i Amir (ill. p. 70, below left); its noble progeny include the Mosque of the Imam (Masjid-i Shah) in Isfahan and the Taj Mahal.

The double-shell dome seems to have been a Timurid invention: examples earlier than the those of the Bibi Khanum Mosque occur in the Shah-i Zinda cemetery, on the late 14th-century Tomb of Shirin Bika Aka and the Tomb of Tuman Aka, of 1385, and also in the city of Turkestan, where the sanctuary of Khvajeh Ahmad Yasavi was built on the order of Timur in 1395 or 1397.

Just as the frame around the great arch of the *iwan* accentuates the beauty of the space to which it leads, so the proud silhouette of domes emphasizes the triumphal character of the building they crown, devised through its splendour and monumentality to proclaim the glory of its illustrious founder.

The Mosque of Bibi Khanum, Samarqand

left The large dome over the prayer hall is superbly decorated: its smooth turquoise cap rests on a zone of *muqarnas* faced with embossed tiles, bands of various types of ornament and inscriptions in cursive script.

top A detail of a shaft of the great *iwan* (cf. p. 67, above). Here too, texts alternate with patterns in multicoloured ceramic.

above A detail of one of the two secondary domes, Each of the ribs rests on a cluster of *muqarnas*, and is decorated in various shades of blue set off against white and brick red. A meticulous restoration has recaptured the original glittering appearance.

The Gur-i Amir, Timur's Mausoleum in Samarqand

At the other end of the city, also around 1398, construction began on a religious complex consisting of a *madrasa* and a *khanaqah* grouped round a square courtyard, preceded by a doorway in the form of a *pishtaq*. To this was soon added a dynastic mausoleum, completed in 1404. That commission was overseen by Muhammad Sultan, Timur's grandson and heir presumptive, but he was killed in battle at the age of twenty-nine, and so was the first to be buried there. He was soon followed by Timur himself, and then by Timur's successors, Shah Rukh and Ulugh Beg. The veneration in which the mausoleum was held protected it over the centuries, whereas other some buildings in the complex have disappeared.

The Gur-i Amir, or Gur Emir, the 'Tomb of the Emir', is 33 metres high, and consists of an octagonal lower structure surmounted by a drum 10 metres tall (15 metres in diameter), and a ribbed dome of swelling profile. This dome has a double skin: the space between the two, about 15 metres high, is filled with timber beams which are fixed to the summit of the lower, inner dome, and which serve to counter the centrifugal thrust of the bulbous outer dome. Underneath is a square funerary hall, 10.20 metres square, with shallow recesses in the middle of the four sides that produce a cruciform plan. The direction of Mecca is indicated by the presence of a *mihrab* in the south-western recess. The furnishings and decoration work together to stress the sumptuous character. In the stucco facing of the walls, heightened with gold and silver, play is made with ornamental motifs and miniature *muqarnas* to obtain glittering effects.

This funerary chamber contains the cenotaphs of the early members of the Timurid dynasty; their actual tombs are in a crypt below – a room no more than 2 metres in height, with walls and vault of exposed ochre-coloured limestone, which presents a striking contrast to the dazzling space above. That upper room soon became a place of veneration, drawing the inhabitants of Samarqand and the surrounding area.

The vast entrance *iwan* of the mausoleum, flanked by two minarets 25 metres high and 33 metres apart, marks the building's façade to the courtyard. The *pishtaq* bears an inscription that identifies the architect, who was, it seems, responsible for the design as a whole; it reads, 'The work of Muhammad bin Mahmud al-banna al-Isfahani'. The phrase following the name means 'builder, from Isfahan'. Thus there is no doubt that this monument, perhaps the most celebrated of the Timurid period, has a Persian pedigree.

opposite, above The interior of the funerary chamber, showing the cenotaphs.

opposite, below left The double-shelled dome on its tall cylindrical drum, and one of the two *muqarnas*-crowned minarets.

opposite, below right A detail of the ribbed dome. The decoration is not yet as sophisticated as that seen on the secondary domes of the Mosque of Bibi Khanum (cf. p. 69, below), and the *muqarnas* are much simpler.

above Looking up at the *mihrab* wall. In this building devised to honour Timur, the art of Samarqand made an extravagant use of gold and lapis lazuli to create a shimmering structure where *muqarnas* contrast with the smooth surfaces of squinches.

THE SUCCESSORS OF TIMUR

In Afghanistan, a land ravaged by successive wars, few monuments have escaped destruction or damage. The Friday Mosque in Herat, founded in 1201, was rebuilt in the 15th century in Timurid style, and its tile facing is modern. The marble dado with its grid patterning contrasts with the leafy tile mosaics above, which symbolize the splendours of Paradise. Amid the geometrical and floral patterns, sacred texts are fitted in on ever-changing scales.

When Timur died in 1404, Khalil Sultan was proclaimed Sultan in Samarqand. Shah Rukh, the conqueror's fourth son, born in 1377, initially kept a low profile; but after strengthening his position in Transoxiana and around the Caspian Sea, he had himself recognized as the legitimate heir in Samarqand in 1409. His dominion extended as far as Iraq, and included Isfahan. He appointed his son, Ulugh Beg, governor of the city of Samarqand, and withdrew to a new capital at Herat, from which he governed until 1447, and where he was very active as a builder. He had married Gawhar Shad in 1388, and in her honour in 1417 he built the immense Friday Mosque. This covered an area of 116 x 64 metres and had a courtyard 50 metres square; a 36-metre-high minaret stood out at every corner, and the dome over the sanctuary was 25 metres in diameter. Under the reign of Shah Rukh and Ulugh Beg Timurid art and culture reached their apogee.

In 1445, Shah Rukh had to put down a rebellion by his son Baysunqur in Isfahan. Two years later, he died at Saveh, in Iran, and the empire was divided: Muhammad bin Baysunqur received Iraq and Fars, Abu'l Qasim Babur received Khorasan, and Ulugh Beg was awarded Transoxiana, but he only reigned there for two years, from 1447 to 1449. There followed a very unsettled time, as various tribes contended for power. The Timurid dynasty fell in 1500 under the blows of Muhammad Shaybani Khan, head of the Uzbek tribe, who seized Bukhara, Samarqand, Balkh and Herat, and reigned until 1507. The Timurid prince Babur was defeated by the Uzbeks, and went on to build a new empire in India. In Iran itself, the native Safavid dynasty emerged in 1501.

The Buildings of Ulugh Beg in Samarqand

The Madrasa of Ulugh Beg in Samarqand, begun in 1417

above left The façade to the Registan displays an impressive *pishtaq* and flanking minarets.

left The minarets have smooth shafts faced with sacred texts, and flaring tops – from which the *muezzin* called the people to prayer – supported on *muqarnas*.

above The stellar decoration on the entrance pavilion alludes to the ruler's passion for astronomy. The large rope moulding framing the arch was originally painted.

Ulugh Beg's architectural patronage was exercised long before the brief two years of his reign: as early as 1417, thirty years before he came to the throne, when he was governor of Samarqand, he began to build his great *madrasa*, and in 1420, at the age of twenty-six, he laid the foundation stone of the observatory, which was to earn him universal fame as the 'astronomer king' (see pp. 84–85).

Ulugh Beg's greatest work is the *madrasa*, effectively a university, that he erected in the Registan or market square (see pp. 230–31), half-way between the Mosque of Bibi Khanum to the north-east and the Gur-i Amir to the south-west. As a ruler, he is remarkable for bequeathing to posterity not a great mosque or a major shrine to attract pilgrims but a place of learning and a foundation dedicated to the study of the universe.

Ulugh Beg's *madrasa* was to have a profound influence on this type of institution, dedicated to religious and scientific study: he refused to restrict its curriculum to the interpretation of the Qur'an, or to jurisprudence and theology, and instead, as a man passionately interested in all areas of knowledge, he also included mathematics and the sciences. Thus for a time his *madrasa* became both the greatest centre of scholarship in the Islamic world and the Timurid university par excellence.

The architectural formula was to be very influential: among its progeny are the simpler *madrasa* built by Ulugh Beg at the same time in Bukhara, and the Shir Dor Madrasa and Tilla Kari Mosque, built two centuries later on two other sides of the Registan. The building measures 81 x 51 metres and covers an area of almost 5,000 square metres. It has four minarets at the corners and a large *pishtaq* 35 metres high; as at the Mosque of Bibi Khanum, the main *iwan* leads to a vestibule which itself opens out through another *iwan* facing onto the courtyard. Two apsed structures placed thus back to back were to become, with variations, a standard formula for entrances. The courtyard, 33 metres square, follows the typical Persian system of four *iwans* facing each other on axis, accentuating the symmetry of the four courtyard ranges, and

punctuating the two tiers of cells for the use of professors and students. There are fifty-two openings, and since each cell held two people, it would seem that the building was intended for about a hundred scholars.

Four domed halls at the corners provided room for teaching in the winter, when the open areas in the *iwans* were no longer suitable for lessons. The two halls on the south-western side flank an oblong space covered with transverse arches alternating with small domes: this is the mosque, 27 metres long and 14 metres wide, which traditionally makes the *madrasa* the instrument for the diffusion of the Word.

The great creator of Timurid architecture was Qavam ad-Din bin Zayn ad-Din Shirazi, who (his name tells us) came from Shiraz in Iran, and who was active from about 1408 to 1440. A master of mathematics, designer and decorator, he began under Shah Rukh, for whom he built the Mosque of Gawhar Shad and the Shrine of Imam Riza in Mashhad. He was a master of the techniques, proportional solutions and decorative manners of the Persian style, and through him Persian forms were diffused beyond the country's borders. For the Madrasa of Ulugh Beg, he worked with the chief of the king's astronomers, the mathematician Ghiyath ad-Din Jamshid al-Kashi – 'from Kashan', so also a Persian – whose treatise on mathematics and astronomy has survived to the present day.

The famous *madrasa* suffered considerable damage during two centuries of neglect, when it became a warehouse, but careful restoration by archaeologists in 1932 and from 1952 onwards returned it to its original splendour, and it stands in the Registan as an example of the care that the Timurids lavished on the world of knowledge and learning.

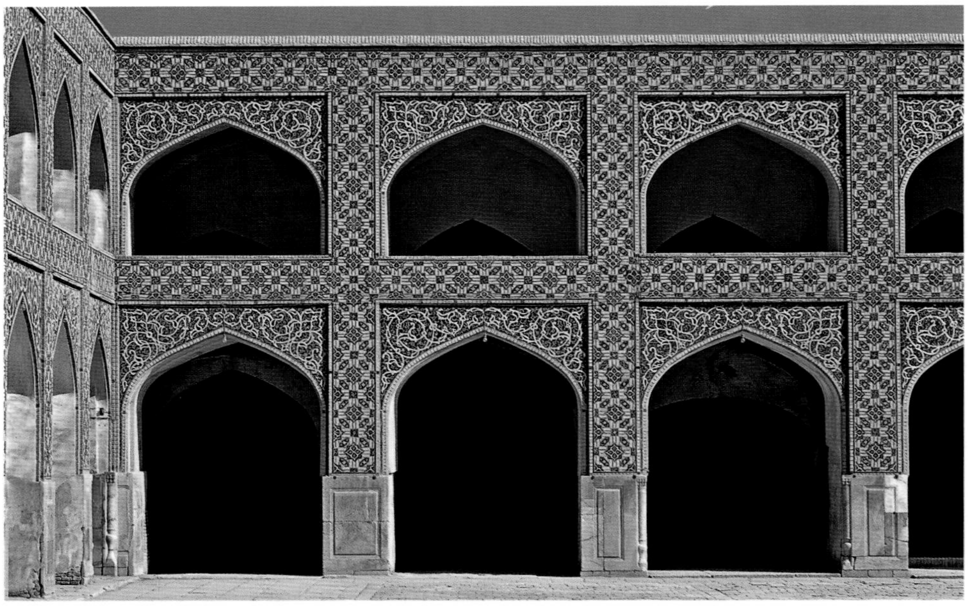

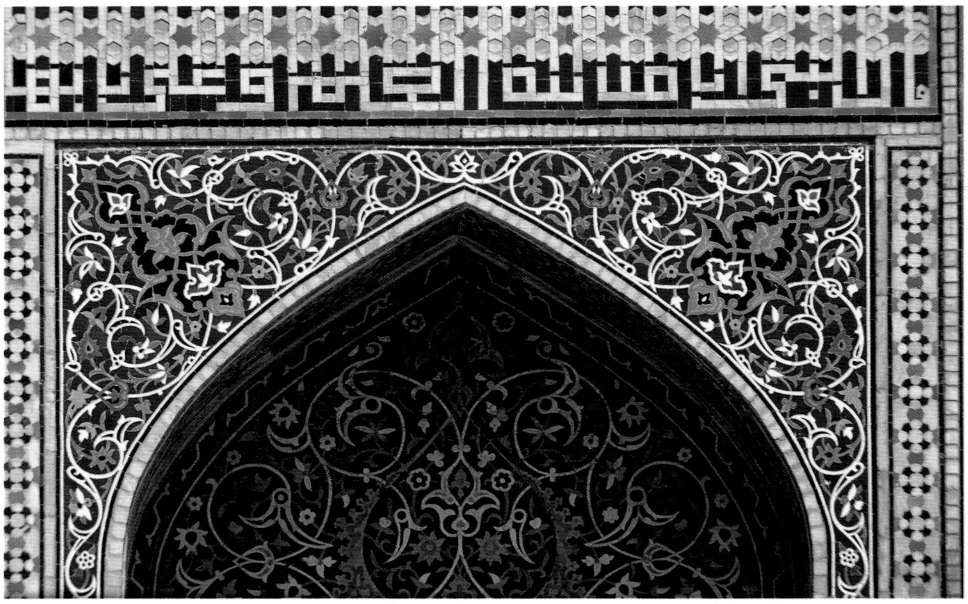

The Friday Mosque in Isfahan, built under the Seljuks and decorated under the Timurids

top Polychrome tiles cover the two tiers of arcades that surround the central court.

centre Tile mosaic decoration on the entrance to one of the winter halls. The delicacy of the arabesque scrolls contrasts with the angularity of the kufic characters in the inscription band.

below A tile mosaic medallion.

opposite The Darb-i Imam at Isfahan, of 1453, has bulbous domes on high drums, showing that the Timurid formula was not confined to Transoxiana. The large stylized writing on the drum is governed by a rigorous process of stylization.

Timurid Decoration

Timurid architecture is remarkable first for the colossal scale of most of the buildings, and then for the quality and richness of their decoration, which covered façades, arcaded courtyards, minarets, *iwans*, *pishtaqs*, and domes. The patterns are both extremely varied and rigorously standardized; and they can be used quite differently depending on the context – an exterior wall, the framing area of an *iwan*, or the interior of a hall. There are glazed bricks forming repetitive motifs on walls, multicoloured tile mosaic based on vegetation or flowers, ornamented *kashi*, and non-figurative, intensely coloured painting, glittering with gilt and lapis lazuli. Such decoration can cover plain surfaces and also areas in relief, such as the cable mouldings that edge the arches of *iwans*, or the *muqarnas* that cover squinches and the bases of domes. Timurid decoration comprises a multitude of techniques and of types of ornament that typically coexist within the same building.

The determination of this splendour-loving dynasty to give religious buildings a special grandeur and lustre led to rivalry between architects as to who would produce the most perfect work, the design that was most unified while fully exploiting a variety of motifs, and a multiplicity of techniques including brick, glazed surfaces, mosaics, pierced screens, and sculptured friezes. The designers unhesitatingly juxtaposed rigorous geometry, borders with repeating patterns, arabesques of twirling stems that spiral out across panels and into corners, and the blaze of gold that heightened the sacred character of the building and evoked the splendours of paradise. Everywhere, with the *horror vacui* that characterizes the art of Islam, motifs multiply until at times the effect of patterns on a minute scale endlessly repeated gives the impression of a plain, smooth and glassy surface, with an unreal sheen, as though solid matter were in a state of dissolution.

Different modes were developed for application in different contexts. On the exterior walls of mosques, *madrasas* and mausoleums, from the beginning of the 15th century on, the Timurid age devised a generalized system of geometrical decoration. Bricks with a glazed black or blue-green face were inserted in rigorous patterns throughout the fabric of the walls, producing the effect of an immense net wrapping round the built forms – a net made up of large squares or rectangles, often

opposite Floral decoration in tile mosaic: the tesserae are cut out with great precision from plain-coloured tiles, then assembled like a jigsaw puzzle, face down, and finally liquid mortar is poured into the cracks to create a complete panel.

below Detail of a frieze of *muqarnas* on a small tomb in Khasvin, built in the early 15th century to honour the Hamadollah Mostowfi, a holy man, historian and geographer who lived around 1350. Timurid features appear here in a simplified form.

bottom A panel on the southern *iwan* of the Friday Mosque in Isfahan includes a large two-handled vase from which scrolling tendrils emerge, a typical Timurid device.

set diagonally, and incorporating inscriptions in highly stylized kufic characters. This repetitive decoration also included sacred names in symbolic form: the words 'Allah' and 'Muhammad' are endlessly repeated, like a litany or a profession of faith directed at God. Plain brick surfaces might also be combined with starry motifs made of coloured ceramic, transforming the flat surfaces that surround the arches of *iwans* into an emblematic sky (see for instance the Madrasa of Ulugh Beg at Samarqand: ill. p. 74, top).

Panels of tile mosaic formed into lancet shapes adorned with vine scrolls and flowers speak out in a brilliant colouristic language. By exploiting the *haftrangi* ('seven colours') technique, an architect could draw attention to particular zones of his design: not only *iwans*, but the spandrels of arches on façades or in courtyards displayed floral motifs – or even, on some *madrasas* under the Shaybanids, animals such as lions, tigers and mythical birds (the *simurgh*).

Moving into three dimensions, this ornament invaded *muqarnas*, cladding their cascading surfaces in mosaic, emphasized the ribs on vaults, took the form of vases alluding to immortality, or sheathed great spiral-twisted columns whose turquoise colour symbolized the springs of life. Windows were filled with pierced screens whose hexagonal links were covered with ceramic, and walls and *iwans* were articulated by bands of writing in large cursive thuluth or naskhi script, whose supple shapes contrasted with the austerity of the Kufic script used for texts from the Qur'an.

All this ornament, drawing on geometry, on floral shapes, on writing and on the principle of rhythmical repetition, is meticulously organized according to the laws of symmetry and duplication. Thus in arcaded courtyards the varied patterns used in the spandrels of the arches are repeated in mirror image on either side of the central axis, or on either side of the two intersecting axes. Invention and the avoidance of monotony are combined with a logic of organization that leaves nothing to chance.

In Samarqand, as in Bukhara, much of this splendid decoration had disappeared, and was restored by the Soviets. An army of skilled craftsmen met the challenge of producing perfect replacements of panels, on the whole based on surviving evidence so that was no need for improvization. In some cases, 'restoration' went so far as to complete parts of buildings that had never been finished in the past: the outer dome of the Tilla Kari Madrasa on the Registan was built because archaeologists argued that it was needed to protect the surviving inner shell, which was crucial to the wellbeing of the gold-leaf and lapis lazuli decoration of the inside of the mosque.

Manuscript Painting in the Timurid Period

below left and right Miniatures from the *Majama al-Tavarikh* (*World History*) of Hafez-i Abru, early 15th century: the emperor of China receiving gifts from ambassadors, and the Caliph Ali with his followers at the beginning of the Islamic era. The style is still stiff and non-naturalistic. (Reza Abbassi Museum, Tehran)

opposite The illustrations of the *Anthology* of Iskandar Sultan, painted in Shiraz in 1410, show a great development in the art of the Persian miniature. The composition of this scene, in which Bahram Gur stands before seven portraits, is remarkably clear and powerful. (Gulbenkian Foundation, Lisbon)

Timur was not, it seems, a patron of miniature painting; but chroniclers report that in the decoration of his pavilions, realized with the help of Persian artists, there were mural paintings which celebrated his conquests and which included landscapes and portraits.

The oldest Timurid manuscript with miniatures was painted in Shiraz in 1393: it too recounts the exploits of Timur. At the beginning of the 15th century, Shiraz was the centre of a brilliant school of painting. Notable manuscripts include the *Anthology* of Iskandar Sultan, governor of Fars from 1409 to 1414, *Kalila wa-Dimna* (a collection of animal fables), and Nizami's *Khusraw and Shirin*. Some of these were made specially for Baysunqur, Timur's grandson. Even more remarkable are a manuscript of the *Shahnama* painted for him, and another made for Muhammad Djuki in 1440.

The school of Shiraz reached its high point with works on historical themes, which, according to the great scholar Basil Gray, are even finer than the manuscripts created in Herat under Timur's son, Shah Rukh. Shiraz painting also developed a fantastical religious repertory, seen in the *Khawar Nama* of Ibn Hussam (*c.* 1480), which includes depictions of Ali and Muhammad – presumably reflecting Persian Shi'ite thought, since they break the commandment against the portrayal of living things.

The most original works of Timurid painting were produced in Herat, where the famous painter Bihzad (1455–1536) illustrated works by Sa'di and Nizami using the most daring compositions and the most harmonious combinations of colours seen until the miniatures created under the Safavids at the court of Shah Tahmasp (1524–76). Bihzad directed the school of Herat from 1486 to 1506 and then moved to Tabriz. He stands among the very greatest Muslim miniaturists, and had a great influence on the artists of Shah Tahmasp.

As the chief painter of Sultan Hussein in Herat (1470–1506), Bihzad developed powers of observation and a naturalistic manner that not infrequently includes touches of humour. His remarkable mastery of composition, displayed both in the arrangement of figures and in the organization of architectural space, is conjoined with astonishing freedom when he wants to escape from the geometrical frame of the image. His miniatures illustrating the *Khamseh* of Nizami are particularly outstanding, but all his works are characterized by intense vitality, elegant movement, and a feeling for nature: they are marvels of freshness and virtuosity without show.

opposite The great Shi'ite Shrine of Imam Reza at Mashhad in eastern Iran includes many Timurid elements – in the outer court of the mosque, in its gilded *iwan* of the late 15th century, and in the golden dome presented by Gawhar Shad, the wife of Shah Rukh.

left A door leading into the Friday Mosque in Kerman. Begun in the 14th century under the Muzaffarids, it was decorated by the Timurids and later by the Safavids, but retains an overall sense of unity.

below The southern entrance to the Friday Mosque at Yazd, begun by the Muzaffarids: the ceramic decoration of the monumental *pishtaq* is thought to date from the Timurid period, while the two slender minarets were added in the reign of the Safavid Shah Tahmasp.

Timurid art in Iran

Art underwent a number of transformations in Iran during the reign of Timur, then under Iskandar Sultan, who governed Fars on behalf of the Timurids from 1409 to 1414, and finally under Baysunqur, who rebelled against the central power and was defeated by his father Shah Rukh in 1447. In 1468 the country fell under the power of Uzun Hasan, chief of the White Sheep Horde, who reigned until 1478. Despite these turbulent events, an original style of architecture emerged, and the creations of the Timurid period are both numerous and precocious. The technique of ceramic mosaic soon became widespread: entire *iwans* and *pishtaqs* were covered with floral motifs, as though permanently overgrown with flowering vines, against which geometrical designs and calligraphic inscriptions formed a counterpoint. We have already seen the very fine tile mosaics of the door of a winter hall in the great Friday Mosque in Isfahan (ill. p. 76, centre); following on from that, the courtyard façades received new Timurid cladding (ill. p. 76, top). The use of polychrome ceramic became widespread, and new, bold forms appeared.

Remarkable early examples of this decoration occur at Yadz, in the large Friday Mosque of 1327. The great *iwan-pishtaq* at the entrance, astonishingly tall for its width, has every surface, including the *muqarnas* in the arch, entirely covered with very fine tile mosaic; the minarets added under Shah Tahmasp give it even more singular proportions. In the mosque's beautiful *mihrab*, of 1375, jasper is combined with ceramic, while the interior of the prayer hall, completed under Amir Chakmak Shami, governor of Yadz in the time of Shah Rukh, is entirely covered with *kashi*. Everywhere, except in the winter hall, which has plain walls and is vaulted with transverse arches, a blue-green polychromy reigns.

In Isfahan the large Shi'ite mausoleum known as Darb-i Imam has a sumptuous portal in midnight blue tile mosaic, where a panel of 1453 showing the Tree of Life springing from a vase representing immortality attests to the freedom and refinement of Timurid tile mosaic in Iran.

The case of the Blue Mosque or Muzaffariah in Tabriz, constructed in 1465 by the daughter of Jahanshah, is unique. The building is a product of the Muzaffarids, Turkmen chieftains of the Kara Koyunlu or Black Sheep tribe, who succeeded in shaking off Timurid guardianship, and combines Turkish-Persian architectural features with Timurid decoration. The prayer hall, which has a large central dome resting on powerful piers buttressed by nine small domes, is peculiar in having the *mihrab* set in an apse. This feature, which came from Byzantine models copied by the Anatolian Turks, has a sumptuous covering of blue tile mosaic. The Tabriz mosque was damaged several times by earthquakes and largely reduced to a ruin. Great restoration work is bringing it back to life, but in only a few areas of the decoration – notably that of the great apsidal doorway – is it possible to get an idea of the original quality.

The notable Timurid buildings in Mashhad, where the Shrine of Imam Reza (ill. p. 82) and the Mosque of Gawhar Shad rose around 1416 to designs by Qavam ad-Din Shirazi, have already been mentioned (see p. 75). Their decoration is distinguished by its exceptionally fine ceramic cladding; and architecturally, while they are still clearly related to the majestic contemporary creations in Samarqand, they already show many elements of the Safavid style in its definitive form.

Knowledge of the Heavens

An enthusiastic astronomer and astrologer, Ulugh Beg founded a vast observatory in Samarqand, intended to outshine the one at Maragheh in Azerbaijan built by the Il-Khan Hülegü for the famous astronomer Nasr ad-Din at-Tusi. With the exception of a gigantic subterranean sextant, *below*, nothing but foundations remains.

Ulugh Beg's observatory was begun in 1420 on a site to the north-east of Samarqand: here, on a hillock, a two-storeyed structure with underground areas was built to serve as a giant astronomical instrument pointed at the heavens. Ulugh Beg has been taught by the astronomer Salah al-Din Musa bin Mahmud, also known as Qazizadeh Rumi, who had himself studied at Bursa in Turkey and who had come to Samarqand to perfect his knowledge, benefiting from the Timurids' liberal attitude towards the sciences. Ulugh Beg had as a child visited the observatory of Maragheh near Tabriz, which had been built under the guidance of Nasr ad-Din at-Tusi by the Il-Khan Hülegü in 1258. He was passionately interested in astronomy and astrology, and as soon as his father appointed him governor of Samarqand he had nursed the idea that he, too, would build one of those giant astronomical complexes that made the fame of their founders.

The interest of powerful men in the stars is explained by an attitude that went back to antiquity, when no distinction was made between astronomy and astrology – the science of reading the future in the stars. Egyptians, Babylonians, Greeks, Alexandrians and Romans believed that the heavens influenced human destiny: just as the moon affects the tides, the inclination of the earth on its axis affects the seasons, and there are connections between climate and the configurations of the stars, so the planets, it was thought, must have an influence, either good or bad, on the future of individuals depending on the year, month, day and hour of their birth or conception. The ancients had divided the heavens into twelve zones, represented by the twelve signs of the zodiac, and had analysed the paths of the planets, and the movements of the heavens were set out in numerous treatises by famous scholars, from Arato to Ptolemy, from Manilius to Publius Nigidius Figulus, and from Balbillus to Trasillus. Their texts, written in Greek or Latin, entered the libraries of Umayyad and 'Abbasid rulers in Arabic translations, and were later studied by the Persians. They gradually attracted commentaries, new calculations, and fresh theories, and were diffused throughout the Islamic world, where they were not condemned as in Christendom. For those in positions of power, knowledge of the future through horoscopes was a great asset: they could make the correct choices in decisions that were crucial for themselves or for their people, choose the most propitious time or place for a military engagement, know the fate of a child or of an enemy, control the future – in short, be the masters of time. This is why, for a long time, astrology was the special province of kings, emperors and sultans, and to reveal a prince's horoscope was punishable by death.

The Timurids fully matched other rulers in their enthusiasm for a field that was considered highly scientific. At Ulugh Beg's observatory. al-Kashi, followed by Qazizadeh Rumi and Ali Kushji, worked to produce the famous astronomical tables issued in 1437: with their greater precision these replaced those of Maragheh, and were in use until the 18th century.

The first designs for the observatory of Samarqand were made by the astronomical theoretician Ghiyath ad-Din Jamshid al-Kashi, who had previously worked, since 1414, for Iskandar Sultan, governor of Fars and of Isfahan. It seems that significant improvements were then made to them by Qazizadeh Rumi.

Archaeological excavations and studies conducted in 1965 and 1967 showed that Ulugh Beg's observatory had a diameter of 48 metres and that its two-storeyed cylindrical structure was about 30 metres tall. Only the foundations survive, but a very important discovery was made in the basement: there archaeologists found a curved trench dug for a gigantic sextant that went down to a depth of more than 20 metres. At the bottom of the trench there were two parallel arcs 63 metres long with gradations engraved in the white marble: these allowed the

far left Muslim astronomers studying the skies, in a 16th-century Ottoman miniature. Equipped with a sighting instrument and a globe, they note the results of their studies.

left A Persian brass astrolabe, typical of the design of this instrument that spread through Iran from the 10th century. Against the background of a solid plate, a pierced plate revolves indicating the ecliptic, in conjunction with the sightings taken by the observer along the projecting alidade. (Iran Bastan Museum, Tehran)

meridian to be determined, thanks to a hole in the vault through which a ray of sun entered at a specific time. According to the account of Ismail Sayili, the chief architect, on the second floor of the building there was a planetarium which showed the movement of the heavenly bodies and which allowed horoscopes to be drawn up with the help of a mechanical contrivance that portrayed the sky at any given moment in the past, present or future.

Scientific progress in the study of the world is inconceivable without developments in both techniques and instruments. To establish astronomical tables, as Ulugh Beg was to do, it was necessary to make precise observations of the sky: the earliest instruments were based on the two-dimensional representation of the celestial and terrestrial spheres. Among these was the astrolabe, which made it possible to work out the position of heavenly bodies at any given moment. The idea of creating a flat (stereographic) projection of the sky goes back to the Greeks. John Philoponus, in the 6th century, described a planispheric astrolabe and explained how it worked. The object, which hangs from a ring, comprises a disk which depicts the sky at the Equator; this is inserted into a base; in the centre a circle turns round, representing the ecliptic; a rule with sights, the alidade, makes it possible to measure angles by means of graduated measures on the rim. Otto Neugebauer, a historian of astronomy, explained the astrolabe as providing a representation of celestial phenomena by means of a rotating network of circles on a disk representing the sky at the Equator, viewed from the south, and explains that the principle derives from a combination of descriptive geometry with trigonometry.

From the 8th century onwards, Arabic-Persian astronomers worked to perfect the astrolabe of antiquity. The Persian mathematician al-Biruni (973–1050) from Khwarezm, who translated Euclid's *Elements* and Ptolemy's *Almagest*, composed a treatise on the construction of the astrolabe. Muslim scholars developed instruments that were ever more precise, while paying attention also to their appearance, with the result that astrolabes produced by Arabic-Persian craftsmen are true works of art.

Some of the instruments used for observation in the great Islamic observatories at Maragheh, Samarqand, etc. were effectively giant astrolabes: ten, twenty or a hundred times larger, they were thought to give results that were ten, twenty or a hundred times more precise. The astrolabe contributed to a better understanding of the heavens and of geography, but more commonly it was used to work out the movement of the planets within the zodiac so as to draw up horoscopes: in this, it became an instrument of power for rulers.

4

The Evolution of the Mughal Style from Babur to Akbar

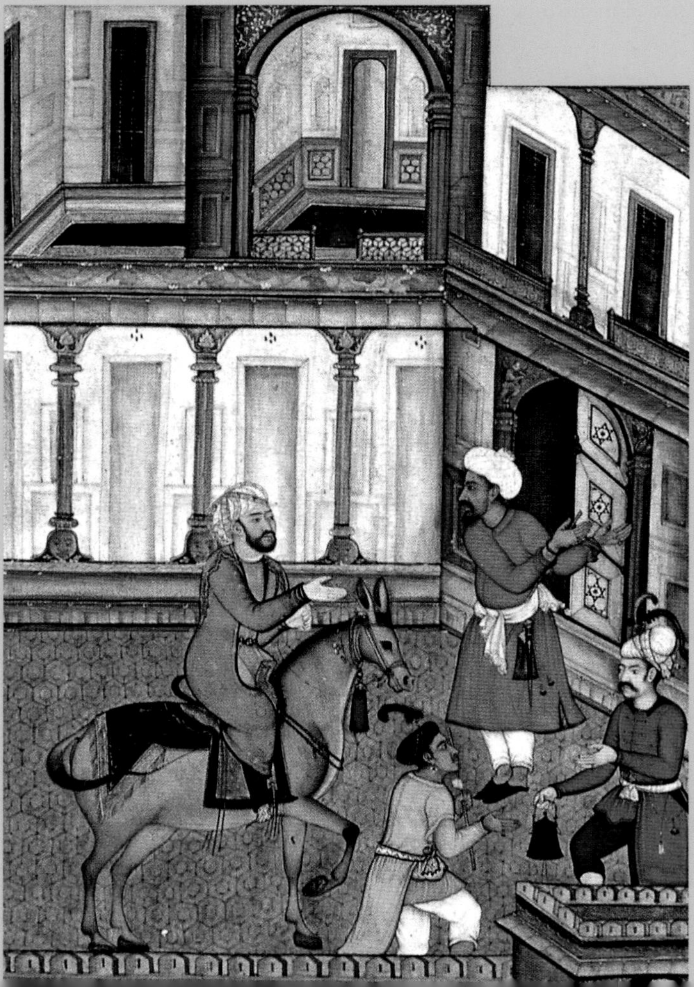

After looking at the extraordinary flowering of Timurid art in Transoxiana and Iran, we now turn back to India to trace an evolution that, after the destruction wrought by Timur, resumed its own course and indeed gathered speed on both political and artistic levels. This transitional phase was first manifested in the Delhi Sultanate, with the Sayyid and Lodi dynasties. Then the Afghan rulers were overthrown and the Hindu troops were defeated by Babur, a Turkish-Mongol conqueror from the Timurid dynasty of Samarqand. Babur founded the Mughal dynasty, giving the Muslim world of India a new unity, and he also fostered a new artistic spirit, strengthening the Persian influence in the subcontinent.

In the wake of the storm that Timur unleashed on India, the last sultans of Delhi made an attempt at recovery with the Sayyid dynasty (1414–51). Khizr Khan ascended the throne of the impoverished capital, claiming to be a *sayyid*, or descendant of the Prophet. His successor, Mubarak Shah Sayyid, commissioned for himself a mausoleum of a distinctive form – an octagonal structure covered by a dome and surrounded by a portico with three arches on each of the eight sides. This pattern had already appeared in the Hauz-i Khass, the tomb of Khan-i Jihan Tilangani, the prime minister of Firuz Shah Tughluq, who had died in 1369, but there it was still in an experimental form. The definitive solution, which would prevail for more than a century, appeared in the mausoleum of Muhammad Shah, who had died in 1434, erected in 1444–50 by his son, Ala ed-Din Alam Shah. It is 22 metres in diameter, and its surrounding portico is marked at the corners by battered piers that counter the thrust of the dome. The portico, open to the outside and covered with a vault, surrounds the funerary chamber proper. On the roof, the dome is surrounded by a series of small pavilions or *chhatris*, derived from Hindu architecture, whose function is purely decorative. These kiosk-like structures appeared for the first time in Muslim architecture during the reign of Firuz Shah, notably on the Kotilal in Delhi of *c.* 1370. On the mausoleum of Muhammad Shah they provide a visual link between the cornice of the building and the central dome, and provide a sense of ascending movement. The dome, with an interior diameter of 7 metres, covers a funerary chamber surrounded by two levels of arcades.

The Mausoleum of Muhammad Shah is marked by the recurrence of the number eight: eight sides, eight arches within the chamber (seven doors and a *mihrab*), and eight *chhatris* on the roof. Like the tomb of Rukn-i 'Alam at Multan (ill. p. 54), it alludes to the venerable Dome of the Rock in Jerusalem (ill. pp. 306–7). That building, with its two concentric galleries for the ritual of circumambulation, through which the faithful do honour to a place or a saint, lies behind the importance of the octagon in the Islamic world. Circumambulation is a sanctifying action: pilgrims on the *hajj* circumambulate the Ka'ba in Mecca, following an ancient pre-Islamic practice that may go back to the time of Abraham. The association of the practice with the octagonal Dome of the Rock led to the choice of that figure for

p. 86, above The white marble dome over Humayun's Tomb in Delhi.

p. 86, below Yahya Barmaki, the vizir of the Abbassid caliph Harun ar-Rashid, was looked to for ethical guidance by Muslim rulers. In this detail from a 17th-century Mughal miniature he arrives on mule-back at a palace and is welcomed. (Reza Abbassi Museum, Tehran)

p. 87 A miniature from the *Baburnama*, of 1598, depicts Babur's visit to Gwalior, where was received *c.* 1500 by Raja Man Singh. The painting, by an artist who signed himself Bura, meticulously renders the complex defenses of the fortified city. (National Museum, Delhi)

opposite, above The façade of the Moth-ki Masjid in Delhi, 1505.

opposite, below The tomb of the Sayyid sultan Muhammad Shah, of the 1340s, inaugurated the tradition in Delhi of octagonal funerary monuments crowned by a dome ringed with *chhatris*.

left A transverse view of the prayer hall in the Moth-ki Masjid in Delhi: each bay progresses upward from a square base to an octagon supporting a dome, by means of cubic *muqarnas* in the corners.

the design of tombs, beginning with the Qubbat as-Sulaybiyya at Samarra, built for Caliph al-Muntasir in 862; we find it again in the Mongol Mausoleum of Öljeitü at Soltaniyeh (ill. p. 51). The Tomb of Muhammad Shah is built of fine white limestone ashlar with red sandstone accents. Its pointed arches are stilted. Under the surrounding arcades, rows of geometrical stalactites make the transition between the square plan and, in alternate bays, small domes and pointed vaults.

Similar buildings were to be erected by other Indian sultans. Also in Delhi, the Lodi dynasty created what they called *gunbad*, after the Persian term for dome which had come to mean a tomb. These are square buildings crowned by domes raised on drums; all the façades are similar, with axial arches framed by panels and two or three tiers of blind arcades. They vary in function, however: sometimes they are mausoleums and sometimes they serve as entrance gates.

At the same time, India saw the emergence of a new type of mosque design, which was to assume its finest form under the Mughals. A characteristic early example is the Moth-ki Masjid, built in Delhi in 1505 by Miyan Bhoiya, the prime minister of Sikandar Lodi (1489–1517). It has a shallow, transverse prayer hall five bays wide, covered by vaults or domes; five great pointed arches open in the façade, and beyond each, in the far wall that forms the *qibla*, is a *mihrab*. The central arch projects slightly to emphasize the entrance, and behind it rises the central dome; further domes mark the two ends. The external appearance seems to be derived from a 12th-century building, which was not a mosque but a Karakhanid mausoleum at Uzegend in Kyrgyzstan: built of brick, this has three openings with stilted arches of which the central one is larger, behind which rises a dome that covers the funerary chamber. The early Indian structures have an archaic appearance and are rather heavy: the arcades rest on squat piers and have three orders of voussoirs. Inside, the pendentives of the domes are covered with rows of crudely geometrical stalactites, composed of cubic elements arranged in a quincunx.

This type of mosque, with its plan expanded in width, conformed to the Arabic ideal of the place of prayer, as established by the Prophet Muhammad at his house in Medina. In the Lodi period, it can be seen again in the mosque that forms part of the complex of the octagonal Mausoleum of Sikandar Lodi (1517).

From the Delhi Sultanate to the Deccan

The tomb complex of Isa Khan in Delhi

above The funerary chamber is a fine example of the art of the Lodi dynasty, continuing Sayyid traditions.

below Section (1) and plan (2).

opposite The funerary mosque displays the characteristic tripartite façade that was to become standard for Mughal mosques. There is still some use of coloured decoration around the central door.

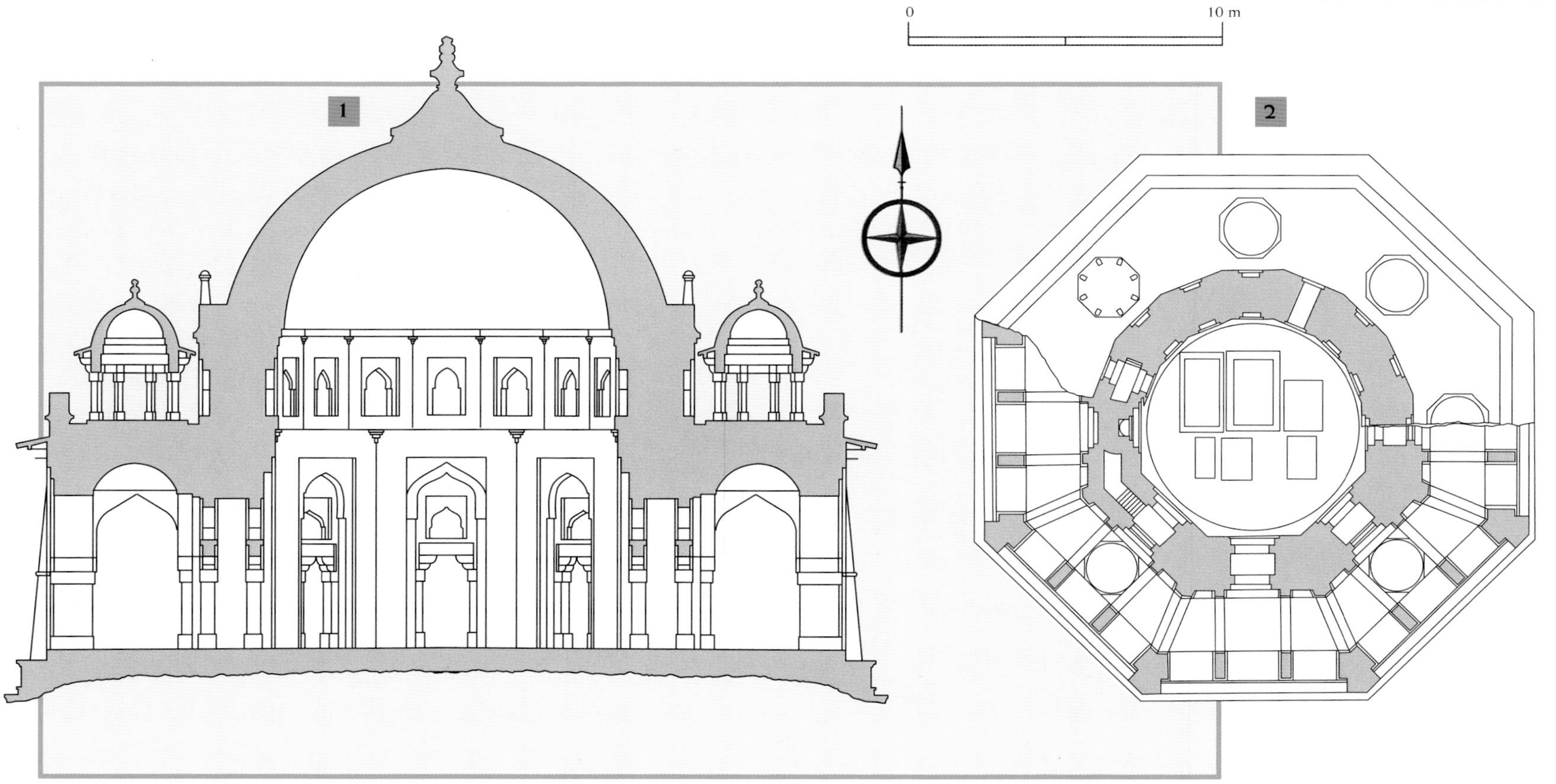

In the mosque of the funerary complex of Isa Khan in Delhi, of 1547, where the entrance door is inscribed in a rectangular frame of red sandstone, the new Indian formula emerges clearly. The decoration makes extensive use of coloured ceramic in blue, green and yellow, and of rosettes made of carved stucco. The play with contrasts between materials – grey limestone and red sandstone – and with the polychromy of the ceramic, here and in the Tomb of Isa Khan, introduced a formula that was to be greatly exploited and developed in India in the future.

Late Lodi architecture includes a number of original designs, although the style was often heavy. India now had a distinctive architectural vocabulary, which would soon be joined by an ornamental repertory that prefigured the great works of the Mughals. As yet, however, there is no sign of the elegance that would come with renewed Timurid and Persian influence.

Islamic penetration of the Deccan continued during the 14th and 15th centuries. Several regional powers became established, most notably the Bahmani Sultanate (1347–1422), centred on Gulbarga, in the heart of the subcontinent, in the area of present-day Hyderabad. The Friday Mosque at Gulbarga was built in 1367 on the orders of 'Ala' ad-Din Bahman Shah within the fortress (now in ruins). Its architect came from the north of Iran, probably Khorasan or Khwarazm. The building is interesting for a number of reasons – for its layout, which is remarkably unified and rational, and for the systematic use throughout of pointed arches, domes and vaults. It is indeed a 'great mosque': 53 metres wide and 65 metres deep, it provides an enclosed area of 3,500 square metres. In a radical departure from the traditional formula, instead of a courtyard there is a vast covered space.

The Persian architect who designed the Gulbarga mosque used a strictly modular system, based on a square of 5 x 5 metres. In width there are 11, in length 14, making a total of 154. In the central hypostyle hall each square is covered by a dome; that area is surrounded on three sides by a zone of 2-unit spaces covered by pointed tunnel vaults. Domes at the corners each occupy 4 units; finally, the large domed space in front of the *mihrab* occupies 9 units. In this work, the rigorous logic of the design is combined with

technical simplicity in the architecture. Mughal builders were to follow a similar principle of repetition.

What, at the beginning of the 16th century, survived in India of the spirit of the Persian builders which had inspired the Ghaznavids and Ghurids? Curiously, very little Persian influence is detectable between 1200 and 1500, despite the fact that Farsi was the language of the Delhi Sultanate and that the Islamic traditions that were introduced into India were Turkish-Afghan rather than Arabic. The most characteristic element of Persian architecture, the courtyard-plan mosque, is nowhere seen, nor is the four-*iwan* scheme; indeed, the *iwan* with its pointed vault posed too many problems for Hindu stonemasons. And as we have seen, brick was replaced by ashlar, in the use of which local builders excelled. Only the arch and the vault, which had initially defeated Indian craftsmen, ultimately became widespread. It is as though India, faced with the repeated attacks of the Mongols, turned inward on itself for protection. It fell into a period of cultural stagnation: between the passage of Chinghiz Khan's hordes at the end of the 13th century and Timur's assault a hundred years later, its seems that Delhi was frozen in a state of shock and grief.

The advent of Babur, founder of the Mughal dynasty, paradoxically led to a cultural renewal and to an extraordinary flowering of the arts, in which Persians were to play a key role. The early years of the presence in India of the Turkish-Mongol clan, soon referred to as 'Mughal', were a time of inconclusive conflicts, interregnums and usurpations. The forty years between the death of Sikandar Lodi in 1517 and the ascent to the throne of Akbar, the second Mughal ruler, in 1556, were a time of chaos but also of rich creativity, when India saw a profound revitalization of the forms and aesthetic principles of Islamic art.

The Friday Mosque at Gulbarga, designed by an architect of Persian origin and built in 1367, reflects a modular and rational system in its plan and in its elegant arches.

left, and below The main dome over the *mihrab* area (to the right in the photograph) takes up 3 x 3 (9) units of the plan, while the smaller domes that buttress the corners of the building occupy 2 x 2 (4) units.

Key

(**A**) transverse section; (**B**) plan

1 Hypostyle hall composed of single modular units
2 Double-unit side spaces
3 Corner rooms covered by 4-unit domes
4 Principal domed hall of 9 units over the *mihrab*

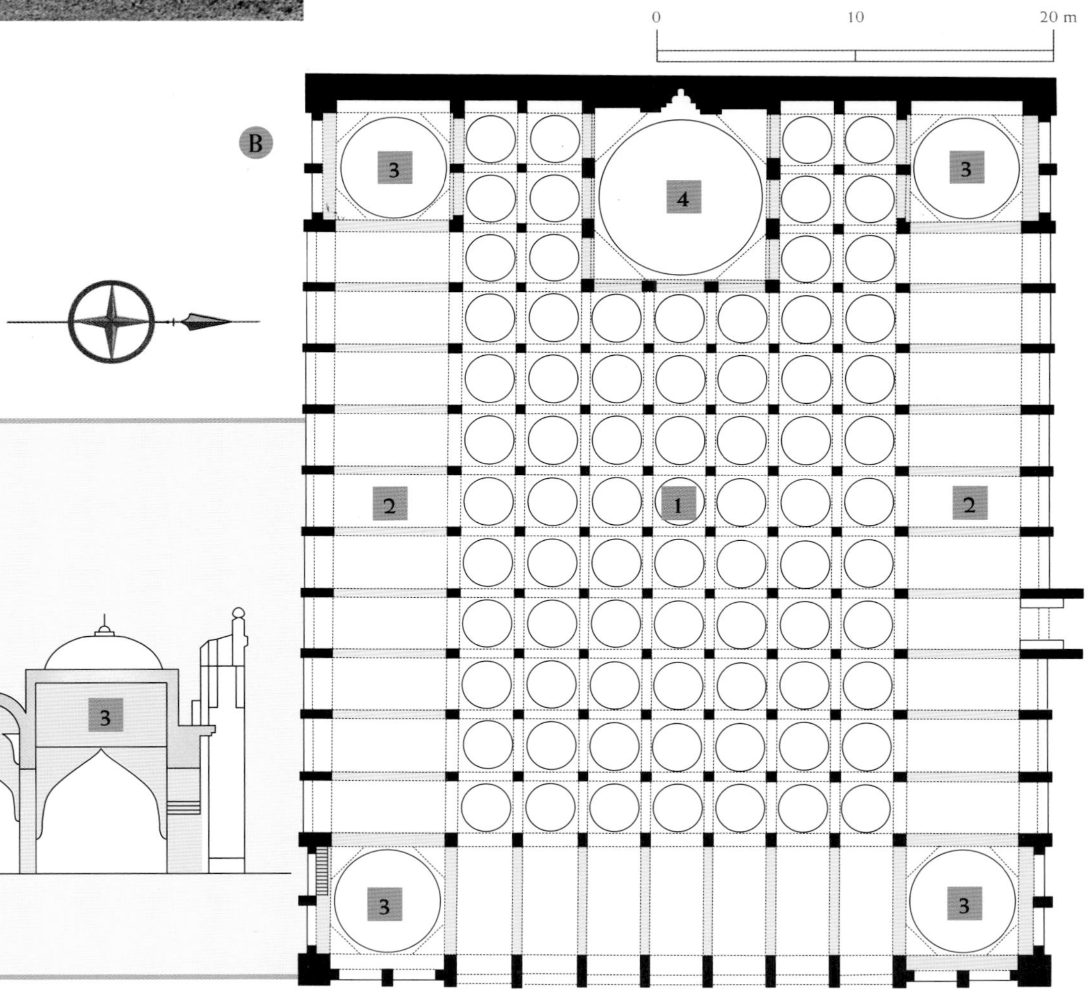

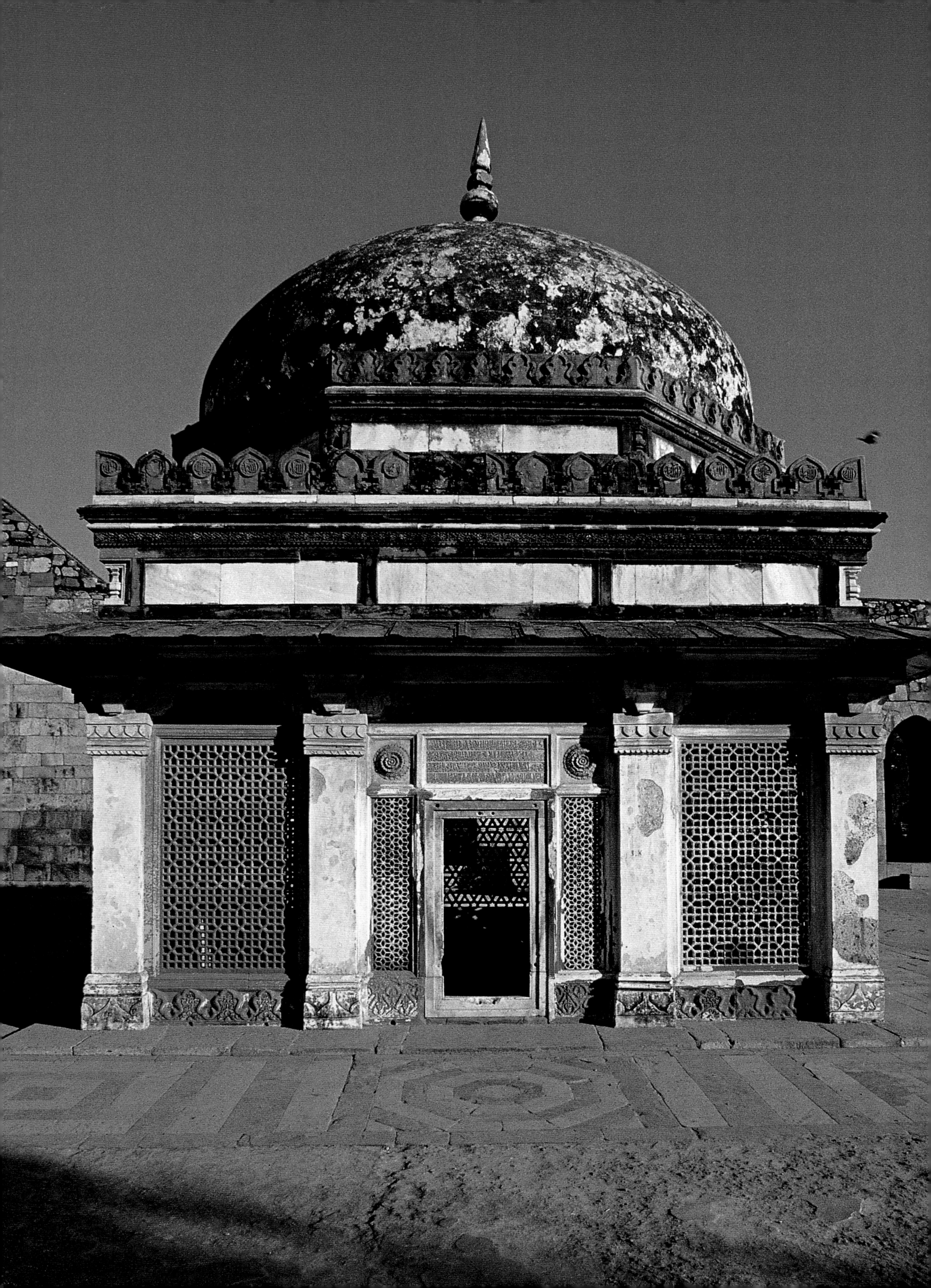

opposite, below, and right The small tomb of Imam Zamin, near the Quwwat al-Islam Mosque in Delhi, completed in 1537. The simplicity of the design and the subtlety of the geometrical elements make this an excellent example of early Mughal architecture, twenty years before Humayun's Tomb (ill. p. 101). Characteristic features are the white marble and red sandstone, the walls consisting of *jalis* or stone screens, and the dome.

below The *jalis* with their geometrical patterns allow light to enter the funerary chamber.

right Section, and plan taken at three levels.

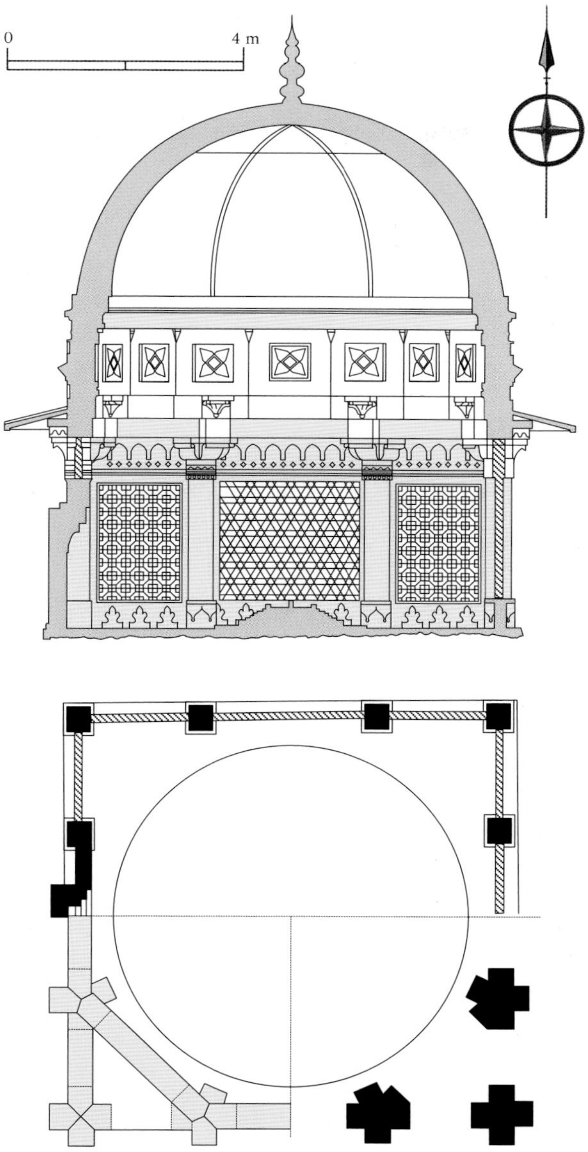

below The octagonal Sher Mandala in Delhi was built in 1545, during the reign of Sher Shah Suri. Humayun turned it into a library and died from a fall there in 1556, shortly after his return from exile.

The Emergence of the Mughal Style

A remarkable artistic development took place between the last decades of Afghan rule and the ascent to power of the third Mughal emperor, Akbar. In Delhi, the Afghan throne was shaken when Sikandar Lodi died, but nothing it seems could stop the great movement that launched India's 'Renaissance'. Mughal art was born when Babur, an adventurer whom the governor of the Punjab had called to his aid, entered the fray, and its development was not affected either by the dramatic events surrounding his defeat of the sultan of Delhi at Panipat in 1526 or by his death in 1530. Humayun, Babur's son, then took power, but he was defeated by a coalition led by Sher Khan Sur, and forced to flee to Iran; there he spent many years at the court of the Safavid ruler Shah Tahmasp and witnessed the flowering of an admirable school of miniature painting.

From 1540 to 1545 Delhi was ruled by the usurper, who took the name Sher Shah. Although he was an Indo-Afghan, and his power far from assured, in his time the first 'Mughal' art seems to have sprung up fully formed. One of the first examples of a successful design in a reinvigorated Indo-Muslim vocabulary is the small tomb next to the 'Ala' i Darwaza gate of the Quwwat al-Islam Mosque in Delhi, dedicated to a holy man, Imam Zamin, and completed in 1537. This is a little square building surmounted by a hemispherical dome that rests on an octagonal drum. It is made of white marble and red sandstone, materials that were henceforth to characterize Mughal architecture. Its walls are formed of pierced stone screens or *jalis* in geometrical patterns of octagons and hexagons in combinations of extreme virtuosity. All of these elements – the polychromy of the stone, the pierced openings, and the transparency of the *jalis* – are distinctive features of the Mughal style.

Other manifestations of this style can be seen in the Purana Kila ('old fort'), a citadel surrounded by wide moats that was begun by Humayun before his exile and completed by Sher Shah. It has straight curtain walls punctuated by towers, and red sandstone gates flanked by round, tapering towers. The decoration is already Mughal in character. Inside the Purana Kila is a curious two-storeyed octagonal building surmounted by a large *chhatri*, known as the Sher Mandal; this housed a library in which Humayun was to meet his death by falling downstairs.

The most significant developments in Mughal art came to fruition after Akbar had succeeded Humayun. But let us now return to the advent of Babur.

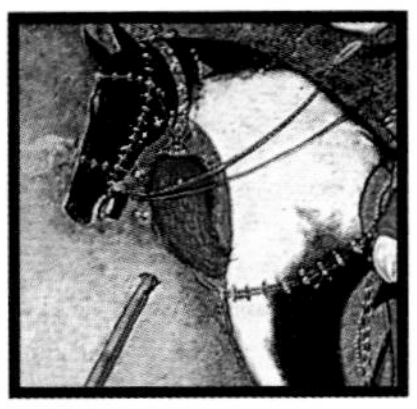

left and below Details of a miniature showing Babur on horseback with his followers, from a manuscript of the *Baburnama*, or *Memoirs* of Babur, illustrated for his grandson Akbar in 1598. (National Museum, Delhi)

opposite The battle of Panipat, fought in April 1526, depicted in Akbar's copy of the *Baburnama*. The troops of Babur (shown with a plumed helmet, advancing from the left) rout the army of Ibrahim Lodi, which includes a fighter on elephant-back. (National Museum, Delhi)

Babur Invades the Subcontinent

The life of Babur ('the Tiger'), founder of the Mughal dynasty, is a real cloak-and-dagger tale. He himself recounted its key moments in his famous *Memoirs*, the *Baburnama*, a narrative throbbing with life and passion. Babur – or, more precisely, Zahir ud-Din Muhammad Babur – was born in 1483 at Andizhan, in what is now Uzbekistan, the son of Umar Shaykh Mirza, Timurid prince of Farghana. As he liked to boast, through his father he was descended from Timur, while on his mother's side he was more distantly related to Chinghiz Khan. He spoke and wrote in Chagatai, a Turkish language (named after the tribal chieftain Chagatai, son of Chinghiz Khan), and was a Sunni, like most of the converted tribal Turkish population of the Timurid world. He also came under the influence of the Shi'ism of Iran, however; he was completely fluent in Persian, and used that language to write the refined poems that were collected together as his *Diwan*.

Babur lost his father when he was twelve, and inherited nothing from him but a title which he was forced to defend with his sword. His first aim was to secure his rich valley, Farghana, against his envious neighbours. Supported by a small group of courageous horsemen, he launched an assault on Samarqand, the capital of his ancestor Timur, and captured it in 1497, when he was only fourteen. He was able to hold it only for a hundred days; but after reconquering his own kingdom in 1500, he again obtained possession of Samarqand. It was wrested from him again the following year by the Uzbeks, led by Shaybani Khan. Undaunted, Babur fled to Tashkent, which was ruled by his uncle, the Mongol Mahmud Khan; there he learned that Farghana had fallen into the hands of his enemies.

Babur decided to concentrate his efforts and those of his three hundred followers on Kabul in Afghanistan, a key centre of communications between Iran, China and India. In 1504 he captured the city, established his general headquarters there, and worked out a strategy. He next took Ghazna, which gave him control of the Khyber and neighbouring passes. Then he went on to take Kandahar in 1516. Babur was now thirty-three years old, and all his ambitions were focused on India. Like his predecessors, the sultans in Kabul, he launched a series of raids on the Indian plains. Beginning in 1519, Babur made three expeditions in two years, getting to know the terrain and the enemy. He also demanded of the sultan in Delhi, Ibrahim Lodi, the return of all the territories that had been conquered by his ancestor Timur – a request that met with a dusty answer.

Ibrahim Lodi had alienated his nobles, however, and in 1524 one of them, Daulat Khan, governor of Lahore, appealed to Babur, offering to support him in return for help in overthrowing the Sultan. Babur immediately launched a campaign in the Punjab and took possession of Lahore. At this point, however, he was summoned to Balkh, which was besieged by the Uzbeks. After relieving Balkh he returned to Kabul, and there in 1525 he prepared the expedition that was to be decisive. At the very first encounter he crushed all Afghan resistance in the Punjab, and moved on towards Delhi to face Ibrahim Lodi at Panipat. The sultan led a powerful coalition with an army of some 75,000–100,000 men and 1,000 elephants. Babur had only 12,000–15,000 men, but his strategy worked miracles: he had enlisted the support of Ottoman artillerymen, with firearms. These were a fearsome novelty on an Indian battlefield, and thanks to them he achieved a crushing victory on the evening of 21 April 1526, leaving the enemy with losses of 15,000 men. Babur took for himself the high-sounding title of 'Emperor of Hindustan', which was pronounced in the *khutbah*, the sermon preached in a mosque in the name of the caliph. During the Friday prayers, he was invested with a sacred legitimacy.

Despite his military success, the country did not fall entirely into Babur's hands. Many Afghans and Hindu Rajputs continued to fight for independence. A coalition brought together 200,000 men,

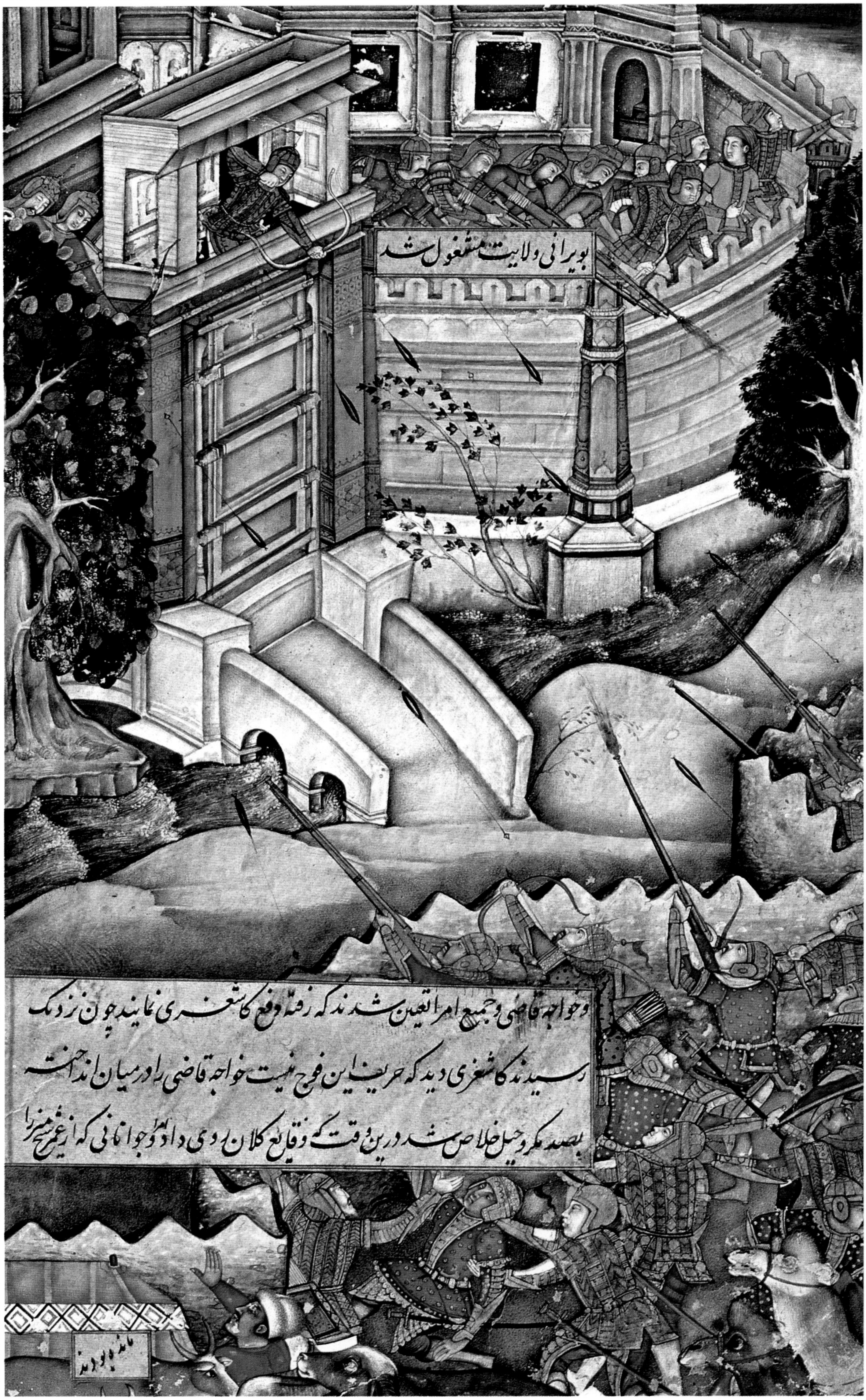
بویرانی ولایت مشغول شد
و خواجه قاضی و جمیع امرا تعین شدند که رفته دفع کاشغری نمایند چون نزدیک
رسیدند کاشغری دید که حریف این فوج نیست خواجه قاضی را در میان انداخته
بصد مکر و حیل خلاص شد درین وقت که وقایع کلان روی داد امرا و جوانانی که از غم سلطان میرزا
مانده بودند

opposite A miniature from Akbar's copy of the *Baburnama* shows the attack by Babur's men on a fort at Kashgar in Central Asia. The artist, Farrukh Chela, depicts the use of firearms in both camps. (National Museum, Delhi)

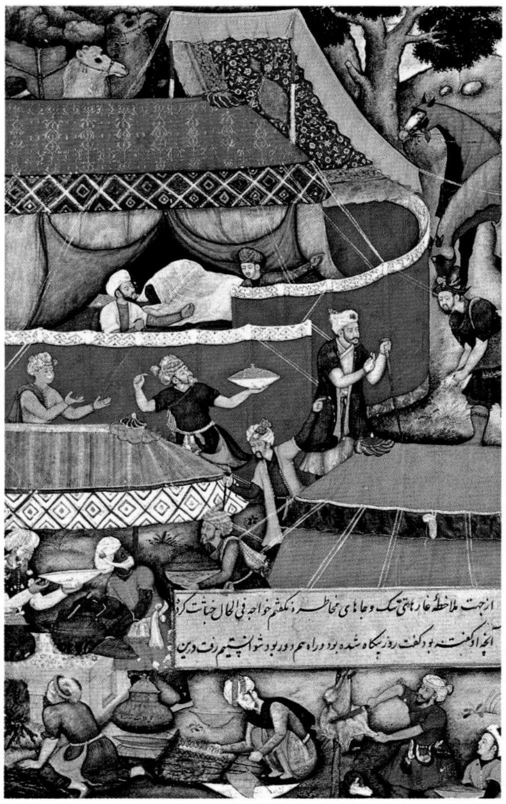

far left Babur's troops celebrate a victory in India in a tented camp formed of multicoloured fabrics. Similar canopies would have been used at Fatehpur Sikri (pp. 244–53). Here, in Akbar's *Baburnama*, the artist has given his colour sense free rein. (National Museum, Delhi)

left One of the crucial moments in the conquest of India by Babur was the crossing of the Indus, when his troops used inflated goatskins to transport their equipment. The painter of this miniature in Akbar's *Baburnama*, Gobind, emphasizes the fact that Babur had elephants. (National Museum, Delhi)

but Babur again overcame them, at the battle of Khanua in 1527. In 1529, after a series of victories over the Afghans, who were often disunited, Babur concluded a peace treaty with his enemies.

In 1530 Babur learned that his son Humayun was gravely ill, and that doctors despaired of saving him. He 'offered to God his own life in exchange for his son's': Humayun recovered, but Babur soon contracted a disease that led to his death at the age of forty-seven. He was buried in Kabul – where, he says in his *Memoirs*, he had been concerned to lay out gardens and create pools for irrigation – in a setting that reminded him of his native Farghana.

Babur's time in power in India was too brief for him to have left a significant architectural legacy, though it is known than he built palaces, now destroyed, as well as fortresses and mosques in the places where his conquests took him. His real contribution to the world of art and thought is in literature, with his *Memoirs*; in their richness and their spontaneity, the *Memoirs* were to have an important influence on Mughal literature. In the third and last volume of his detailed and lively journal he describes his feats of arms and his impressions of India. Manuscripts of the *Baburnama* long provided opportunities for miniaturists to display the refined Timurid aesthetic that had been introduced by famous Persian artists who were brought to India. One of the finest examples is the manuscript of 1598 commissioned by Babur's grandson, the Mughal emperor Akbar (now in the National Museum, Delhi: ill. pp. 96–99, 102). Written in Persian, it includes 144 full-page miniatures in a format of 13 x 21 centimetres, executed by 49 different artists.

When he was in exile at the court of Shah Tahmasp, Humayun persuaded two miniaturists from Tabriz and Qazvin to follow him to Kabul, and then on to India when he was restored to the throne in Delhi. This explains the strong Persian influence on an art that was to reach great heights under the Mughals. Mughal miniatures, like those produced in Iran and Transoxiana, also show a number of distinctively Chinese features – curiously shaped clouds, picturesque rock forms, faces and galloping horsemen treated in a particular way, etc. This is not surprising in an art that derives from the great Timurid masterpieces, which were painted at a time when contacts between the Chinese and Persian empires were encouraged by the presence of Turkish-Mongol rulers who looked to both sources.

Among the miniatures in the *Baburnama* there is a scene where Babur is concerned with a peaceful activity – laying out a garden with artificial watercourses, square pools and ornamental plants (cf. ill. p. 102). Knowledgeable about hydraulic installations, of which there were many in Farghana, he organized plantations and planted trees throughout his realm. His successors followed his example in laying out gardens on the four-part *chahar bagh* pattern, as we shall see.

At the battle of Panipat both Ibrahim Lodi and the old Raja Vikramajit of Gwalior lost their lives. The raja's widows and children were in Agra and tried to flee: Babur had them arrested, but treated them with courtesy, and in gratitude they gave him a precious stone of inestimable value, the Koh-i Nur, or 'Mountain of Light', one of the finest diamonds in the world. The Hindu rajas of Gwalior had built an impregnable fortress on a rocky spur rising out of the middle of the plain, crowning the cliffs with walls reinforced by semicircular towers. The site retained its strategic importance under the Muslims. In his *Memoirs* Babur describes a visit to Gwalior: 'I went to see the palaces of Man Singh and Vikramajit. They are extraordinary structures, built of massive, irregular blocks of stone. The most beautiful buildings of the rajas are those erected by Man Singh. Some have four storeys, of which the lower ones are very dark. The buildings are roofed with domes covered with gilded copper plates or green faience tiles. The walls too are adorned with faience tiles. We also visited the garden that Rahimdad had laid out south of the fortress.'

Humayun

When his father Babur died in 1530, Humayun was twenty-three years old. At first he ruled without opposition; soon, however, he found himself threatened by the intrigues of his three younger brothers. At the same time he had to deal with pressure from the Afghans. He managed to defeat Mahmud Lodi, but then he had to face a more fearsome enemy, Sher Shah Suri. While things began well, as Humayun captured Gaur, the capital of Bengal, in 1539, on his way back to Agra he was defeated first at Chausa and then at Kanauj in 1540. He was forced to give up the throne, leave India, and seek help from his brother in Kandahar. That proved a vain hope, and Humayun turned to Shah Tahmasp of Iran: there he found himself among friends, for his father had formed an alliance with Shah Ismail, the founder of the Safavid dynasty, and relations between the two families were excellent. Humayun remained away from India for fifteen years, first in Qazvin and then in Kabul, where he made plans to recover his throne.

Sher Shah ruled in Delhi for six years, extending his empire in Rajasthan and Sind. He feared Humayun's return, and prepared himself against it by building a line of fortifications in northern India. A decisive man who liked efficient organization, he reformed the administration, centralized the government, improved the system of taxes on agriculture, extended the road network, and built more than a thousand caravanserais. In Delhi he continued the architectural revival, as we have seen (p. 95), with buildings in which red sandstone is set off by white marble. Islam Shah Suri, who succeeded his father in 1545, pursued the same intelligent policies until his death in 1554.

In the meantime, Humayun, established in Kabul, was waiting for an opportunity to recover his kingdom. With 12,000 soldiers lent to him by Shah Tahmasp, he reconquered Kandahar and Lahore and prepared to retake Delhi. Once again the decisive battle took place at Panipat, in 1555. Humayun's triumph was short-lived, however: in 1556, at the age of forty-nine, he fell down the stairs of his library in the Purana Kila (ill. p. 95) and died.

Humayun's son, Akbar, was not yet thirteen when he came to the throne, and was placed under the guardianship of one of Humayun's officers; Bayram Khan conducted an effective regency until the day of Akbar's eighteenth birthday, but then the prince, incited by his relatives, rejected him: suspected of treason, Bayram Khan was put to death. Akbar later regretted his action, and built a magnificent tomb for his tutor in Delhi.

Humayun's body was to rest in a temporary tomb until 1565, while the splendid mausoleum in Delhi commissioned in 1557 by his widow, Hajji Begum, was under construction. For its design she turned to a Persian architect, Mirak Mirza Ghiyas, who came from Herat, had worked in Bukhara, and had been in the circle of Babur and Humayun in Kabul. His style belongs to the Persian-Timurid tradition, and reflects the distinctive Persian approach to architecture. Looking at this vast mausoleum makes one realize how suddenly the architecture of Islamic India emerged, in terms both of its scale and of its stylistic features. Humayun's Tomb was to have a great influence on all Mughal architecture, and in particular on the Taj Mahal. We shall look at it again in more detail in Part II (pp. 238–43).

The tomb is square in plan, and crowned by a white marble dome. Each side features a large axial *iwan* set back between projecting corner blocks; these are not arranged in inward-facing pairs, as in a courtyard mosque; rather, they face outwards, while emphasizing the symmetrical composition. Within is an octagonal funerary chamber covered by a low dome. As at the Gur-i Amir in Samarqand, built a century and a half earlier, the double-shell principle allows the construction of domes with quite different profiles inside and out.

opposite At the court of Shah Tamasp in Iran, where he spent his years of exile, Humayun learnt the importance of the art of the miniature through manuscripts such as this *Anthology* of Iskandar Sultan, painted in Shiraz in 1410: here Alexander the Great is shown watching the sirens bathing. (Gulbenkian Foundation, Lisbon)

below Humayun's monumental tomb in Delhi, commissioned by his widow in 1557, was designed by the Persian architect Mirak Mirza Ghiyas. Positioned in a huge, geometrically laid-out garden, the tomb proper stands on a square platform and is crowned by a double-shelled dome of white marble.

The Art of Princely Gardens

Approaching Humayun's Tomb, one is immediately struck by the marvellous geometrical garden that surrounds it. Gardens play a crucial role in Islamic, and particularly in Mughal, architecture. They provide the setting for palaces and tombs, and express the love of their creators for landscapes in which nature has been disciplined by man. They often required major works: in the area that was to become a garden, earth was moved to form terraces, enclosing walls were erected, water was brought in and a complex irrigation system devised, and channels and basins were dug, like a reenactment of the actions of God in creating the world.

Babur in his *Memoirs* describes the making of a garden in Kabul – a passage illustrated by a lovely miniature in the copy of the *Baburnama* produced for Akbar (ill. p. 102). He comments on its beauty, and in analysing it he concludes that its charm derives as much from its natural setting as from the benefits it yields in the way of fruit, flowers and aromatic plants. Here is what he wrote:

> In the year 914 [1508–9], I laid out a park known as the Garden of Fidelity. I situated it on a height, facing south, with a river flowing at the foot of the slope. It produces oranges, lemons and pomegranates in abundance. The year when I captured Lahore I brought back banana trees and had them planted there: they took very well. The following year, I added sugarcane that I had had brought from Bukhara, which also took very well. The garden on the height has sufficient running water and enjoys a very mild climate. In the centre is a little hillock; a stream that turns a mill flows through the garden and around this little hill which is covered with a lawn. To the southwest, a ten-sided pool, surrounded by orange and pomegranate trees, lies in the centre of a clover meadow. This is the most beautiful corner of the garden, and it is at its finest when the oranges are ripe. This garden is indeed admirably placed.

Unfortunately, in India Babur did not find such good conditions for garden-making as he had in Kabul, and he did not hide his disappointment, concluding: 'The cities and villages of India are completely devoid of charm.' Elsewhere he is more specific:

> given that one of the great disadvantages of India is the lack of running water, I always intended to have waterwheels set up, to run water through them, and to lay these places out in an ordered and symmetrical way. . . . Several days after my arrival in Agra, I crossed the Jumna to inspect sites that might be suitable for a garden. The places were so detestable and so desolate that I went on my way, with a hundred shudders and unpleasant impressions. But since there was nowhere else in the vicinity of Agra, it was there that

below Babur supervising the completion of a pool in Kabul, about which he wrote in his *Memoirs*, from the illustration in Akbar's *Baburnama*. (National Museum, Delhi)

opposite A holy man, protected by angels, meditates in a pavilion which suggests the Persian idea of paradise and its magnificent palaces. This superb miniature painted by Djami in Herat in 1553, during the reign of Shah Tahmasp, comes from a manuscript of the *Gulistan* or *Rose Garden*. (Arthur Sackler Gallery, New York)

> I undertook to lay out a park. I began by having a large well dug, whose water was to feed the *hammam*, and I had land prepared that is now planted with tamarind trees arranged around an octagonal pool. At each corner, I planted lovely beds of roses and narcissus in perfect alignment. Thus in this India devoid of charm and regularity, ordered and symmetrical gardens appeared.

The ancient Egyptians are known to have laid out pleasure gardens, and some are attractively depicted in wallpaintings in tomb chambers. The most famous written account of gardens in the Orient is Xenophon's description of the creations of the Achaemenids, where he speaks of vast parks filled with trees and animals and irrigated by watercourses. Lysander praises the geometric layout of the park that Cyrus had laid out at Sardis. At Pasargades, archaeologists have found the regular pattern of irrigation channels that flowed through the green spaces surrounding the palaces. And the plantations of Persepolis are pictured in the reliefs of the Apadana.

It is now known that Persian gardens go back to the gardens of the Sumerians, the Babylonians (with the famous hanging gardens of Babylon) and the Assyrians. These were characterized by regular, symmetrical layouts and by a great use of artificial channels and basins.

Similar characteristics can be found in Greek and Roman gardens, and they were perpetuated in the Islamic world in the Umayyad gardens of the palace of Medinat az-Zahara, near Cordoba in Spain. The latter included a basin in the middle of which was a small island with an emblematic pavilion. The 'Abbasid parks at Samarra functioned as botanical gardens, aviaries and zoos: according to the accounts left by Christian embassies, wild animals such as gazelles and deer moved about in them freely.

Investigation into the meaning of these gardens has shown that they were simulacra of Paradise. In the Islamic world, this interpretation is based on the text of the Qur'an that promises resurrection of the elect: 'God has promised to believers, both men and women, gardens watered by streams. They will dwell there forever. He has promised them delightful dwellings in the Garden of Eden' (*Sura* 2). Another passage in *Sura* 56 develops the theme further:

> Those who will be closest to God will inhabit gardens of delights. They will rest on seats adorned with gold and gems, leaning on their elbows, facing each other. They will dwell among lotus trees without thorns and under banana trees laden with fruit, under far-reaching shade, beside a spring of running water, in the midst of abundant fruit. Whoever is among those close to God will know rest, pleasure. and gardens of delights.

Among the traditions of ancient Iran revived by the Timurid rulers were palace gardens, which were to inspire Mughal gardens in India from Babur onward. Their popularity was great, and no major building in the lands of Islam is without a garden. In the West, the most famous of them are, perhaps, those of the Alhambra in Granada, whose symbolism was expressed in the Arabic writings of Ibn Zamrak in the time of Muhammad V, between 1362 and 1391.

The palace garden as an image of Paradise is a model of the universe, as the walled gardens or *pairidaeza* of ancient Iran were a microcosm. The various 'climates' and the structure of the world can be experienced there, divided by the four Rivers of Paradise into as many regions that contain the different 'kingdoms' of the world, from rocks through plants, trees and flowers, fruit and spices to fish in vivaria and birds in aviaries, and on to domesticated and wild animals. The Persian carpet pattern called 'four Paradises' depicts this symbolic arrangement, with its watercourses that flow out in the four cardinal directions.

This paradisiac environment was created by means of a number of ingenious elements: among the 'marvels' that went into the creation of this idyllic picture were murmuring streams, shady waterfalls, and – an even greater wonder – fountains whose perpetual play was made possible by a knowledge of hydraulics developed in antiquity, with siphons, pressurized conduits and aqueducts that made running water fall like beneficial rain. The enchanting sound of fountains delighted the inhabitants of dry countries. Is not the ability to make rain a divine prerogative? The ruler had such power, and he used the garden to perform court rituals, placing his throne as Ruler of the Universe on a little island in the midst of water representing the primordial ocean. This arrangement occurred not only in Akbar's ephemeral capital at Fatehpur Sikri but also in Delhi, Lahore and Agra. The garden had become more than a princely luxury: it was the setting for ceremonies that reflected the semiology of the imperial court, as well as an image of the paradisal world promised to believers in the *suras* of the Qur'an.

AKBAR, AND HIS DREAM OF MUSLIM-HINDU FUSION

Humayun owed the recovery of his throne to the Persians and his mausoleum was the work of a Persian architect. His son, Akbar, was surrounded in childhood by an atmosphere that was closer to that of Qazvin than of Delhi. Yet once Akbar was emperor, his patronage was marked by a relative neglect of Persian forms in favour of Indian ones.

The personality and works of the 'Great Mughal' Akbar (1556–1605) are very attractive. His fundamental aim was to unify his empire, to effect a lasting bond between the Hindu communities and the Muslim conquerors whose leader he was: only thus, he thought, could the various elements of Indian society live harmoniously together. In this architecture played a remarkable role, as his novel policy was expressed in his buildings.

Akbar was more than a conqueror, although the campaigns that he launched on all fronts enabled him to found a true empire: in that empire he created new institutions, set up a centralized administration, and promoted fresh cultural and artistic initiatives. He had a thirst for knowledge, and was extremely learned, although having come to the throne so young he never learned to read or write. He possessed a large collection of books, and to feed his passionate interest in philosophy and religion he had the works of the best authors read to him. Indeed, his love of books led him to encourage calligraphy and manuscript painting.

Once he had grasped the reins of power, Akbar embarked on a series of conquests in continuation of the expansionist policy of his tutor, Bayram Khan. He took possession of Rajasthan, captured the fortress of Chittor in 1567, and Gujarat in 1573. In Bengal he brought to heel the turbulent Afghan princes who had staged repeated uprisings ever since the death of Sher Shah; their defeated leader was put to death in 1576. To the north, on the border of Transoxiana, he fought the Uzbeks. To be closer to the centre of operations, he moved temporarily to Lahore. He then took Kashmir in 1586, and Sind in 1590. Turning his attention to the Deccan, he sent ultimatums to the southern princes in 1591. Several kingdoms were acquired by means of persuasion and active diplomacy. Overall Akbar added greatly to his inheritance, so that just before 1600 his empire extended from Kabul to the centre of the Indian peninsula and from Baluchistan to Bengal.

To this vast territory Akbar applied an intelligent conception of government, with the establishment of a solid economic, legal and social infrastructure. From the account left by his biographer, Abul Fazl, it is clear that his interests were wide-ranging: among other achievements he regulated mining, and the making of weapons and war machines; improved the organization of the army, and reformed the treasury and tax-collection; took a great interest in schools and issued guidelines for teaching; and laid down court protocol and ceremonial procedure. Akbar applied

opposite A portrait of Akbar with the globe symbolizing his universal power is displayed by his son Jahangir, the third Mughal emperor of India, in a 17th-century miniature by Abul Hasan Nadir az-Zaman and Hasim. (Musée Guimet, Paris)

below A Muslim ruler distributing gifts to the poor of a town he is visiting, watched by the governor standing on the walled town's drawbridge. This 17th-century Mughal miniature comes from the *Book of Barmaki*. (Reza Abbassi Museum, Tehran)

centralized planning and set standard prices for basic goods, forced commerce to comply with precise rules, and initiated a plan for production and exchange. He applied to the whole empire a single set of laws and a single set of weights and measurements, and minted coinage that would be legal tender in all provinces. These centralized state structures were to remain in effect until the arrival of the British.

Akbar was a careful observer of the world, and he was concerned, as his grandfather Babur had been, to understand India. He studied its natural resources and its diverse communities, and took equal interest in philosophical principles and in game management or the cultivation of dry areas through irrigation. There was nothing concerning India that he did not care about, from the customs of its peoples to their languages. He was obsessed by the idea of unity. He longed for syncretism on a vast scale, and he promoted a single language that would be comprehensible to everyone – Hindustani, which combined Persian, Arabic and Urdu and which could be written equally well in Arabic-Persian script or in Devanagari (used for Sanskrit and Hindi).

In the sphere of religion as well, Akbar was anxious to eliminate antagonism and fanaticism. India comprised the most diverse religious persuasions. Among the dominant Islamic community most were orthodox Sunnis, like other peoples of Turkish-Mongol origin; what Shi'ites there were generally came from Iran. Among the indigenous peoples, the majority were Hindu (Shaivites, Vaishnavites, etc.); but there were also Jains, a few Buddhists in the north, and Mazdaeans who had fled from southern Iran. Finally, there were Christians, in the form of Jesuit missionaries from the European trading post in Goa. These differences led to strong intercommunal tension. Akbar wanted to promote tolerance, and to find a solution to religious antagonisms. Under his own roof there were many confessions: some of his wives were Muslims, others were Hindus from the Rajput nobility, and yet others professed Mazdaism; for the latter he went so far as to build a fire temple in his palace.

Akbar's prime concern was to reconcile the two branches of Islam: Sunnism, which he inherited from the Timurids, and the Shi'ism of the Persians. Convinced that the Law applied to all, he wanted to establish universal tolerance throughout his empire, and he dreamed of a syncretic union between Sufism (the mystical current within both Sunnism and Shi'ism) and the Vaishnavite vision native to India. When his liberal policy outraged the *ulamas* (literally 'the learned'), the doctors of the law who guard the purity of Muslim rules, he deprived them of all their prerogatives to govern and dispense justice.

Akbar then proceeded to set up meetings among representatives of the various religions, so as to get a clearer idea of the nature of each faith: his court became a place where Buddhists, Hindu sages, Zoroastrians, and both Nestorian and Catholic Christians met to engage in vigorous debates under the direction of the emperor himself. It was a time of spiritual unease: the millennium of the Muslim religion was approaching, and fear of the Last Judgment intensified the anxiety of the faithful. Tension was further heightened by Millennarian Shi'ites, who looked to the return of the twelfth Imam – the 'hidden Imam' or Mahdi, the 'Master of Time'.

In this climate of uncertainty, Akbar ended up by founding his own religion, the Din-i Ilahi or 'Divine Faith', in which the positive elements of all the various faiths were combined in an unprecedented syncretism. Akbar was its founder and leader, and the representative of God on earth. He decreed that muezzins should henceforth hail the appearance of the sun with the ritual Islamic phrase *Allah'u akbar*: traditionally this means 'God is great', but it could also be taken to mean 'Akbar is God'. Another decree, in 1593, declared the equality of all men, Muslims and Hindus, within the empire. Going further, he sought to abolish the caste system. It is not difficult to imagine the fierce resistance that met these attempts to reform the immemorial traditions of India. Yet Akbar remains remarkable for his humanistic vision and for the breadth of his views, in his desire to unify the people over whom he reigned.

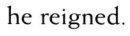

The Jahangiri Mahal in the Red Fort in Agra, built *c.* 1575 by Akbar for his son and heir

Top With its gate in the form of a *pishtaq* and the *chhatris* at the corners, the palace combines Persian and Hindu architectural styles.

Centre In the inner court brackets between the first-floor arches support terraces above.

Below A hall opening onto the court has, instead of Persian arches and vaults, corbelled arches with pendants, and lintels supporting brackets.

Akbar the Builder

Akbar's reform of the judicial and religious systems and his reorganization of the country resulted in a modern realm with a strong regime, and the wealth generated by his good management was invested in a formidable number of construction projects, as he fostered the creation of civic and religious building of outstanding quality and originality. The purpose of this architecture went beyond the normal one of demonstrating the ruler's power and providing a setting for his state: for Akbar, it was part of his program to unify the empire. The style that Akbar promoted drew equally on Persian-Timurid sources and on Hindu traditions. Architecture became part of the system of government, an agency of social cohesion.

This can be clearly seen if one looks at a few celebrated examples. In Agra, which was renamed Akbarabad, the 'City of Akbar', the emperor commissioned a new fort, with a circle of high, red sandstone walls set on the foundations of the Lodi fortifications. The stone of which the Red Fort is built is superb, and the quality of the masons' work is outstanding. Construction began around 1565. The walls punctuated by semicircular towers rise out of deep moats; the whose ensemble bristles with crenellations, and has arrowslits at regular intervals. The projecting angle towers have platforms on their roofs for artillery – henceforth a determining factor in a siege.

In the gates, reached through outer systems of protection, defensive features are combined with decorative elements in marble and coloured stone inlay, which somewhat soften the severity of the military works. The palace buildings were substantially renewed by Shah Jahan, Akbar's grandson, some sixty years later (from 1628), so little remains of Akbar's imperial palace in Agra

to tell us of the organization of the court and of state ritual. The only palace structure surviving from his time is the one that he began in 1572 for his son Jahangir, the heir to the throne, and this clearly illustrates his architectural preferences. The Jahangiri Mahal occupies a site measuring 80 x 88 metres that overlooks the Jumna River. At its corners there are octagonal towers topped by *chhatris*; inside is a court surrounded by two storeys of apartments, with porticoes to north and south. This arrangement, similar to that in Jodh Bai's Palace at Fatehpur Sikri, forms a symmetrical, centripetal structure that comes as close to the spatial arrangement of Hindu architecture (e.g. in the palace of Gwalior) as as to that of Iran. Throughout, this makes use of bracket-and-lintel construction, inspired by the Hindu architecture of Bengal and Gujarat. The entrance door has a large Persian arch, but everywhere else the forms are derived from wooden architecture – joists, corbels and brackets, tie-beams and corbelled out balconies all rendered in red sandstone. Rectangular piers with capitals in the form of corbels set at right angles to each other are combined with rows of brackets that support overhanging terraces. In this combination of the true arch and of corbelling Akbar was enunciating a political program: his determination to bring the vital traditions of India together to form a new nation. The Jahangiri Mahal is indeed closer to Hindu constructional forms than to the Persian-Timurid forms of Humayun's Tomb (ill. pp. 100–101), although that was built some fifteen years earlier.

above The southern entrance to the Red Fort in Agra. At this point the inner entrance, the Akbari Darwaza or Akbar Gate, is protected by a barbican entered through an ornamented gate set at right angles to the main wall, the Amar Singh Darwaza. This structure, and one of the round mural towers (left), are seen over the low outermost wall and gate added by Aurangzeb, Akbar's great-grandson.

A New Capital for Akbar: Fatehpur Sikri

Akbar invited many Hindus to work with the Muslim ruling class; in his desire not to cut himself off from the roots of India he manifested great tolerance and a synthesis-seeking spirit which are apparent in his architecture, and especially in his palaces. Fatehpur Sikri is a particularly clear manifesto of his socio-political aims. Just as two hundred and fifty years earlier Muhammad ibn Tughluq had decided that Daulatabad would be the new capital of Muslim India, so Akbar conceived the grandiose project of building a city on a virgin site 40 kilometres to the west of Agra, from which to direct his empire. Personal reasons lay behind his choice. At twenty-three Akbar was still without an heir, and his wife had just lost twins; in his concern, he decided to consult a holy man, Shaikh Salim Chishti (1480–1572), who was living a life of seclusion at Sikri. The shaikh predicted the birth of a son, and on 30 August 1569 the child was born, under the sage's protection. It was indeed a boy: with the birth of the future Jahangir, the continuation of the dynasty was assured.

In gratitude, Akbar decided to fix the centre of his empire at Fatehpur Sikri – 'Sikri, City of Victory'. In the buildings of this 'ideal city' he further developed the Indo-Persian-Timurid character of his architecture. (For a detailed look at these buildings, see Part II, pp. 244–53.) Fatehpur Sikri was provided with all the structures necessary for court life, administration, and Islamic worship, with a fine mosque and Halls of Private Audience (Diwan-i Khass) and Public Audience (Diwan-i Amm). Some features, however, remain mysterious, in particular a square tank with a small open-air island in the centre where the emperor's throne could be set up. Here, seated under a canopy, Akbar assumed the aspect of the Ruler of the World. But how should we understand this 'imperial cult'? Was it because Akbar had founded a religion and as such had become divine in his own lifetime? or was he the god-king, in the tradition of antiquity? What is certain is that, seated under a canopy on a cosmic island, Akbar was the embodiment of omnipotence.

This airy canopy, set up temporarily for the performance of a specific court ritual, is a reminder of the ephemeral architectural structures used by the Mughal armies (ill. p. 99 left). Between the openwork elements that survive at Fatehpur Sikri – piers, lintels, brackets and pierced stone grilles – we must imagine an 'architecture of cloth'. With its position on a slight elevation above the plain, the city felt the slightest breath of air, and the architects exploited that, as they made provision for screens, hangings, carpets and curtains thanks to which the inhabitants could live on the flat roofs and enjoy the evening breeze. The Eastern habit of sleeping under the stars was here systematized, as Akbar looked at local customs to make his capital more comfortable. For the Mughals, too, life under canvas had a long history, going back to the days when their ancestors were nomadic Mongols in Central Asia; in Samarqand Timur still preferred a tent to a palace.

In the *Ain-i Akbari* Abul Fazl, the chronicler of Akbar's reign, describes mobile camps that accompanied the emperor when he moved thrugh the country. His royal camp was, like that of the Turkish-Mongol khans, a folding city, which could be loaded on waggons or taken to pieces and carried on camelback. Akbar claimed to have invented a system of modular tents as large as the buildings in a real city. In this too he was following a time-honoured tradition, one that stretched back to the Achaemenid and Hellenistic rulers and which derived both from antiquity and from the tribes of the steppe.

above left The white marble mausoleum in the court of the Great Mosque – rebuilt and embellished during Jahangir's reign – was dedicated to the memory of Shaikh Selim Chishti, whom Akbar venerated, and who had predicted the birth of the emperor's first son.

opposite The Anup Talao, with a small square island reached by four walkways. Here Akbar performed elaborate court rituals.

left and below This curious pavilion of red sandstone held the emperor's Diwan-i Khass or Hall of Private Audience. It is said that Akbar organized religious debates there between representatives of the different faiths in his empire, including Christian missionaries. The rows of brackets that support the projecting balcony are a feature from Hindu architecture.

According to Abul Fazl, the emperor's camp comprised various elements: a square enclosure containing 54 rooms, each measuring 24 x 14 metres, surrounded a courtyard of 150 x 150 metres, in the centre of which stood the royal pavilion. The rooms were separated by hangings. Awnings, each some 12 metres long, provided shelter; some were of waxed cloth to give protection from rain. The palace area, with a temporary Diwan-i Khass and Diwan-i Amm, extended over a length of 1,500 metres. There were also tents for officers and tents for soldiers. Moving all this required 100 elephants, 500 camels, 400 carts and 100 men, escorted by 500 horsemen and by 1,000 waggon drivers, 500 water carriers, 50 carpenters, 50 tent assemblers, 30 leather workers, 50 torch bearers and 150 sweepers.

This lightweight architecture provided a novel and functional setting for living, and Akbar was justifiably proud of it. Clearly it underlies the layout and the buildings of Fatehpur Sikri. Despite all the emperor's care, however, his city proved not to be viable. Just as Muhammad ibn Tughluq's bold enterprise at Daulatabad ended in disaster, so the 'artificial' capital at Fatehpur Sikri was doomed. A lake had been created to the north-west of the city, but it proved inadequate to supply the inhabitants with water. As early as 1585, the decision was taken to abandon the 'ideal city'.

The Mughal court moved as a body to Lahore, leaving all Akbar's structures behind. From the laying of the first stone to the city's final abandonment was a period of no more than fourteen years. The relatively good state of preservation of the remains is explained by the distance of the site from any city and by its near-total isolation for three hundred years. Thus at Fatehpur Sikri we can see an almost perfect ensemble dating from the second half of the 16th century, infused with the generous and utopian spirit of a Turkish-Mongol ruler with grandiose aspirations.

5

Architecture, Manuscript Painting and Carpets in Bukhara and under the Early Safavids

p. 110 Decorative details from Shaybanid *madrasas* in Bukhara.

p. 111 A *simurgh* – the Persian mythical bird akin to the phoenix, symbol of resurrection – on the façade of the Nadir Divan Beghi Madrasa in Bukhara, of 1622 (see p. 115).

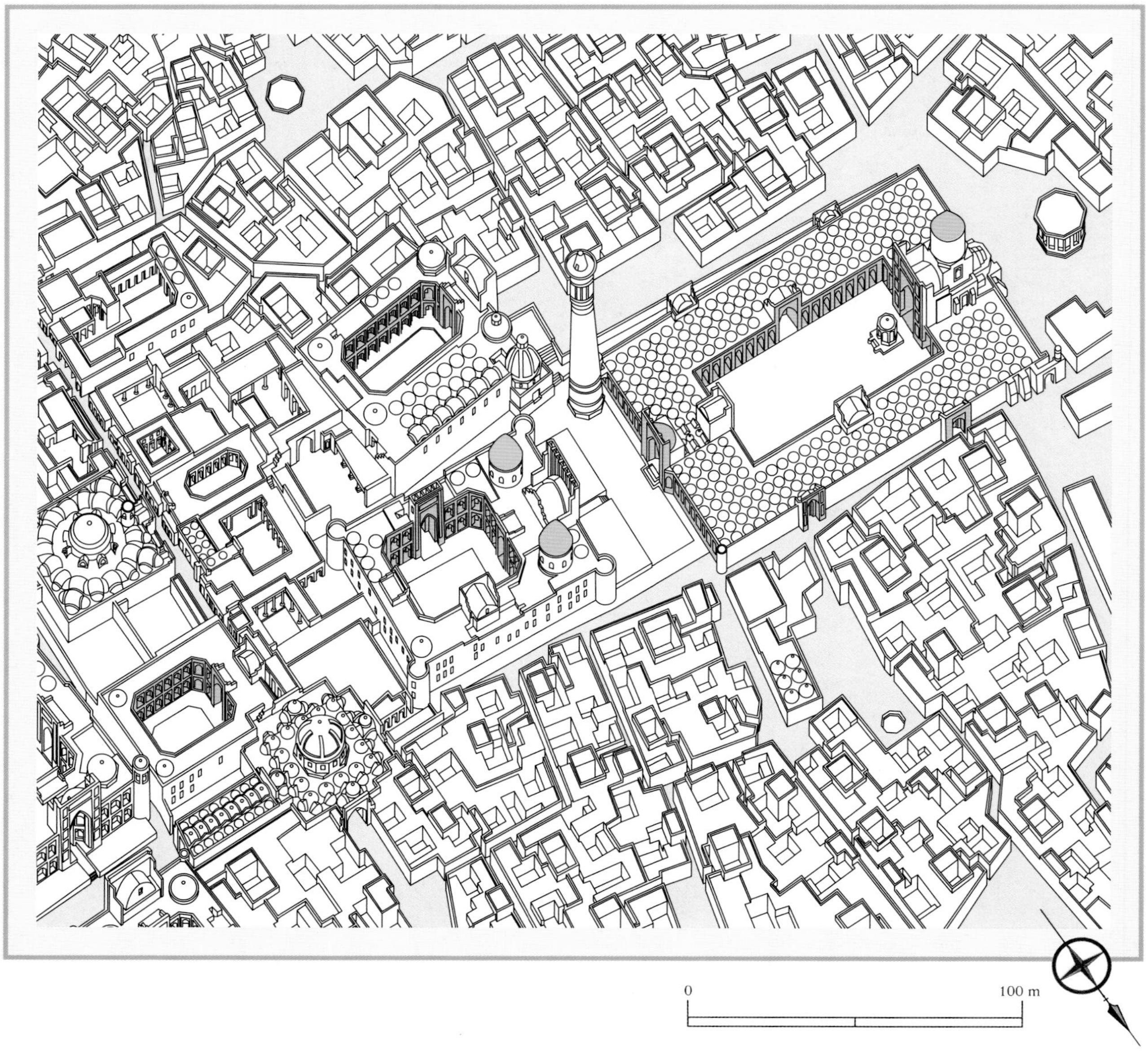

The period that begins with the Shaybanids of Bukhara, who succeeded the Timurids in Transoxiana, is expressed in a number of buildings in which the formulas developed in Samarqand are maintained but also taken further and revitalized. Around 1511 the Uzbeks – one of the tribes of the Golden Horde, descended from the Turkish-Mongol Chagatai tribes – took over Transoxiana, and their chief, Shaybani Khan, moved the capital from Samarqand to Bukhara. Bukhara had already been attacked repeatedly by Ismail I and Persian troops, who had captured it in 1510. Both Bukhara and Khiva were to fall to the Safavids in 1599, and were again subjected to Iran after a raid by the Persian adventurer Nadir Shah (1736–47).

The Shaybanids actively maintained Timurid styles in art and architecture: they were responsible for the two great 17th-century *madrasas* that flank the Timurid Registan in Samarqand (see Part II, pp. 230–37), and the Shaybanids enriched Bukhara, which they held from 1510 to 1599, with many Sunni religious buildings. The hostility between Iranian Shi'ites and Turkish-Mongol Sunnis led to frequent wars between Iran (including Khorasan) and Transoxiana, but they did not prevent cultural contacts, or inhibit the influence of the 'Persian style' on the architecture of the Shaybanids. The post-Timurid legacy consists essentially of religious buildings.

In Bukhara, the Kalyan Mosque is dominated by an ancient Seljuq

The Kalyan Mosque in Bukhara, 1512–39

left, above An axonometric view showing the mosque (on the right) in context. It is separated by a court dominated by a tall minaret from the Miri Arab Madrasa, which was built in 1535 in imitation of the great Qur'anic schools of the Timurids. (After Klaus Herdeg)

left, below The entrance *pishtaq* and the Kalyan Minar, a Seljuk minaret.

minaret datable to 1127, known as the Kalyan Minar. Free-standing like an Italian campanile, this is a slightly tapering cylinder 50 metres tall. Its geometrical brick patterning recalls that of the Tomb of Ismail Samani (ill. p. 27, below), highlighted by occasional touches of faience.

The Kalyan Mosque built by the Shaybanids in 1512–39 is similar to the Mosque of Bibi Khanum in Samarqand (ill. pp. 66–69), though on a smaller scale. It is a symmetrical and axial structure entered through a large *pishtaq*, with the classic arrangement of a courtyard bordered by arcades (here single-storeyed) punctuated by four *iwans*. The largest of these leads to the prayer hall, which is further emphasized by a handsome dome, and contains a lovely *mihrab* faced with tile mosaic. The two side *iwans*, which mark the transverse axis in the standard Persian arrangement, are not treated monumentally. The court is surrounded by covered spaces, in which square piers support small brick domes. In front of the prayer hall is the ablutions fountain, in the form of an octagonal kiosk.

above View from the top of the minaret. The court is of the four-*iwan* type; the largest *iwan*, leading to the prayer hall, is topped by a dome over the *mihrab*. Hypostyle spaces covered with small domes surround the perimeter of the court.

The Persianization of Transoxiana

The Madrasa of Mir-i Arab forms a majestic counterpart to the entrance front of the Kalyan Mosque in Bukhara, in the same way as the Madrasa of Shir Dor faces that of Ulugh Beg in Samarqand (ill. p. 230). This arrangement characteristic of Transoxiana is known as *kash*. The vast Mir-i Arab Madrasa has the same general arrangement as the Shir Dor Madrasa: on either side of the centrally placed entrance, domes crown halls – here used for teaching – at the corners. But whereas those in Samarqand have thick projecting ribs resting on *muqarnas*, those here are covered with smooth faience; very slightly swelling in profile, each rests on a drum crowned by a band of *muqarnas* above a beautiful inscription in thuluth script on a blue ground. Within the great entrance *pishtaq* the back wall takes the form of a tree-sided apse, as in the Kalyan Mosque. This move to replace the flat end wall at the back of the *iwan* or *pishtaq* by a space with chamfered corners is characteristic of the style of Bukhara. It is seen again later, in Isfahan, in the Mader-i Shah Madrasa, of the early 18th century.

One can categorize this feature as part of the 'baroque' character that emerges in Shaybanid mosques and *madrasas*, although they remain relatively simple and always symmetrical in plan. This trend is particularly noticeable in the tile mosaic decoration of the surfaces surrounding the great *iwans*. In Samarqand, the Shir Dor Madrasa displays a pair of lions holding the disk of the sun, symbolizing the strength of light; and the Khodja Akhrar Madrasa has tigers chasing gazelles, alluding to a legend about the capture of the soul (ill. p. 233). In Bukhara, the

left and below The Miri Arab Madrasa in Bukhara, of 1535. Two domes faced with smooth blue glazed bricks flank the *pishtaq*. The polychromy of their *muqarnas* produces a shimmering effect, particularly in the warm colours. The two tiers of arcades give access to rooms used by teachers and students. Their ceramic decoration, and that of the *pishtaq*, has recently been restored.

madrasas show a variety of living beings, whose presence is unexpected in the Islamic world. At the Nadir Divan Beghi Madrasa, of 1622, above the arch of the *pishtaq* are two *simurghs* (see also ill. p. 111) flying towards each other, a Persian symbol of eternal life and resurrection; the association is emphasized by the green colour of their plumage. The *simurgh* plays a key role in an early 13th-century mystical poem by Attar. Persian iconography saw no difficulty in using figurative symbols or depictions of living beings, even in the decoration of religious buildings. This tolerant attitude to images, which was a product of Shi'ite thought, became accepted in the art of the Persian-influenced Sunnites of Transoxiana. It is reflected even more spectacularly in manuscript painting.

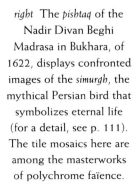

right The *pishtaq* of the Nadir Divan Beghi Madrasa in Bukhara, of 1622, displays confronted images of the *simurgh*, the mythical Persian bird that symbolizes eternal life (for a detail, see p. 111). The tile mosaics here are among the masterworks of polychrome faïence.

Bukhara also has a handsome Madrasa of Ulugh Beg, which is a simplified version of the one that Timur's grandson built in the Registan of Samarqand (ill. pp. 74–75). Subsequently, the new capital was to witness a brilliant development of the courtyard-plan *madrasa* in the 16th and 17th centuries. The same general formula can be traced in the Madrasa of Abdullah Khan (1588–90), which faces the Madrasa Mader-i Khan (1566), in that of Abd al-Aziz (1651), and in that of Kokaldosh or Kukeltash, which stands within the Liabi Khauz complex. In that complex, where two buildings face each other across a pool edged by fine plane trees, the building to the south is a *khanaqah*, dating from 1620. *Khanaqahs* have a hall where members of spiritual confraternities gather to perform exercises with a mystical dimension, such as dancing and singing. Since they have an enclosed meeting place, they do not necessarily have a courtyard, but their *pishtaq*-style façades belong to the tradition of *iwans* surrounded by ample frames covered with geometrical motifs in polychrome faience. In these tile mosaics the artists gave free rein to their sense of design and to their search for a meaningful expressive language for Islam.

above The façade of the Madrasa of Kokaldosh or Kukeltash in Bukhara. In the 17th-century Liabi-Khauz complex, as in the Registan (though on a more modest scale), three sides of an open space are lined by buildings whose designs are interrelated.

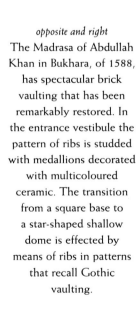

opposite and right The Madrasa of Abdullah Khan in Bukhara, of 1588, has spectacular brick vaulting that has been remarkably restored. In the entrance vestibule the pattern of ribs is studded with medallions decorated with multicoloured ceramic. The transition from a square base to a star-shaped shallow dome is effected by means of ribs in patterns that recall Gothic vaulting.

right, above The funerary complex of Chor Bakr was built *c.* 1560 in a former cemetery on the outskirts of Bukhara. Three linked buildings stand side by side: a *khanaqah* (monastery), a *madrasa* set slightly back, and a mosque, accompanied by a free-standing minaret.

right, centre and below The remarkable mosque in the Bakhauddin complex near Bukhara (a site dedicated to the memory of a holy man named Baha al-Din, who died in 1389) has a centralized plan but no courtyard. Four large *iwans* open to the exterior, and serve to buttress the dome which is strengthened by massive projecting ribs. The dome inside is covered with a delicate tracery of ribs.

opposite Detail of a screen window lighting the *khanaqah* in the Chor Bakh funerary complex. The hexagonal openings are formed naturally by the shape of the assembled bricks.

Funerary Architecture

Other buildings in and around Bukhara were designed for specific ritual purposes: these are the funerary complexes, with places of prayer built to accommodate the veneration associated with a burial – expressions of the important role played by the dead in Islam. In the cemetery of Chor Bakr, constructed outside the city between 1560 and 1563, there is a very interesting group that brings together three *iwans*, which seem a far-off reminiscence of the great Sasanian *iwan* at Ctesiphon (ill. p. 298). The three buildings, all oriented towards the Ka'ba at Mecca, are linked: to the left is a *khanaqah*, with a graceful swelling dome on a drum; in the centre, set back beyond an open space that is like half a traditional courtyard, is a *madrasa*; and to the right, on the same alignment as the *khanaqah*, is a very austere mosque. In front of the courtyard, a small minaret provides a vertical accent in this vast complex dominated by horizontal lines.

Another notable funerary site is that of Bakha al-Din, or Bakhauddin, which dates from 1546 and lies a dozen kilometres east of Bukhara. Here the faithful come on pilgrimage on commemorative feastdays, and, following the tradition of the ancient *agape*, gather in rooms for collective meals. Kitchens are provided for groups of the pious who have sacrificed the ritual lamb, who thus share the food provided by the family of the deceased. The Bakhauddin complex is centred on a vast square mosque with a great depressed dome of which the exterior displays ribbing that indicates the structural lines of force.

Other types of prayer hall, surrounded by porticoes with tall wooden columns, belong to the the tradition of domestic architecture expressed in houses and palaces. These verandas and galleries, known as *talar*, may be used in structures for religious purposes or for everyday life, and they can be traced back to the architecture of the Achaemenids and their predecessors: they are clearly depicted in the reliefs of the great rock-cut tombs of the Persian kings at Naqsh-i Rustam. Derived directly from vernacular housing, it was a natural indigenous form, appropriate for a time when great forests of conifers still covered large sections of the Persian world.

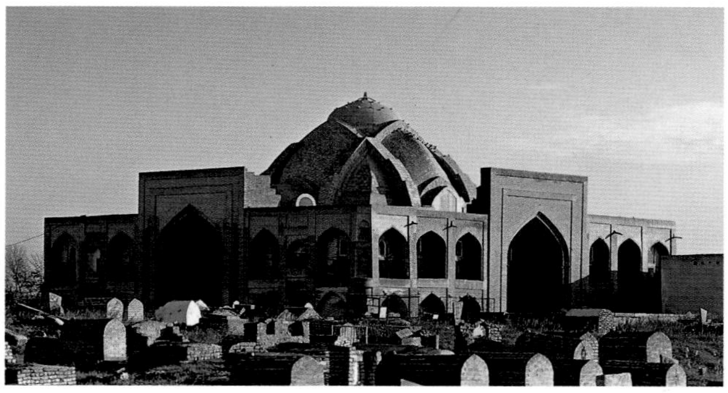

از زمینش بر داشت و بالای سرش برد و فرو کوفت
که غریو از خلق بر آمد ملک فرمود تا استاد را خلعت

Miniature Painting in Herat, Shiraz and Tabriz

After the fall of the Timurid empire, the art of making books continued to develop both in the quality of the works produced and in their significance as symbols of knowledge and taste, to the point where the principal dynasties were honour-bound to support painters and calligraphers. Baysunqur, the son of Shah Rukh of Herat, is said to have been an artist himself. The city of Herat was to remain an important centre for the production of Persian miniatures, although the famous artist Bihzad chose to live in Tabriz, the capital of Shah Ismail, founder of the Persian Shi'ite dynasty. At the same time, from 1528 onwards, Bukhara again attracted court artists: Ubaid Allah Khan (1512–39) commissioned al-Harawi, a painter from Herat, to produce a series of illustrations for a *Diwan* of Sa'di. Some twenty years later, Shiraz became famous when Murchid al-Attar (active 1523–52) illustrated a manuscript of the *Marvels of the World* by Qazvini. That refined and delicate work contrasts with a later manuscript from Shiraz, of the *Khamseh* of Nizami, where the dense image takes the form of interlacing vegetation among whose branches almost mannered figures appear.

In the meantime, however, a patron who had unerring taste and was a great lover of art ascended the Persian throne in the person of Shah Tahmasp (1513–76). In the first decades of his reign he took a particular interest in the creation of important new works, and he left a magnificent collection of illustrated manuscripts of unequalled quality, especially large-format copies of the *Shahnama*, where, thanks to artists such as Dust Mohammed, Mirza Ali, Aqa Mirak and Muzaffar 'Ali, a subtle sense of composition and an interest in picturesque detail are combined with a sensitivity and freshness of colour that made the Tabriz school one of the most fertile art centres of the Islamic world.

All the characteristic features of Persian miniature painting were now combined in a style that would remain unchanged for several centuries, which from Tabriz exerted its influence on the court art of the Ottomans in Istanbul and the Mughals in India. Despite their extreme 'realism', these paintings invite the observer into a world of dreams, in an ethereal or dramatic atmosphere. It is an inward vision that naturalism cannot satisfy: by its handling of space in stepped receding planes, by its use of 'leitmotifs' such as picturesque rocks, gardens full of flowers, or interiors curiously formed of flat planes richly decorated with repeating motifs, it conjures up an unreal world of unmistakable character. Heirs to the notable developments made under the Timurids, the Safavid miniaturists produced a utopian perfection conveyed through lyric illusionism. The painter's invention becomes a refuge where the powerful are tempted to withdraw. That was not the case with Shah Tahmasp; after 1545, according to Anthony Welch, he lost his interest in painting and dismissed almost all his artists, who went off to search for new patrons elsewhere in Iran or in India, where they were responsible for the beginning of Mughal painting. His attitude can be explained by the difficulties he experienced in his struggle against the Ottomans.

The art of the book did not regain its prestige at court until the reign of Shah 'Abbas I. A manuscript of the *History of the Prophets* dedicated to Shah 'Abbas around 1600 shows that a certainly sobriety was favoured, but its relatively unadorned style may be due to remote Timurid influence via a model now lost. The art of the miniature now began to lose its impetus, and painters did not hesitate to copy. In a *Shahnama* of 1614 that belonged to Shah 'Abbas, swarming with details, plagiarism achieves greatness, according to Basil Grey, through the refinement of observation and the luxurious ornamentation: the illustrations in this manuscript were inspired by those in a *Shahnama* painted by Baysunqur almost two centuries earlier. Under the late Safavids, miniature painting often did little more than repeat the old formulas. Contacts with the West disturbed its development, and awareness of 17th- and 18th-century European art led to increasing confusion between Persian painting's vision in superimposed planes and frontal depiction of architecture and the European conventions of optical perspective.

opposite A page from a manuscript of the *Gulistan* or *Rose Garden* by the great Persian poet Sa'di shows two wrestlers performing before a ruler and a select audience. It was painted in Bukhara in the mid-16th century. The city's school of painting remained active through the 17th century. (Bibliothèque Nationale de France, Paris)

above The building of the fort of Khawarnak, shown in a miniature painted in Herat by the celebrated Bihzad in 1494. Activities represented include the making of bricks, the transportation of materials, and the construction of a vault with scaffolding. (British Library, London)

CARPETS, BETWEEN TRADITIONAL FORMS AND THE 'PERSIAN STYLE'

The art of the carpet forms a specific category within the 'Persian style'. Its origins go back to a time long before the present era. Its earliest history is uncertain, but thanks to Soviet excavations in the Siberian Altai in 1949 and to finds recovered by archaeologists from the site of Pazyryk, half-way between Iran and China, it is known that knotted carpets were already being made in the 5th century BCE. Within a *kurgan* or mound, the burial of a Scythian tribal chieftain was found intact, preserved by the permafrost. Among the contents – the body of the deceased and his clothing and rich ornaments, skeletons of horses, remains of chariots and harnesses, etc. – the archaeologists were amazed to discover a complete large carpet, of which the size alone (200 x 183 centimetres) indicated remarkable technical skill. Its design corresponded to the traditional formula with which we are familiar: a central area, which here featured 24 rosettes in juxtaposed boxes (6 x 4), and, around the central panel, five borders, some with geometrical motifs and others with alternating 'processions' of animals. The innnermost border featured a long line of reindeer (or deer?) with imposing antlers, moving in single file in a clockwise direction. Another zoomorphic border, separated from the last by a row of abstract motifs, consists of horses in harness, led by men (grooms or riders?) walking alongside them, all moving in the opposite direction to the reindeer procession. These horses are curiously similar to part of the relief of the *Procession of Tribute-Bearers* at Persepolis, an Achaemenid work contemporary with the Pazyryk *kurgan*.

The art of the knotted carpet here appears in a remarkably developed form (with 3,600 knots in a square of 10 x 10 centimetres), and the width of the loom used is striking. Carpet-weaving is traditionally associated with nomadic or semi-nomadic peoples, who used narrow looms no wider than 1.2–1.4 metres. At Pazyryk, however, we are suddenly in a different world: such great square carpets were produced by sedentary craftsmen with broad looms which were far too heavy and cumbersome to be moved by their owners.

The existence of wide looms indicates that the technology had been developing for a long time, especially when one considers the associated depiction of complex motifs and, more remarkable still, living beings. Whatever its origins, it seems certain that already in antiquity the art of carpet-making used a repertory of images that was closely related to that of floor mosaics, whether Greek, Hellenistic, Roman or Byzantine. In the present state of knowledge it is difficult to be certain which came first, but the resemblance between the designs of concentric borders used in both genres leaves no room for doubt of their interconnection. The Pazyryk carpet survived because it was preserved in ice for 2,500 years; elsewhere, because of the fragility of textiles, no ancient carpets have survived. We have literary evidence, however: in the very early days of Islam, in the 7th century, the Arabs who had just captured the Sasanian capital of Ctesiphon found a large carpet that they called 'Khusrau's Spring'; its borders were covered with flowers, leaves and precious stones, and they surrounded a field representing a pool of water, at the bottom of which you seemed to see pebbles. It is safe to assume that this was a floor carpet. The 'Abbasids liked to have carpets in their palaces and before long, starting in the 9th century, Fars in southern Iran became famous for work of this type, of which unfortunately none survives. A few rare fragments are known, and

top Central motif of a Persian carpet with the garden pattern known as *chahar bagh*. (Carpet Museum, Tehran)

above Detail of a Persian carpet bearing an inscription indicating that it was intended for Shah Tahmasp, mid-16th century. It was made in the imperial carpet factory and measures 505 x 240 centimetres. A further inscription names the design as 'enclosed garden of tulips': it includes trees, beasts of prey, dragons and bears. (Poldi-Pezzoli Museum, Milan)

opposite A carpet with a central medallion design, from Saruk in southern Iran. It was made in the mid-19th century of wool on a cotton base, and measures 314 x 208 centimetres. The decoration in the centre is of the 'Shah 'Abbas' type.

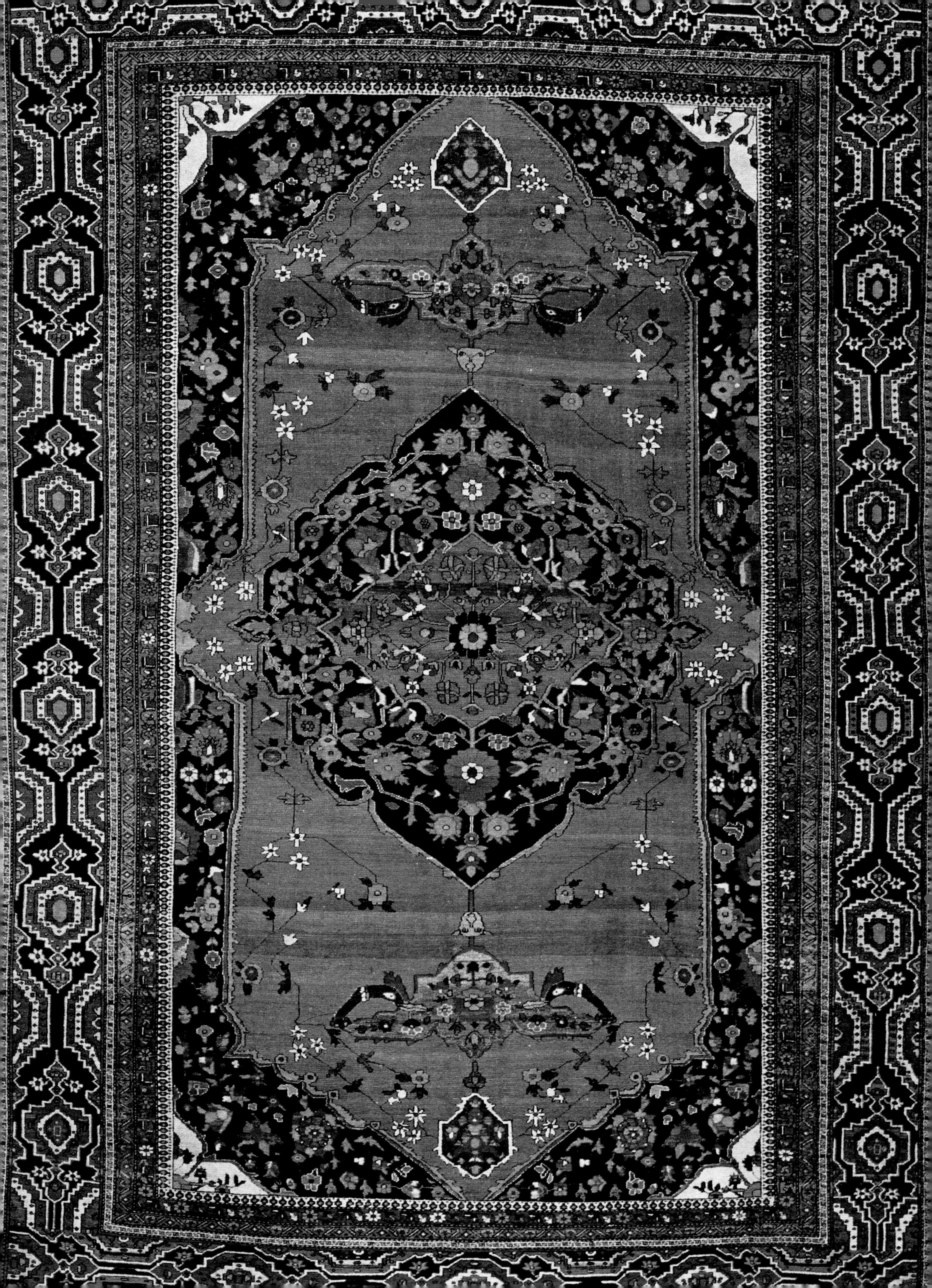

left A silk carpet made in Tabriz in the 19th century, measuring 190 x 140 centimetres. It has an off-white background and a large floral medallion; the borders include rich interlace motifs, and there are inscriptions at the two ends. (Carpet Museum, Tehran)

opposite Two details of floral motifs from a large 'vase' carpet, with stylized carnations or tulips on a white background – a late 19th-century copy of a 'Vienna' carpet made in 1600.

carpets are depicted in medieval Western paintings, thought it is not often that one can distinguish woven from knotted textiles. From the 15th century on, paintings by masters such as Memling and Holbein show the existence of superb carpets with geometrical designs, probably from the Caucasus.

According to a tradition that went back to the Mongols and the Timurids, technicians, craftsmen and artists were considered part of the booty that could be removed from captured cities. Like the miniaturists and painters captured by the Ottomans at Tabriz in 1514 and taken back to Anatolia, specialists in carpet-making were sought after for their talents. The same was true of potters, especially those who made tiles for architectural decoration, whom the Turks had the habit of bringing back from successful campaigns in Persia: these 'consultants' were to found the celebrated workshops of Iznik.

The Austrian imperial collections were inspired in part by the fascination aroused by articles left behind after Suleiman's hasty abandonment of the siege of the city in 1529. Among the riches in his camp were magnificent Persian carpets, which greatly stimulated an art already prized in the West. Not one of those survives in Vienna today. The carpets now known sometimes as 'Vienna carpets' are products of Persian workshops in the second half of the 16th century and the 17th century which can be seen in the Museum für angewandte Kunst.

Carpets are accessories of the Islamic religion in mosques: prayer carpets, whose central motif represents the *mihrab* towards which the faithful are turned, are modest personal items charged with meaning and often very meticulously executed. But the carpet-maker was more often in the service of the powerful. In the Safavid period, in the 16th and 17th centuries, the imperial workshops at Tabriz, Kashan, Shiraz, Isfahan and Ardebil produced remarkable creations, notably immense floor carpets measuring as much as 6 x 4 metres, 8 x 4 metres, or even in one exceptional case 11 x 5.35 metres. The size is amazing, but the fineness of the weave is even more so. One large wool carpet, measuring 5.5 x 3 metres, has no less than 7,400 knots per 10 x 10 centimetre square, while some small prayer carpets (typically measuring 1 x 1.6 metres) sometimes count more than 10,000 knots. In India

in the 17th century carpets knotted on silk might have an incredible 20,000 knots.

The decoration consists of floral motifs and plant forms that scroll out symmetrically, as on tiles (*kashi*) or on the tile mosaic panels that clad the surrounds of *iwans* in mosques and *madrasas*. Carpets became true works of art. In the 'Persian style', carpets harmonize with other decorative media in an architectural context. They could reproduce the mythical gardens of Paradise, displaying a *chahar bagh* pattern which consists of four parts separated by the four rivers of paradise, with a central pool that recalls the ablution basins of Persian mosques of the Safavid period. In Bukhara, carpet design was influenced by the proximity of the nomad-haunted steppes: large knotted carpets have juxtaposed octagonal medallions within whose geometrical forms it is possible to make out a stylized spider with eight legs: they are a charm against tarantulas, a very basic wish for protection that goes back to the carpets used in the tents of nomadic tribes. Carpets became early ambassadors for the art of the orient, as they moved with trade along the famous Silk Road: through them the Persian style filtered out to the dwellings of lords and burghers and into the choirs of churches. They should never be underestimated as vehicles for the transmission of the aesthetic vision of the Middle East.

Clearly, not all Persian carpets were made in court workshops. In the shadow of the masterpieces, there are a host of folk products that drew both on traditional motifs and on the vine-scrolls, foliage, flowers and vases seen in the decoration of architecture. Between these two extreme styles there are many intermediate forms, and the technology used affected the appearance of the products. Nomad carpets, made on narrow looms, usually have designs confined to geometrical and repeating motifs, in very stylized forms that in some ways recall those of *kilims*, which are flat-woven rather than knotted, in a technique that goes back to very ancient tapestry-weave textiles of Pharaonic and Coptic Egypt.

Only very fragmentary evidence survives from the whole realm of textile art, which included floor carpets, hangings and door-curtains, ornaments for draft and riding animals, parts of the tents of nomadic peoples, and the light enclosing walls of portable dwellings. Some state tents have survived, while others are portrayed in miniatures. Canopies are mentioned in surviving texts, both for their richness and for their iconography. On the edge of the steppe, the life of settled peoples was influenced by the lifestyle of nomadic tribes. Iran and Transoxiana were never far removed life from the legendary land of Turan and its elusive horsemen.

The finest of the splendid 16th- and 17th-century Persian carpets that form the nucleus of the collection of the Österreichisches Museum für angewandte Kunst, which include extremely rare masterpieces, give one a better understanding of the role carpets played in the courts of great men. One of the outstanding pieces in the collection is a large fragment of a carpet made in Tabriz around 1600, with a pattern known as 'vases on a white ground'; the fragment measures 248 x 150 centimetres, and the original must have measured at least 470 x 380 centimetres. It was published for the first time in 1896, then taken up in several specialist works. Around 1906, the designer Tahir Zadeh Bihzad of Tehran made a copy of its pattern, and before 1910 several superb full-size reproductions were made, signed by craftsmen in Kerman. What makes it particularly interesting is that it shows us the design of imperial carpets in the time of Shah 'Abbas I: indeed, the composition of stylized large flowers and branches on a plain off-white background is very similar to that seen in faience on the façades of Safavid mosques.

Iran under the early Safavids

Iran had been left ravaged and fragmented by Timur, and when the last Timurids disappeared it had to rebuild itself completely, both materially and politically. No local ruler was powerful enough to unify the whole country, as Shah Rukh had done in eastern Persia between 1404 and 1447. Northern and western Iran were the setting for the trials and confrontations of two semi-nomadic Turkmen tribes: the Ak Koyunlu, or White Sheep tribe, led by Uzun Hasan (1453–78), and the Kara Koyunlu, or Black Sheep tribe, led by Jahan Shah or Jihan Shah (1435–67). The former were located to the east of present-day Turkey, in the triangle between Sivas, Mardin and Erzurum south of Armenia, while the second occupied the area between the Caspian Sea and the Tigris River; together, they presented a grave threat to the sedentary culture of Iran.

Meeting little opposition from the weakening authority of the Timurids, Jahan Shah set out from Azerbaijan and captured Soltaniyeh and Qazvin, entered Isfahan in 1453, and eventually extended his power as far as Iraq. At the same time, the Shi'ite movement, favoured by the so-called Safavid current, which was concerned to promote spiritual renewal, exploited the antagonisms between the Turkmen princes and the last of the Timurids to impose its mystical vision on Iran.

The Safavid dynasty, which ruled from 1502 to 1722 or 1736, took its name from Shaikh Safiy al-Din, who died in 1334. A descendant of the Caliph Ali, he had spread Shi'ism through the Ardabil region by means of a Sufi order called the 'Safaviyeh', whose doctrine was to constitute the basis of the dynasty's religious policy.

The troubled decades that preceded the advent of the Safavids saw the defeat of the Kara Koyunlu in 1468 and the Ak Koyunlu in 1478, but their power was not really dissipated until 1503. These inter-tribal struggles favoured the development of a strong Persian power. The Safavid spearhead was formed of soldiers known as the *qizilbash*, or 'Red Hats', who wore a head-covering with twelve pleats to proclaim their allegiance to Twelver Shi'ism. Their leader was Ismail I, who was to rule Iran from 1502 to 1524. He promoted the 'Shi'ite revolution' to consolidate a national power in Iran based on the religion of the descendants of Ali, in opposition to his two formidable Sunni neighbours, the Ottoman Turks to the west and the Uzbeks, Central Asian semi-nomads, to the north-east. Shah Ismail entered Tabriz in 1502 and had himself crowned king. He proclaimed Shi'ism the state religion, with the intention of uniting the majority of the population around its ruler and of promoting a stronger sense of Persian identity. For the first time since the arrival of Islam, Iran had a king who founded a native dynasty, and whose religious loyalties corresponded to those of a large part of the population.

The first concern of Ismail I was to reconquer the entirety of Iran as far as Mesopotamia: he began by seizing the provinces of Gilan and Mazandaran, and by 1508 he controlled a powerful kingdom that stretched from Baghdad to Armenia and from the Upper Euphrates to Khorasan. Beginning in 1514, however, the Ottomans led by Sultan Selim I launched a series of campaigns against Iran, in which fortune was to swing back and forth between the two nations. The first battle, fought on the site of Chaldiran in 1514, went to the Ottoman forces, who were well equipped with modern armaments. Firearms, in the form of artillery and muskets, had begun to make their mark in war.

When Ismail died in 1524, his son and successor, Tahmasp, was only ten years old. In the early years of his long reign, which was to last fifty-two years, Iran was disturbed by internal struggles between various factions of the *qizilbash*. Shah Tahmasp (1524–76) – a fantastical and introverted character, at whose court Humayun was to find sanctuary – succeeded in preserving the unity of the country despite reverses in his conflicts with the Ottoman sultans Süleyman the Magnificent and Selim II. They attacked Azerbaijan, where they occupied Tabriz and captured many craftsmen and artists whom they carried off to Anatolia, and then seized Baghdad. Nevertheless, through the Treaty of Amasya, Tahmasp secured thirty years of peace with the Sublime Porte.

opposite A detail of a Safavid miniature of 1650 shows court life: a young lord, his wife and their retinue refresh themselves in the palace gardens. (Museum of Islamic Art, Cairo)

above The Safavid rulers were objects of great interest in the West, and some were portrayed by Italian painters. This profile of Ismail Sefi (1629–42), the grandson and immediate successor of Shah 'Abbas, hangs in the Uffizi Gallery in Florence.

A Style Emerges

Few buildings from the time before Shah 'Abbas I survive to help us trace the evolution of forms that culminated in the flowering of Safavid art. In Isfahan two works are of significance: the group of mausoleums known as the Darb-i Imam, of 1453, and the Tomb of Harun Velayat, of 1513. They are key links between the post-Timurid style and that of Shah 'Abbas.

The Darb-i Imam complex was built in the reign of the Kara Koyunlu ruler Jahan Shah, in honour of the Imamzadeh (descendants of the Imam) Ibrahim Batha and Zain al-Abedin. The French scholar André Godard has called it 'one of the masterpieces of the coloured architecture of Iran' and 'a gem', chiefly on the basis of the *iwan* that leads to the funerary chamber. The dome over one of the tombs was restored under Shah 'Abbas and then again under Shah Suleiman, so that it is difficult to know how much remains of the original appearance. The large-scale inscription in geometrical script that stands out against a light brick background on the drum is very similar to that seen on Timurid buildings in Samarqand (ill. p. 66) and Muzaffarid buildings in Bukhara, whereas the vine scrolls on the dome are clearly in the style of Shah 'Abbas. The second dome is much later in date (Qajar?), with a slender profile not seen before the 19th century; there too, however, the drum may be original, since this part of the structure was not so vulnerable to weather as the faience on the curved domes.

The same uncertainty surrounds the date of the dome of the Tomb of Harun Velayat, a holy man of whom nothing more is known than his name and the fact that 'Muslims, Jews and Christians all claim him as their own'. Here between the drum and the slightly overhanging dome there is a frieze of palmettes (descendants of the *muqarnas* on Timurid domes) of which a significant amount seems to be original. Again, the most important feature of the building is

left, centre The Tomb of Harun Velayat in Isfahan was built in 1513, at the start of the Safavid era. In its decoration purity and refinement are united to achieve perfection: tile mosaic lays a luxurious surface over forms of limpid clarity.

left, below The dome of the Tomb of Harun Velayat still displays a Timurid palmette frieze above the drum, though it seems that the faience cladding was renewed in the 17th century. The tall, slender minaret of Ali dates from the Seljuk period.

the *pishtaq*, of which André Godard considered that the transparent, vibrant glazes were among the best extant examples. The *iwan* is especially notable for an ingenious system of interlacing based on two squares overlapping at a 45-degree angle, a formula that is also seen in the Mosque of the Imam . The Tomb of Harun Velayat was built by the Grand Vizier Durmish Khan in the reign of Shah Ismail I and is dedicated to the ruler himself. An inscription on the entrance alludes to Ali, the venerated Imam: 'I am the city of Knowledge, and Ali is the gate.'

One of the great buildings of Isfahan earlier than the time of Shah 'Abbas is the Masjid-i Ali, a mosque with the typical four-*iwan* plan, which dates in part from the 12th century and is topped by a great dome of 1522. With its grandeur and scale, it exercised a strong influence on buildings that came after it.

Thus the technical and aesthetic vocabulary of Safavid architecture was already fully developed before Shah 'Abbas came to the throne. All that was needed for Isfahan to achieve its full splendour was the grandiose vision of a ruler obsessed by the glory of Iran.

opposite, top Detail of the decoration of the Darb i-Imam in Isfahan, of 1453. The building continues the style of the Timurids, while showing developments that were to lead to Safavid architecture.

above The fine *iwan* of the Darb i-Imam is beautifully decorated with Timurid polychromy. The corners skilfully formed of *muqarnas*, the pierced openings, and the intersecting ribs anticipate styles in use two and a half centuries later.

6

The Flowering of Safavid Iran: the Masterpieces of Isfahan

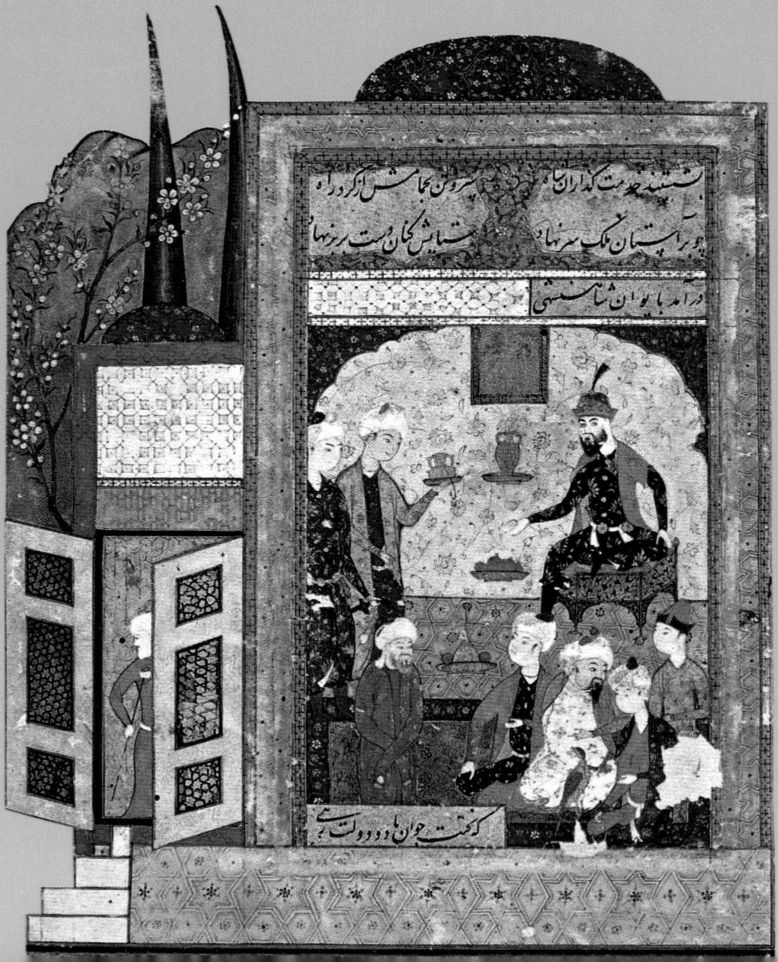

The Ottoman capture of Tabriz forced Shah Tahmasp to move his capital to Qazvin. When he died, after years of illness, he was followed briefly by Ismail II (1576–77), and then by Muhammad Shah (1578–87). Then, for more than forty years, the Safavid empire was in the hands of Shah 'Abbas I (1587–1629), and under him Iran reached its greatest heights, from a cultural and artistic as well as from a diplomatic and military point of view.

Shah 'Abbas's reign had begun badly, with the loss, in ten years, of Herat and of Mashhad in Khorasan. But the east was recaptured, and the Persians went so far as to take Balkh, on the border of Transoxiana. To the south, they occupied Luristan and strategic islands in the Persian Gulf. Shah 'Abbas then confronted the Ottomans; he retook Azerbaijan in 1602, and extended his domain over Georgia and Mesopotamia. Iran was once again as large as it had been under the pre-Islamic Sasanians.

Once he had strengthened the position of Shi'ism, Shah 'Abbas drew a clear separation between religious and temporal powers. The country was efficiently centralized under an authoritarian administration and bureaucracy. The post of *wazir* or vizier was instituted, as the highest government office after the shah. The vizier's title was Itimad ud-Daula or 'Pillar of the State' – a title adopted by the Mughal court in India, which was profoundly influenced by Iran.

Under the Safavids Iran experienced an age of greatness that lasted for two hundred years. The capital, initially at Tabriz, had been moved to Qazvin; Shah 'Abbas, however, decided to place his court even more centrally, and moved the capital to Isfahan in 1598. He then transformed this ancient Seljuq city, radically altering its urban structure with a new network of streets and squares on a scale unprecedented except in Timurid cities, and erecting a series of great religious monuments and sumptuous palaces set within vast gardens on the *chahar bagh* model. The emperor required a setting on the scale of his ambitions, where he could receive neighbouring princes and ambassadors from distant nations.

Shah 'Abbas determined on a dynamic foreign policy, and established relations between Iran and the West. Ambassadors were sent to Europe and were received with great pomp by the courts of Moscow, Prague, Valladolid and Lisbon and by the Pope in Rome. He did not neglect London, or wealthy merchants coming from France. As Akbar had done in India, he decreed tolerance, especially in religious matters, and received Christian missionaries. Carmelites, Augustinians and Capuchins were allowed to found monasteries; and the Armenians had their own quarter at Julfa, outside the city walls, where they had a cathedral built in pure Safavid style.

When it came to his army, Shah 'Abbas knew that he needed to adopt the most up-to-date techniques. For this he turned to an Englishman, Sir Robert Sherley, who, with his brother and about sixty of his fellow countrymen, turned the Persian troops into an effective fighting force on the European model. Cannon foundries were established, so the country need not depend on foreign supplies of artillery. Shah 'Abbas also set up a permanent army that was very large for the time, consisting of 15,000 cavalry, 12,000 infantry, 3,000 imperial guards and 500 cannon. The professional soldiers included corps of *qizilbash*, though he was anxious to keep their violent power under control. According to Y. Bomati and H. Nahavandi, the Shah could muster some 120,000 men, thanks to whom he was able to reconstitute the empire.

In the realm of the arts, the reign of Shah 'Abbas was unquestionably a great age. Architecture reached a rare level of perfection; and painting and the arts of the book (miniature painting, calligraphy, and binding), ceramics, the production of carpets and textiles, and fine jewels made Persia the admiration of Europe. The 'Persian style' was widespread throughout China and the Near East, and 'Persian taste' was looked to as both distinctive and novel.

What the Timurids had begun in Samarqand was carried on in Isfahan, and the Safavid city became a cultural centre that dazzled visitors from the West. The reports of European travellers, fascinated by this phantasmagoric capital, are full of hyperbolic praise: they describe the polychrome faience domes, the portals with their cascades of stalactites, the colourful bazaars where products from all over the world were displayed side by side, and the gardens cooled by streams and pools that were so unexpectedly to be found in this oasis set in a desert surrounded by arid mountains.

p. 130 above and p. 131 Details of the Lutfullah Mosque in Isfahan.

p. 130 below A miniature from a 16th-century manuscript of Sa'di's *Bustan*. (Reza Abbassi Museum, Tehran)

opposite, above Detail from a 16th-century *Shahnama* in Shiraz style.

opposite, below A late Persian miniature of Shah 'Abbas with a hawk. (Reza Abbassi Museum, Tehran)

above Byzantine troops defeated by warriors of the Prophet (shown top right), in a 16th-century miniature from Tabriz. (Reza Abbassi Museum, Tehran)

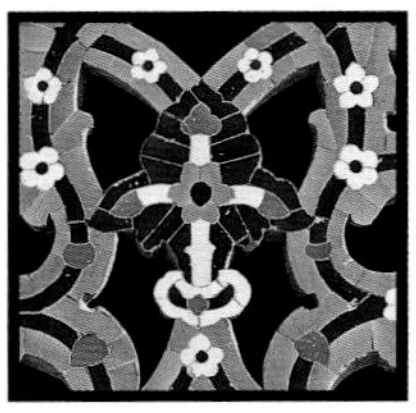

Shah 'Abbas Creates a New Isfahan

When Shah 'Abbas chose Isfahan for the centre of Safavid power, it was already a vast and populous city. In the 12th century the Spanish traveller and rabbi Benjamin of Tudela visited it and reported that it covered some 18 kilometres. It had been the capital of the Seljuqs long before it was that of Shah 'Abbas; destroyed by the Mongols, it was rebuilt in the traditional way: the old city presented a labyrinthine pattern of low houses, each with a small courtyard, a characteristic feature of Persian houses. It would retain this character on the edge of the new quarters and thoroughfares. The urban fabric was of a type seen throughout the Middle East. The houses were of sun-dried brick, reinforced in places with fired brick; there was a dense pattern of streets, combined with a system of canals and streams that provided water for the inhabitants. In addition, a meandering covered bazaar street ran like a spinal column through the city, its twists marked by major buildings that clustered along its path.

The vaulted bazaar led past caravanserais, markets, small mosques and *madrasas* from the Friday Mosque to the shah's new planned city. The ancient mosque, built by the 'Abbasids, altered by Malik Shah in the 11th century and then embellished by the Mongols and Timurids in the 14th and 15th centuries, stood next to a vast open space, the Maidan-i Kadim, which was the centre of the original town. This was 400 metres long, and oriented on the line the *qibla* of the Friday Mosque. Beyond it lay the gardens of the Old Palace, the seat of Seljuq power, of which nothing now remains.

When he decided to enlarge and remodel his capital in 1598 Shah 'Abbas was barely twenty-seven years old, but he been in power for a decade and large-scale projects held no terrors for him. He chose as the site a stretch of open land between the old city and the course of the Zayandeh Rud, the 'Life-Giving River', that flowed round to the south.

The work of remodelling Isfahan began with a great formal north-south avenue 2 kilometres long, the Chahar Bagh. The neighbourhood through which it ran, also called Chahar Bagh, linked the old city to the banks of the river, which provided water for the houses and for public fountains. The name came from the twenty or so square gardens that flanked the avenue: all measured about 160 x 160 metres, and each had the traditional Persian layout alluding to the 'Four Gardens' (*chahar bagh*) of Paradise – divided into four green squares by watercourses intersecting at right angles. Within this leafy setting, the sumptuous residences of court dignitaries formed a consistent and imposing ensemble close to the ruler's palace.

The Chahar Bagh itself was a very wide tree-lined avenue with, running down its centre, a straight channel enlivened by jets of water and little cascades. It led directly to the Zayandeh Rud, which it met at right angles. At this point the river was crossed by the Bridge of Thirty-Three Arches, also known as the Allahverdi Khan Bridge in honour of a Georgian general who had commanded a corps of *qizilbash* and who later became governor of Fars. On the other bank lay the Armenian suburb of New Julfa.

above Detail of a pierced tilework panel in the Mosque of Shaykh Lutfullah.

below Isfahan, seen from an outlying caravanserai. In the foreground are tombs, outside the walls. Beyond that, the domes and minarets of the great mosques appear above the trees of the oasis, which hide most of the city. In the distance rise the parched mountains. This view is from Pascal Coste, *Les Monuments modernes de la Perse* (1867).

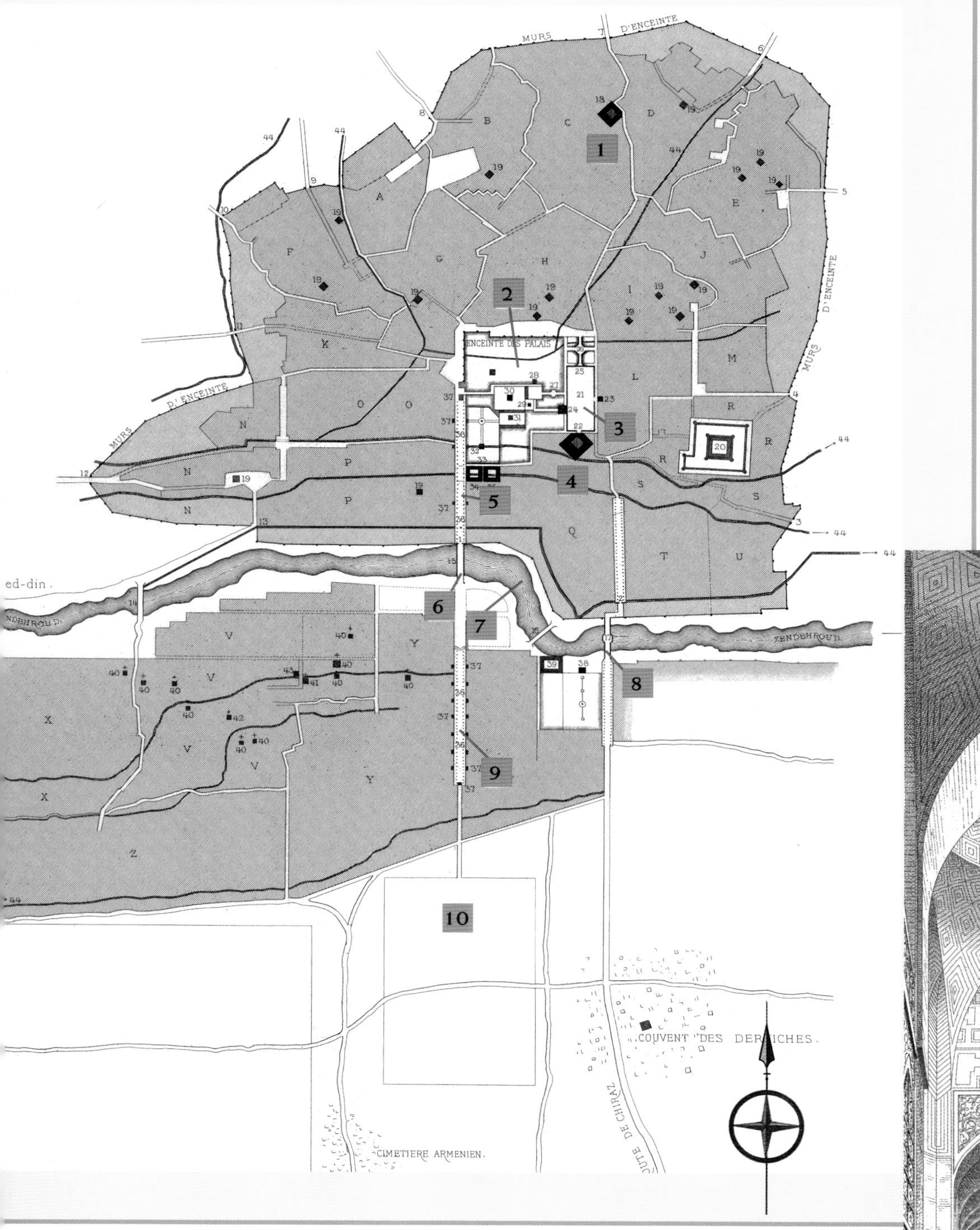

Key

Plan of Isfahan from Pascal Coste, *Les Monuments modernes de la Perse* (1867)

1 Friday Mosque
2 Palace area
3 Maidan-i Shah
4 Mosque of the Imam (Mosque of the Shah)
5 Chahar Bagh
6 Allahverdi Khan Bridge
7 Zayandeh Rud
8 Khwaju Bridge
9 Road to the palace of Hezar Jerib
10 Site of the palace of Hezar Jerib

right The Bazaar of the Tailors, a vaulted corridor-like space lit by openings in the tops of the domes. From Pascal Coste, *Les Monuments modernes de la Perse* (1867).

A New Maidan

Shah 'Abbas's other great urban set-piece was devised to link the old city with a group of new buildings that he planned to erect in an area which it seems already had a few buildings and a square. This second axis on the east side of the city was on a different alignment from the existing one of the old bazaar, and linking the two called for skill.

The first part of the new scheme was a vast square called Maidan-i Shah, the Royal Square (now sometimes known as the Maidan-i Imam). In the middle of its northern end, the handsome *pishtaq* of the Qaisariyeh linked it to the southern end of the bazaar. The new square was created by enlarging an older open space, the Nakh-i Jahan, which had started out as a camp site in the Timurid period. Shah 'Abbas had grander ideas, and his square measures 512 x 159 metres. It served as a gathering place for the great caravans that came to the city to stop over and to satisfy the desire for exotic products; it was also a place for polo matches, of which Shah 'Abbas was very fond; and it served for executions and for military parades.

The open space of the Maidan-i Shah is enclosed by uniform rectilinear ranges two storeys high that house some 180 shops and produce an effect of great majesty. A water channel flows in front of them. The area thus became a perfect place for animals to rest and for merchants from distant parts to sell their goods. Caravans comprising hundreds of camels gathered in this

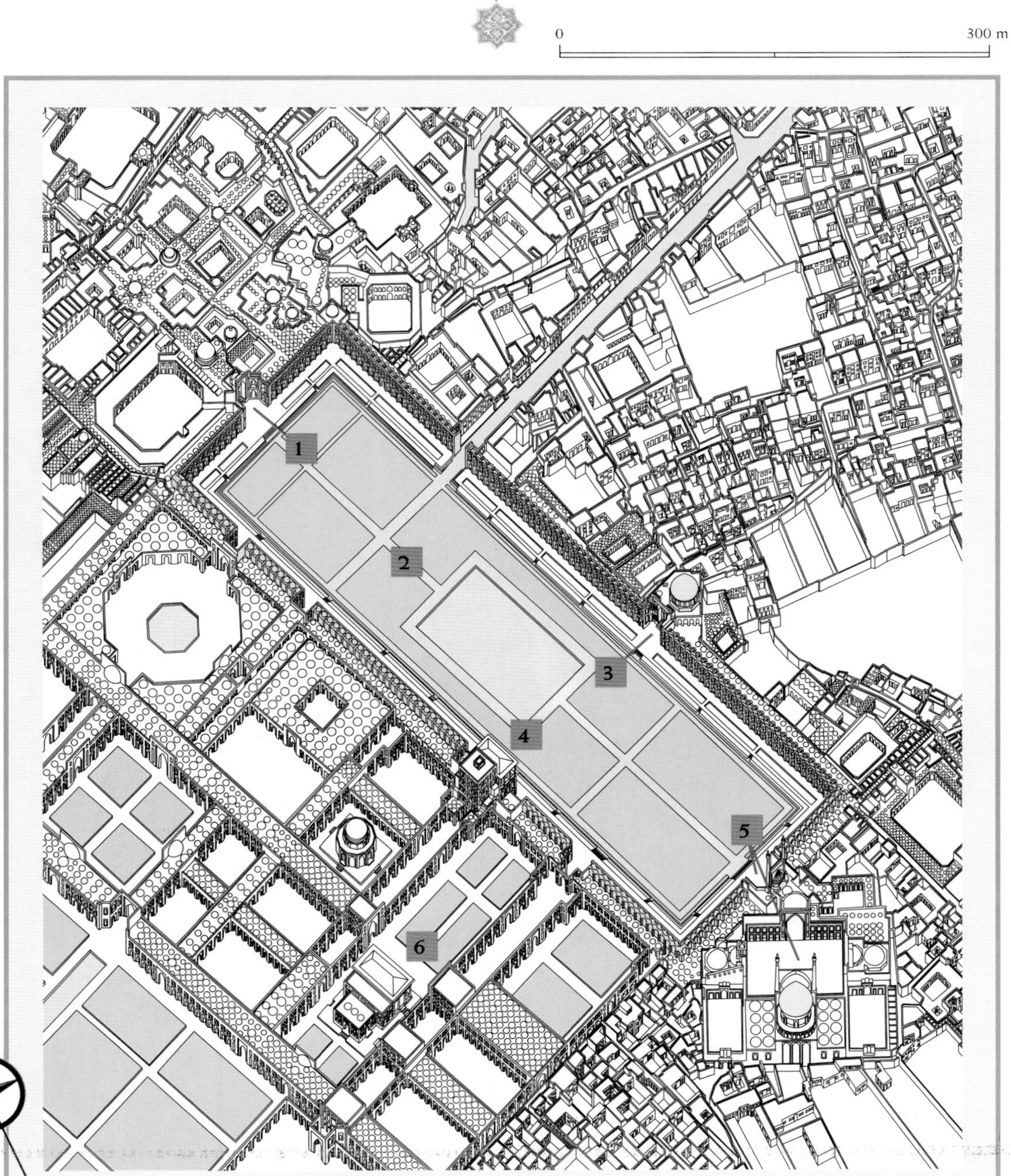

Key

Axonometric view of the centre of Shah 'Abbas's new Isfahan (Courtesy Klaus W. Herdeg)

1 Gate to the bazaar, or Qaisariyeh
2 Maidan-i Shah, or Royal Square
3 Mosque of Shaikh Lutfullah
4 Ali Qapu Palace
5 Mosque of the Imam (Mosque of the Shah)
6 Palace area

meeting place, in a cheerful and lively atmosphere. On days when polo was played, all had to make way for the riders.

Along the edge of the Maidan, going south from the Qaisariyeh, there are a number of majestic buildings that are landmarks of the new Isfahan. First of all, on the west side, is Ali Qapu ('the Gate of Ali'). A gate leading to the palace was first erected in the Timurid period, and Shah Tahmasp is said to have lived there in the mid-16th century. Shah 'Abbas transformed it into a belvedere, with a raised terrace under a roof supported by tall wooden pillars – a scheme known as *talar*; from this veranda 33 metres up, he could follow the progress of polo matches. Ali Qapu was also the official entrance to the gardens surrounding the Chihil Sutun, or Palace of Forty Columns. In that luxurious reception pavilion, the Shahinshah or King of Kings sat enthroned in an *iwan* decorated with *muqarnas* set with mirrors that glittered with a thousand reflections (ill. p. 145 below).

Exactly opposite Ali Qapu is the royal mosque and oratory dedicated to Sheykh Lutfullah (Maisi), a much respected Shi'ite theologian, whose daughter Shah 'Abbas had married. In this, one of the most important monuments of his reign, begun in 1602, several novel ideas were conceived and applied. The entrance portal and the dome offset beyond it to the right announce what was to characterize Shah 'Abbas's religious architecture in Isfahan: the rejection of symmetry and the absence of ostentatious monumentality. The *pishtaq* that opens on to the Maidan is covered with tile-mosaics and with *kashi* that are predominantly blue in colour; behind that superb creation, the position of the dome over the prayer hall makes a deliberate statement in favour of asymmetry, with a result that is disconcerting to Western eyes.

opposite, top A *kashi* in the Mosque of the Imam (Mosque of the Shah).

above Aerial view of the Maidan. In the foreground is the Mosque of the Imam (Mosque of the Shah), with its splendid dome and twin minarets over the entrance *pishtaq*; at top right is the dome of the Lutfullah Mosque; at top left, the *talar* of the Ali Qapu Palace.

That asymmetry is seen again in the main building of the complex, the great Mosque of the Imam – formerly known as the Mosque of the Shah – which is set at the southern end of the Maidan, on the axis of the Qaisariyeh. Here too the offset at first sight seems incomprehensible. The immense blue portal enclosing a great niche filled with *muqarnas* stands in the middle of the end of the square, and it is further emphasized by two elegant minarets that frame the *pishtaq* with its sumptuous faience decoration. But beyond this symmetrical entrance, the large dome with its bulbous profile, itself set between two more minarets, is again placed asymmetrically, and very markedly offset to the right. The explanation here, as in the smaller Lutfullah Mosque, is the need to orient the *qibla* towards Mecca, which lies to the south-west of Isfahan, on a different axis from that of the great square. It might have been possible to mask the skewing round of the two mosques by a *trompe l'oeil* adjustment; but instead, Shah 'Abbas's architects boldly decided to conceal nothing of the constraints that ritual placed on the construction of religious buildings.

Thus around the vast rectangle of the Maidan-i Shah Isfahan received a new urban centre where significant cultural, royal and economic aspects of the city came together. There are the two mosques, of which the first, the Lutfullah Mosque, served the ruler and those close to him, while the mass of Shi'ite worshipers gathered in the great Mosque built by the Shah and dedicated to the Mahdi or Twelfth Imam, whose return Persians expect at the end of time. There is the gate known as Ali Qapu, leading to the Chihil Sutun pavilion, where the Shahinshah appeared at his most majestic. And finally there was the new bazaar, with warehouses, caravanserais and baths that met the practical needs of urban life.

opposite Detail of a star on the drum of the Lutfullah Mosque, with a stylized kufic inscription giving the names of Allah, Muhammad and Ali.

below The Maidan, looking towards the Lutfullah Mosque on the left and, on the right, the Mosque of the Imam (Mosque of the Shah). There the entrance *pishtaq* faces north on the central axis of the square, whereas the main *iwan*, in front of the dome, faces north-east. Note the two storeys of shops that enclose the square. From Pascal Coste, *Les Monuments modernes de la Perse* (1867).

SPACE AND ORNAMENT IN THE LUTFULLAH MOSQUE AND THE MOSQUE OF THE IMAM

The oratory mosque of Shaikh Lutfullah was built over a number of years: the *pishtaq* facing the Maidan dates from 1602; the interior decoration was finished in 1616, and the *mihrab* in 1618. No minaret signals the presence of the mosque, and it has only a relatively low dome. Remarkably for Iran, it does not have a courtyard; but its unified internal space, with a dense atmosphere of meditative tranquillity, is a unique work of art.

The building overall is not large – it has a total depth of 40 metres, and its prayer hall measures 18 x 18 metres – but it conveys an extraordinary sense of spaciousness. You pass through the handsome portal, below blue faience *muqarnas*, make a 45-degree turn to the left, and discover a dark corridor faced with tiles and roofed with a series of small domes. At this end of this first section, the corridor bends to the right. A further turn, at right angles, leads to a door from which you suddenly see the interior in all its harmony. Thus to reach the sanctuary you have gne along a twisting path that has made you lose all sense of direction – a quarter-turn to the left, then a half-turn to the right, and then another half-turn to the right before you find yourself facing the *qibla* wall. The architect devised an ingenious spatial journey that leads the faithful into the sanctuary facing the *mihrab*, rather than bringing them in from the side, which enhances the importance of the *mihrab* and makes it the immediate centre of attention.

The square prayer hall is entirely faced with tile mosaic and roofed by an elegant depressed dome. The eight great arches that surround the hall are given a remarkable sense of vitality by turquoise-glazed spirally twisted mouldings that seem to spring up organically from the ground. In the corners, where one might expect *muqarnas*, there are smooth surfaces with triangular motifs. Above them at the base of the drum runs a band with an inscription in thuluth characters on a blue ground. The drum is pierced with sixteen grille windows that diffuse a soft, quiet light that encourages meditation. The dome itself is covered in a delicate pattern of lozenges. In the decoration, throughout, buff natural brick (seen also outside, on the dome, where arabesque floral trails run across it) is used to set off turquoise and ultramarine blue, alternating with white inscriptions. The *mihrab*, in a rectangular frame, has sharp, refined *muqarnas* covered with flowers on a deep blue ground.

Outside, between the windows in the drum there are inscriptions in large white kufic lettering framed in black on a turquoise background. Inscriptions in geometric characters are also skilfully combined into seemingly decorative star-shaped medallions that in fact bring together the names of Allah, Muhammad and Ali (ill. p. 138). The grilles of the sixteen windows in the drum are formed of twisting stems and flowers in a seemingly infinite variety of patterns (ill. pp. 131, 140–41).

opposite, above The Mosque of Shaikh Lutfullah is reflected in a (modern) pool in the Maidan. The offset alignment of the *pishtaq* and dome is clearly visible.

opposite, below The fine *pishtaq* of the Lutfullah Mosque. The *muqarnas* here are covered with very sophisticated tile mosaic that seems to multiply the delicate network of honeycomb-like spaces.

above On the dome of the Lutfullah Mosque, ornamental trails stand out against the plain brick background. The drum below is ringed by an ultramarine band filled with thuluth script; the large stylized inscription between the grille-windows here bears the invocation 'O Allah' in white tiles framed with black.

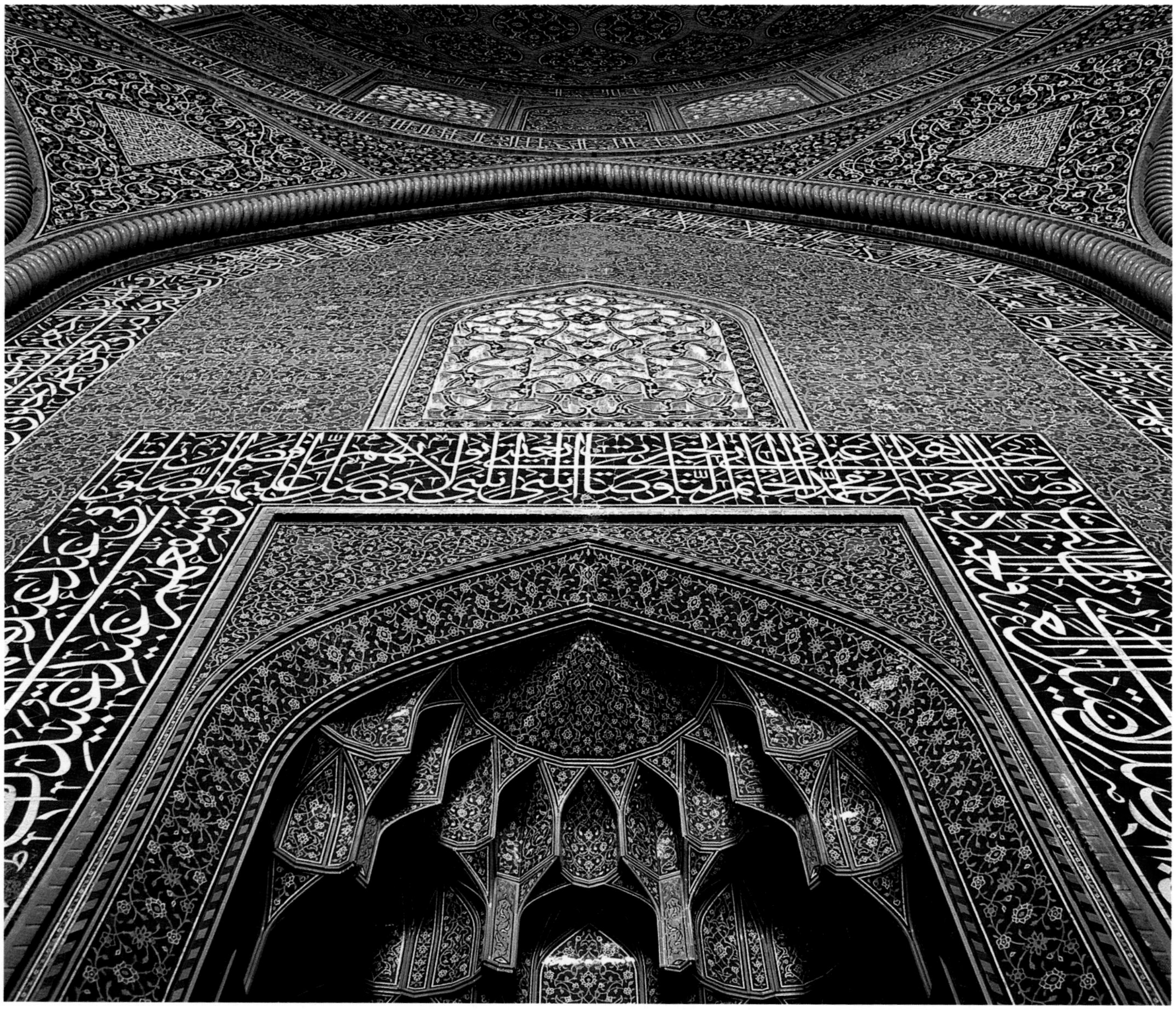

Looking up past the *mihrab* of the Lutfullah Mosque, the holy-of-holies, towards the drum and dome. Light filters softly in through the grille-windows. The complex *muqarnas* of the *mihrab* and its inner surround are covered with fine tile mosaic, and framed by verses from the Qur'an in large cursive script.

As has already been said, the Lutfullah Mosque was built as a private place of prayer for the ruler and his court; with its modest size, it could never have served the greater urban community. The same is not true of the great Mosque of the Imam, formerly the Mosque of the Shah, at the southern end of the Maidan (for a more detailed look at this building, see Part II, pp. 258–73). This fronts the square with a fantastic statement in the form of a monumental *pishtaq* 35 metres wide dominated by minarets 45 metres tall, built between 1612 and 1616. The *iwan* within is an enormous apsed niche like a shadowy grotto, covered with sumptuous blue *muqarnas* that suggest a frozen waterfall (ill. p. 258 below). The outer face of the *pishtaq* is covered with tile-mosaic panels of great refinement; but the decoration of the concave surfaces of these *muqarnas* is even more astonishing, as one looks at detail after detail – at the precision of the network of ribs with its endless subdivisions, and at the exquisite floral motifs with their poppies, buttercups and lotus flowers caught among vine scrolls.

Over the door leading into to the mosque is a tympanum made of a single slab of red Yazd marble. Its austere simplicity serves to heighten by contrast the rich profusion of vegetation framed by a twisted moulding around the doorway. This motif, which we have just seen in the Lutfullah Mosque and which appeared earlier in Timurid *madrasas*, springs like the stem of a vine from vases derived from a distant classical source which in Islam symbolize immortality.

As in the Lutfullah Mosque, the path from the entrance to the sanctuary in the Mosque of the Imam is full of surprises. The entrance portal faces the Maidan, but here too there is a difference of 45 degrees between the axes of the square and of the mosque. To conceal this fact, the architect made it impossible to go directly from the entrance into the courtyard (see the plan, p. 259). Instead, you first enter a vestibule; from here, through an arch of which the lower part is blocked, you can get a slimpse from the back of the northern *iwan* into the sacred space. But to go further, you must turn right (the more direct route) or left (along a corridor with kinks as in the Lutfullah Mosque). Either way, you enter the courtyard through a modest opening in one or other side of the northern *iwan*. The effect then is dazzling. Emerging from the narrow dark corridor, you suddenly see the whole of the marvellous space of the courtyard with its central pool and its four *iwans*, and the enormous swelling dome framed by two 50-metre-tall minarets. All the surfaces are faced with tiles in shades of blue and green: these cover the two levels of arcades around the courtyard, the smooth frames surrounding the great *iwans*, the shadowy surfaces within them, and the shining sphere of the dome, like a turquoise bubble against the azure sky. Rarely in the history of architecture has a designer shown such subtlety in contriving the initial impact of a building.

The interior of the prayer hall is entirely covered with tiles, as are the two hypostyle spaces at the sides, each covered by eight small domes. Their predominant shades of blue contrast with the golden yellow of a sunburst

The smooth-surfaced squinches in the prayer hall of the Lutfullah Mosque are framed by a twisted moulding whose turquoise spirals contrast vividly with the overall gold colour of the background of the room. The decoration is typical of the Safavid period: everywhere, inscriptions alternate with floral motifs.

in the apex of the large dome and harmonize with the high, smooth dado of yellow Yadz marble. The materials are luxurious, but the effect is never excessive; and the main *mibrab* and the *minbar* are admirably simple. The Mosque of the Imam presents a striking contrast to the Timurid buildings in Samarqand with their interiors covered in gold and lapis lazuli. Here the overall effect is one of restraint and modesty, despite the lavish and omnipresent floral ornament. Magnificence never overwhelms meaning in the decoration. Taken as a whole, the great cathedral-mosque of Isfahan devised by Shah 'Abbas is a work of dazzling splendour, in a context of outstanding grandeur and majesty.

In Part II we shall look more closely not only at its architecture but at its use of symbolism; for it demonstrates how Persian art became the vehicle of symbolic meanings that shed light on Shi'ite mysticism in the Safavid period. What matters here is to stress that the Mosque of the Imam is a paradigm of the 'Persian style'. It is entirely governed by the characteristic Persian formula of the court with four *iwans*. The prayer hall is surprisingly bright, lit both from the main *iwan* and from large arches in the sides of the drum. The dome, in Timurid fashion, has two shells separated by an unlit void about 10 metres high. The inner shell is 30 metres high and rests on a drum with eight grille-windows similar to those of the Lutfullah Mosque. The outer shell, with its pronounced swelling shape, measures 52 metres to the top of its gilt bronze finial with the image of the moon, which symbolizes the calendar of the Islamic world.

It is impossible not to remark on the close similarity in shape between the dome of the Mosque of the Imam in Isfahan, completed around 1628, and that of the famous Taj Mahal in Agra, which was begun in the very year 1628. Might the timing suggest the origin of the unknown architect of the Taj Mahal, or at least the school to which he belonged, since there can be no doubt of the strong Persian aesthetic reflected in the Indian design?

Palaces, Pools and Gardens

The palaces of Persian and Timurid kings were not places of monumental architecture, with the exception of great entrance gates, like the huge *pishtaq* that led into Timur's park at Shakhrisabz (p. 59). The palace buildings themselves were fairly sober, recalling a time when the Turkish-Mongol rulers had not yet completely settled down: they were temporary structures of wood, or even cloth canopies or tents. In Iran, however, that tradition met and fused with one that went back to a time long before the advent of Islam, when the ruler's residence was also the setting where he displayed his power, made his ritual appearances, established his majesty. Examples are the palaces of Persepolis and Ctesiphon. Hence Safavid palaces were often built in permanent materials. To these the builders added wooden galleries or *talar*, on the old Achaemenid model seen in the reliefs of Naqsh-i Rustam. The *iwan* might be made of light materials, but it took on a major role.

In Isfahan, the old palace of Ali Qapu facing the Maidan (which, as we saw, was built on an earlier structure) contains halls for receptions, music and dance, and rooms where the royal wives gathered. These include delicate rooms with ceilings made of carved and painted stucco composed of many small tiny openwork domes fitted together like the component niches in *muqarnas*.

Gradually Ali Qapu became less a palace than a belvedere or loggia from which the ruler and his court watched polo matches. It was given a *talar* with a roof supported on tall columns each made of a single tree-trunk, like those of the Chihil Sutun, or Palace of Forty Columns.

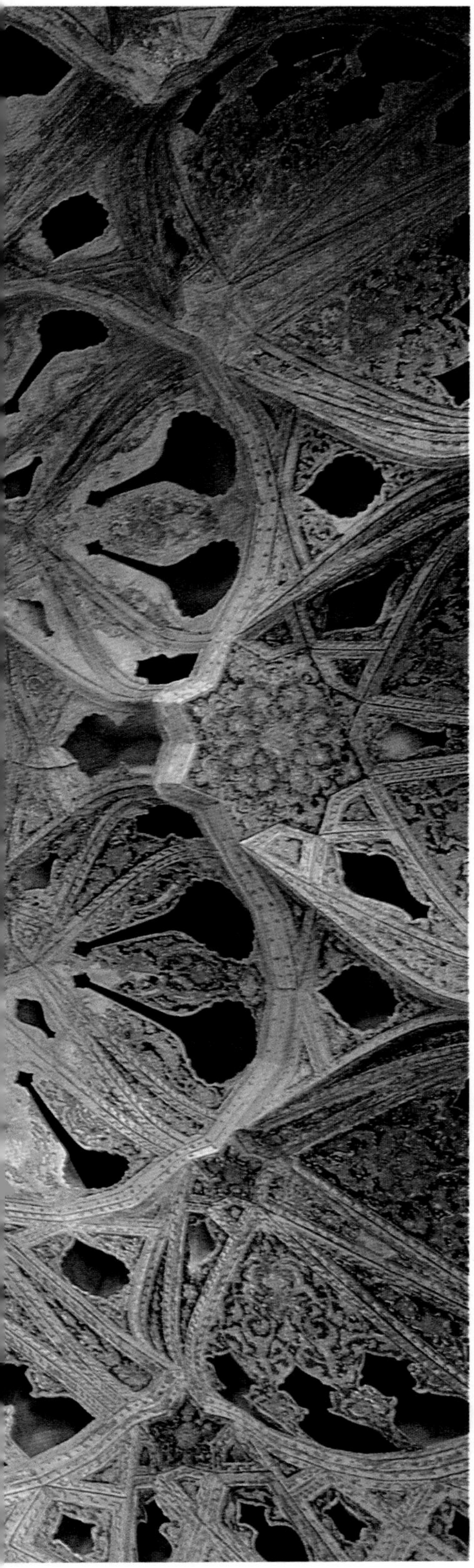

above and below The Chihil Sutun (Palace of Forty Columns). The *talar* was used for receptions and courtly ritual. Reflected in the long pool, its twenty wooden shafts are doubled in number. In the gold and mirrored *iwan* (*below*), Shah 'Abbas II held court and received important guests with characteristic Safavid pomp.

right, top The palace of Ali Qapu (the Gate of Ali) stands in the middle of the long west side of the Maidan. From its terrace in *talar* form, Shah 'Abbas I keenly followed polo matches played in the square below (the pool there is a modern addition).

above The intricate *muqarnas* ceiling of a music room in Ali Qapu. The fragile stucco is supported by a wooden framework and covered with ornament in gold and colour.

The Chihil Sutun stands in a lovely wooded park, on the edge of a pool 70 metres long. It was built in 1647 on the order of Shah 'Abbas II (1642–67), perhaps on the site of an older pavilion built by Shah 'Abbas I. It is a single-storeyed building with twenty columns, but they are reflected in the pool and produce the magical effect of a structure with forty columns.

In the middle of the forest of three rows of six wooden shafts that support the roof of the terrace is a handsome rectangular basin. Behind this, the building is of masonry; two wings project on either side, and between them, beyond the pool, two columns flank the entrance to a deep axial *iwan*. This is the focal point of the palace, designed for the ruler's formal audiences. Everything here is devised to create a setting with as much pomp and lustre as possible for official receptions, and the architecture becomes a jewel box filled with light: the walls and the apse over of the *iwan* form an alcove-like space entirely clad in mirrors; the ceiling is covered with stalactites, of which each cell is formed from a multitude of tiny mirrors held in place by a network of gilded rods. The atmosphere is one of dreamlike fantasy. As the mirrors sparkle in the shadowy interior and reflect the light outside, one can imagine the atmosphere at a state occasion where the King of Kings, in ceremonial robes, is surrounded by high dignitaries arranged according to a strict etiquette, among torches and courtly music. Formal speeches are made, and then virtuoso performers and female dancers come to entertain the onlookers, while servants bring round fine wines from Shiraz, exotic fruit and exquisite dishes.

This is not a historian's imaginary reconstruction: such a scene is depicted in a great wallpainting in the

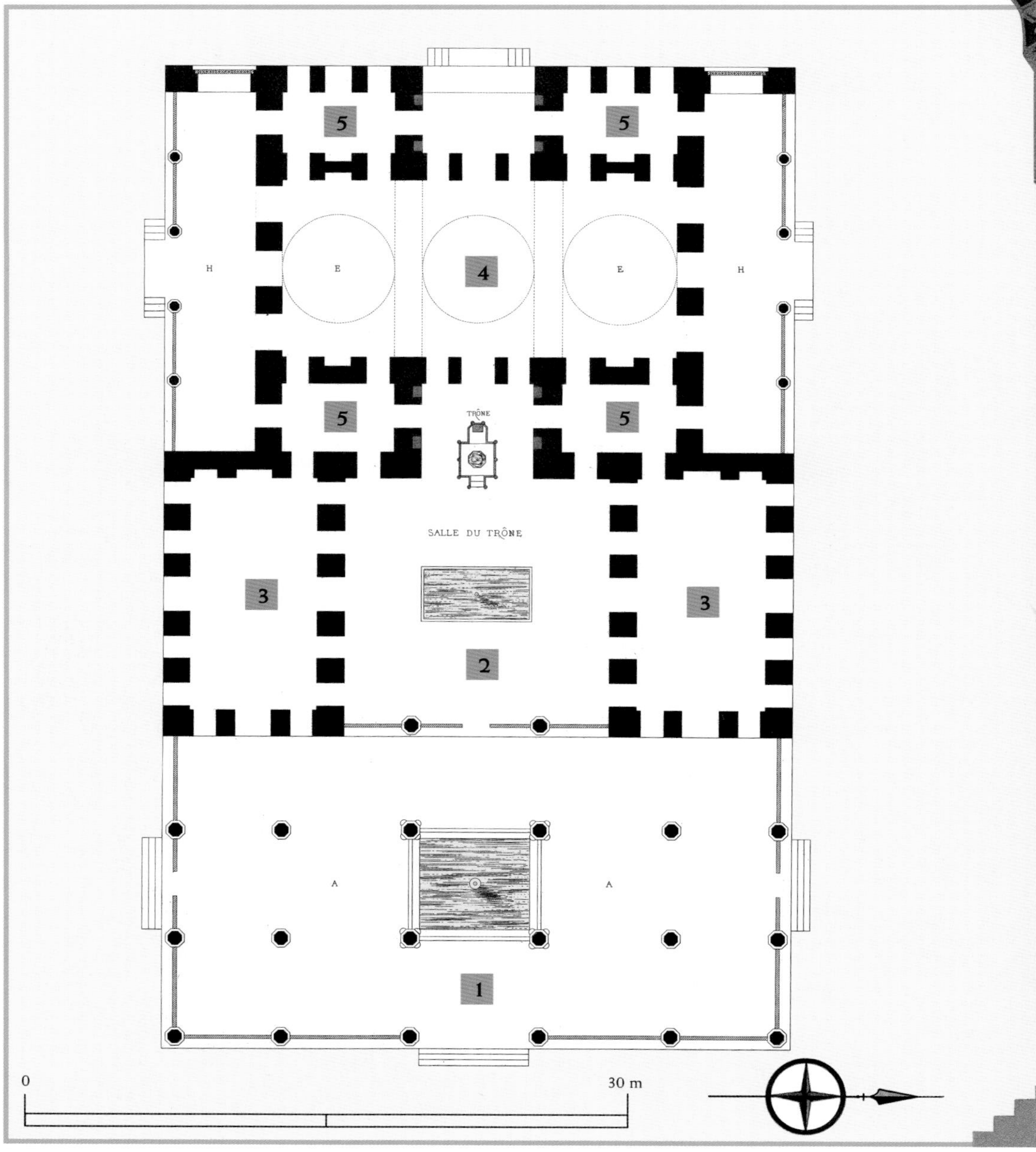

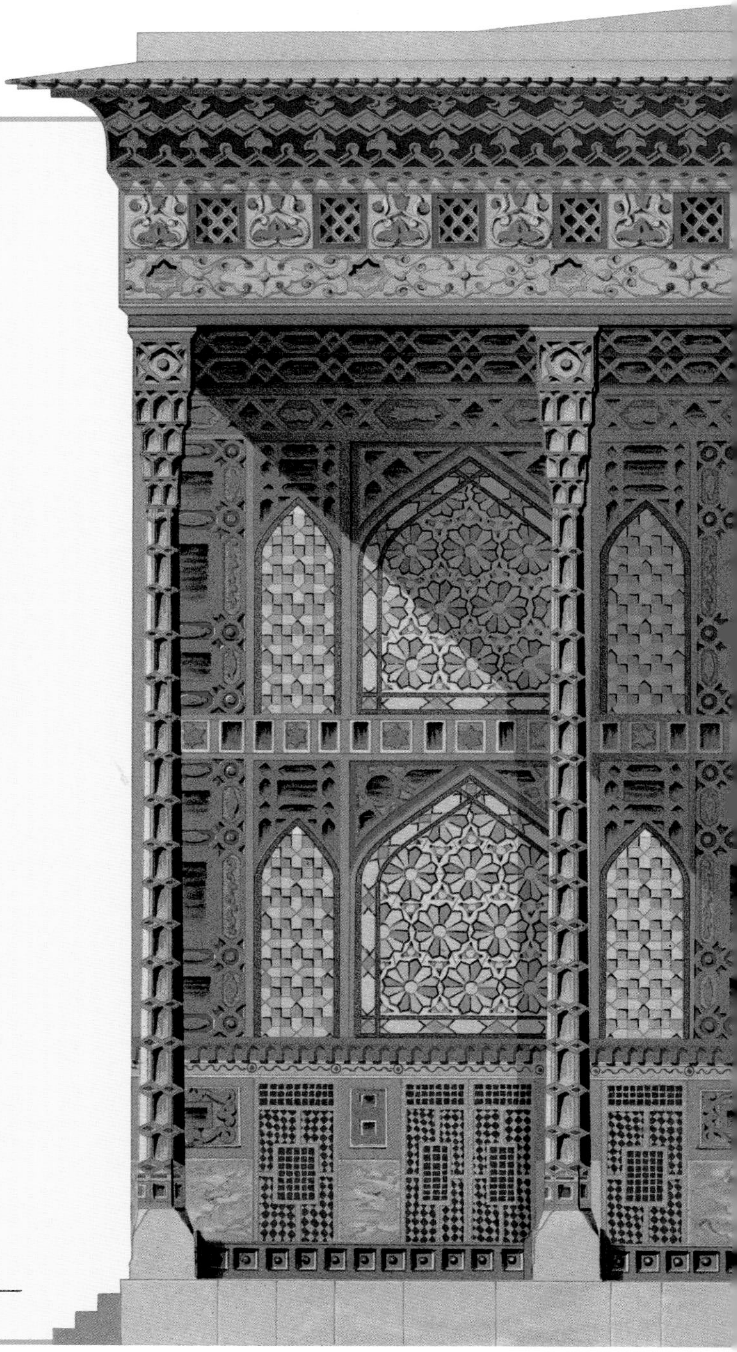

Key

Plan of the Chihil Sutun Palace

1 *Talar* with central pool
2 Throne room in the form of an *iwan*
3 Side rooms of the palace
4 Great domed reception hall
5 Service rooms

reception hall of Shah ʻAbbas II. This oblong room, 22 metres wide and 10 metres deep, was once crowded with a throng of important guests brilliantly clad in gold brocade, taffeta and damask, who moved about among the silver-gilt serving vessels, golden ewers, and Chinese porcelain plates.

Elsewhere in the palace, a small room with coloured glass windows is faced with dazzling *kashi* that depict a scene in a flower-filled garden: a young prince is paying court to a princess languidly stretched out on a carpet of grass dotted with carnations, while servants bring them yellow pears and fine wine in splendid long-necked Chinese porcelain bottles. The theme is one favoured in contemporary miniatures, enlarged to a scale of 2 x 1 metres and coloured in the vivid tones of glazed ceramic.

The Chihil Sutun palace was the setting for sumptuous receptions in 17th-century Isfahan, but it was also the setting for much more important events: the ceremonies when the ruler offered himself to the gaze of his courtiers, who in a ritual of vassalage made an act of formal sub- mission to him – as the deified Sasanian kings had done in the great *iwan* at Ctesiphon, more than a millennium earlier.

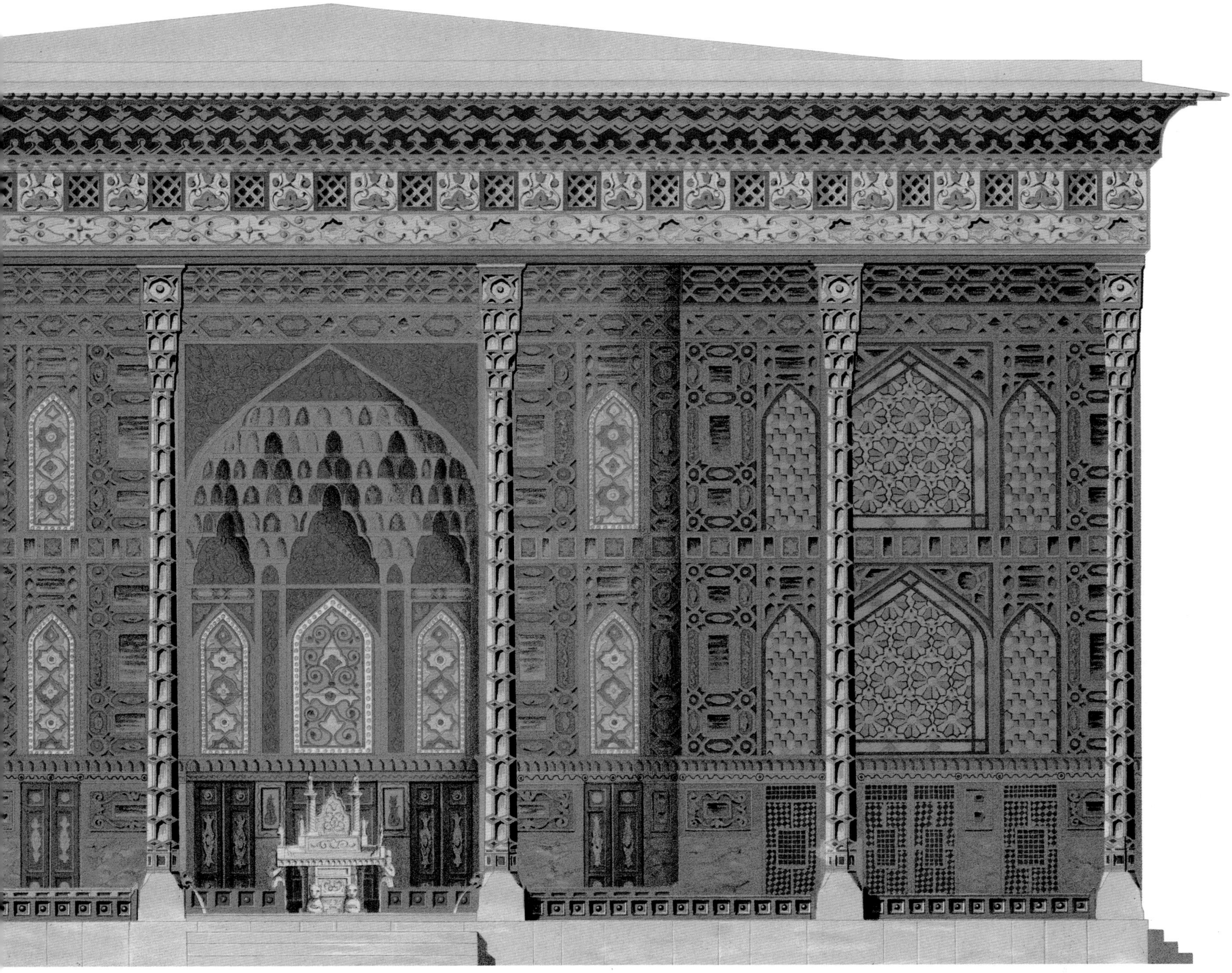

The Chihil Sutun

opposite, above Dancers at a reception in the time of Shah 'Abbas II, 1647.

above Transverse section with the decoration reconstructed, from Pascal Coste, *Les Monuments modernes de la Perse* (1867). We are looking at the *talar* and, through it, at the *iwan*, where Coste shows a throne.

below A tile picture in the palace, depicting a couple in a garden, with servants bringing wine and exotic foods.

The Delicate Pavilion of the 'Eight Paradises'

Not far from the Chahar Bagh is a park covering an area of 400 x 320 metres, which contains one of the best examples of a Safavid royal pavilion – the pavilion of Hasht Bihisht, or 'Eight Paradises'. This two-storeyed palace, built about 1670 under Shah Suleiman, has a rectangular plan with chamfered corners; it stands in the middle of a handsome garden, from which it is separated by a narrow channel that runs right round it and flows out on the main axes to feed four square pools with jets of water. As with all pavilions of this type, the architecture is lightweight, and consists chiefly of wooden structures and thin plastered walls on a brick core. The polychromy of the walls everywhere includes gold leaf, so as to create a glorious setting for the ruler, as in the Chihil Sutun.

The Hasht Bihisht has four verandas, of which the main one faces east; there and in the two at the sides pairs of wooden columns support flat roofs into which countless mirrors are fitted. The verandas lead to a central hall which is open in all four directions. In this octagonal space four great arches admit light and support a dome entirely covered with wooden *muqarnas* and crowned by a

above The Hasht Bihisht (Eight Paradises) pavilion, built about 1670 in a wooded garden for Shah Suleiman.

below The pavilion as Pascal Coste recorded it in *Les Monuments modernes de la Perse* (1867). The light structure stands on a podium. A centrally placed waterfall feeds a narrow channel from which spring jets of water. Beyond the *talar*-like main veranda lies the domed central hall.

opposite Longitudinal section and plan by Pascal Coste.

Key

1 Pools connected by a channel
2 Large *iwan* with pool and fountain
3 Smaller lateran *iwans*
4 Central domed room and octagonal pool
5 Octagonal chambers
6 Stairs

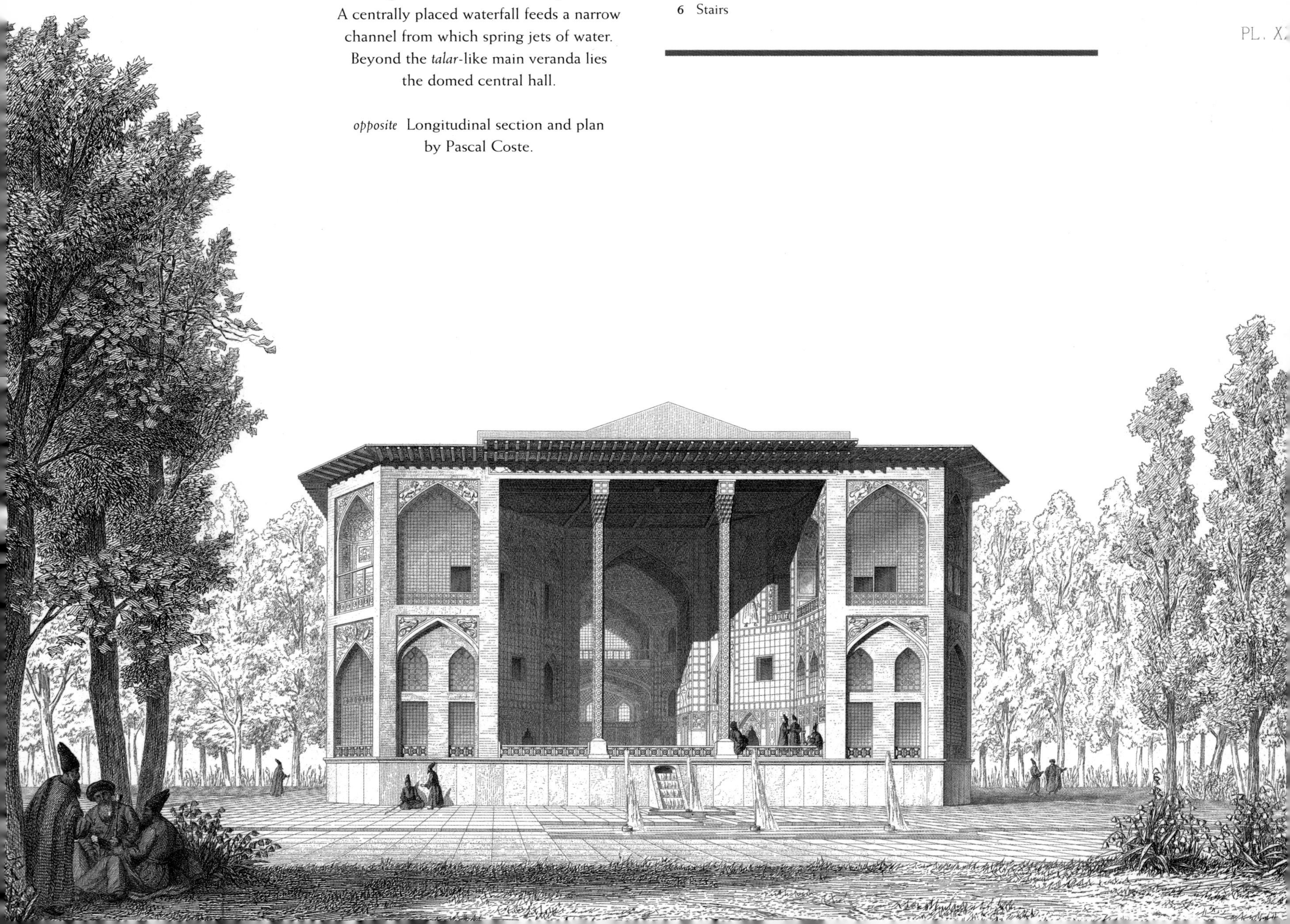

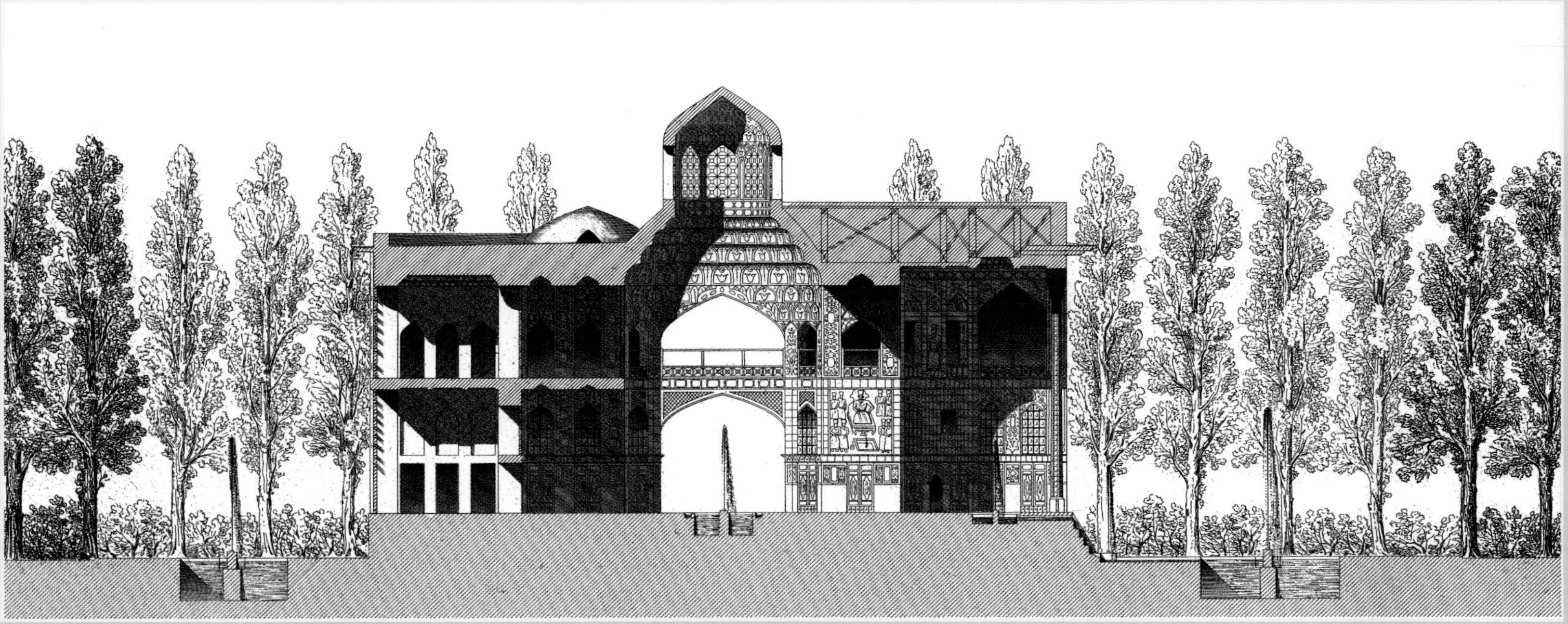

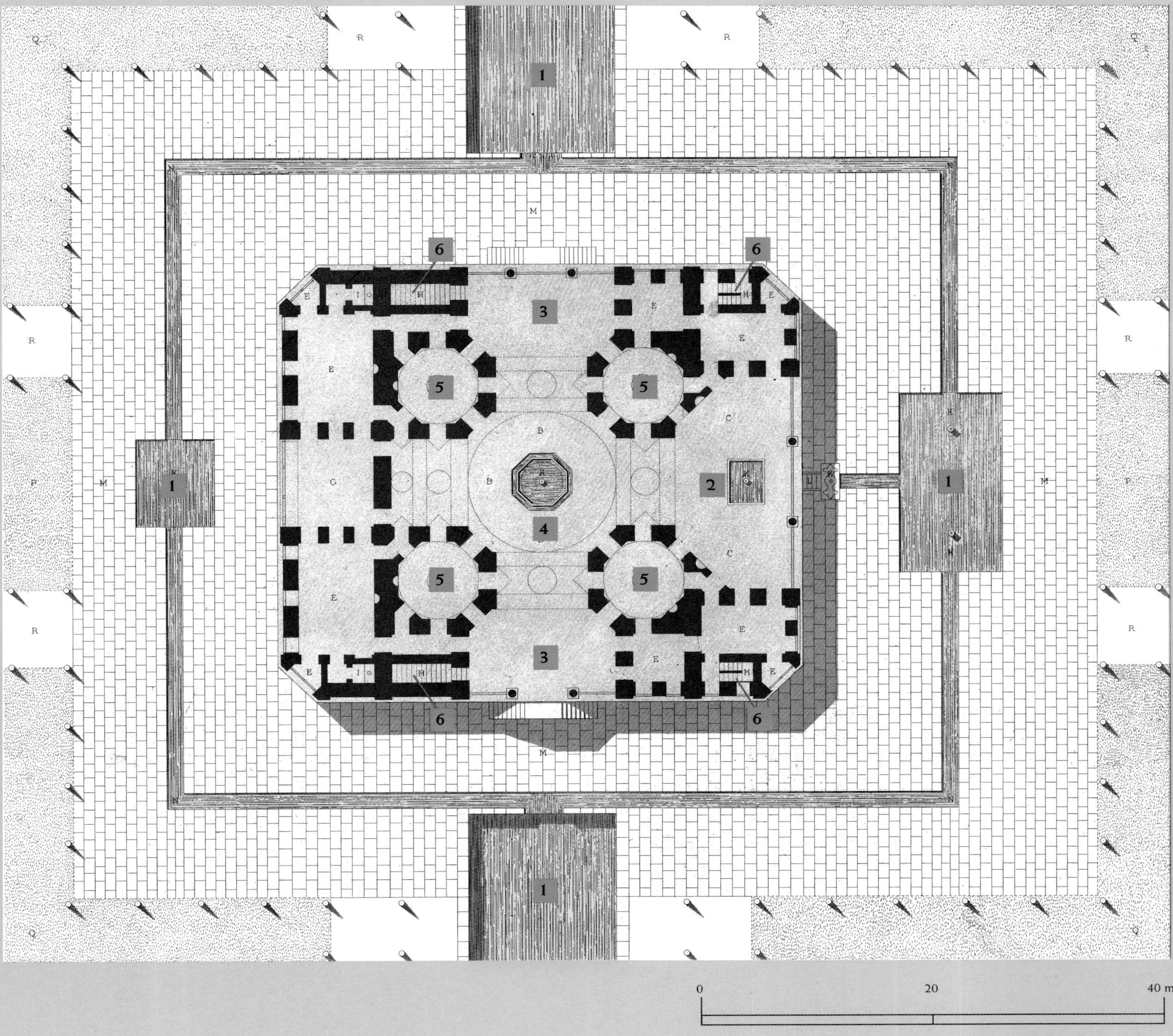
1
2
3
4
5
6
0
20
40 m

opposite, below, and right
The extraordinarily rich decoration of the Hasht Bihisht pavilion was recorded by Pascal Coste in *Les Monuments modernes de la Perse* (1867): his illustrations include the central room (*below*) and a detailed drawing of its elements, from the double entrance arch up to the lantern (*right*). That decoration has now been superbly restored by an Italian team. A detail (*opposite*) shows *muqarnas* covered with gold leaf and paint surrounding a little dome lined with tiny convex mirrors, like those used in the Mughal architecture of India.

lantern. The octagonal lantern is echoed by an octagonal basin with a fountain in the floor, whose water once spread coolness and a refreshing sound. On this level there are four small circular rooms in the diagonals, and stairs in the corners of the building lead to the upper level where there are further small apartments. Those rooms are covered with shallow *muqarnas*, and they have niches in the walls which would have held ceramic vessels. The decoration, on a gold ground, includes extremely fine floral motifs that recall the most spectacular products of the miniature painter's art.

From the mid-17th century onward, Safavid architecture took on a 'rococo' character, seen here in the plan of the pavilion, with its chamfered corners, circular rooms, and *talars* with elegant wooden columns, as well as in the decoration, where mirrors are combined with gilded surfaces to heighten the ruler's ceremonial lustre.

The Bridges

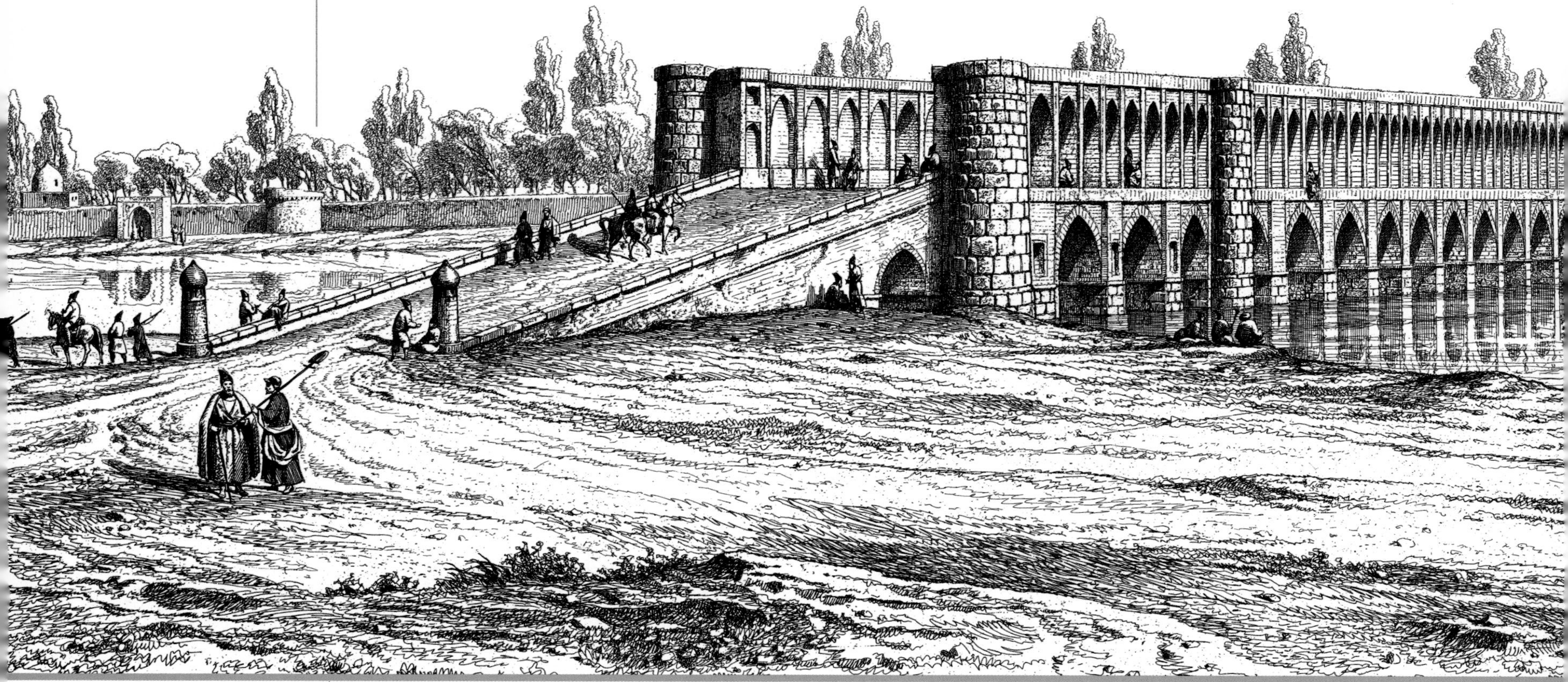

Isfahan grew up next to the Zayandeh Rud, which feeds the oasis where people had first settled in prehistoric times. To carry the line of the Chahar Bagh across the river (ill. p. 135), Shah 'Abbas built the Bridge of Thirty-Three Arches or Allahverdi Khan Bridge. Almost 300 metres long, this rests on a continuous stone platform to counter the risk of its supports being undermined by the current, which can be violent during the spring thaw. The parts of the piers in contact with the water are built of stone; everything above is of fired brick. The thirty-three arches are, like all others of their time, of the four-centered Persian form. The bridge is 13.5 metres wide, and consists of a central roadway for carts and caravans, flanked by covered passages whose slender arcades provide welcome shade for pedestrians when the sun was at its most intense.

Some 1,500 metres downstream from the Allahverdi Khan Bridge, another great work was created around 1650, in the reign of Shah 'Abbas II: the Khwaju Bridge. This stands on the line of the Maidan, and performs a dual function: it regulates the course of the river, by means of

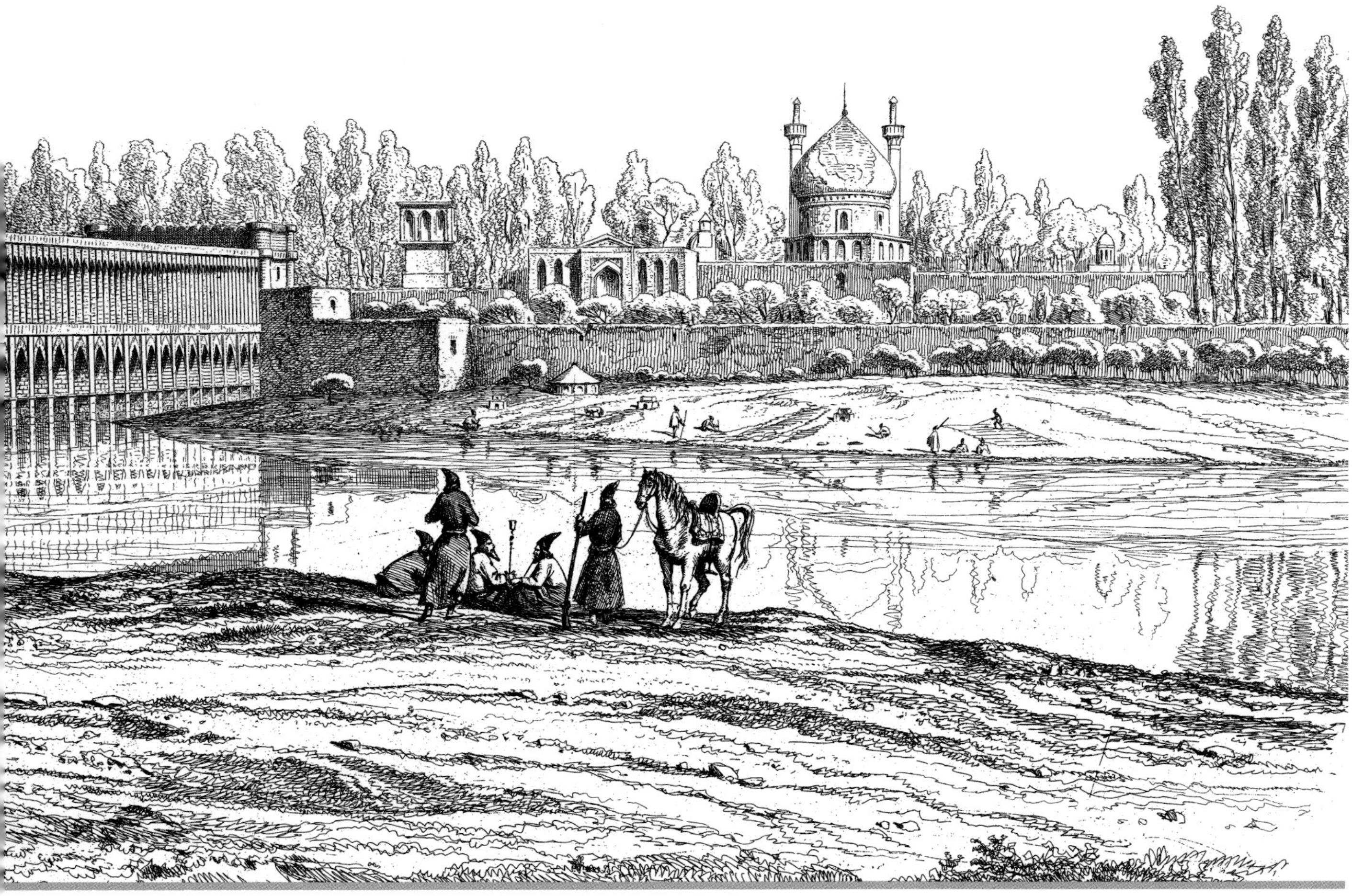

opposite, above Aerial view of the Khwaju Bridge on the Zayandeh Rud, built by Shah 'Abbas II to supply Isfahan with water.

above The Khwaju Bridge, from Pascal Coste, *Les Monuments modernes de la Perse* (1867). The central feature, set on a wider footing, helped the bridge to resist the pressure of the water.

opposite, centre Aerial view of the Allahverdi Khan Bridge or Bridge of Thirty-Three Arches, built by Shah 'Abbas I to carry the line of the new Chahar Bagh across the river to the palace known as Hezar Jerib (cf. the plan p. 135).

left The Allahverdi Khan Bridge, from Pascal Coste, *Les Monuments modernes de la Perse* (1867). Here we are looking towards the centre of the city, to the Madrasa Mader-i Shah with its swelling dome and twin minarets.

floodgates that can block its eighteen arcades to create a dam, and it provides a river crossing with flanking covered passageways for pedestrians, as on the Allahverdi Khan Bridge. To help the bridge resist the pressure of the water when the floodgates are closed, the engineer provided wider sections at the two ends of the roadway, and a massive pair of semi-octagonal structures in the centre on specially substantial foundations. The base on which the bridge stands has locks at this point. A vaulted passage that runs along the base below the roadway gives access to the floodgates. Technology and hydraulic engineering here came together to produce a work with the crucial purpose of providing water for a constantly growing population and for an ever-increasing number of pools and fountains in the city.

The Armenian Cathedral in Julfa

above Aerial view of the cathedral in the Armenian quarter of Julfa.

below Interior looking east. The cathedral was built c. 1655 in Safavid style.

right The decoration of the dome combines Persian motifs in gold leaf and polychromy with painted scenes from the Bible and seraph heads.

The suburb of New Julfa grew up on the south bank of the Zayandeh Rud to house Armenian refugees taken in by Shah 'Abbas. An active community of merchants and craftsmen developed, and the ruler's policy of toleration was put to the test: the Armenians were allowed to build a cathedral. Surprisingly, in architectural style it differs little from contemporary mosques. Built around 1655, it has an unadorned brick dome; inside, it is richly decorated in Safavid fashion – but its decoration also includes paintings with Christian subjects which stand out in startling fashion. This is especially striking on the interior of the dome: he we find interlacing patterns and floral motifs that would be perfectly at home in a mosque, but dotted about among them are angels, seraphs, and scenes from the New Testament. Around 1710, Persian ceramics and wall-paintings sometimes used the forms of Western art.

We have been looking at Isfahan as it was at the height of its fame; since then, invasions and the passage of time had greatly damaged its splendid monuments. In the 1920s, however, thanks to the determination of the French scholar André Godard, work began on a series of exemplary salvage operations and restorations. Specialized areas of Persian craftsmanship were revived, and Godard's team, later assisted by Italian restorers under the aegis of UNESCO, succeeded in recovering the city's magnificent appearance in the time of Shah 'Abbas.

At the dawn of the third millennium, one can only hope that the pressures of modern development will weigh lightly on the city of Isfahan, that great treasure which has so miraculously survived into our own time.

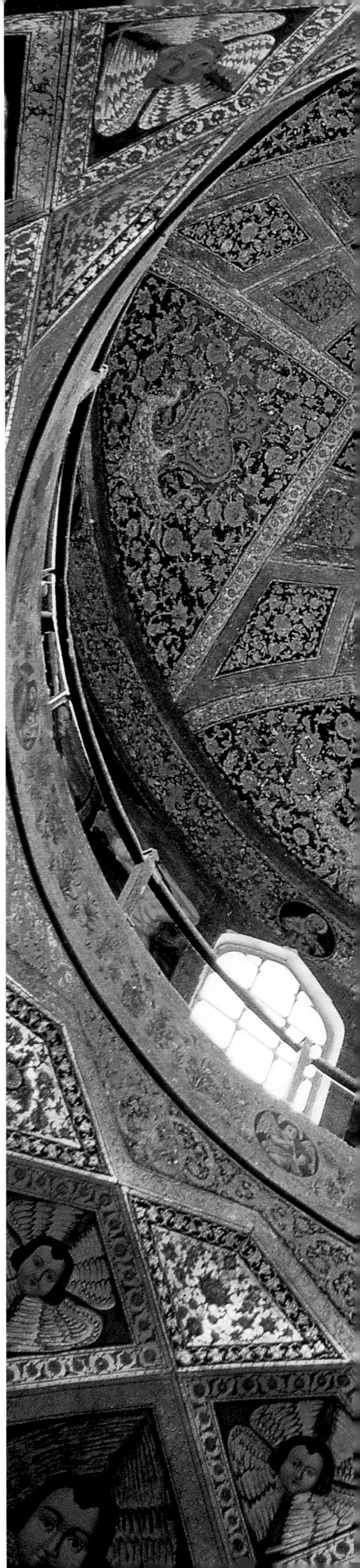

7

Jahangir and Shah Jahan: the Great Age of the Mughals

When the Safavids were at their height in Iran under Shah 'Abbas I, in India the Mughal throne was occupied by the Emperor Jahangir. He had neither the stature of his father Akbar nor the love of magnificence that would characterize his son, Shah Jahan, and his reign forms a sort of transitional period. Persian influence became stronger, and it is safe to ascribe to the presence of the 'Persian clan' the extraordinary artistic flowering that took place under Shah Jahan.

Akbar had moved the court to Lahore for strategic reasons after the failure of Fatehpur Sikri in 1585, and that city (now in Pakistan) served as a third Mughal capital after Agra and Delhi. Inside the fort, Jahangir built a palace quarter of which the Diwan-i Amm, or Hall of Public Audience, survives. This an elegant hypostyle structure is known by the Persian name of Chihil Sutun ('Forty Columns', as in Isfahan): its façade displays paired columns, while in the interior three rows of ten octagonal piers support arcades, forming an open reception area where the ruler sat enthroned. The load-bearing elements are more slender than in Akbar's time, and the architecture is consequently more elegant. To cope with problems of statics, use is made of techniques that involve arches set at right angles to each other, and the structure is further stiffened by iron rods at capital level. The design is extremely severe, and the entire building is of red sandstone without any decoration. The Mughals were later to erect a series of splendid buildings in Lahore – the Tomb of Jahangir, the sumptuous palaces of Shah Jahan, and finally the immense Badshahi Mosque commissioned by Aurangzeb.

Three years before he died in 1605 at the height of his power, Akbar had selected his burial place, and work had begun on his mausoleum, of which he had developed the design with his architects. His tomb was to be at Sikandra, to the west of Agra, beside the road to Fatehpur Sikri. The building displays the same originality as the monuments of the abandoned capital, with the same fusion of indigenous and Timurid techniques. Akbar's intentions were respected to the end, although it was Jahangir who completed the tomb in 1614.

Only a year after Akbar's death, Jahangir continued his father's policy and made use of the Hindu architectural vocabulary. Along with openwork stone panels or *jalis* he favoured sinuous brackets supporting overhanging eaves, which recall the shape of the struts that support projecting stone elements in the medieval temples of Khajuraho or Ranakpur. This feature too had been used by Akbar. We shall look at it more closely in Part II (pp. 254–57), as an expression of the strong personality of the tomb's designer and intended occupant.

Jahangir (1605–27), whose name means 'Conqueror of the World', was thirty-six years old when he succeeded his father in Lahore. His chosen ceremonial name showed him to be a proud descendant of Timur. Mughal power was now secure. The reign of Jahangir coincided, however, with the rise of a new religious movement, Sikhism, which had been founded at the end of the 15th century by Guru Nanak in the Punjab. This monotheistic system, created from the fusion of Islamic Sufism and Vaishnavite Hinduism, resembled the syncretic form of religion to which Akbar had aspired; but tension between the followers of Sikhism and the Mughals led in time to repeated bitter clashes.

Some writers saw Jahangir as a 'wise, benevolent and generous man', whereas others accused him of weakness, and even called him a drunk. The fact is that he held the reigns of power until 1622, and then gradually began to lose control – because of poor health, or because of excessive indulgence in alcohol and opium? His favourite wife, Nur Mahal ('Light of the Palace'), who was of Persian origin, exercised more and more power: eventually with her father, Itimad ud-Daula ('Pillar of the State'), and her brother, Asaf Khan, she took over the running of the empire and began to style herself Nur Jahan, 'Light of the World'. The family governed secretly, while imposing the Persian language at court. At the same time, in architecture, Akbar's syncretic forms were replaced by a return to Timurid forms and Persian traditions.

p. 156 above Decoration in the Tomb of Itimad ud-Daula, Agra.

p. 156 below Decoration of the Tomb of Shah Jahan, Agra.

p. 157 Persian tile mosaics in the Tomb of Afzal Khan, Lahore.

above Miniature of a shaikh in meditation, 1615. (Musée Guimet, Paris)

opposite The birth of Rustam, from a *Shahnama* commissioned by Jahangir, 1610.

بکافید بی رنج پهلوی ماه
بتابید مر بچه را سر ز راه
چنان بی گزندش برون آورید
که کس در جهان آن شگفتی ندید
یکی بچه بد چون گوی شیرفش
به بالا بلند و به دیدار کش
شگفت اندرو مانده بد مرد و زن
که نشنید کس بچهٔ پیل تن

The Lahore Palace and Hiran Minar Hunting Pavilion

opposite A detail of the wall of the fort at Lahore. The red sandstone *jali* has patterns chiefly based on hexagons and octagons. Below it is a tile-mosaic frieze depicting a triumphal procession; in the spandrels above are winged victories holding long-handled fans or *flabella*.

below The tile-mosaic decoration on the Lahore fort includes figures of foot-soldiers and cavalry on parade.

left, above The hunting park near Lahore created by Jahangir in 1607, seen from the top of the tower known as the Haran Minar. In the middle of the artificial lake stands an octagonal pavilion crowned by a *chhatri*: this was used for court festivities, and reached by guests across the gated bridge.

left, centre Jahangir's private apartments in the fort at Lahore are reflected in a square pool. There a platform in the centre, enclosed by a white marble parapet and reached by two walkways, symbolizes the cosmic island.

Jahangir built few monumental works. He began by having the wall of the fort of Lahore embellished with a series of ornamental motifs in tile mosaic that recall the decorations on the walls of the Rajput fort of Gwalior. Some of the panels show elephant-fights, others depict military parades with horsemen, while others, in the spandrels of the arches, have winged victories echoing an antique motif. Large openings in the walls, filled with *jalis* in red sandstone, prove that there was no longer any fear of riots or insurrections. The troubled times of the early decades had now given way to real stability.

In the royal quarter, Jahangir built a private palace for himself that rises beyond a square pool with a central island made of marble. The building is strictly functional, with a heavy, unadorned appearance. While no per-manent bridges lead to the island in the pool as at Fatehpur Sikri (ill. p. 108), its openwork marble parapet shows that it was used for court rituals.

In 1607 Jahangir established a hunting reserve some 40 kilometres from Lahore, which comprised gardens and an artificial lake that served as a reservoir. Here he captured an antelope which was quickly tamed and placed at the head of the royal herd; he became very attached to the animal, and when it died he erected a tower to its memory, called the Hiran Minar, from which the reserve then took its name. From the top of this tower, the view extends out over the rectangular lake: here a gated causeway leads to a central island, on which rises an octagonal pavilion with an open gallery at first-floor level, surmounted by a *chhatri*. Such pavilions surrounded by water are a recurrent motif in Indo-Persian design.

The tomb of Jahangir at Lahore, built by the emperor's widow after 1628, during the reign of Shah Jahan

left The entrance to the tomb complex. The *iwan*, vaulted with *muqarnas*, is of red sandstone alone; everywhere else, the sandstone is set off against rich, abstract decoration in white marble.

opposite, far right The cenotaph of Jahangir seems to glow in the half-light; it is superbly decorated with semi-precious stones inlaid in white marble in floral patterns similar to those at the contemporary Taj Mahal in Agra.

opposite, below The tomb in its garden. At the corners are four-storey minarets. The unusual design inspired some of the features of the Taj Mahal (ill. pp. 274–75).

Jahangir's Tomb at Lahore: A New Type of Mausoleum

When Jahangir died in 1627, after a few initial obstacles his eldest son ascended the throne triumphantly under the name of Shah Jahan, 'Ruler of the World' (1628–59). That was in Agra; but it was in Lahore that the tomb of Jahangir was erected by his widow, to a design said to have been made by Jahangir himself. The complex includes a walled garden 480 x 480 metres square, of the Persian *chahar bagh* type, composed of sixteen units separated by channels and fountains, similar to that of the garden around the Tomb of Humayun (which had thirty-six units: ill. p. 239). On either side, the garden is entered through monumental axial gates of red sandstone, whose *iwans* are vaulted with *muqarnas*. The tomb itself stands in the middle: it is a low square building measuring 75 x 75 metres, with at the corners four tall octagonal minarets, each with four tiers of balconies, surmounted by elegant *chhatris*. Double arcades surround the tomb, intended for the rite of circumambulation: the outer ones have thirteen arches on each side, the inner ones eleven. In the middle of each side a corridor leads in to the funerary chamber containing the white marble sarcophagus of Jahangir.

The balconies of the minarets rest not on *muqarnas* but on brackets. These are the only elements in the Hindu-inspired style of Akbar's time: everywhere else we find Persian arches, and vaults covered with a fine net of purely Persian *muqarnas*. Another Persian feature appears below the arcades of the tomb: a magnificent plinth is covered with tile mosaic in floral and vegetal motifs that suggest Trees of Life on a golden yellow background, evoking a Paradise garden. The use of coloured tile decoration on such a scale is a Timurid device, and here reflects Safavid influence.

Jahangir's mausoleum looks strange today, for the vast platform between the four corner minarets is completely empty. It now looks something like the open space on top of Akbar's Tomb at Sikandra;

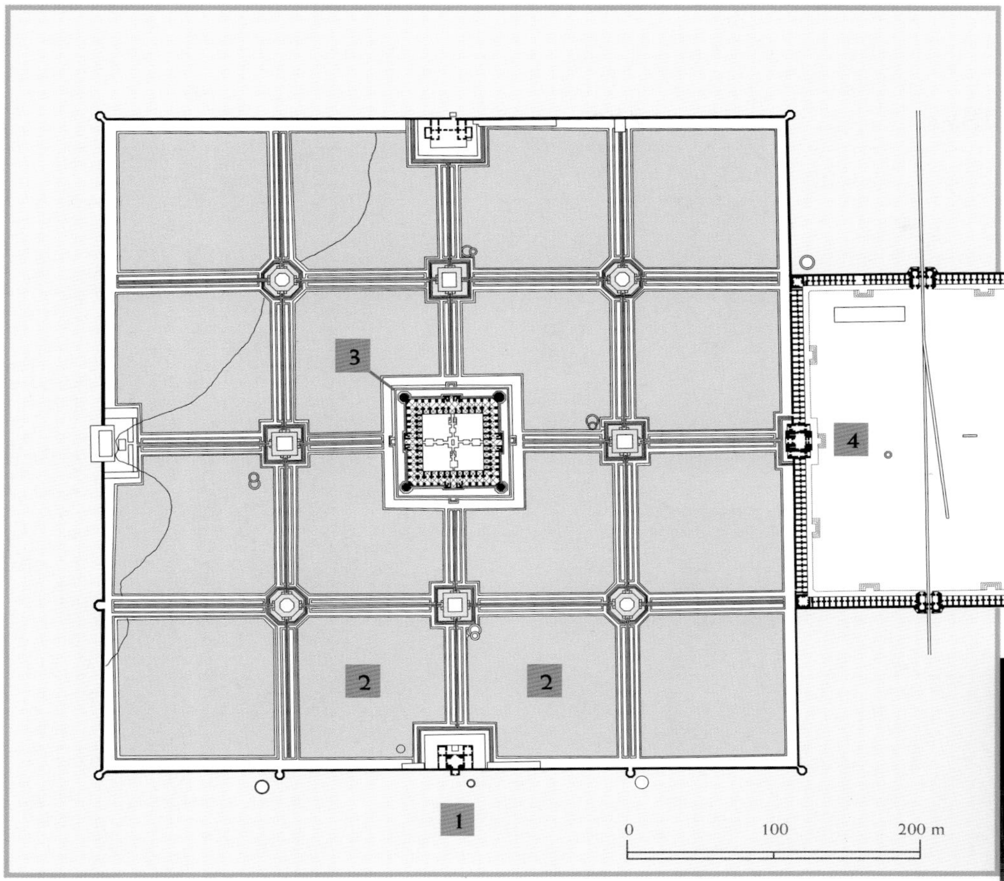

Key

Plan of the tombs of Jahangir and Asaf Khan, Lahore

1 Entrance in *pishtak* form
2 Garden of *chahar bagh* type
3 Tomb of Jahangir
4 Court of the old *zenana*, used as a caravanserai
5 Tomb of Asaf Khan

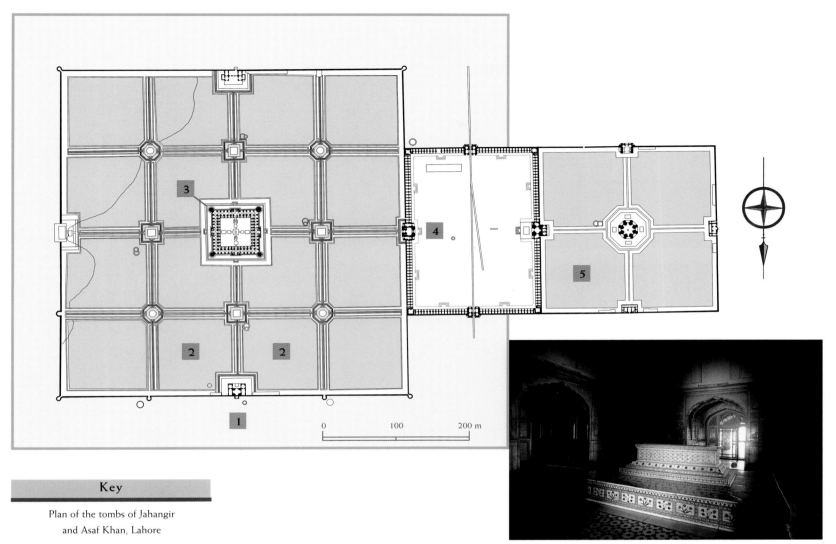

but at Lahore the original appearance was quite different, for in the centre of the platform was the building's focal point, a marble kiosk lit by marble *jalis* and containing the cenotaph of the emperor, similar to that on the top of the mausoleum of Itimad ud-Daula at Agra (ill. p. 164, top). Both kiosk and cenotaph were later destroyed.

The tomb complex eventually included a caravanserai built by Shah Jahan, the old *zenana* or seraglio, with 180 rooms for pilgrims. Beyond that on the same axis the tomb of Nur Jahan's brother, Asaf Khan, was added in 1641. It too stands in the centre of a *chahar bagh* garden, divided into four sections by axial paths leading to four gates. The tomb is an octagonal structure of purely Persian type covered by a bulbous dome that comes up to a slender point. It has lost much of its characteristically Persian tile mosaic cladding, but its *iwans* and gates, and the vault of the funerary chamber, still show remains of this type of decoration which was clearly executed by superbly skilled craftsmen. This glazed tile work is of the purest Persian-Timurid type, brought to India with workers from Samarqand and Isfahan by the Persian clan at the Mughal court.

THE TOMB OF ITIMAD UD-DAULA AT AGRA

We must return now to Agra, which was to be Shah Jahan's capital. In many respects the Tomb of Itimad ud-Daula, begun in 1621 and finished in 1628, the year when Shah Jahan came to the throne, is related to the work of his reign. Its resemblances to Jahangir's mausoleum in Lahore make it an interesting transitional introduction to the new style of Indo-Islamic architecture in its full maturity.

Itimad ud-Daula, 'Pillar of the State', was a great figure of the last years of Jahangir's reign: a Persian adventurer called Mirza Ghiyas Begh, he was the father of Jahangir's empress Nur Jahan, who appointed him treasurer and court vizier. When he died in 1621, Jahangir gave Nur Jahan unlimited means from the private imperial fortune to build her father a tomb in Agra on the bank of the Jumna. It stands in a *chahar bagh* garden, but one on a miniature scale, since he was not of royal blood. The tomb itself is nonetheless regarded as one of the wondrs of Mughal architecture.

The mausoleum that Nur Jahan erected for her father and mother occupies a site 165 metres square. It is surrounded by a wall, which is pierced on axis by two gates in the form of tiered pavilions, built of red sandstone with decorative details of white marble.

The garden is crossed by marble channels with pools and fountains. In the middle is a low plinth covered with inlay in geometrical patterns. Axial staircases lead up to the tomb, which is relatively small (27 x 27 metres) and has a square plan emphasized by towers at the corners, miniature versions of octagonal minarets, crowned by *chhatris*. The ground floor is subdivided into nine spaces: the central funerary chamber contains the tombs of the vizier and his wife, while four rooms in the corners were to receive the tombs of their relatives. Stairs in the towers lead to the upper platform, where a square pavilion forms a canopy over the cenotaphs of Nur Jahan's parents. This room has *jalis* of remarkable quality, and the floor, which in the room below containing the real tombs has a geometrical pattern, is here decorated with coloured marble inlay in patterns of flowers and vine trails that recall Persian carpets, which obviously served as models for the Mughal craftsmen. Exquis-

left, above The tomb, entirely faced with dazzling white marble, stands on a platform in a garden surrounded by red sandstone walls with elaborate gateway pavilions.

left, centre The two tombs of Itimad ud-Daula and his wife lie in the central chamber at ground level, below a vault with flattened *muqarnas*. The floor is paved with coloured marble in a star pattern.

left, below A detail of white marble inlay in red sandstone: the bottles refer to the wine promised to the elect in paradise (Qur'an, 83:25).

above The northern pavilion, seen from the tomb. Beyond is the Jumna River.

itely refined and superbly executed decorations in coloured marble inlay cover all the walls of the mausoleum, down to the smallest detail, with interlace, octagonal motifs, Greek key and geometrical friezes, and the pierced patterns of the *jalis* are exceptionally fine.

Not far from the tomb of Itimad ud-Daula there is a wholly Persian building, the Chiniki Rauza or Ceramic Tomb, erected to the memory of Afzal Khan, finance minister under Shah Jahan, who died in 1638. This brick building, now mostly ruined, retains some notable examples of tile mosaic: there are bouquets to suggest the ever-blooming vases of flowers symbolic of immortality, which resemble tile work on the Tomb of Asaf Khan, Nur Jahan's brother, in Lahore. The technique of tile and brick, easier to work than stone and marble, is another reminder of the Persian origin of members of the ruling family.

After looking at so many mausoleums, one might assume a morbid streak in Indo-Persian culture, but that would be wrong: the tombs built by the dynasties of Islamic India for great figures from their society are never gloomy or sad. On the contrary, they reflect the certainty that the dead will live in this sort of paradisal setting. The gardens promised to believers in the Qur'an are places of joy that prefigure eternal happiness:

> He [Allah] will reward them for their steadfastness with a garden and a raiment of silk. Reclining therein on couches, they will find there neither excessive heat nor excessive cold. Its trees will cover them with their shade, and its clustered fruits will be brought within easy reach. And vessels of silver will be passed round among them and also goblets of glass, bright as glass but made of silver, which they will measure according to their own measure. And therein will they be given to drink a cup tempered with ginger, from a spring therein named Salsabil. And there will wait upon them youths who will not age. When thou seest them, thou thinkest them to be pearls scattered about. And . . . thou wilt see there a bliss and a great kingdom. On them will be garments of fine green silk and thick brocade. And they will be made to wear bracelets of silver. And their Lord will give them to drink a pure beverage. 'This is your reward, and your labour has been appreciated.' (76:16–23)

opposite Shah Jahan, on a white horse, listens to a delegation of Afghans asking for mercy outside the fortified city of Kandahar, which had just surrendered to him in 1638. The illustration comes from a *Padshahnama* of 1640. Ten years later, the Persians re-took the city. (Musée Guimet, Paris)

right A posthumous portrait of Shah Jahan, painted *c.* 1720. The emperor is shown with a halo to indicate his superhuman nature. He has a beard and long moustache, unlike Akbar (ill. p. 104), and wears a brocade coat. (Musée Guimet, Paris)

Shah Jahan: the Age of Masterpieces

The full flowering of Mughal art in India took place during the reign of Shah Jahan, between 1628 and 1659. It followed on from, and was influenced by, the great artistic renewal fostered by Shah 'Abbas I in Isfahan between 1587 and 1629. A number of connections can be traced – most notably in the resemblances between the Mosque of the Imam in Isfahan and the Taj Mahal in Agra.

The 'King of the World' was thirty-five years old when he ascended the Mughal throne. His first action was to launch a vast operation to recover the places that had been lost in recent decades. He attacked the Portuguese trading settlements in Bengal and neutralized their power, then moved on the sultanates in the Deccan, where he succeeded in annexing Golconda and Bijapur. Turning northward, he faced the Persians and retook the city of Kandahar, a key point between Iran and the Indian plain.

He dreamed of rebuilding the Timurid empire and set out to conquer Turkestan, but reverses at Balkh limited his success. Nevertheless, he had acquired an immense territory, and over it he ruled unchallenged: under Shah Jahan Mughal power reached its climax. In architecture and art it was a time of superb achievement. Sumptuous imperial palaces were created, as well as the undoubted masterpiece of his reign, the world-famous Taj Mahal.

The Mughal capitals of Agra, Delhi and Lahore display a series of buildings of great beauty and outstanding importance, in which the generalized use of white marble almost completely supplanted the red sandstone used by Akbar. The age of Shah Jahan was, one might say, the classical age of Mughal art. The Persian-Timurid architectural vocabulary, transposed from brick to the finest marble, was fully established: four-centered Persian arches, arcaded porticoes, single- or double-shelled domes of simple shape or with a swelling outline, *iwans* and *pishtaqs*, *chahar bagh* gardens, and much else – and all displayed the decorative Persian motifs of arabesques, vine scrolls, inscriptions on a monumental scale, *jalis*, *muqarnas*, latticework and interlace.

Palaces in the Image of Paradise

Driven by construction mania, Shah Jahan commissioned many remarkable buildings, most of which have survived intact. In addition to mosques and mausoleums, he also conceived of a centre of power in each of his capitals: the Red Forts in Agra and in Delhi and the fort at Lahore proclaimed his wealth and celebrated the symbolic nature of his authority. The same elements are found in all of them. First came the Diwan-i Amm, or Hall of Public Audience, a vast space for official court ceremonies – feasts, the reception of allied and subject princes and members of the diplomatic corps, and solemnities surrounding the awarding of honours. Next came the Diwan-i Khass, or Hall of Private Audience, where the ruler held private meetings with his ministers or eminent members of the imperial 'clan', took official or secret decisions, and promulgated laws. Then there was the Khass Mahal, the emperor's private palace; and finally the emperor's private mosque or oratory. These buildings were accompanied by gardens for the emperor, with their own pavilions, laid out on a *chahar bagh* plan.

In addition to these buildings that provided for the pomp of the imperial court, each of the forts included buildings for utilitarian activities – ministries, a mint or treasury, guardhouses, armouries, etc. There were also more general places for relaxation and enjoyment: luxuriant gardens crossed by the Nahr-i Bihisht or River of Paradise, with fountains, little cascades, and pools that reflected palaces and pavilions.

A distinctive quality of all these palace complexes is that none of the structures within them is really monumental. In form these low, almost modest, buildings are not at all showy, apart from their remarkable aesthetic quality and the extraordinary care with which they were built, using the most precious materials. This reserve, this rejection of the colossal, reflects the ancient Persian tradition of preferring pavilions and kiosks for rulers and reserving the grandest structures for worship. As in Isfahan, the palaces are not proud or overscaled: rather, they are closely integrated into nature and the designed landscape.

The architectural elements within the forts in the three capitals are very similar. Rather than looking at each site in turn, therefore, it will be more interesting to describe an ideal palace complex of the age of Shah Jahan, with all the typical ingredients – halls for public and private audience, the residence of the emperor, the

The Red Fort at Agra

opposite, above The walls looming high over the Jumna were built by Akbar; in the 17th century the fort was remodelled to accommodate Shah Jahan's palace.

opposite, below Shah Jahan's Diwan i-Amm, or Hall of Public Audience begun in 1628. It is nine bays long and three bays deep, with columns – doubled along the perimeter – linked by cusped arches.

right, above and centre The Musumman Burj pavilion projects out from the riverside wall. Its marble structure is richly carved and further embellished by delicate inlays of coloured semi-precious stones, techniques that reached a peak of subtlety in the time of Shah Jahan. The pavilion was enjoyed during her lifetime by the empress Mumtaz Mahal. Later, Shah Jahan, imprisoned by his son Aurangzeb, is said to have spent his last years there.

below The Diwan i-Amm in the Red Fort at Delhi. While the one in Agra (ill. p. 170, below) is made entirely of marble, here the pavilion is of red sandstone and only the emperor's canopied throne, at the left, is of marble.

mosque for congregational prayer and the ruler's private oratory, and the most characteristic types of gardens.

Not all the buildings within the forts were built at the same time. Some additions were made to Shah Jahan's original schemes by later rulers; and all too often Mughal buildings were replaced in the 19th century, confusing the palace layout, by military structures for the British colonial power.

Sadly, this is especially true of the Red Fort in the emperor's new extension to Delhi – Shahjahanbad, the City of Shah Jahan – which was the most remarkable from a semiological point of view. As at Agra, the fort stands on the bank of the Jumna River, but here it is a regular rectangle in plan (apart from a wedge-shaped extension to the north, built for strategic reasons), measuring 600 metres from north to south and 400 metres from east to west. The walls are reinforced by towers and the gates are fortified. On three sides the walls were surrounded by a moat, while on the fourth they plunge down to the river, which provides a natural defense against attack from the east. Within the fort, the space was divided orthogonally on symmetrical lines, and the resulting sub-spaces were treated according to a strict hierarchy.

The most prestigious area was that on the wall above the Jumna. Here, from private pavilions on a height, the ruler could enjoy extensive views and catch any cooling breeze. Next in prestige came the gardens around the buildings for private and public audience; then followed further gardens, formally laid out and filled with rare aromatic plants; finally there were the administrative buildings, flanking the access road. A bazaar street separated the imperial quarters from the service area, crossed at right angles by a covered market. The area to the west contained the guards' barracks and servants' quarters.

The chief palace building at Agra is the Diwan-i Amm, or Hall of Public Audience. It is the finest surviving example of this type of prestige building used as a setting for imperial ceremonies. Shah Jahan ordered its construction at the very beginning of his reign, in 1628. It stands within a rectangular open space measuring 180 x 120 metres, which is surrounded by porticoes and entered through monumental gates on the south and north and laid out as a luxuriant garden. The Diwan-i Amm rises at the east end of the transverse symmetrical axis; built entirely of white marble, it is a spacious pillared hall, three bays deep and nine bays wide.

The Diwan i-Amm in the Red Fort at Agra, begun in 1628. The marble columns are doubled on the façade, and quadrupled at the corners. Visible in the distance are the domes of the Moti Masjid or Pearl Mosque, beyond a row of *chhatris*. Inside, the elegant columns support cusped arches in both longitudinal and transverse directions. Here Shah Jahan staged royal entertainments for distinguished guests.

With its forty columns, it corresponds to the Persian Chihil Sutun, or 'Palace of Forty Columns'. The columns support beautiful cusped arches that meet at right angles to support a flat roof. In the centre at the back a triple arcade forms a sort of balcony, on which the emperor displayed himself in majesty to the gaze of his subjects. The marble columns – paired on the façade to make the structure more rigid – have straight twelve-sided shafts, square bases, and capitals with *muqarnas*-like facetting. Brackets support the broad eaves, which are also of marble. Only the platform on which this marble forest rests is of red sandstone.

The building is large (65 x 25 metres), but the lightness of its design gives it an etherial grace, and the pale marble catches the light. One can easily imagine its splendour during official receptions, filled with brightly coloured costumes – the brocades and silk veils, the uniforms of the imperial guards, the picturesque costumes of foreign visitors – and with the sound of music without which no court ceremonial would be complete. For the Diwan-i Amm was always the place of choice for celebrations and ceremonies, where the Mughal emperors displayed their wealth and their munificence, in a setting of pageantry for which India has a special gift.

The Diwan-i Amm in the Red Fort at Delhi is made not of marble but of red sandstone; but it contains the famous throne of Shah Jahan (ill. p. 169, below), which is entirely made of white marble and ornamented with superb *pietra dura* decoration of foliage, vine scrolls and flowers, further enhanced by a *bangla* roof (a curved roof derived from the Hindu architecture of Bengal, transposed into stone) supported on four small columns and forming a bower or emblematic canopy over the emperor.

While Mughal court ritual was of almost inconceivable refinement and ostentation, and the architecture is of great richness in detail, it never becomes heavy or pompous. This paradox lies at the heart of Mughal art: settings for festivities out of the Thousand and One Nights never lose their human scale. The explanation lies in the tradition of light-weight, portable constructions, which Akbar had effectively turned to stone: the buildings of the Mughal court reflect their origin in the world of the steppes and the encampments of Central Asia, or the ceremonial tents of the Achaemenids.

The Diwan-i Khass or Hall of Private Audience in Delhi, also known as the Daulat Khana-i Khass, stands on a square marble platform each face of which has six piers linked by cusped arches. Through the building runs the Nahr-i Bihisht, the River of Paradise, cooling the room where the imperial council met. As if to emphasize the line of this artificial watercourse that flows over carved white marble slabs, on the northern and southern façades of the Diwan-i Khass the central arch of the triple hierarchical arcade is larger than the others. The piers of this exquisite building are faced with panels inlaid with *pietra dura* flowers and leaves framed in delicate foliage trails. The roof has projecting eaves and, at the corners, four delicate *chhatris* of white marble.

top The Machhi Bhawan garden in the Red Fort at Agra lies in front of the white marble Diwan i-Khass, the emperor's Hall of Private Audience. Laid out in 1637, it forms a private space surrounded by arcades.

above The Musamman Burj at Agra, like other rooms in the imperial palace, was designed to catch the slightest breath of air, and a fountain further cooled the atmosphere as it splashed in the carved marble basins. Niches in the walls here served to hold vases and bottles

below Shah Jahan's Diwan i-Khass in the fort at Lahore. Like that at Agra (*top*) it looks out over a garden in *chahar bagh* style, laid out around a pool, but its structure is even more delicate.

At Agra, the Diwan-i Khass lies beyond an enclosed garden that is visible only to those granted access to the ruler's private quarters. The same arrangement occurs in the fort at Lahore. There the Diwan-i Khass has marble supports of unparalleled delicacy and structural boldness: instead of stones the full thickness of the arch, here what look like cusped arches are formed from a sheet of marble only a few centimetres thick, which is nevertheless substantial enough to ensure the stability of the whole. The floor is inlaid with stars so that it seems to reflect the heavens. A passage runs round three sides of the room, while in the centre there is a tiny fountain. On the fourth side, openings filled with *jalis* lead to a row of alcoves, of which the middle one contains the imperial throne. Here around the figure of the Great Mughal councillors and ministers were grouped according to a strict protocol.

The unreal appearance of this transparent structure, like a palace in a dream, was explained by Shah Jahan in an inscription over the entrance to the Diwan i-Khass, in verses of wholly Persian character and sentiment: 'If there be a Paradise on Earth, it is here, it is here, it is here!'

top The Anguri Bagh gardens in the Red Fort at Agra, laid out in *chahar bagh* form, are overlooked by the Khass Mahal, which is flanked by two pavilions with curved *bangla* (Bengali-style) roofs.

above The Musammad Burj in the Red Fort at Agra has a cool interior with a central fountain, and looks out over the walls across the river.

left and above The Shish Mahal or Palace of Mirrors in the fort at Lahore. The emperor's brilliant reception room is enclosed within a marble and sandstone envelope of great refinement, precision and clarity. Inside, the dazzling decoration dissolves the material nature of the walls and ceiling. The floor has a star pattern that echoes the design of the roof, which springs from shallow *muqarnas*. The mirrors are further highlighted by coloured motifs.

In addition to the public areas, Mughal palaces also contained the ruler's private residence. At Agra, the Khass Mahal or private palace stands on top of the wall overlooking the Jumna, with distant views over the landscape beyond the river. The buildings form a celestial environment in the midst of cruciform *chahar bagh* gardens: their raised floors are paved with marble, and within them you find fountains with elegantly shaped basins. The Khass Mahal has a portico with cusped arches and, within, an oblong room with openings that admit the breeze and softly filtered daylight. On either side are elegant canopied pavilions with curved *bangla* roofs. To the north of this complex is the Musamman Burj, an octagonal pavilion said to have been the residence of Mumtaz Mahal, the wife of Shah Jahan, which projects out over the wall of the fort, providing striking views from its surrounding gallery (ill. p. 169, top). Within is a polygonal room with countless niches in its marble walls where the empress could keep the vases, boxes, jars and bottles that contained the necessaries for her toilette. Behind that projecting room lies another, running sideways, which has further marble niches and a beautifully carved pool whose fountain must have lulled the monarchs to sleep.

There is a Musamman Burj in Delhi as well, but there it was a place where the ruler made formal appearances. It is a transparent half-octagon that seems to have been spun out of marble by some magical spider, with walls made of large *jalis* that leave it open to the winds from the plain – an extreme example of dematerialized architecture, as if devised to convince all beholders that they are in a realm of dreams.

There are similar etherial residences in the fort at Lahore, of which the main one is the Shish Mahal, or Palace of Mirrors, where the decoration is of almost inconceivable refinement and virtuosity. Behind an arcade of five arches opening onto an enclosed court is a sumptuous space for living and entertainment. This is a luminous jewel box of which the walls and ceiling are covered with panels made of a mosaic of small mirrors that confuse the eye and dissolve any sense of enclosure. This glittering space owes its effect to a novel technique of breaking up

the light by means of small faceted mirrors that catch the slightest gleam. Like a firework it plays with light and colour, setting reflections against the subtlety of flowers made of coloured glass, and paintings inset above the marble dado. As a setting for the apotheosis of the Great Mughal it has no parallel: nowhere else has human imagination, in its desire to exalt the superhuman nature of the sovereign, been so successful in transfiguring the world, dematerializing the physical setting, and evoking Paradise on earth. There can be no doubt that the model was the the mirrored *iwan* in the Chihil Sutun in Isfahan (ill. p. 145, below).

The Western observer stands bemused in front of this imperial architecture made up of kiosks dotted about in gardens, where order and imagination meet. Is this the splendour for which the Mughals are famed? Everything is light; there are no impressive façades, vast vistas or grandiose structures. The 'palace' of the emperor is nothing like the palaces of Renaissance or Baroque princes in Europe: it consists of a series of relatively small units (such as the Diwan-i Khass), or of buildings that are light and airy even when they are large (such as the Diwan-i Amm). The Mughal ideal – like that of the Safavids in Iran and the Ottomans in Istanbul – was to set the structures symbolic of power, the royal residence, and places for entertainment in a designed version of nature.

With their show of splendour and luxury, these freestanding pavilions that made up the palace complex fulfilled the age-old dream of the Mughal rulers who longed for a residence on a human scale. In ancient Rome, motivated perhaps by a desire to escape the teeming city, Nero in his Golden House and Hadrian in his villa at Tivoli produced something similar. They fled the Palatine, the hill of palaces, to enjoy the pleasures of nature and of an architecture of pavilions.

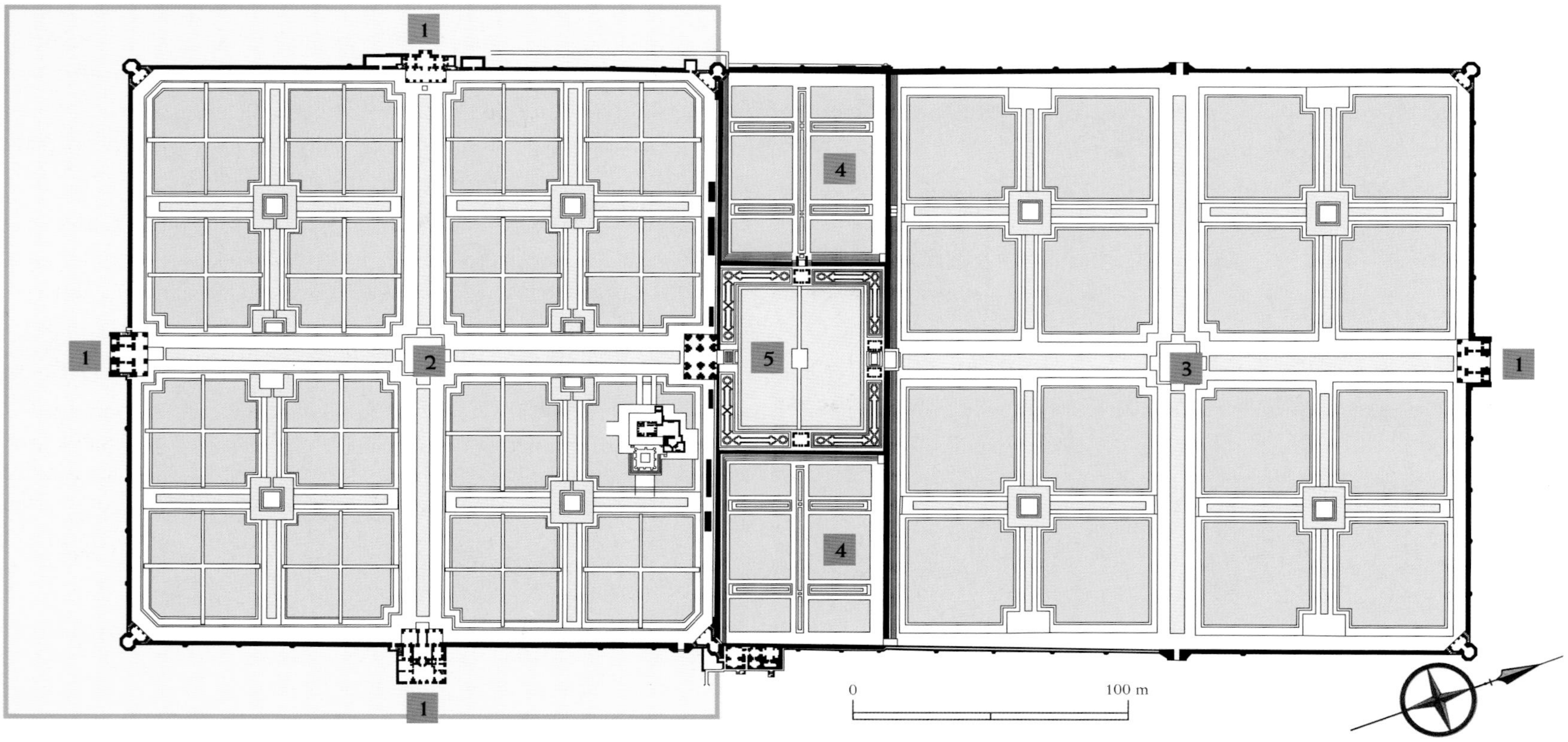
1
1
2
5
3
1
4
4
1
0
100 m

The Shalimar Gardens in Lahore: Heaven on Earth

left Dozens of jets spurt into the large pool in the middle of the gardens. A central axis leads from the marble platform in the foreground into the distance, past a small island of white marble reached by two walkways, which served for the performance of Mughal cosmological ritual.

above and below The pools in the gardens are surrounded by pavilions of white marble and red sandstone, realizing Shah Jahan's conception of Paradise on earth.

Key

1 Entrance gates
2 Southern garden in *chahar bagh* style
3 Northern garden in *chahar bagh* style
4 Intermediate zone
5 Large pool with fountains

To get an idea of the great Islamic gardens of which Arabic and Persian poets sing, there are two chief places where the Western visitor can go: to the celebrated gardens of the Generalife at the Alhambra in Granada in Spain, and to the Shalimar Gardens in Lahore. The latter are one of the finest surviving Mughal ensembles, and they perfectly illustrate 'artificial nature', that paradox which is at the heart of the Islamic concept of gardens, and which originated in Irann.

The Shalimar, or 'Residence of Love', was created by Shah Jahan in 1642. Here the *chahar bagh* is translated into the materials and techniques of the Indian subcontinent, in an area measuring 200 x 450 metres. The plan takes the traditional four-squares arrangement but uses it in a tripartite layout: the gardens consist of two 200-metre squares separated by a dip that helps the water to drain away. Between the two quadripartite gardens, a middle band 50 metres wide contains a vast rectangular pool and also a *hammam*, or Turkish baths. The two *chahar baghs*, each of which covers an area of 4,000 square metres, are divided into four parts, each of which is subdivided into four units, and in the case of the southern garden again subdivided. The subdivisions are demarcated by paths, orthogonal channels, and centrally placed pools. A wall surrounds the entire complex, with small octagonal towers at the corners. Axially placed gates and pavilions complete the architectural furniture.

In the space between the *chahar bagh* gardens there is a magnificent pool 50 metres wide, from which dozens of fountains spurt up, their splashing filling the air and giving a sensation of coolness. At its centre is the now classic 'island', here in white marble, reached by two footbridges. Here, the ruler was the focus of a solemn ritual, in which the ceremony introduced by Akbar at Fatehpur Sikri was perpetuated but also developed further. The Great Mughal in majesty, in his role as Master of the World, was perpetuating a courtly tradition that went back to the rulers of Greek and Roman antiquity.

Places of Prayer

However much the Mughals may have sought comfort and pleasure in life, their spiritual concerns were in no way diminished. Courtly splendour was balanced by prayer; like their Turkish-Mongol brothers, they followed Sunnite orthodoxy. Palaces therefore had to provide spaces for prayer.

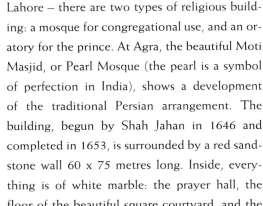

The whole of Muslim existence is governed by the precepts of the Qu'ran, and the ruler is the leader and spokesman of the community. He looks to the sacred text for guidance in his everyday actions as well as in the expression of his faith in the mosque, which is the place of prayer and meditation. In all the Mughal centres of power – at Agra, Delhi and Lahore – there are two types of religious building: a mosque for congregational use, and an oratory for the prince. At Agra, the beautiful Moti Masjid, or Pearl Mosque (the pearl is a symbol of perfection in India), shows a development of the traditional Persian arrangement. The building, begun by Shah Jahan in 1646 and completed in 1653, is surrounded by a red sandstone wall 60 x 75 metres long. Inside, everything is of white marble: the prayer hall, the floor of the beautiful square courtyard, and the arcades that surround it are all blindingly white. On three sides of the court there are monumental gates that evoke the principle of the Persian mosque with cross-axes and *iwans*. The main entrance is to the east, with secondary entrances to north and south. On the western side is the prayer hall, an oblong hypostyle space 50 metres wide, which is three bays deep and seven bays long; inside it, eighteen cruciform piers support cusped arches, forming bays that are alternatively covered by domes and flat vaults. The courtyard façade is surmounted by a series of slender *chhatris*, behind which there rise three bulbous domes raised on high drums. The apex of each dome is surrounded by a ring of foliage, above which rises a gilded bronze spike with the crescent moon – which, as we have seen, governs the Islamic calendar.

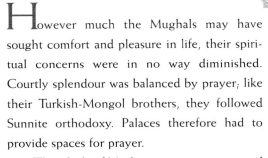

Shah Jahan's tiny oratory, the Najina Masjid, is also signalled by three bulbous domes. This is a jewel carved of marble, an extraordinarily delicate pavilion whose cusped arches are on such a small scale that their cusping reads more like a lace edging, yet where grace never leads into frivolity.

Finally, there are the two great urban mosques, the Friday Mosques in Delhi and Agra. These are vast buildings, whose essential purpose was to provide a place for congregational Friday prayers in the imperial capitals, and their grandiose proportions well display the majesty of Mughal art in its finest phase. In Delhi, the Friday Mosque is contemporary with the Red Fort. Great flights of steps, and an enormous gate as at Akbar's mosque in Fatehpur Sikri, lead to the court, which is almost 100 metres square. The façade of the oblong prayer hall is framed by two tall octagonal minarets with three tiers of balconies, surmounted by *chhatris*. Five arches that open on either side of the centre lead in to the hypostyle room, while the main *iwan*, on the central axis, leads to the *mihrab*. Above the *mihrab* rises the main dome, which is raised on a drum and has an elegant swelling profile. Secondary domes to left and right are positioned so as to give the whole design a sense of harmonious balance. Red sandstone is used for the main structural elements, while the domes and façade are of white marble. Panels above the arcades display fine inscriptions by the Persian Nur Allah Ahmad. The domes are given a vigorous plasticity by ribs emphasized by vertical black lines, like the lines of longitude on a globe – the first signs of the emergence of a 'baroque' character in Mughal art. This intensely white sacred architecture suggests the purity of believers' hopes for the bliss of Paradise.

opposite, above The tall minarets and ribbed domes of the Friday Mosque in Delhi overlook a vast court surrounded by arcades.

opposite, centre The Friday Mosque in Agra, less impressive than that in Delhi, looks forward to late Mughal architecture of Aurangzeb's time.

above and opposite, below The Moti Masjid or Pearl Mosque in the Red Fort at Agra is built entirely of marble in a design of great purity. The prayer hall, fronted by an arcade of seven cusped bays, is crowned by three bulbous domes and a row of airy *chhatris*. Within, cusped arches frame bays where shallow domes alternate with vaults. The court has a central pool; the centres of the sides are marked by *iwans*, in the Persian manner.

The Romance of the Taj Mahal

Domes, *iwans*, palaces, mausoleums, all lead finally to the pearl of India, the Taj Mahal – a legendary monument built by a legendary emperor, and the epitome of Mughal art. Among the tombs erected in Islamic India for the rulers of a dynasty whose power lasted for three centuries and controlled a continent, the Taj Mahal at Agra represents absolute perfection. Its worldwide fame is due to the combination of outstanding qualities: the harmony of its forms, the articulation of its component elements, and the beauty of its materials, further enhanced by its setting, in a superb *chahar bagh* garden; all come together to make this grandiose mausoleum the paradigm of the Mughal aesthetic.

Everyone knows the Taj Mahal, but it still retains some mystery. It is the object of mistaken beliefs and absurd legends, and visitors and even distinguished specialists have gone astray in interpreting it, so it is worth analysing it more closely before going on to consider the refinement of its design and the confusions that have arisen from its very celebrity. A close examination of the building will be found in Part II (pp. 274–85). At the end of our introductory look at it here, we shall attempt to refute some of the baseless myths that surround it by considering a hitherto unpublished argument concerning the person whose tomb it was intended to be.

The Taj Mahal's fame has isolated it in the public mind, but it must be seen in the direct line of the great Mughal mausoleums, especially the tomb of Humayun in Delhi (see pp. 100–101, 238–43), begun less than a century earlier, which it closely resembles. In that 'prototype' we find many of its characteristic features, including the bi-axial symmetry, the dome flanked by four *chhatris*, the great framed *iwans* in the centre of each façade, the square plan with chamfered corners, and the vast substructure on which the tomb stands. Most of the tombs that we have considered so far represent stages in an evolutionary process that culminated in this design. The Taj Mahal has four corner minarets as in the tomb of Jahangir at Lahore (ill. p. 163) – paraphrased in the corner towers of the small tomb of Itimad ud-Daula at Agra

(ill. p. 164) – but here they no longer have any organic link with the central building. The overall concept comes from the tomb of General Khan-i Khanan in Delhi (ill. p. 282), begun in 1626, shortly before Shah Jahan came to the throne. Its red sandstone has now completely lost its original white marble facing, but one can see in it numerous analogies and solutions that the architect of the Taj Mahal adopted and made his own.

Thus the great mausoleum at Agra is not unique: it belongs to a line of emblematic Mughal buildings which were themselves derived from Timurid Transoxiana and Safavid Iran. It is impossible to give any credence to the notion, based on old colonialist ideas, that the Taj Mahal could not have been the work of a Persian or Indian architect, and that it was devised by a European. Setting that idea aside, historians have put forward as possible designers names mentioned in documents, but most of those refer merely to executant builders, whose names are known because they were paid salaries and thus figure in the accounts. There is clearly no hope, in the present state of knowledge, to assign a name to the 'onlie begetter' of this wonderful mausoleum. One thing seems certain: the Taj Mahal reflects a purely Persian style, and it would not be impossible for the architect to

opposite, above The tomb, seen from the top of the south-western minaret. Clearly visible from here are the building's chamfered corners, lateral *iwans*, and dome resting on a high drum.

opposite, below A vast marble terrace surrounds the tomb. The isolated minarets at the outer corners, which stand on the diagonals of the plan, are a distinctive feature of the Taj Mahal.

above A closer view of the dome, one of the *iwans*, and a chamfered corner crowned by a *chhatri* shows the subtle harmony of the whole, as the forms combine with the great variety of types of decoration – inscriptions around the *iwan*, arabesques in the spandrels, floral friezes in *pietra dura*, and zig-zag patterns on corner shafts and pinnacles.

left Detail of a marble *jali* with hexagonal motifs.

The flattened *muqarnas* in the *iwans* of the Taj Mahal are one example of how the Timurid architectural vocabulary was transformed in the great art of the Mughals.

have been Persian, summoned to India for the commission, as with the mausoleum of Humayun. Perhaps he was in the circle of the architects of Isfahan, given the close resemblance between the dome of the Taj Mahal and that of the Mosque of the Imam (ill. p. 137).

What is really original about the Taj Mahal, beyond the use of marble for the most important elements (as in Shah Jahan's work in the palaces of Agra, Delhi and Lahore), is the composition with four minarets effectively detached from the main structure, and the siting of the mausoleum at the end rather than in the centre of the *chahar bagh* garden. In other respects – the high quality of the design as a whole, its equilibrium and harmony – it is the end product of an aesthetic process initiated in India by the Persian architect Mirak Mirza Ghiyas, designer of Humayun's Tomb, who was himself working in a Persian-Timurid tradition.

Wherein lies the aesthetic value of the Taj Mahal? Chiefly in an extraordinary sense of measure, in an absence of vain ostentation, and in a sort of mystical quality that accords with the Muslim vision of the heavenly cities of the next world that await the faithful. The dematerialized surfaces of the luminous marble, reflected in the waters of the Gardens of Paradise, conjure up the image of an eternal and radiant universe. The Taj Mahal seems to glow with a radiance expressive of divine perfection, as it were a proof of the existence of God.

For some three hundred years the Taj Mahal has been thought to be the tomb of the empress Mumtaz Mahal, who died in childbirth; her inconsolable husband, the Great Mughal Shah Jahan, it was said, raised this matchless mausoleum in her memory. It is an engaging and moving story, but one might question whether its romanticism is in character with the Oriental world. The idea that the Taj Mahal was built for a woman has given rise to the most far-fetched interpretations. In the West, the reports of 17th-century travellers that the great building was intended to immortalize Shah Jahan's love for his favourite wife, who had died at the age of thirty-eight in 1631 giving birth to his fourteenth child, made it a monument to femininity, the embodiment of the disconsolate emperor's love. This touching fable was suitable for a century obsessed with the loves of kings and queens, but it is not consonant with the mentality of Muslim rulers, or – to an even greater extent – with the symbolism of a building celebrating the authority of the Great Mughal. The story shows a fundamental ignorance of Islamic custom and of the traditions prevalent when the Mughal empire was at its height. To make it more plausible, a poignant myth was invented: Shah Jahan was said to have planned to build a second mausoleum, identical but in black marble, on the opposite bank of the Jumna, for himself.

With its grand scale and splendour, there can be no doubt that the Taj Mahal was intended for the emperor himself. Mumtaz Mahal happened to die before he did, so she came to be buried first in this monument to his reign. This statement will disappoint the lovers of romantic fiction, but it is easy to prove. The attribution of this illustrious tomb to Mumtaz Mahal is essentially due to a confusion of words, which the first travellers unwittingly passed on. The empress was often known as Taj Bibi, 'the Lady of the Crown', meaning the wife of the emperor. The mausoleum was called Taj Mahal or 'Palace of the Crown'. The similarity between the two names led to the monument being thought of as 'the Palace of the Lady of the Crown'. And there the fables started.

There is another major argument to add to the debate: it centres on the date of the transfer of the dead empress's remains. Mumtaz Mahal, who had married Shah Jahan in 1612, died in 1631, when the emperor had been on the throne for four years. Her death occurred at Zainabad, where the court was resident at the time, and her remains were transferred to Agra six months later. How could the Taj Mahal, which according to this account had begun on her death, have been

On the walls marble panels carved in shallow relief with an endless variety of flowering plants are framed by bands of *pietra dura*.

sufficiently advanced a mere six months later to house her body with dignity?

The whole argument hinges on this six-month lapse. Let us imagine what the sudden decision to build such a mausoleum would have entailed. After the emperor had taken the decision, it would have been necessary to conceive a general idea, to work out schemes within a particular typological tradition, to chose a design, to draw out the plans and have them approved by the emperor, and to translate the plans into models or scale drawings for the builders to use. All this work would have had to be done before work began. It would also have been necessary to select the site, to acquire the land, to prepare it with special regard for the gradient needed for the correct functioning of the hydraulic system in the gardens, and to level the soil over an area of 17 hectares, 9 of which were laid out in *chahar bagh* form, where a change in level of as little as a few centimetres would affect the flow of water. Finally, it would have been necessary to build the formidable substructure, involving 120,000 tons of material, on which the mausoleum was to stand and within which a funerary crypt would be created. That crypt would have had to be finished when the remains were transferred, since it is inconceivable that the empress's body would have been moved a second time.

All these operations could not possibly have taken place in six months, even with a workforce of 20,000, as reported by Jean-Baptiste Tavernier, and even if the architects did everything short of the miraculous to satisfy their patron. Without machinery, 120,000 tons of earth and alluvial deposits could not have been moved and levelled in the time.

The origin of the Taj Mahal and its intended purpose have thus been mythologized to satisfy a feeble desire for romance. The truth is that Shah Jahan had begun the project well before 1631. His decision to erect a tomb for himself which would express the greatness of his reign was taken in 1628, and work must have started as soon as he came to the throne. If construction had been under way for three or four years before Mumtaz Mahal's death, her remains could well have been transferred at the time recorded in dynastic histories. It is impossible to avoid the conclusion that the Taj Mahal was not built for her.

Many people will be disappointed by this correction of the 'facts', since they have been thrilled by the thought of the empress's place in the heart of the Mughal emperor and by the importance conferred on women by the creation of such a mausoleum. But, alas, historical truth forces us to reject this account and to render to Shah Jahan that which is Shah Jahan's. Sometimes the reexamination of history entails painful revisions, and the loss of much-loved myths.

8

The Last Creations: Late Iran, the Khanate of Khiva, Aurangzeb, and the Rajputs

Throughout the 18th and 19th centuries interesting works of art continued to be produced – in Iran under the last Safavids and, the Qajars; in Khwarazm under the khans of Khiva; and in Mughal India under Aurangzeb and the Hindu princes of Rajasthan. Paradoxically, though times were difficult politically, rich forms continued to be created; but all exploited existing trends rather than inventing something radically new. In every region there was a move towards what one might call a 'baroque' aesthetic: it can be seen in the famous Madrasa Mader-i Shah in Isfahan, in the *madrasas* of Bukhara and Khiva, in the late Mughal works in Lahore and Delhi, and in the palaces of the Rajput rulers and the last observatories built in India.

The later years of the Safavid dynasty under Shah Sultan Husain (1694–1722), before the Afghan invasion and the capture of Isfahan, were not a period of decline. There is no sense of exhaustion in the late productions of Iran (or of Mughal India), but rather a progressive change in the forms of expression. The buildings yield nothing to earlier works in scale or in the richness of their ornamentation. However, very much less was produced, since major undertakings became rare in Iran after the fall of Isfahan. The 18th century was a period of recession in Iran, as the country entered on a political and military decline that Shah 'Abbas II was unable to stem. Explanations lie in the excessive centralization of the state under the last Safavid ruler and also in a reduction in the number of *qizilbash*, which left the army incapable of putting down revolts in the provinces or preventing incursions of armed bands from the east. A split developed between civil and religious authority: Shah Sultan Husain was a bigot, and the government became filled with *imams*, leading to sectarian policies such as a withdrawal of trust from the Armenian minority, whose energetic activities had enriched the country.

Four years after the fall of Isfahan the shah was beheaded, and a series of heirs, usurpers and puppets competed for power until Nadir Shah seized power. Nadir had been a military commander in the service of Shah Tahmasp II. He took Mashhad in 1727, but for his own gain, and went on to defeat the Kurds who were threatening to take Isfahan. In 1730 he began the reconquest of Fars, western Iran and Azerbaijan, then drove out the Afghans and restored order in Khorasan and Herat, while Tahmasp II, who had taken on the Ottomans, lost Tabriz and Hamadan. Claiming that the shah wanted to launch an expedition against him, Nadir entered Isfahan and organized a great show: he pretended to be reconciled with Tahmasp and invited him to a gathering, but once there he forced the shah to abdicate in favour of his son, who ruled briefly as Shah 'Abbas III. From 1736 on, Nadir was shah of Iran, and was to remain so until 1747. He launched a series of conquests that culminated in a raid on India, from which he returned laden with treasure in 1739. Nadir Shah embarked on great military adventures in the style of Mongol and Timurid rulers. He turned on the khan of Bukhara and seized land beyond the Amu Darya, then occupied Khiva and challenged the Uzbeks. In 1747, threatened by insurrections and rebellions, he signed a treaty with the Ottomans, but in a palace coup his guards assassinated him in July of that year.

Nadir Shah's death plunged the region into a period of political confusion that was to last until the advent of the Qajars. In the meantime, Karim Khan Zand headed a handful of tribes in the south and established his capital at Shiraz, but he

p. 182, above A royal lion in the Gulistan Palace, Tehran.

p. 182, below Ornamental motif from a carved marble panel in the Badshahi Mosque in Lahore.

p. 183 A tile picture of a vase of flowers in the pilgrimage shrine at Mahan.

opposite, above Detail of the decoration of the Madrasa Mader-i Shah, Isfahan.

below left A portrait of Fath Ali Shah by Mirza Baba, 19th century. (Private collection)

below right Nadir Shah, in an 18th-century miniature. (Victoria & Albert Museum, London)

was not able to rule the country as a whole. The Qajars owed their success to a superior military organization, and established themselves in Azerbaijan. Fath Ali Khan was succeeded by his son, Muhammad Hasan Khan Qajar, who held power from 1751 to 1759, but it was Agha Muhammad Shah (1779–96) who defeated Karim Khan Zand and reunited the country. The problem of nomadism remained acute, however: it is estimated that between a third and a half of the population of Iran consisted of tribes that lived a nomadic existence. Cities shrank, and did not recover until the 19th century. That recovery was due to Fath Ali Shah (1797–1834), under whom peace returned to the country, although clashes with the Russian tsars Peter I and Nicholas I, who succeeded Catherine the Great, led to the loss of Georgia and Armenia. Tehran did not become the capital of the country until the reign of Muhammed Shah Qajar (1877–96).

Decades of insecurity had led towns to surround themselves with walls and to build fortresses, and cities that were already fortified restored their walls, within which they enjoyed a false sense of security.

The vast court of the Qajar ruler Fath Ali Shah. Among the dignitaries are European ambassadors. (Royal Asiatic Society, London)

Features of the Late Style

The most important work of this period in Iran, the Madrasa Mader-i Shah, built in Isfahan by the last Safavid ruler shortly before the Afghan invasion in 1722, is the subject of a special study in Part II (pp. 286–95). Here we shall be concerned to look at a few distinctive features of the building that show an interesting evolution in architectural forms and decoration.

At first sight, the *madrasa* erected in honour of his mother by Shah Sultan Husain between 1706 and 1714 is very similar to the Mosque of the Imam, built by Shah 'Abbas. First of all, one is struck by the great similarity between their domes, both in overall form and in decoration, to the point where it is not always easy to tell them apart out of context. The main difference is that the dome of the *madrasa* is smaller than that of the mosque.

One of the most impressive technological achievements of Safavid architectural decoration is the creation of large-scale patterns on the external surfaces of domes. The regularity and formal perfection of the scrolls and fronds disposed symmetrically all over the turquoise blue majolica surfaces of the vast bulbous shapes called for a very skilled technique. How were these immense motifs created? Looking closely at the domes, one is forced to the conclusion that such jigsaw puzzles could never have been assembled *in situ*. And indeed, the answer is to be found in one of the halls of the *madrasa*: there, lying on its side, is an enormous curved segment of vault made of brick; on its inner side, at one end it comes to a point for the top of the dome, while at the other it flares out and corresponds to the curve where the dome meets the drum. It is as it were a cast of one-eighth of the dome.

On the inner face of this 'cast' – on which probably a drawing had been made – the coloured tiles composing the design could be assembled. Turquoise, buttercup yellow, white and black bricks were precisely fitted together, on the level, without having to cope with the problems posed by weight or gravity, sloping surfaces, etc. When an eighth of the dome was complete, parts held together with whitewash could be removed and put in place precisely where required on the surface of the dome, to which they were fixed with a relatively liquid mortar.

The coloured surface of the dome was put in place in eight identical operations, and the joints made invisible, leaving no hint of the technique that had been used.

A more careful look at the ensemble of the Madrasa Mader-i Shah reveals differences between it and the Mosque of the Imam. Everywhere here the corners are chamfered; where in the mosque the *iwans* have rectangular vaults with smooth concave surfaces only slightly marked by delicate grids of tracery, here they have vigorously modelled *muqarnas*, of which some of the cells even have what look like pendant keystones. In the corners of the courtyard there is an extra refinement, as in the *madrasas* of Bukhara: the walls do not meet at right angles, but at 45 degrees; and the openings there lead into small octagonal courtyards that look like stage sets with the sky as a backdrop (see the plan, p. 289). Vestibules or *iwans*, themselves vaulted recesses, have further vaulted recesses carved into their sides. Some domes are not hemispherical but depressed, with a flattened profile that suited the new fashion for flattened vaults.

The decorative language becomes much more varied, both in technique and in appearance. Instead of *kashis* you often find a revival of the earlier technique using bricks glazed in a single colour, and these are frequently used to produce geometrical, almost pointillist, ornament rather than scrolls and flowers. Contemporary with this 'kinetic' style, where rhythms and contrasts go to create puzzles that make dazzling play with light, in a way that looks forward to 'concrete' art, is a manner that makes use of realistic, almost sentimental, motifs. Here and there it is still possible to find floral panels of great refinement made in traditional tile mosaic, in contrast to the new formulas. The latter are more graphic, and make use of black lines and borders that outline the volumes of *muqarnas* and set up optical vibration in surfaces and spaces. This was something new. It would prove very popular in some of the regions that took up the 'Persian style'.

Increasing complexity can also be seen in a utilitarian work like the *hammam* of Ganj-i Ali Khan in Kerman, in south-eastern Iran. This has an intricate plan with a multiplication of octagonal structures, shallow domes with projecting ribs, and

The Madrasa Mader-i Shah in Isfahan, begun by Shah Sultan Husain in 1706: detail of the *muqarnas* on a minaret (*opposite*), transverse section (*below*) from Pascal Coste, *Les Monuments modernes de la Perse* (1867); and an ornamental motif in coloured tile mosaic.

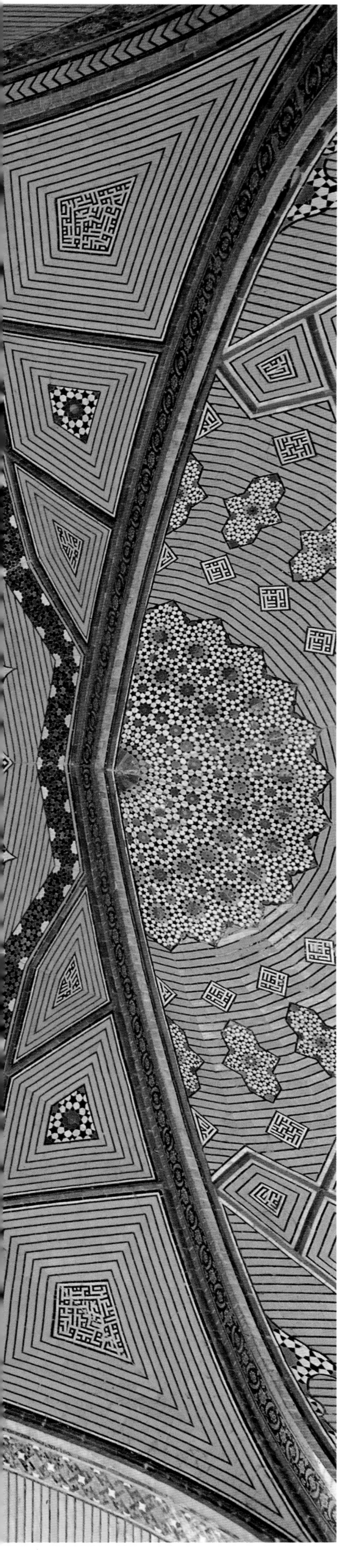

opposite and top The Madrasa Mader-i Shah in Isfahan, 1706–14. In the shallow dome over the entrance hall, of a type resting on ribbed pendentives that has Timurid ancestry, Safavid-style floral decoration has become subtly geometricized. The vine scrolls that adorn the surface of the main dome are in the tradition of those on the Mosque of the Imam (ill. p. 137), some hundred years earlier in date.

above and below Rooms in the *hammam* at Kerman built by Ibrahim Khan Zahirol Doleh, governor of the city under the Qajars in the 19th century. The rooms are lit from above, and covered with ribbed vaulting and *muqarnas*.

chamfered corners. The architect has created a maze of rooms tightly intersecting with each other, most of which are illuminated only by oculi in the vault. The bathing pools reflect a diffused light, adding to the voluptuous atmosphere of these Roman-style baths. *Hammams* were designed for large numbers of customers, and their plans became increasingly complex, while the rooms became bigger, with alcoves and subordinate spaces where the domes, in a display of technical bravura, are supported only by slender columns. The art of living in 18th- and early 19th-century Iran took on a character of extreme refinement, reflecting a high standard of living and widespread advances in comfort and luxury.

The Shrines of Mahan and Qazvin

In the 14th century a poet and mystic called Shah Ne'matollah Vali left Samarqand, travelled through Herat, and settled in Yazd. He came to be regarded as a saint and venerated, and a shrine to him soon grew up at Mahan. It attracted many pilgrims; buildings were erected on the site of his tomb, and they evolved over the centuries in a setting of lovely gardens with pools.

The central tomb, which was enlarged several times, is flanked by two courtyards. These are entered through gates surmounted by curious pairs of minarets with very slender shafts, which have instead of balconies for the muezzin small pepper-pot-like structures – decadent but not unattractive features that date from the Qajar period. The various rooms that surround the tomb were built at the same time. Inside, they have domes covered with a fine network of ribs and lit by oculi. One of these ancillary rooms contains a *mihrab* of which the niche with *muqarnas* is carved from a single stone, and surrounded by attractive late tiles with floral motifs. The tomb proper goes back to the Timurid period; its dome, with superb white star motifs on a turquoise background, seems to date from the time of Shah 'Abbas I, though it may have been restored again in the Qajar period, when the rest of the shrine was remodelled.

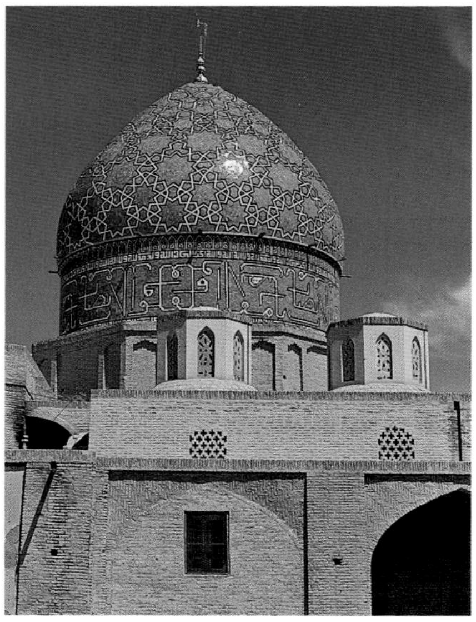

The complex of the mausoleum of Shahzadeh Hossein in Qazvin also includes buildings in Qajar style. The new forms appear in the entrance façade, which rises above a pool at the end of extensive gardens: it has six minaret-like features, the lower parts of whose cylindrical shafts are engaged in the wall, while the upper parts emerge like pinnacles. The whole is covered with tile mosaic and *kashis* in which geometrical motifs alternate with intensely 'rococo' realistic bouquets

opposite, centre and bottom Interior and dome of the shrine at Mahan, near Kerman, dedicated to Shah Ne'matollah Vali, founder of the order of dervishes. The dome, in Timurid style, seems to have been renewed by Shah 'Abbas I, and perhaps again under the Qajars, when the rest of the shrine was remodelled. The later structures have a characteristic complexity.

below, and opposite, above The pilgrimage shrine of Shahzadeh Hossein in Qazvin has the distinctive 'rococo' appearance of Shi'ite sanctuaries of the Qajar period. An unusual outer gate (*below*) with minaret-spires stands at the end of an avenue with pools. Behind it rises the dome of the mosque. On the mosque itself (*opposite, above*) the *talar* is completely faced with mirrors.

of flowers. The mosque itself, beyond this screen, has rounded 'pediments' and a *talar* entirely covered with mirrors, even the wooden columns, in an admittedly rather debased version of Persian art. This flavour characterizes all the decorative vocabulary, from the tilework to the stucco on the domes, but the overall effect of decadent splendour is not without its attraction.

Here at Qazvin, an enfilade of courtyards provides space for the multitude of pilgrims moving freely about in the gardens. In these shrines a new form of piety grew up, as popular faith expressed itself through the celebration of national identity.

right, above A fine princely house in Tabriz of the Qajar period, recently restored. Its wide *talar*-type veranda, with a colonnade supporting arches, overlooks an internal garden cooled by pools and fountains.

right, centre A wealthy town house in Zavareh, built in the Qajar period. The inner court with its multi-lobed pool is a handsome sober design in exposed brick. Around it cluster two storeys of bedrooms and reception rooms.

right, below An ornamental motif in Qajar *kashis*: four tiles combine to form a bouquet of flowers in a wide-mouthed vase. (Private collection)

opposite The Gulistan or Palace of Roses in Tehran, built in the early 19th century. The side elevation of one of the wings (*opposite, above*) draws on the Persian-Timurid tradition of painted tiles and coloured bricks and mosaics to produce a 'Shah 'Abbas Revival' style. Further decorative ceramic covers the shallow domes of an airy room with a central fountain (*opposite, below*).

Qajar Secular Buildings

Houses and palaces survive in a number of towns and cities, though they have often been undervalued, and much of the urban environment has been and continues to be lost to property speculators.

Isfahan, Yazd, Kashan, Tabriz and other cities can still show good examples of this traditional architecture, which reflects the existence of a well-to-do society. At Tabriz, in Azerbaijan, several of these 19th-century 'palaces' have been intelligently restored so that it is now possible to experience what they were like originally. They typically have a façade with a portico of slender columns, in the manner of a *talar*, which may be decorated with carved stucco. Behind the colonnade is an elegant and shady space that leads into the reception room. That room has a glazed window which is sometimes fitted with coloured glass. Carpets and hangings, sofas, cushions and lamps scattered throughout the interior create a luxurious atmosphere. In the tradition of inward-facing houses, the façade looks onto enclosed gardens with pools, which are the the last descendants of the *chahar bagh*.

Yadz and its environs are notable for houses with ventilation towers designed to catch the slightest breeze or to release hot air from the interior (on the high plateaux bordering the deserts of Lut and the Great Kavir it can be extremely hot in summer). Their bristling skyline recalls that of a medieval Italian city.

In Teheran, the Qajar rulers lived in the Gulistan, or Palace of Roses, built at the beginning of the 19th century. Here there are still *kashis* on the façade and mosaics of coloured glazed bricks on the insides of the domes, but there is now a European flavour. The bouquets of flowers are increasingly realistic, and heraldic lions wielding swords symbolic of power decorate the curved pediments and the bases of the columns. (The Gulistan contained the famous Peacock Throne

that Nadir Shah had plundered from the Red Fort in Delhi. Before its destruction it served for the coronation of Persian kings; known from copies, it was a ceremonial high-backed chair entirely encrusted with precious stones, a late Mughal work of ostentatious magnificence in a decadent 'orientalist' style.)

A simpler residence, though for a well-to-do family, survives at Zavareh. The house, built entirely of exposed brick, centres on a lovely octagonal courtyard covered by a dome with a central oculus; a multi-lobed pool below the opening is like the *impluvium* in ancient Roman houses. Around this are two storeys of rooms which open through tall arches onto the small courtyard shaded from the fiery rays of the sun.

Also at Zavareh an example survives of a type of architecture that emerged in the late period to accommodate performances organized by the Shi'ites of scenes from the miraculous lives of the Imams or Imamzadeh. During great feasts and religious commemorations, these sacred mysteries were performed in covered halls big enough to accommodate large crowds. Typically these are vast spaces of plain undecorated brick, in which octagonal piers or cylindrical columns support shallow domes with central oculi, and round or octagonal stages make it easier for the actors to be seen by the audience. They are not strictly speaking secular buildings, but they are closer to secular types than to the specialized structures of mosques and *madrasas*.

Caravanserais and Citadels

Caravanserais were an essential institution in desert regions to ensure communication between one point and another within a territory, and to promote trade over long distances. The Silk Road is especially famous, but in Iran and neighbouring countries there were many routes used by travellers and merchants. To provide safe staging-posts, rulers built hostels along the route, which were fortified to a greater or lesser extent depending on the region. Merchandise, which included foodstuffs, spices, goods and slaves passed along this chain of way-stations, spaced out every 30 kilometres or so – the distance a camel could cover in a day – ensuring that the cities were kept regularly supplied.

In addition, taxes collected on the frontiers of the empire represented an important source of revenue for the state, which thus had an interest in providing secure amenities that would attract large-scale international trade. On the old Khorasan road, near Lasdjerd, there is a relatively sophisticated caravanserai of fired brick with walls strengthened by arcading which must date from the late Safavid period.

Another protective building erected throughout the area of Persian influence is the type of fortress known as *Ark*. The ancient stronghold of Bam in far south-eastern Iran, in the direction of Seistan and near the edge of the deserts of Baluchistan, is now in ruins, but for a long time it was the key to Iran, protecting the region of Kerman against invaders from what is now Pakistan and Afghanistan. Here, in a dominant position, a little citadel grew up, with powerful crenellated walls of mud brick, reinforced by semicircular towers. Overlooking the settlement from a height is a keep, fortified by several outer lines of walls and towers, from which you can look down on the remains of streets and a few ruined mosques and *madrasas* among heaps of collapsed houses. It seems the town was abandoned after a punitive attack in 1794 by the ruler of Iran, Agha Muhammad Qajar, on Loft Ali Khan, ruler of the Zands, who had taken refuge there.

There is another *Ark* at Bukhara. The Shaybanid capital, which occupied a key position on the road to China, had an impressive *glacis* above which, here too, a stronghold was erected, with regular, battered walls. Like all structures made of rammed earth or mud brick, these had to be rebuilt a

number of times, and the walls we see today are relatively recent, but they follow a model of ancient defensive walls that goes back to the time of Alexander, as was shown by the investigation of the remains of Afrasyab (Samarqand).

The structures at the highest point of the *Ark* of Bukhara were reserved for military and administrative institutions. A few buildings made up a sort of palace on a small scale, where the leader could withdraw with his elite corps. Here too was a small mosque, in a prominent position; it has *talar*-like porticoes surrounding a square room with a flat timber ceiling painted with geometrical motifs.

Many of the early strongholds were destroyed during the Mongol invasions in the 13th century and never rebuilt.

above and opposite, top The abandoned city of Bam lies on the edge of the desert in southeastern Iran. The citadel (*above*) makes the most of the height on which it stands, and its walls and towers of mud brick bristling with crenellations were carefully designed to withstand a siege.Looking down on the town from the citadel (*opposite, top*) reveals a ghostly landscape of empty houses and streets.

opposite, centre and below The citadel or *Ark* in the centre of Bukhara, with its battered walls and semicircular towers, offered a place of last resort for the ruler and his court. Its brick architecture looks back to models older than the age of Chinghiz Khan, perhaps to the time of Alexander the Great. Within the citadel is a small mosque (*opposite, below*), in which wooden columns support a wooden ceiling. The forms, traditional in Persian architecture, originated in Achaemenid buildings.

The Khanate of Khiva

top Tombs cluster round the Mausoleum of Pahlavan Mahmud, defender of the Khiva Khanate in the 12th century. The green dome was built in 1918 by Muhammad Rahim Khan over structures dating from the 14th to 18th centuries.

above The Friday Mosque in the walled city is a wooden building in the tradition of hypostyle halls with columns made from tree trunks resting on stone bases. The 212 columns, originally erected in the 10th century, have been restored many times.

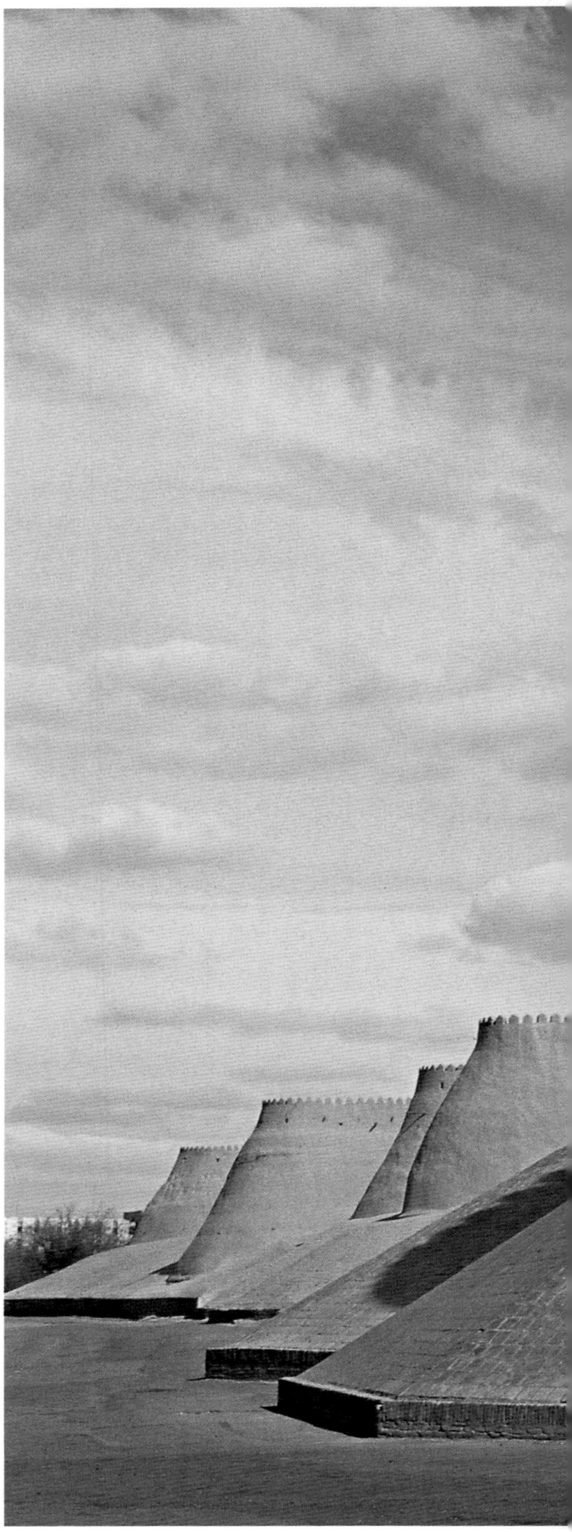

far left The minaret beside the Madrasa of Islam Khoja looks like a Seljuk building, but dates from 1908–10.

left One of the single-pillared *iwans* faced with blue tiles in the harem of the Tash Khwali (Stone Palace), decorated around 1830.

above The city of Khiva retains much of its defensive brick walls with towers spaced out at intervals. The fortifications were the subject of constant maintenance from the 10th century on.

The city of Khiva lies south of the Aral Sea on the northern bank of the Amu Darya. The last capital of Khwarazm, it managed to keep alive the architectural and artistic traditions of the cities on the Silk Road right up to the beginning of the 20th century. Up till then, as in Bukhara, you could see great caravans with between 1,000 and 4,000 camels, who negotiated the Black Sea and the Tarim desert before making their way through Dzungaria and Mongolia and ending in Beijing.

Khiva is enclosed within mud-brick walls similar to those that we have just seen. Its monumental buildings – mosques, *madrasas*, *khanaqahs*, minarets, *talars*, caravanserais, etc. – were erected by Allah Kuli Khan (1825–42), whose wealth allowed him to compete with Bukhara. Though it is entirely 19th-century in date, his architecture is essentially the same as that of the 17th and 18th centuries: forms and techniques went on without a break.

The tallest minaret in the city was built by Esfandyar Khan in 1908–10. Next to it are hypostyle mosques in wood which go back to the medieval period in conception but which were, it seems, rebuilt more than once after Mongol, Timurid and Uzbek invasions. In these buildings the carpentry and carving have a delicate freshness; they are combined with large panels of *kashis*, predominantly blue in colour, in which the Persian technique is maintained. The same successful combination can be seen in the courtyard-centred buildings of the harem (1830) and the wooden *iwans* of the palace of Tash Khwali (1855), as well as in the audience courtyard of the palace of Kohna Ark (1804).

Paradoxically, the 'Persian style' survived everywhere right up to the beginning of our own time: in Iran, the Qajar period went on until 1925; in Uzbekistan, traditional architecture came to an end with the advent of the Bolsheviks in 1920; and in India the last rajas, who had succeeded the Mughals, went on erecting their dream palaces until independence in 1947.

Aurangzeb and the Last Mughals

Shah Jahan, under whom the Mughal dynasty achieved supreme glory, came to a pitiful end. After exercising absolute power for some thirty years, the ruler of the Empire of the Indies fell victim to a family coup engineered by his son, Aurangzeb, who imprisoned his father in the Red Fort at Agra. Shah Jahan was to spend seven dreary years in this palace-prison from which he could see the Taj Mahal, the mausoleum where Mumtaz Mahal already lay and which would soon be his own last resting-place. This impious act has been explained by the fact that Aurangzeb was by then forty years old, and tired of waiting for the imperial throne.

Aurangzeb chose as his official title Alamgir, 'Head of the Universal Empire'; after having his three brothers eliminated, he retained power for almost half a century, from 1658 to 1707, and died at the age of eighty-nine. An able administrator and a brilliant fighter, he spent twenty-six years warring in the Deccan to complete the conquest of southern India, took Golconda, and defeated the sultan of Bijapur. Under him the Mughal empire reached its greatest extent. His expansionist policy provoked revolts, insurrections and uprisings, which he crushed with bloody reprisals.

A fanatic Muslim, Aurangzeb was constantly at war with the Hindu princes, with the Nayaks of Tamilnadu, the Jats of Bharatpur, and the Sikhs of Amritsar. In consonance with his strict Sunni faith, he revived the *jiziya*, or poll tax, imposed on non-Muslims, and applied it to all Hindus and Jains. Also in the purest Sunni tradition, *sharia*, or Islamic law, was rigorously applied. Aurangzeb was austere by disposition, and he enforced Islamic prohibitions against alcohol and prostitution, and banned the cultivation of poppies so as to eliminate opium. The *ulema*, the orthodox theologians, persuaded him to order the destruction of many Hindu temples. His rejection of any frivolity extended to banning music – except for military marches. In many respects he was the exact opposite of his predecessor: where Shah Jahan loved the arts and luxury, courtly pomp and splendid feasts, Aurangzeb demonstrated asceticism, austerity and rigour.

This austere and bigoted man was intent on promoting piety in an atmosphere of national security, and he was all the more determined to impose order because his policies aroused vigorous opposition. The building types he favoured were fortifications and places of worship. The army was in the service of religion. In Lahore in 1673 he built an imposing new entrance to the fort, known after him as the Gate of Alamgir, a bastion with two towers crowned with *chhatris*.

Opposite the gate is the Badshahi Mosque, an immense building covering 3.6 hectares which is the biggest mosque in India and among the largest in the world. It stands on a raised platform:

opposite and right, above and below The immense Badshahi Mosque in Lahore, of 1673. The monumental red sandstone gate (*opposite*) stands at the top of a steep flight of steps. Inside is a square courtyard with a superb marble ablutions fountain (*right, above*). The bulbous dome over the *mihrab*, behind the central *iwan*, is flanked by two smaller domes also of white marble. The prayer hall (*right, below*) is often decorated with carved stucco rather than marble, but the effect is still one of Mughal splendour.

right, centre The Moti Masjid (Pearl Mosque) in the fort at Lahore was Aurangzeb's private oratory. It is build entirely of marble, in a sober style that reflects the austere character of the emperor.

great staircases lead up to a monumental door similar in function to the Buland Darwaza at Fatehpur Sikri, which in turn leads in to a square courtyard measuring 190 x 190 metres surrounded by high walls marked at the corners by three-storeyed minarets. In the centre of the courtyard is a sumptuous white marble ablutions fountain.

The walls and paving of the structure containing the prayer hall are of red sandstone, with the exception of the three beautiful bulbous domes covered in gleaming white marble. Five arches on either side flank the central *iwan*, which is surrounded by a frame delicately decorated with trailing lines and vine scrolls in white. At its corners this building has octagonal towers which echo the four minarets at the corners of the courtyard.

The complexity of the Badshahi Mosque's upper parts looks forward to the Mughal baroque of the 18th century, but in its elements there is nothing that was not already present in the Friday Mosques of Delhi and Agra (ill. pp. 176). In its vast size Aurangzeb's mosque fully reflects its creator's mind: it is on the scale of the empire, which had never before been so vast.

Given its size, the delicacy of the applied decoration is even more surprising; the motifs, however, are rather stiff and cold. Inside, where the other great mosques had marble reliefs here we find stucco, its sinuous shapes outlined in colour which disturbs the unity of the whole.

In the Red Fort in Delhi Aurangzeb built a small oratory for his own use which is known as the Moti Masjid or Pearl Mosque, as in the forts at Agra and Lahore. It should not be confused with the lovely mosque of the same name in Agra (ill. pp. 176–77), however: it is an elaborated version of the Najina Masjid there. The small 'chapel', preceded by a courtyard surrounded by a white marble wall, has three minute naves topped by three exaggeratedly bulbous domes, which are divided into swelling segments emphasized by filets. In their exaggeration and affectation these decorative motifs, which recall the style of the age of

Late works in the Red Fort at Delhi

above left The Moti Masjid (Pearl Mosque), a small oratory built for Aurangzeb in 1622: from the white marble enclosure rise ribbed bulbous domes where Mughal forms are taking on a baroque character.

above right The Shah Burj fountain pavilion, built for Muhammad Shah in 1725, shows the baroque quality of late Mughal architecture. A cascade effect would have spilled down the inclined plane into the multi-lobed pool.

below The Sawann Pavilion, in the gardens, has an arcade of cusped arches supported on exaggeratedly swelling columns with have bulbous bases and lush foliage capitals typical of 18th-century Mughal architecture.

opposite The central room of the Rang Mahal, on the walls of the fort, was cooled by a fountain springing from this carved marble basin on the course of the axial water channel known as Nahr i-Bihisht (River of Paradise).

Louis XIV in France, illustrate the 'baroquization' of Mughal art, apparently under Western influence. Every detail shows how the style was changing: cusped arches now have mouldings that accentuate their edges; we find abaci with lush leaf motifs, where formerly foliage appeared only discreetly.

In the later buildings in the Red Fort at Delhi this overelaboration becomes ever more marked. In the Rang Mahal, or 'Coloured Palace', built in 1725 in the reign of Muhammad Shah (1719–48), we see columns which have an exaggeratedly swelling shape, large bulbous bases decorated with foliage, and floral capitals of complex and overwrought design. The language of Mughal art is transformed by multi-lobed ribbed pools, cascades gushing from the walls, distinctive shallow vaults of *bangla* type, and the use, to decorate walls, of panels with heavy frames. The Rang Mahal forms part of the complex known as the Shah Burj. This includes a tower containing a *noria* or Persian wheel, where oxen walking in a circle turned a mechanism to supply water to the channel known as the Nahr-i Bihisht, or River of Paradise. The same stylistic features recur in the Sawann Pavillon, at the northern end of the Hayat Bakhsh Bagh, a garden of *chahar bagh* type whose name means 'Garden that Gives the Gift of Life'. This architectural management of water – with bubbling cascades, fountains, and pools in complex shapes – reflects the refined lifestyle of the 18th century. This is the Delhi of the last Mughals, burning with its final flames, marked by languid nostalgia and open sensuality. The martial, pious age of Aurangzeb might never have existed.

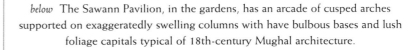

opposite Though it was built at the end of the Mughal period, the tomb is powerful in design, with corner towers and an axial *iwan* crowned by a splendid dome.

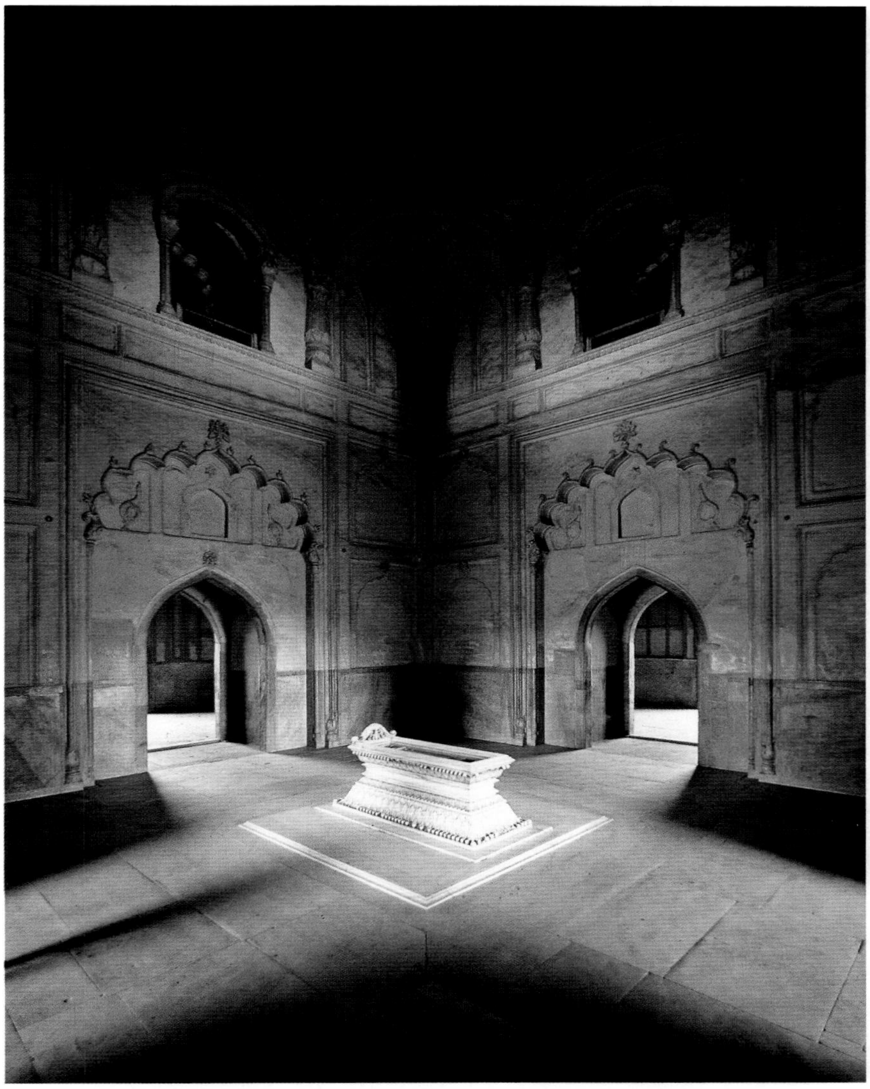

left The cenotaph of Safdar Jang stands in the middle of the square, double-height funerary chamber.

below The vestibule, with a central dome and two buttressing half-domes, is covered with shallow *muqarnas* in stucco, in a striking display of virtuosity right at the end of the Mughal period.

Safdar Jang's Tomb, the Last Mughal Mausoleum

Mughal India was dealt a fatal blow in 1739, when, in a sudden brutal raid, Nadir Shah (1736–47) – the Turkoman adventurer who had usurped the throne of Iran – entered Delhi and sacked the city. When he withdrew he carried off an enormous amount of booty, including splendid works in Mughal baroque style.

Muhammad Shah had foreseen the imminent end of his dynasty, but the true swan song of Mughal art was sounded by the tomb in Delhi of his Grand Vizier, Safdar Jang (later to become nawab of Oudh at Faizabad), completed in 1753. This was long regarded as a variant on the Taj Mahal, whereas in fact it is a bold and coherent building in which the Mughal style is treated with elegance and originality. It repeats neither the freestanding minarets of the Taj Mahal nor the chamfered corners of Humayun's Tomb. It rises boldly from a terrace supported on a handsome arcade, and is crowned by a bulbous dome faced with white marble. At the corners are four small towers surmounted by airy *chhatris*. Two tiers of open loggias buttress the great axial *iwan*, which contains what looks like a ceremonial balcony.

The refinement and rigour of the design are even more striking in the interior spaces. The oval entrance vestibule has a dome with pendentives covered with *muqarnas* of remarkable lightness, whose motifs recur in the two apses that buttress it on either side. The square funerary chamber is unlike those in most of the great Mughal tombs: it is a handsome double-height room with doors decorated with cusping and upper-level openings under an ornate inner dome. Within it stands the sober white marble cenotaph. An empty space separates the inner and outer shells of the dome: the one visible from outside is very tall, in a tradition that includes not only the Taj Mahal in Agra (ill. p. 275) but the Gur-i Amir in Samarqand (ill. p. 57). The setting is a typical *chahar bagh* garden in the best Persian tradition.

Around the time of the tomb's completion, Delhi was struck in 1756 by a new incursion of Afghan tribes. In a pattern going back to the days before the Mughals, these mountain people from the north multiplied their raids for plunder on India, which had lost its cohesion and was unable to defend itself. In the following year, 1757, the English established themselves in Bengal; they occupied Delhi in 1803, and the next half-century was punctuated by recurrent confrontations, notably the war against the Sikhs in 1845 and the Mutiny in 1857, which was bloodily repressed.

Hindu Rajas and the Mughal Style

left, top and below The palace of Amber. It was built to defend a strategic pass, but abandoned in favour of Jaipur during the reign of Jai Singh II in 1727. Within its walls are *chahar bagh* gardens (*left, below*) and a pavilion in Bengali style (*left, top*).

left, centre In the palace of Udaipur, the ornate façade of the Mor Chowk (Peacock Court) dates from the reign of Sangram Singh II in the 18th century. The large-scale figures in the upper tier of decoration, above the peacocks, are related in style to Rajput miniatures.

Udaipur and Lake Pichola. On the right is the City Palace, begun by Udai Singh in the 16th century and continued through the 18th and 19th centuries. On the left is the Jag Nivas Palace of 1746, like a marble boat on the lake.

In the story of the spread of the 'Persian style' there is a very curious chapter, of which the central figures are the rulers of Rajasthan, the mountainous region west of Agra and Delhi, who remained faithful to Hinduism but fostered art, architecture and miniature painting that might be taken for Mughal. Already in the 16th century Rajasthan was showing signs of what was to become one of the most remarkable examples of mimicry in the history of art. Not one of the rajas of these small Hindu states could resist the powerful attraction of the Mughal style, and from the 17th to the early 20th century they challenged one another as to who would build the most beautiful 'Mughal' palace in north-western India.

The Rajput princes long remained independent. After fighting the first Muslim invaders, they put up a heroic resistance to the early Mughals, but after contending with Babur for control of the Delhi Sultanate, the Rajput confederation was defeated at Khanwa in 1527. As part of his attempt to establish peace and concord in India, in 1562 Akbar married a Rajput princess, the daughter of Raja Bihari Mal of Amber, a gesture that succeeded in establishing bonds between the Mughal court and the Hindus of Rajasthan. The Rajputs fought side by side with the Muslim forces and formed a sort of elite corps in the service of the emperor. Raja Man Singh I (1589–1614) of Amber, head of the leading princely family of Rajasthan, supported Akbar's policy of harmonization, and it was he who introduced the Mughal style. Attracted by the setting and by the way of life of the Mughal rulers, the Rajputs created palaces with *diwan-i amm* and *diwan-i khass*, princely apartments, *shish mahals* covered in mirrors, and *chahar bagh* gardens as fine as any of their models.

The palaces of Amber, Jaipur, Udaipur and many others demonstrate the fascination exercised by the Mughals on the splendour-loving Rajput kings, who took from their Muslim overlords not only structural forms and decoration but court ritual and all the symbolism that accompanied the expression of Mughal power.

The maharajas of Amber constructed one of the most beautiful of these palaces in the 17th

and 18th centuries. Set in a fortified pass, above an artificial lake created to supply it with water, from outside it appears an austere citadel; inside, however, is a surprise, for here the buildings can compete in delicacy and charm with the most sumptuous palatine structures in the forts at Lahore, Delhi or Agra, and they have the same baroque flavour as the late works in the Delhi fort. There are a host of buildings dedicated to the symbolic proclamation of royal power: halls where marble columns carved with leaves on their swelling shafts support intersecting arches; elegant cusped arcades; pavilions with curved *bangla* roofs; mirrored halls that reflect the glory and splendour of the ruler; Paradise gardens laid out on terraces or on a peninsula in the artificial lake; and yet more. Everything is in the purest Mughal taste, in the ideal tradition of the 'Persian style'.

The dream palace of the maharana of Udaipur consists of two distinct parts – on the shore of Lake Pichola, and on a number of islands in the lake. The main fortified parts of the vast City Palace, surrounded by high walls punctuated by towers, and provided with a guardhouse, stretch out for a distance of 500 metres along the shore. The complex was begun in the reign of Udai Singh (1537–72) and several times enlarged and embellished. It makes provision for courtly and administrative activities, and also includes, on the upper storeys, idyllic rooms with decoration that stops just short of being mannered.

Out on the lake there are pleasure pavilions like the Jag Nivas, built in 1746, which seems to float on the water like a ship in a mirage. These served for courtly outings, where princely guests enjoyed an enchanted existence. Rivalling one another in splendour and ostentation, they indulged in fantasies where imagination gives form to an unreal world.

opposite, above The decoration in the Diwan i-Khass of the palace at Amber, created by Jai Singh I in the 17th century, rivals that of the Taj Mahal at its finest, both in the shallow carving of flowers in white marble and in the *pietra dura* work.

opposite, below The façade of the Diwan i-Khass in the palace at Jaipur, built by Jai Singh II, seems to have three storeys of rooms, but on the top floor there is nothing behind the *jalis* except the sky.

above Detail of the Peacock Gate of the palace at Jaipur. The peacock symbolizes immortality (like the Persian *simurgh*) and the divine nature of the Hindu rulers of Rajasthan.

Observatories in Jaipur and Delhi

The shahs of Iran were passionately interested in astrology and astronomy: an observatory was built at Nishapur in 1074; the Il-Khans built another, for Nasr ad-Din at-Tusi, at Maragheh around 1259; and Ulugh Beg (1448–49), the Timurid ruler of Samarqand, built a vast centre for the study of the heavens of which the enormous instruments had an architectural character (see pp. 84–85). These giant observatories were to provide sextants and astrolabes ten, twenty, or a hundred times larger than those currently in use, so as to obtain measurements that were ten, twenty, or a hundred times more precise. The aim was to track the movement of the planets and the signs of the zodiac more accurately, so as to draw up more reliable horoscopes.

Since the days of Graeco-Roman antiquity, astrology had been important for rulers: it served to legitimize their authority by enabling them supposedly to predict the future by reading in the stars the fates of men, and especially the fate of the ruler himself. No major decision – to found a city, set out on a journey, sign a treaty, declare war, engage in battle, etc. – was taken without consulting the court astrologer as to whether the heavens were propitious or unpropitious for the projected date. The Mughals, who belonged to the Persian-Timurid tradition (itself partly based on the culture of antiquity) and were familiar with the Hindu traditions of *mantra* and *yantra*, had similar concerns. Yet it was the Hindu rajas and not the Mughals who took practical steps to pursue this 'scientific' quest: at a relatively late period, they built extraordinary observatories for themselves and for their Mughal overlords.

The dream was realized by Jai Singh II (1699–1743). The Amber court had moved to Jaipur, and there, beginning in 1728, he built a series of gigantic 'machines' in a special area set aside for the study of the sky. His constructions followed on from apparatuses devised in the West by Tycho Brahe at Uranienborg in 1576, and further developed in Leiden in 1632, in Paris in 1667, in Greenwich in 1675, and in Berlin in 1705 – for Jai Singh II knew not only the works of Islamic scholars but European scientific publications, of which he obtained copies to study.

The instruments that he built of masonry in Jaipur are among the most disconcerting creations in all cultural and scientific history, like buildings in a fantasy world, with graduated surfaces inscribed on marble, curved 'wings', spherical and cylindrical sections – hemispheres half-buried in the ground, openwork cylinders that stand out like crowns against the sky, inclined discs, sighting instruments designed to spot the signs of the zodiac, enormous dials, and gnomons tens of metres tall. In these instruments, the dreams of ancient scholars became reality: through Arab scholars and translators, works including Ptolemy's

opposite and right, above Within the Jantar Mantar, the great observatory in Delhi begun by Jai Singh II for Muhammad Shah in 1734, is the Ram Yantra, with its three tiers of arcades that make it look like an amphitheatre. Some 20 metres in diameter and centred on a graduated pillar, it enabled observers to study the movement of the stars across the sky.

left, centre and below The Jantar Mantar in Jaipur was begun in 1728 by Jai Singh II. In the general view (*below*), the instruments in the foreground are the Rasi Valaya Yantra, which served to follow the movement of the signs of the zodiac. The Jai Prakas (*centre*) comprises concave hemispheres where astrologers could go down into the spaces between the marble sections.

Almagest, Euclid's *Elements*, Plato's *Timaeus*, Geminius's *Isagog*, the *Phainomena* of Aratus and Cicero's essays on divination became part of the heritage of Islamic science, on which the observatory of Jaipur was based, like those in Iran and Transoxiana.

The Mughal emperor Muhammad Shah became intrigued by the work of Jai Singh II and asked him to build a similar observatory in Delhi, on an even larger scale: this was the Jantar Mantar, begun in 1734. With its enormous 'machinery', its openwork towers, its concave hemispheres within which observers could move about, it seems a futuristic vision. Its structures reflect not only a scientific system that led to a better understanding of the universe, but also a society that was fascinated by geometry and by fate. The last representatives of the declining Mughal dynasty founded all their hopes of renewal on the stars: scrutinizing the configurations of heaven, they hoped to see signs of a fundamental change of direction, and to be assured that the future was not black.

Alas, history did not confirm their hopes, but the masterpieces they left behind still move aesthetes and all who are fascinated by the marriage of arts and sciences.

Postscript
The Primacy of Architecture in the 'Persianized' World

From our explorations of the masterpieces of Iran, Khorasan, Transoxiana, Afghanistan, Pakistan and India, on the long journey from Tabriz to Agra via Isfahan, Bukhara, Samarqand, Lahore and Delhi, one thing stands out, and that is the importance throughout of the 'Persian style'.

In the story of the influence of the art and culture of Iran, architecture plays a pre-eminent role – architecture not merely as building, but as a way of thinking about and representing the world, a system of reference. It reveals a civilization's philosophy and conditions a person's place in the universe; it is the cultural web that a civilization spins around itself, and the framework within which it blossoms.

Taken in this sense, architecture is essential to many other forms of art – painting, calligraphy, manuscript painting, and decoration, where both colour and sculpture are involved (in *muqarnas*, interlace, capitals, etc.).

The spatial vocabulary of the 'Persian style' includes a number of original inventions. Chief among these is the *iwan*, which features in many buildings of the Persian world. As a space it is neither indoors nor outdoors. It need not be a passage: it can provide a setting for theological instruction or for a display of majesty. As a key accessory of thought and ritual, it enriched architectural syntax and soon attracted decoration, in the form of a sumptuous frame that enhanced its monumental shadowy recess.

To the feature of the courtyard, which goes back to the very first mosque founded in Medina by the Prophet Muhammad, Iran added the four *iwans* that govern the cruciform plan derived from the *chahar bagh*. Through this division the structure of the world, based on the four Springs and the four Rivers of Paradise, was made manifest. The physical structure of the mosque could now be interpreted in transcendent terms.

We have seen the importance of the Persian four-centered arch as an ingredient of the style. It was more than a mere technical feature: it was the bearer of symbolic meaning, to such an extent that it was imitated even in areas where masons were technically incapable of constructing it (e.g. in the Quwwat al-Islam Mosque in Delhi). Particular forms and spaces developed under the Il-Khans in Iran and the Timurids of Samarqand were diffused through conquest on a continental scale. Individual empires might be short-lived, but they gave birth to an art which often proved infinitely more durable than they themselves, and which still moves us today, after more than half a millennium.

It is extraordinary to think that the 'Persian style' produced its two most distinguished masterpieces in the same decade of the 17th century, in the reigns of Shah 'Abbas and Shah Jahan, 3,000 kilometres apart: the Mosque of the Imam in Isfahan, with its sumptuous bulbous dome covered with turquoise ceramic (ill. pp.136–37), and, far away to the east, the Taj Mahal (ill. pp. 274–75), with its gleaming marble dome that draws all eyes to the Mughal city of Agra.

What makes this 'Persianized' architecture recognizable everywhere is the meaning that underlies it. In Iran it aimed at more than merely local expression, and took on elements that made it part of a larger history. Some features come from Arabic Islam: the *mihrab* and the *minbar*, the minaret and the ablutions fountain. To these were added the *talar*, whose light and airy structure goes back to the Achaemenids, and the *chahar tak*, a dome resting on four supports derived from Sasanian architecture, whose juxtaposed repetition was to give rise to the domed hypostyle hall: the pre-Islamic past lived on into the future. Thus Persian architecture has its roots deep in history and in 'national' traditions.

In addition to the built structures, there is the decoration applied to them: here Iran took colours and motifs and infused them with a brilliant new life. As we have seen, Persian art stands in the tradition of Sasanian and Achaemenid art, from which it took both the techniques of sculpture and stucco mural decoration and the plant forms depicted (palmettes, flowers, vines, etc.) which were known before the arrival of Islam. Decoration gradually spread out from the *mihrab* and furnishings until under the Timurids and Safavids no surface was left unadorned.

First came abstract themes – elements repeated rhythmically, interlace, rinceaux and arabesques; these were then joined by floral motifs, prompted by the spiritual vision of the mosque as a centre of life, an image of Paradise, and a pathway to resurrection. In this respect Persian, Timurid and Mughal ornamental panels have a profound kinship. This vision was soon projected downward as well, as in carpets geometrical motifs were replaced by multi-coloured flowers on a plain background. The knotted carpets of Tabriz, Kerman, Agra and Lahore competed as to which could best echo underfoot the great spiralling vine scrolls on the walls and the curved surfaces of domes. Here too, styles came to have so much in common that with 17th- and 18th-century carpets it is sometimes difficult to tell at first glance whether a piece comes from Iran, Anatolia (Ushak), Ottoman Cairo, Pakistan or India. In this genre, Turkey joined its neighbours in a profound artistic union.

In miniatures too, Persian influence created an aesthetic community that extended from Tabriz to Shiraz, from Baghdad to Isfahan, from Mashhad to Herat, and that included the school of Istanbul and that of Agra, so that (as with carpets) it is not always possible to identify the origin of a manuscript.

My concern in this study has been to draw attention to a great aesthetic impulse whose effects can be felt throughout an entire region of the globe. Notions of 'national identity' have no place here, but one must acknowledge the immense influence exercised by the Persian world.

Iran is animated by its own particular way of thinking, its own philosophy, its own language and its own literature. In the arts its contribution has been decisive, and its distinctive approach to science and learning should not be underestimated. Yet this legitimate recognition of its genius does not in any way justify nationalistic or religious claims: the artistic contribution of Iran extends well beyond the Islamic sphere, and springs from infinitely older and deeper sources, demonstrating how a particular identity becomes manifest in history, regardless of – or despite – any specific religious conditions. It is this deep-lying constant that I have sought to trace through an interdisciplinary study independent of any current movement or regime, regardless of that regime's assumptions and doctrines.

What matters, surely, is that 'vital instinct', and the fact that we owe to it the rich heritage of the 'Persian style' over a period of a thousand years – a heritage which we must always be prepared to defend. From Isfahan to Agra, an inspired art has created marvels which, now more than ever, are a source of wonder and admiration.

Part II

KEY MONUMENTS IN THE PERSIAN STYLE

p. 212 Timurid tile mosaic on the Friday Mosque in Isfahan.

pp. 212–13 Tile decoration of the Friday Mosque.

above Aerial view of the mosque, largely built under the Seljuqs in the 11th century. Hypostyle halls roofed with small domes surround the court with its four traditional *iwans*.

opposite, above Detail of a Timurid tile mosaic in relief on the southern *iwan*.

opposite, below The court, looking towards the prayer hall, from Pascal Coste, *Les Monuments modernes de la Perse* (1867).

Isfahan: The Friday Mosque, from the Seljuqs to the Timurids

Among the many Seljuq monuments in Iran, the most remarkable is probably the Friday Mosque in Isfahan, which stands in the heart of the old city, at the beginning of the sinuous covered bazaar that runs to the edge of the new Maidan of Shah 'Abbas (map p. 135). The building as we see it today reflects campaigns and alterations carried out over a number of years, but chiefly in the Seljuq period, when the city was for the first time the capital of Iran.

A mosque on the site had been built under the 'Abbasids, in the 9th–10th centuries, but in a simpler form, consisting of vast hypostyle spaces around a square court and covering an area of 130 x 85 metres. The main prayer hall seems to have been 7 bays deep with 19 piers in each row, hence with more than 120 brick columns; in addition, there were halls 3 bays deep at the sides and, to the northeast, a secondary hall with 5 bays, making a total of some 300 piers. The scale was justified by Isfahan's wealth as a central oasis in the Persian plateau, with a large and active population.

By the time of the Seljuqs, Persian builders had become more sophisticated in their handling of space and their knowledge of technology, and their new skill was displayed to the full in this monumental structure. Under the influence of the circle around Nizam al-Mulk, the distinctive features of the Persian mosque were incorporated: the court was given four *iwans* facing each other in pairs on the two axes that cross at the centre of the ablutions fountain. These *iwans*, set within great emblematic frames, are each treated in a different way. The northern one has a simple pointed tunnel vault, almost 25 metres deep; the eastern has a more elaborate system of buttressing, in which arches mingle with small domes; and the southern one, which leads to the domed prayer hall, is framed by two cylindrical minarets and vaulted with *muqarnas*. The western one is the most unusual and complex of all, with a large-scale *muqarnas* vault in which the juxtaposed spherical triangles are not only decorative but functional in a very original way, making up a system as ingenious as that of Buckminster Fuller's 20th-century geodesic domes.

The same principle of spherical triangles is used in the mosque's two domed halls, both of

which predate the western *iwan*. One of the domes, 14 metres in diameter, is over the space in front of the *mihrab* and was designed by the architect Abul Fath. The other, 10 metres in diameter, known as the Gunbad-i Khaki, or 'Dome of Earth', covers a northern extension of the mosque which was built to house the tomb of Malik Shah (who died in 1092) or his wife. In both cases the passage from square plan to circular dome is resolved with remarkable logic: in each corner a small squinch supports a tunnel vault extending inward; that vault is flanked by little vaults in the form of spherical triangles; and the four elements taken together reduce the square plan to an octagon that supports the curve of the dome. The spherical triangles resemble those of the western *iwan*: the architect has taken a rational and effective solution and generalized its application to the point of

left The southern *iwan*, crowned by two minarets, is reflected in a pool with multi-lobed basin.

below The façades of the two-storeyed arcade that surrounds the courtyard are covered with coloured tile decoration which has been restored many times.

opposite Detail of a Timurid gate, with decorations signed by Sayyed Mahmud and dated 1447. They are notable for the fineness of the scrollwork and inscriptions, showing the art of coloured mosaic at a peak of virtuosity. The Persian arch frames a tympanum with lush arabesques.

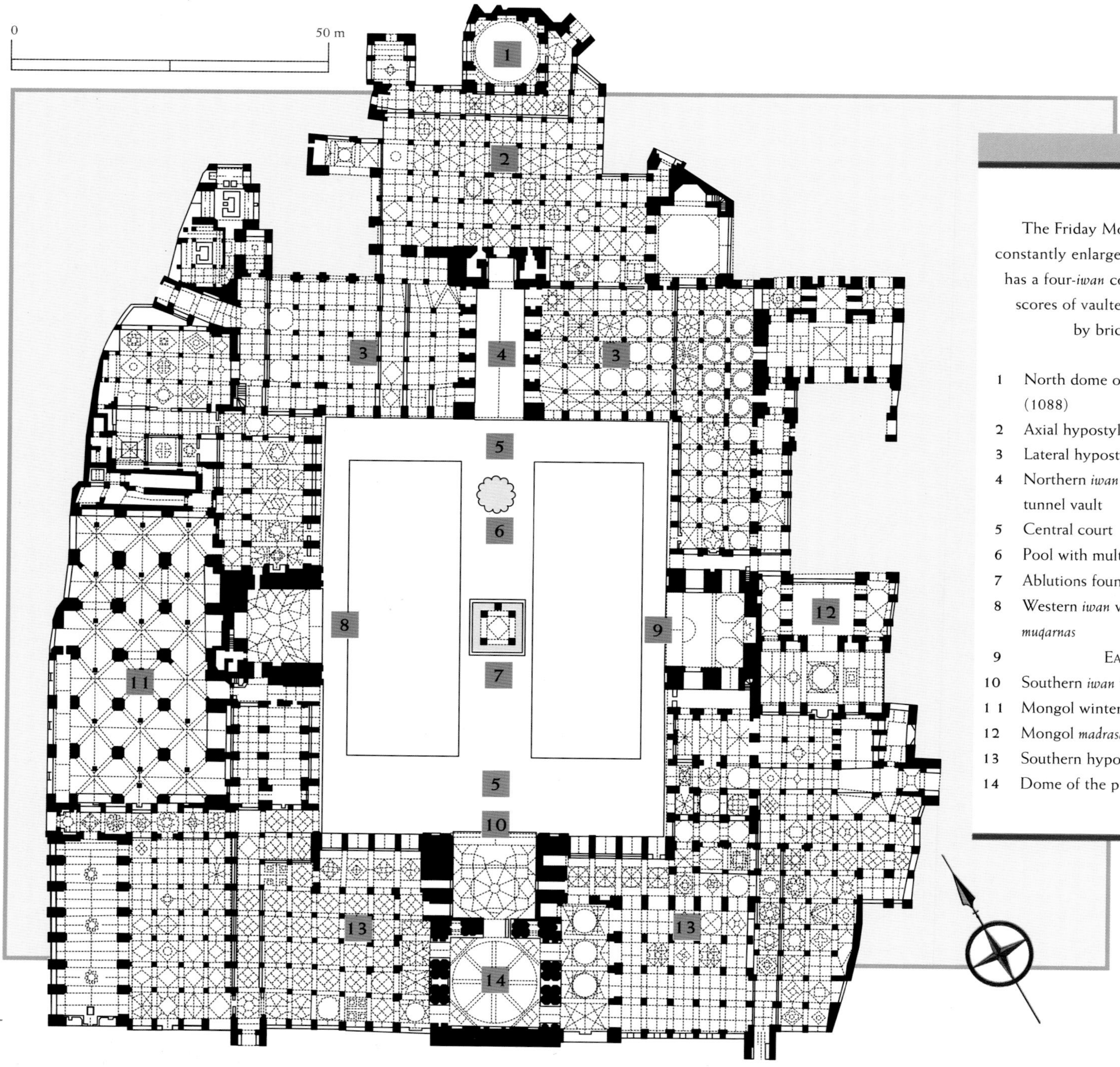

Key

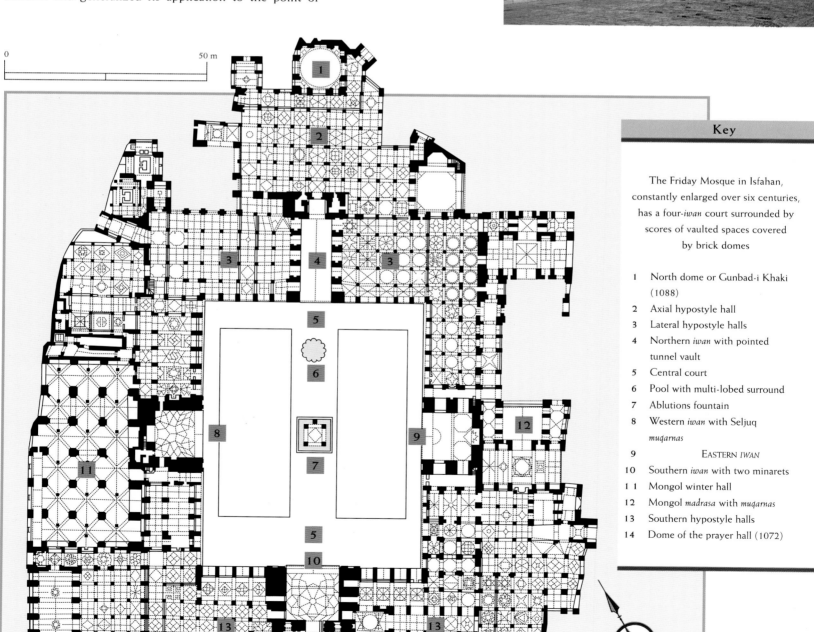

The Friday Mosque in Isfahan, constantly enlarged over six centuries, has a four-*iwan* court surrounded by scores of vaulted spaces covered by brick domes

1 North dome or Gunbad-i Khaki (1088)
2 Axial hypostyle hall
3 Lateral hypostyle halls
4 Northern *iwan* with pointed tunnel vault
5 Central court
6 Pool with multi-lobed surround
7 Ablutions fountain
8 Western *iwan* with Seljuq *muqarnas*
9 Eastern *iwan*
10 Southern *iwan* with two minarets
11 Mongol winter hall
12 Mongol *madrasa* with *muqarnas*
13 Southern hypostyle halls
14 Dome of the prayer hall (1072)

opposite Direct light on the western *iwan*, a Seljuq masterpiece. Composed of large triangular *muqarnas* that buttress one another, this displays a typically Persian brickwork technique.

right, above The *mihrab* of the Mongol *madrasa* to the east of the mosque, built in 1366, takes up the theme of *muqarnas* on a smaller scale. Coloured ceramic decoration is here contrasted to natural brick.

right, below Part of a hypostyle hall with brick columns. The square bays between the four-centered arches are covered with a great variety of domes. Altogether, the mosque has hundreds of small domes.

using it to articulate a vast concave surface. The western *iwan* has a further interesting structural feature: on the back it displays a remarkable composition based on ribs that serve to stabilize it.

The same fertility of invention and experimentation appears in the small domes that cover the hypostyle halls: there are scores, if not hundreds, of these, and they show the extraordinary delight that Persian builders took in playing endless variations on the theme of a dome resting on four arches, which André Godard associated with the ancient Sasanian formula of the *chahar tak* or kiosk.

The mosque has winter halls that are enclosed, to provide shelter from the harsh climate of the high plateaux. Here too Persian technology found new solutions. The hall next to the western *iwan*, built under the Mongol Il-Khans in the 14th century, has large transverse arches supporting a low roof in such a way as to allow light to come in from the side without weakening the structure; at the back of the room is a beautiful carved plaster *mihrab* created for Il-Khan Öljeytu in 1310 (ill. p. 47, below). To the south of the western *iwan* is a squat, dark room built in the Timurid period which seems even more suited to its function as a winter hall (ill. p. 46). Massive pointed arches spring directly from the ground and support great pointed vaults with slightly concave triangular webs. The room is lit only dimly, through alabaster slabs set in the apex of each bay.

In the Timurid period the architects of Isfahan, like those of Samarqand and Bukhara in Transoxiana, made use of sumptuous coloured tile mosaics to decorate the surfaces of their buildings. Vines and interwoven branches strewn with flowers created a perpetual garden, transforming the mosque into an image of

Paradise. A particularly notable example of this is a doorway facing the courtyard, dating from 1447 and signed by its maker, Sayyed Mahmud, who was legitimately proud of his creation (ill. p. 217).

Timurid decoration, with its profusion of luxuriant vine trails, its kufic and thuluth inscriptions, and its geometric borders, perfectly suited the virtuosity of Persian mosaicists. Further instances of their work can be seen on the southern *iwan*, with its supremely elegant vases symbolizing immortality.

left, above and centre The ceramic decoration of the western *iwan* combines elements of different periods. Floral and geometrical forms are juxtaposed to later Shi'ite inscriptions which use stylized forms of the names of Allah, Muhammad and Ali.

left, below A palmette motif in relief on an 18th-century panel in the courtyard.

opposite Timurid decoration on the right jamb of the southern *iwan*. The panel on the left has a vase symbolic of immortality from which spring the fronds of a Tree of Life. The motifs include paeonies, bellflowers, stylized carnations and vine scrolls.

opposite The Qutb Minar, begun in 1199, seen from the court of the Quwwat al-Islam Mosque. This immense 'victory tower' celebrated the triumph of Islam over the local Hindu and Jain cults in the region conquered by Qutb ud-Din Aibak

left, above Detail of the Qutb Minar showing Qur'anic inscriptions and floral patterns running round the alternately sharp and curved surfaces of the lowest storey.

left, centre The mosque combines elements re-used from demolished Hindu and Jain temples with imitations of great Persian arches, which local craftsmen working for the Muslims reproduced in the Indian technique of corbelling.

left, below The courtyard façade of the mosque has delicate arabesque and geometrical ornament. In the art of carving, Hindu sculptors were masters.

Delhi: The Quwwat al-Islam Mosque, the First Islamic Monument in India

Construction of the great Quwwat al-Islam ('Might of Islam') Mosque began in 1193, almost immediately after the Muslim capture of Delhi, It was the first Islamic building in India. Started by Qutb ud-Din Aybak, the successor of Muhammad of Ghur and first sultan of Delhi, it is flanked by an extraordinary minaret, the Qutb Minar, constructed in 1199. The mosque, repeatedly enlarged, reached gigantic proportions: 250 metres wide by 150 metres deep, it is the largest place of worship on the subcontinent.

Initially it was a courtyard mosque, oriented to the west, with a *qibla* 45 metres wide and 64 metres deep. Three sides of the courtyard are bordered by hypostyle halls 3 bays deep and 20 piers long; to the east is a supplementary prayer hall 3 bays deep and 10 piers long; to the west is the main prayer hall, which is 4 bays deep and 10 piers long. In all there are 240 piers. These are very unusual for a mosque in being re-used elements from demolished Hindu and Jain temples – 27 temples in all, pulled down with the help of elephants. The piers are monoliths covered with carving, where any figurative motifs have been defaced. With this gesture, the Muslims clearly proclaimed the victory of the new religion over the beliefs of the past.

The great arcade in front of the prayer hall shows the uncertainty of the architects and the technical ignorance of local masons. It is associated with the tradition that three years after the building was finished Qutb ud-Din built a tall façade on the courtyard with five large pointed-arched openings. This symbolic arcade reproduces on a much-enlarged scale the appearance of a *mihrab* indicating the direction of Mecca and representing the presence of God. Here the architectural notion of the *iwan*, associated with the idea of prayer, makes its first appearance in India. The local masons in Delhi, however, did

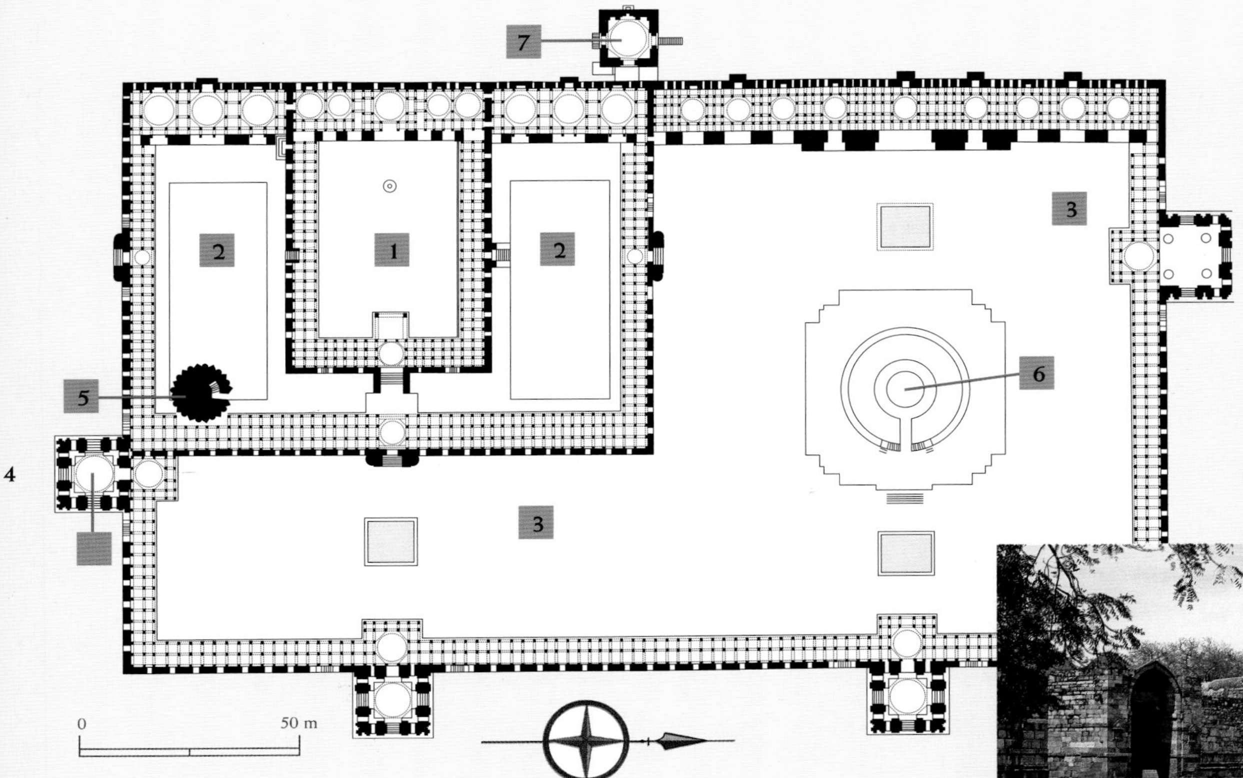

Key

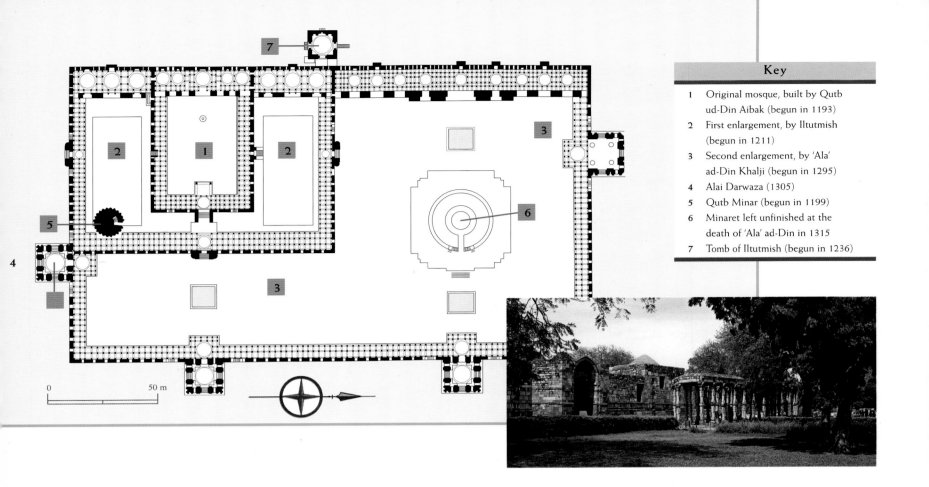

1 Original mosque, built by Qutb ud-Din Aibak (begun in 1193)
2 First enlargement, by Iltutmish (begun in 1211)
3 Second enlargement, by 'Ala' ad-Din Khalji (begun in 1295)
4 Alai Darwaza (1305)
5 Qutb Minar (begun in 1199)
6 Minaret left unfinished at the death of 'Ala' ad-Din in 1315
7 Tomb of Iltutmish (begun in 1236)

not know how to build a true arch composed of voussoirs: instead, they confected the arches by means of rows of corbelled horizontal courses. What mattered – the shape – came through clearly. The central one of the five openings, which is almost twice as high and wide as those on either side, recalls an *iwan* in a Persian mosque. The arches also have the distinctive four-centered shape of the Persian arch; in addition, the shape tapers slightly towards the top.

This screen-wall is enhanced by a rich carved ornamentation: the courtyard façade is covered with Greek key, rinceaux, decorative mouldings, and borders with fine Arabic inscriptions.

A similar engagement between symbolism and technique operated when it came to building the domes in front of the *mihrabs* in the *qibla*. It had become customary to have a dome above the prayer niche, like a sort of honorific canopy. In India, however, the same unfamiliarity with shaped courses meant that this had to be a 'false dome', achieved by means of corbelling. Again, the eye was deceived, and meaning preserved.

A major mosque requires a minaret spectacular enough to serve as a sort of lighthouse, signalling its presence from afar to the faithful summoned by the muezzin's call. The Qutb Minar is not just a minaret: it is also a victory tower, commemorating Muslim supremacy in India, and it stands separate from the mosque proper, like the famous minaret of the Great Mosque of Samarra. The Qutb Minar is essentially circular in plan, and consists of a number of slightly conical superimposed sections separated by projecting balconies corbelled out on *muqarnas*. Originally there were four stages. The lowest section was finished when Qutb ud-Din died; the next three levels of the original four-storeyed design were completed by his successor. The lower three of those original levels survive, each with a different design: in the lowest, rounded and angular vertical shafts alternate; in the next, all the shafts are rounded; the third is star-shaped. The top two sections, which are cylindrical, are later additions. The total height of the tower is 72.5 metres; the diameter at the base is 15 metres, tapering to 3 metres at the top. Bands with Qur'anic inscriptions in Arabic-Persian script run around the circumference, providing the only decoration apart from the *muqarnas*.

After the death of Qutb ud-Din in 1210, another career soldier took control of the Sultanate: Iletmich or Iltutmish, who reigned from 1211 to 1235. The mosque proved too small for the rapidly expanding population of the Muslim capital of India, and Iltutmish decided to enlarge it. Between 1211 and 1229 its surface area more than tripled, from 3,000 square metres to almost 10,000, and the mosque eventually covered an area 115 metres wide and 85 metres deep. Courtyards were added on both sides, a new pillared hall linked them across the front, and there was a new entrance. One effect was to bring the Qutb

above, left, and opposite
Monolithic columns from Hindu and Jain temples destroyed by the Muslim conquerors are used for the halls of the mosque. They retain their original decoration, and form a link of a sort between past and present.

Minar, to the southeast, within the new enclosure. Three secondary *mihrabs* were created on either side beyond the original *qibla*. The shape became a transverse rectangle, more in keeping with the traditional format. The Turkish-Afghan rulers of India now had a great mosque worthy of their power.

The idea of a monumental tomb had at first shocked the guardians of Muslim ritual, since the creed was initially egalitarian, and Muhammad himself had condemned the construction of tombs. Later, however, an exception was made for the tomb of the Caliph al-Muntasir in Samarra, built in 862–64 at the special request of his mother (who was of Byzantine origin, and Orthodox). Thus the 'Abbasid period saw the earliest Islamic mausoleum. Others were to follow, especially in India, where the first Islamic tomb was that of Sultan Iltutmish, built in 1236 next to the Quwwat al-Islam Mosque. The structure is entirely of red sandstone. In plan it is a square which measures 13 x 13 metres on the outside. Inside, the square turns octagonal, with squinches to support a dome that has now disappeared. Four arches at a 45-degree angle bridge the corners above the squinches, and alternate with arches framing slightly recessed spaces. The interior is a 9 x 9 x 9-metre cube, alluding to the Ka'ba in Mecca. In the centre is a

The Mausoleum of Sultan Iltutmish, begun in 1236

The *mihrab* niche (*left, above*) is set within an outer frame carved with Qur'anic inscriptions and rich ornamental motifs; its decoration and polygonal colonnettes supporting a cusped arch echo those within. The square funerary chamber has lost its dome, which was supported on complex squinches (*above*). In the centre stands the marble cenotaph of the sultan (*left, below*), its translucent whiteness contrasting with the building's red sandstone walls. All the walls are covered with delicate geometrical carved decoration.

carved white marble cenotaph, and on the west wall is a handsome *mihrab*.

The internal surfaces are covered with an elaborate decoration of geometrical grids, interlace and arabesques, and texts alternately in kufic and thuluth scripts. The *mihrab* stands in a niche with a cusped arch supported on two small columns; within that is a rectangular frame, and within that is yet another cusped arch on colonnettes: the intention was to create the illusion of an infinite succession of gates – smaller and smaller and farther and farther away – leading to the divine presence.

The large arches of the octagon are still constructed by means of corbelling, showing how slowly Hindu craftsmen learned the technique of the true arch. The true vault was unknown until the beginning of the following century, when it made its appearance in the gate known as Alai Darwaza, erected in 1305 to the south of the mosque.

The last enlargement of the mosque was a titanic undertaking ordered by Sultan 'Ala' ad-Din Khalji of the Khalji dynasty and realized between 1296 and 1315. The building again tripled in area, to 225 metres wide by 130 deep, or a total of 30,000 square metres. The enlargement was not carried out symmetrically around the existing building: rather, it extended to the north and east. The *qibla* wall was lengthened 110 metres to the north, and given nine further *mihrabs*, making a total of twenty.

On the south side of the new perimeter wall, the superb gate known as Alai Darwaza gives access to the courtyard. This is a cubic structure surmounted by a dome; in the jambs of the doorway are a pair of columns, one of red sandstone and one of white marble, with details in yellow lime-

The Alai Darwaza, of 1305, leads from the south into the prayer space of the Quwwat al-Islam Mosque. A square building covered by a dome, it makes masterful use of coloured stone and strictly controlled geometric decoration.

opposite, above A white marble *jali* with patterns based on the hexagon creates a subtle counterpoint with the rhythms of the ornament carved in the stone. The coherent organization of the Alai Darwaza affirms the decorative authority of the Islamic style.

opposite, below Identity of forms and contrast of colours in the jamb of the main door. This visual dialectic is the basis of the art of the Delhi Sultanate; it continued under the Mughals and even under the Hindu rulers of Rajasthan.

stone. The decoration of the building as a whole is strictly geometrical, with blind rectangular panels in red and white frames at the upper level, and narrow pointed windows below. The coloured stone is minutely carved with garlands, interlace and arabesques, and with inscriptions that stand out in relief. The octagonal colonnettes have identical bases and capitals, alluding to the vase symbolic of immortality.

As has already been said, in the Alai Darwaza the Hindu stonemasons showed that they had mastered the technique of the true arch, with radiating voussoirs. Over the windows, the pointed arches have cusped edges that give a delicate effect. In the openings are *jalis*, pierced stone screens on the model of the openwork windows of Hindu temples. The motifs are based on the octagon and square, and on the hexagon and six-pointed star.

In the centre of the new courtyard of the extended mosque is the base of an enormous minaret, begun by 'Ala' ad-Din Khalji. This was to have been a colossal structure, 25 metres in diameter and 120–150 metres tall, but it was never finished.

There was no longer any thought of re-using elements from Hindu temples: here, at the beginning of the 14th century, Islamic architecture and ornament were fully mature. The play of vigorously contrasting colours and geometric patterns worked into the stone creates a perfect harmony – a success due as much to the overall conception of volumes and façades as to the strictly managed details of the polychrome decoration.

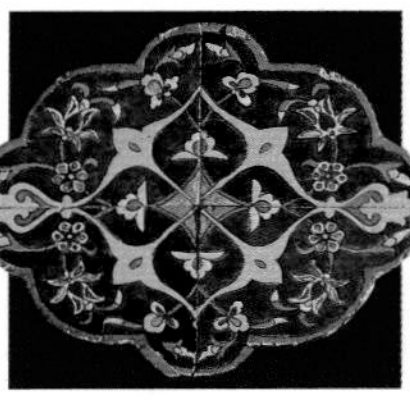

Samarqand: the Registan, a Timurid Royal Square

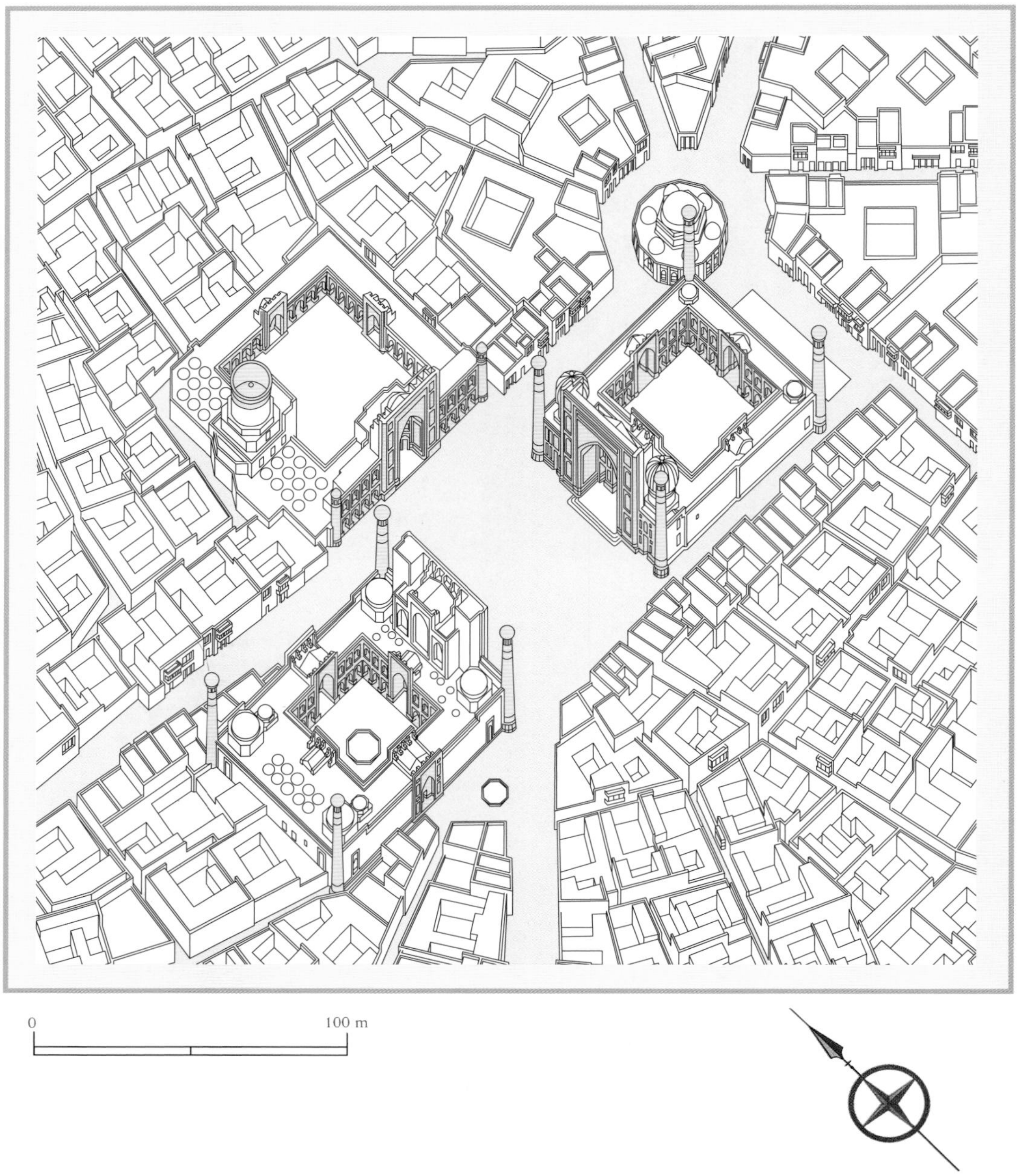

left, top Tile decoration in the Shir Dor Madrasa.

left, centre Axonometric view of the Registan. Its three great buildings were erected between the 15th and 17th centuries. Clockwise from lower left, they are the Madrasa of Ulugh Beg, the Madrasa-Mosque of Tilla Kari, and the Shir Dor Madrasa. (Courtesy Klaus W. Herdeg)

left A view of the square from a similar angle, showing the effect of the tall pishtaqs. One of the minarets of the Madrasa of Ulugh Beg is just visible at the left; in the centre is the Tilla Kari Madrasa, with the dome of its mosque; on the right is the Shir Dor Madrasa.

Two of the four *iwans* that punctuate of the courtyard façades of the *madrasa* begun in 1417 by the astronomer and future Timurid sultan Ulugh Beg. The unified handling of symmetrical forms and the use of two arcaded storeys are features that were to be taken up by the Shaybanids in Bukhara and the Safavids in Iran.

The Registan is a vast open space in the centre of the Timurid city of Samarqand, measuring 70 x 85 metres. It is given a formal and grand character by the fact that three of its sides are occupied by buildings that are similar in size and virtually identical in design, almost like three wings of a palace, with symmetrical façades marked on the central axis by a large *iwan*. Two of these face each other like mirror images. This is the heart of the city founded by Timur, the setting for the flamboyant ceremonies and pomp of the lords of the steppe, where troops drawn from the tribes of Transoxiana passed on parade.

This splendid space was conceived as a unit from the start, although it was not built all at once, and the three buildings we see today came into being over a period of 230 years. The earliest, which determined the scale, appearance and layout of the two that followed, is the great Madrasa of Ulugh Beg, begun in 1417 (see above, p. 74). Opposite this, on the other side of the square, is the *madrasa* known as Shir Dor, of 1619. Finally, the north side is closed by the combined Madrasa and Mosque of Tilla Kari, of 1647. But the character of the space had already been determined: for where the Shir Dor Madrasa now stands, Ulugh Beg had built a *khanaqah*

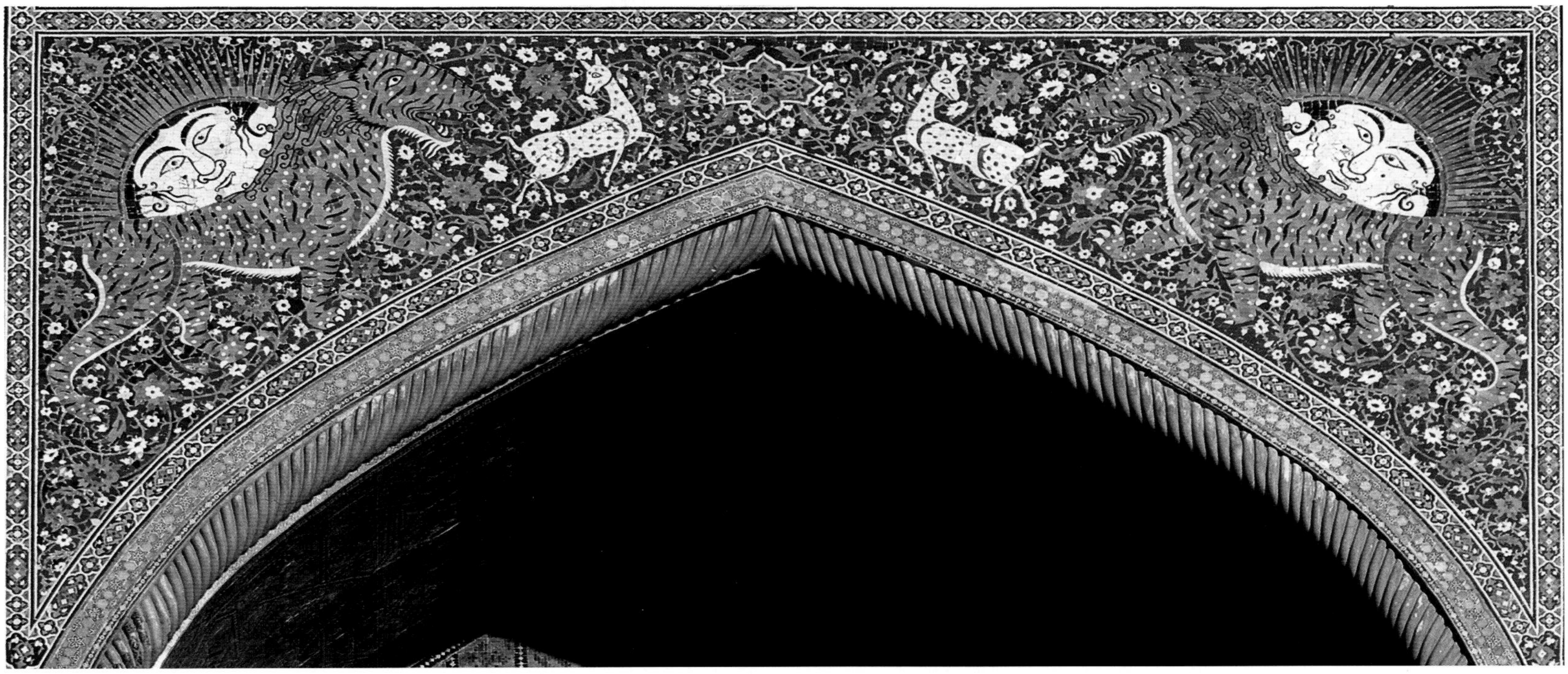

The Shir Dor Madrasa, built in 1619 by masters from Bukhara

opposite Ribbed domes rise above the two arcaded storeys of the courtyard.

above The *pishtaq* displays two 'solar lions' chasing gazelles, using ancient symbols from the Persian bestiary – in defiance of the prohibition on the depiction of animals – to express the omnipresent power of Islam.

below The ceramic decoration here, as on other Timurid buildings in Samarqand, has been restored in modern times; typically it combines tile mosaic, *kashis* of Persian origin, and natural brick.

that faced his *madrasa*; and at the back of the square, where the Tilla Kari Madrasa-Mosque is now, was the caravanserai of Mirza, which was demolished to make way for it.

The Timurids, whose energy is reflected in Ulugh Beg's grand creations, were followed by the Shaybanids, Uzbeks who ruled from 1450 to 1599 before succumbing to the Persian Safavids. At the beginning of the 17th century, Turkish-Mongol power became established in Bukhara, with Nadir Diwan Begi and then Abd al-Aziz Khan.

It is in this last period that the governor of Samarqand, Yalantush Bahadur, erected the two buildings that gave the Registan its final appearance. The architect he chose, Abd-al Jabbar, drew inspiration from the grand Timurid style to give the space its triumphal character, and his two buildings are faithful to the spirit of Ulugh Beg. The Registan complex as a whole, with all its buildings, covers an area of 190 x 260 metres. Using the Ulugh Beg Madrasa as a model, Abd-al Jabbar created a highly original urban set piece, which is open at the corners and yet seems to close in on itself.

The Madrasa of Ulugh Beg occupies an area of 81 x 56 metres. It has a square courtyard (measuring 33 x 33 metres) which is a typically Persian bi-axial space, with four *iwans* and two arcaded tiers of cells for students and professors. At the corners there are halls, and accents in the form of four tall minarets.

This scheme was taken up almost verbatim in the Shir Dor Madrasa. In both cases, the *iwans* facing the courtyard are flanked by wings each of which has three bays of arcades on two levels, making a total of 48 cells. If one assumes that each housed two students, that would make a total of 96 researchers and theologians or jurists. There are a few differences between the Shir Dor Madrasa and its model. Where the Ulugh Beg Madrasa had entrances at the sides, through *iwans* placed back-to-back with those in the courtyard, here there are none. And at the Shir Dor Madrasa the two corner rooms behind

The Madrasa-Mosque of Tilla Kari, built in 1647 under the Shaybanids of Bukhara

left, above On the façade, the monumental *pishtaq* encloses an *iwan* with a polygonal rear wall, whose two levels of arcades reflect those of the wings.

left, centre Looking up in the entrance *iwan*. The vault is a showpiece of tile mosaic (for a detail, see *opposite*). Its interlacing ribs, which emphasize the half-octagon plan, blossom above a band of thuluth script.

left, below The corner turrets are a feature of Timurid fortresses; they give the *madrasa* a martial air in keeping with what was a troubled time in Transoxiana.

opposite Detail of the tile mosaic on the entrance *iwan* (cf. *left, centre*). The vine scrolls and flowers are a subtle echo of Safavid decoration in Isfahan.

the façade have bulbous domes with large ribs, a design that comes from the Mir-i Arab Madrasa in Bukhara, built by the Shaybanids c. 1535, which stood in a similar mirror-image relationship to the Kalyan Mosque (ill. p. 112, above).

The Tilla Kari Madrasa-Mosque differs from the two *madrasas* that face each other across the Registan in having only a single tier of cells opening onto the courtyard. However, it was kept in keeping with the ensemble through architectural trompe-l'oeil: the façade has two tiers of arcades flanking the great axial *iwan-pishtaq*, suggesting the existence of two floors of cells as in the other two buildings – a device that gives great visual unity to the square.

On the west side of the courtyard (in the direction of Mecca) a great *iwan* leads to the prayer hall and principal *mihrab* of the Tilla Kari Mosque. Wings in the form of hypostyle halls flank the *qibla*; above it is a dome on squinches ornamented with *muqarnas*, which catch the light in a glittering display. The decoration here, with its profusion of painted motifs and sumptuous polychromy of gold leaf and lapis lazuli, has been meticulously restored. Above this inner dome there should have been a second, higher dome that would have been prominently visible from outside, but it was never realized. It was finally erected by the modern restorers, both to complete the intended effect and to protect their work in the hall below. The effect has been to enhance the splendour of a structure created at a time when princes and khans still enjoyed a fabulous income from the Silk Road, but when that source of income had already begun to be threatened by the opening of the sea route between Europe and China.

The emergence of a sort of 'baroque' in post-Timurid architecture is apparent at the Tilla Kari Madrasa-Mosque in the showiness of the decoration, and also in the treatment of the space within the entrance *pishtaq*, where a half-octagon plan gives rise to a pattern of ribs that is very like those in contemporary Safavid buildings in Isfahan. A similar play with angled corners had already been exploited in Bukhara under the Shaybanids, at the Mir-i Arab Madrasa, where the corners of the courtyard are set at a 45-degree angle to enhance the sense of spatial continuity; and that device is also seen in several later *madrasas*, especially in Khiva. Both projecting and re-entrant angled corners occur in contemporary Mughal works in India and in the last Safavid creations in Isfahan, such as the Mader-i Shah Madrasa of 1706 (ill. p. 293.

The architect Abd al-Jabbar, who devised the Registan in its final form, was no mere 'imitator' of the style of the time of Ulugh Beg, but a highly interesting innovator.

The sumptuousness of 17th-century post-Timurid art reaches a peak in the Tilla Kari Madrasa-Mosque.

opposite Around the gilded *mihrab*, ultramarine blue, red, and gold leaf blend in the miniature *muqarnas*, the vine trails and the Qur'anic inscriptions.

below The dome above the *mihrab* is covered with tiers of dazzling *muqarnas*. Thanks to a thorough restoration, carried out shortly before Uzbekistan became independent in 1991, the decoration has recovered its splendour.

Delhi: Humayun's Tomb

One of the earliest of the great Mughal buildings in India already shows a very strong Persian influence at work: this is the tomb of the second emperor, Humayun (on the tomb and its gardens see also above, pp. 100–101). Begun in 1557, it is a revolutionary work. A few figures will give an idea of the scale of the enterprise. The tomb is surrounded by a walled garden inscribed in a square with sides 350 metres long. This garden is strictly oriented to the points of the compass, and divided into a regular chequerboard with 36 (6 x 6) squares, which are outlined by irrigation channels and pools. The tomb stands in the centre, occupying 4 squares. This emblematic organization of the space, and

top A decorative motif combining a square and an octagon, composed of white marble inlaid in red sandstone.

above The gate leading into the gardens: its wings, set at 45-degree angles, are topped by two small *chhatris* – an Indian motif added to the Persian architectural vocabulary.

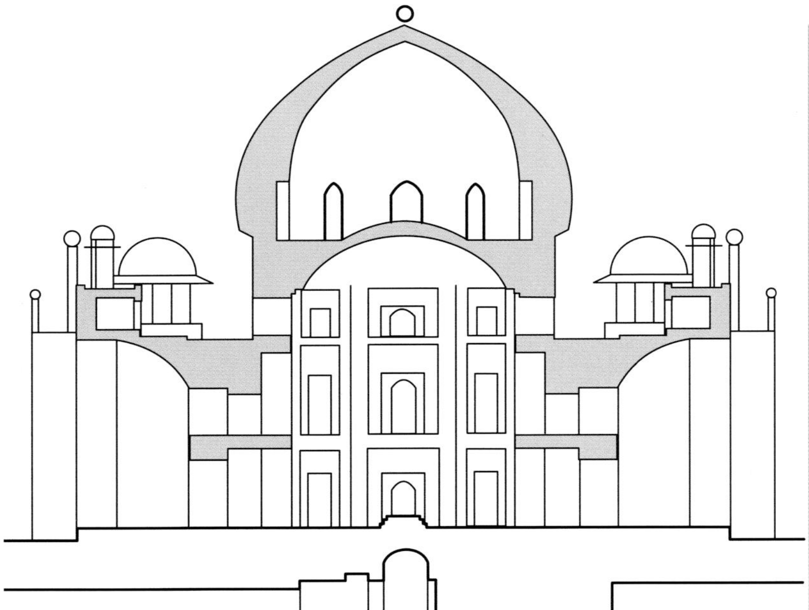

1

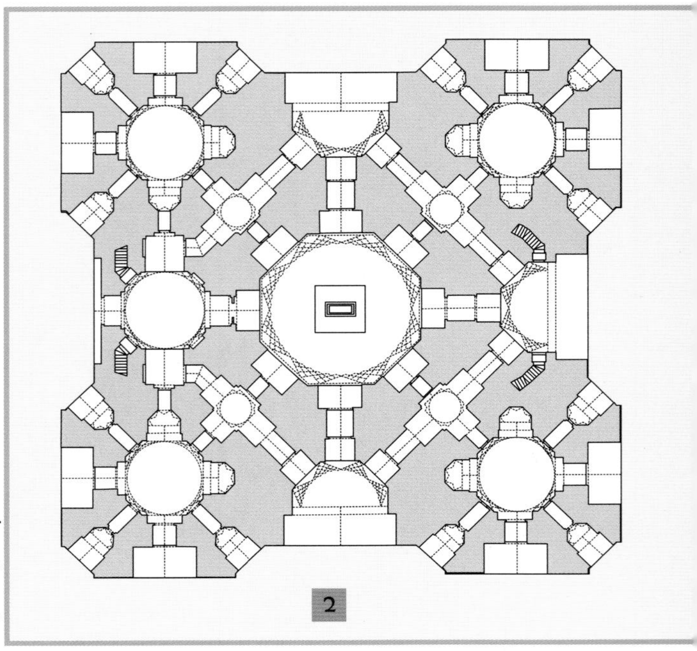

2

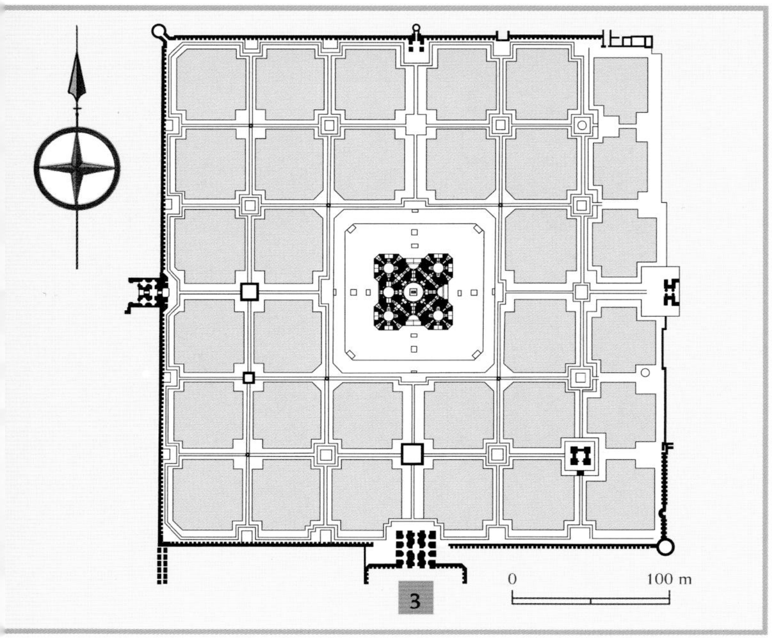

Key

1 Transverse section, showing the double-shelled dome
2 Plan of the tomb, with an octagonal central funerary chamber and four halls on the diagonal axes. There is symmetry on the east-west axis but not on the north-south axis: on the west side (left), instead of a half-octagon iwan there is a domed hall
3 Plan of the complex: the tomb lies in the middle of gardens intersected by a grid of irrigation channels and paths

above The magnificent façade of Humayun's Tomb, built between 1557 and 1565 by the Persian architect Mirak Mirza Ghiyas. A plinth surrounded by arcades (leading to rooms for guests and pilgrims) supports the square central building, which is crowned by a white marble dome framed by *chhatris*.

above The compact volumes of the tomb are articulated by four chamfered corner features that project outward from the core and seem to brace the central dome. Decorated surfaces and shadowy recesses are skilfully balanced, as is the dialogue between marble and sandstone.

opposite, above The terrace level is reached by a stairway that emerges in front of the entrance *iwan*. The *iwan* is a half-octagon in plan, while the corner pavilions are octagons with alternating long and short sides.

opposite, below A *jali*, finely carved from red sandstone in a subtle design of staggered octagons. In Islamic art a passion for geometry produces decorative formulas of endless variety.

the fountains, are again a reference to the Persian *chahar bagh*, or 'four garden', layout. The area is indeed divided into 4 quarters, each of 9 parts (3 x 3 units). The scheme is a associated with a cosmological vision of the universe watered by the four Rivers of Paradise.

The garden, enclosed within a wall and entered through four gates on the two intersecting axes, is thus an image of Paradise, the place of delights promised to the faithful in the *suras* of the Qur'an – a recurrent theme in Islamic architecture, to which we shall return. In the centre of this green space is the mausoleum proper, which measures 47 x 47 metres and is set on a square plinth with chamfered corners that measures 96 x 96 metres. Around the plinth, rows of arches frame small *iwans* which lead to rooms for guests and pilgrims, effectively serving as a caravanserai. There are 17 arches on each side and one at each corner, making a total of 72 arches corresponding to as many rooms. Their silhouette is that of the classic four-centered Persian arch.

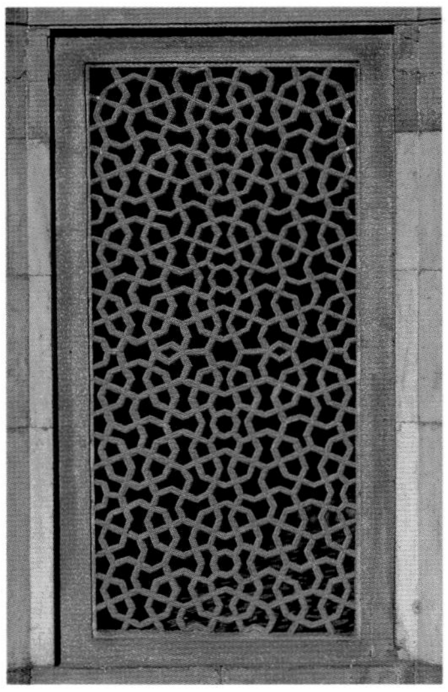

The platform is reached by a staircase within the solid mass of the plinth. The visitor thus passes through darkness before emerging into the light in front of the tomb. It is impossible not to feel the resulting sense of illumination, with its symbolic undertones.

The mausoleum itself is a skilfully articulated mass of hollows and projections, punctuated by large and small *iwan*-like niches. The plan is symmetrical along two axes, and also has a radiating arrangement. Looked at closely, it is a delicate openwork square, where solids and voids are perfectly balanced; glanced at, it suggests the crystalline structure of a snowflake. The game is a very complex one, played with pieces which are themselves symmetrical, as niches, *iwans*, axial and diagonal passages, octagonal rooms, and corridors designed for circumambulation are repeated on each side. The centralized plan, with axes crossing in the funerary chamber, is governed by a scheme of squares combined with diagonally set squares to produce octagons.

The octagonal funerary chamber focuses on the white marble cenotaph of Humayun. His tomb is in a crypt below.

The external appearance of the mausoleum is also centralized and symmetrical. The middle section is marked on each side by a large *iwan* set in a tall, flat frame. Above that is a bulbous dome faced with white marble, topped by a gilded bronze spike. Although the rest of the building is relatively low in proportion, it nevertheless has a marked vertical feeling.

The use of a double-shell system, with the lower shell over the funerary chamber, helps to reconcile exterior and interior. The idea had already been explored in Timurid art – notably at the Gur-i Amir mausoleum in Samarqand – and made a timid appearance in India in the Lodi period. Aesthetics demanded on the outside a high dome that would make a proud effect, and on the inside a dome that would be in proportion to the hall it covered. The first requirement was met by inserting a drum that lifted the dome up and made it more prominent. But if you looked straight up into such a structure from inside, what you would see was a disproportionately tall space ending in darkness; so to meet the second requirement, a lower dome was needed inside. The result is a windowless, inaccessible void which exists to satisfy visual concerns. The double-shelled dome was used in many Timurid buildings in Transoxiana and Safavid buildings in Persia, and again in the Taj Mahal at Agra, where the void between the two shells is greater still.

From the octagonal hall at the heart of the Mausoleum of Humayun, diagonals lead out to four chamfered corner structures each of which contains a subsidiary hall. These are like satellites around the central core, and they stress the horizontal quality that had already been established by the platform on which the building is set. The unity and cohesion of the whole are cleverly achieved by reducing the height of the corner elements in relation to the axial *iwans*. A pyramidal movement is given to the upper level by the presence of four *chhatris* set on the flat roofs of the 'satellite' structures, which provide a visual link with the dome. (Throughout the tomb complex, *chhatris* are the only element taken from Hindu architecture.) Seventy-five years later, we find essentially the same composition in the Taj Mahal, but with an emphasis on verticality (compare ills. pp. 239 and 275).

This magnificent monument to the second Mughal emperor is a truly innovative work. The

architectural elements do indeed have a Persian-Timurid ancestry, but their transposition into new materials – red sandstone and white marble – radically transforms the overall effect, which is one of sober grandeur. The architect's virtuosity is especially apparent in the decoration: here, instead of the multicoloured patterns in ceramic of Iran and Transoxiana, there are simple marble inlays expressed as black lines and broader areas of white against the background of red sandstone. This rigour is what gives Mughal architecture its remarkable purity. The creative genius of Mirak Mirza Ghiyas shines through the formal clarity of Humayun's Tomb.

above Looking up in the entrance hall: the dome has a simple decoration of ridges linked to the periphery by ribbing.

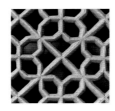

Fatehpur Sikri, An 'Artificial' Capital

After living in Agra for a time, in 1569 Akbar decided to create a build a new capital, Fatehpur Sikri, about 40 kilometres away (see above, pp. 108–9). Where the palace at Agra was fitted within the defensible Red Fort, here there is a purely symbolic perimeter wall 6 kilometres long, and the buildings are spaced out in a seemingly free arrangement below a natural ridge that runs in a south west to north-east direction and forms the northern edge of the city. They stand a vast paved open space, not along streets or paths but – with the exception of a few peripheral elements – strictly oriented to the cardinal points of the compass. The orientation is fixed by the *qibla* of the rectangular mosque, the main building to the south. While the buildings are not set on any grid, they obey a rigorous system, with axial connections between most of them – palaces, residences, reception halls, etc. Yet there is a sense of freedom in the placing of open spaces, courtyards, enclosed structures and porticoes as you wander through the ghost town of Fatehpur Sikri today.

The Panch Mahal, an extraordinary five-storey pyramidal building, consists of superimposed hypostyle halls, open to the air. Its function remains mysterious. Akbar is said to have used it to watch *pachisi*, a board game somewhat similar to chess, which was played with real people as the pieces. Indeed, the purpose of most of the secular buildings in the city remains uncertain. The House of Raja Birbal has a skewed symmetrical plan,

opposite, top Detail of a *jali* in the shrine of Shaikh Salim Chishti.

opposite, centre and below In the Palace of Jodh Bai, built around 1570, traditional Indian structural techniques are used, with piers supporting lintels braced by brackets, and the carved decoration is similar to that of Hindu and Jain temples. All expresses Akbar's desire to marry the innovations of Islam with the ancestral customs of India.

above The entrance to the Palace of Jodh Bai, with light *chhatris* and corbelled balconies, combines features of defensive architecture with those of emblematic gates. The openings are now Persian arches built in the correct way.

with four square rooms in the centre of the ground floor and two rooms at the ends; on the upper floor there are two rooms placed at alternate corners and each covered by a dome, producing a remarkably sculptural effect. Of equally uncertain purpose are the House of Miriam and that of the Turkish Sultana, with its sumptuous geometrical and floral motifs delicately carved in negative relief in the sandstone. Everywhere one seems to be looking at petrified panelling.

A leitmotif throughout Fatehpur Sikri is the treatment of lintels as though they were joists, and various forms of joints and combinations of elements inherited from Hindu carpentry techniques are a recurrent feature.

Key			
1	Bazaar street	12	Caravanserai
2	Taksal	13	Mosque court
3	Diwan-i Amm court	14	Prayer hall
4	Diwan-i Khass	15	Tomb of Shaikh Salim Chishti
5	Court	16	Mausoleum of Islam Khan
6	Hospital (?)	17	Buland Darwaza
7	House of Miriam	18	Badshahi Darwaza
8	Panch Mahal		
9	Anup Talao		
10	Palace of Jodh Bhai		
11	Hiran Minar		

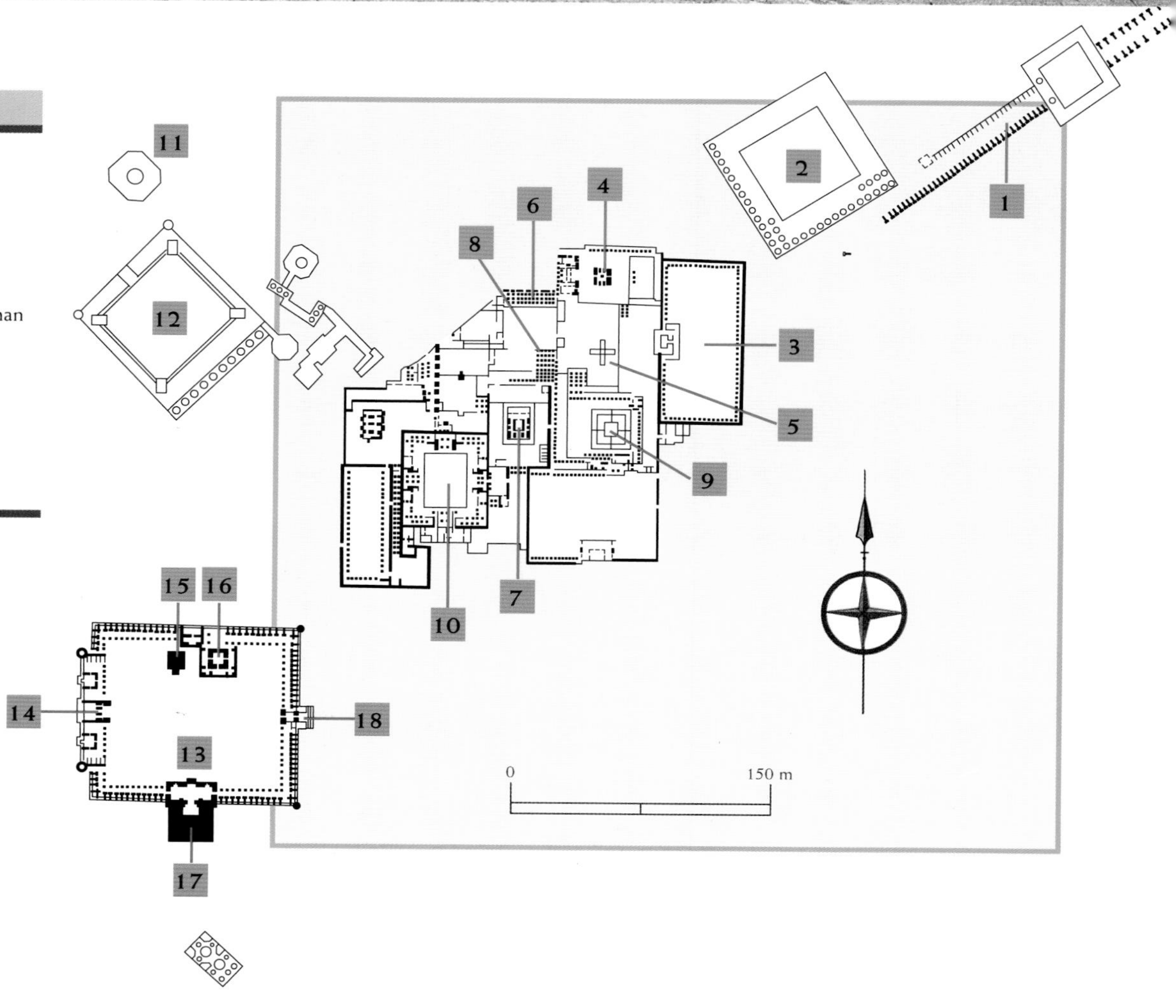

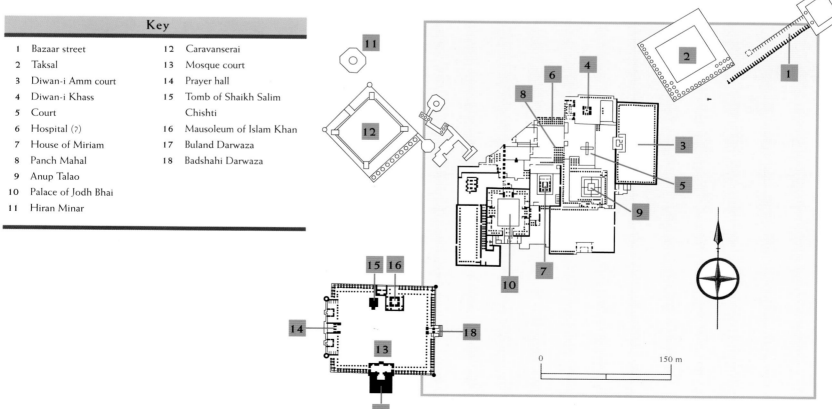

opposite The Anup Talao pool has a square platform in the centre reached by four stone walkways. On this artificial island that symbolized the centre of the world Akbar would sit under a canopy in the role of Cosmocrator.

below The Panch Mahal, built in 1570, has a curious pyramidal composition of five levels decreasing in size. From the *chhatri* at the top Akbar is said to have watched outdoor games of *pachisi* where the pieces on the board were living people.

The most important buildings are in the heart of the city: the great mosque, the palace buildings, and the traditional apparatus of government – the Diwan-i Amm or Hall of Public Audience, preceded by a vast courtyard, and the Diwan-i Khass or Hall of Private Audience. 'Imperial' structures include a platform surrounded by water, where Albar's throne was set up under a canopy; the emperor's workroom; his apartments; and the harem, called the Palace of Jodh Bai. It must be said that in the absence of documents or inscriptions some of these names are conjectural. The 'artificial capital' is completed by administrative buildings, a caravanserai, what may have been a hospital, a *hammam*, a quarter for craftsmen, a market, and immense stables.

right The house of Raja Birbal has two identical asymmetrical façades placed back-to-back. Inside there are six intercommunicating rooms. Those on the upper storey have double-shell domes in the Timurid tradition, supported on corbelling.

Among the surviving buildings we shall look at the most remarkable. The Diwan-i Khass is completely unexpected: it stands on the north side of a vast paved open space, a cubic building with two storeys encircled by a continuous balcony supported on stone brackets. Above the upper floor are projecting eaves, and then a roof of which the corners are accentuated by *chhatris*. The rigorous symmetry on two axes is emphasized by doors in the centre of each of the four sides, flanked by windows with sandstone *jalis*, while on the upper floor there are three windows on each side. The interior is particularly surprising. Within its cubic space is a central mushroom-like structure: this consists of a square pier which turns into a column, which in turn supports an enormous circular 'capital' formed of a series of radiating brackets corbelled out one above the other; these in turn supports a circular platform with a stone balustrade. The platform is connected to the four corners of the room by diagonal walkways that open off a gallery running round the inside of the walls. Stairs within the thickness of the wall give access to this level.

The raised platform held Akbar's throne. From there he promulgated laws, issued decrees, and discussed matters of policy with his ministers. For him discussion was a fine art; he loved dialectics, philosophical and theological disputations. From his raised throne he engaged in debates with guests or opponents, sought out controversy, arbitrated debates, investigated grievances and rendered justice: like a Roman emperor on the raised tribunal in the Aula Regia, he represented the ultimate authority.

In this highly emblematic position, the emperor on his throne was like the sun at its zenith, and he reigned over the four cardinal directions, at the centre of the world. He was the Cosmocrator, the Ruler of the World, like the caliphs of Baghdad and Samarra, in the tradition of the imperial magnificence of Byzantium and antiquity.

A similar cruciform structure lies to the south of the courtyard. Here, in the centre of a square pool known as Anup Talao, is an island bordered by openwork sandstone balustrades connected to the 'land' by four axial stone walkways. Akbar's throne was set up in the middle, under a canopy (such canopies are portrayed in miniatures in the *Baburnama*: they are draped over the emperor when he is receiving delegations and vassals, and over his encampment; cf. ill. p. 99, left). This island out in the open air, set in the midst of water representing the primordial ocean surrounding the universe, embodied the notion of universal power to which the Mughals laid claim. It was a magnificent ritual, of which the origin seems to go back to the Hellenistic-Roman world by way of the 'Abbasids of Baghdad.

The Diwan-i Khass, or Hall of Private Audience

opposite The square building is surrounded by a balcony resting on a battery of far-projecting brackets, and has four delicate *chhatris* – a Hindu motif – on the roof. (In the foreground is the House of the Astrologer, where stone brackets support lintels in a technique derived from carpentry.)

above and below The audience room is covered by a square false dome. A central pillar with radiating brackets supports a platform, from which Akbar presided over ecumenical talks with representatives of India's various religious communities. The platform is reached by four diagonal walkways from a surrounding gallery, itself reached by stairs within the wall.

Key

1 Transverse section
2 Elevation
3 Plan of the upper storey at the level of the central platform

1

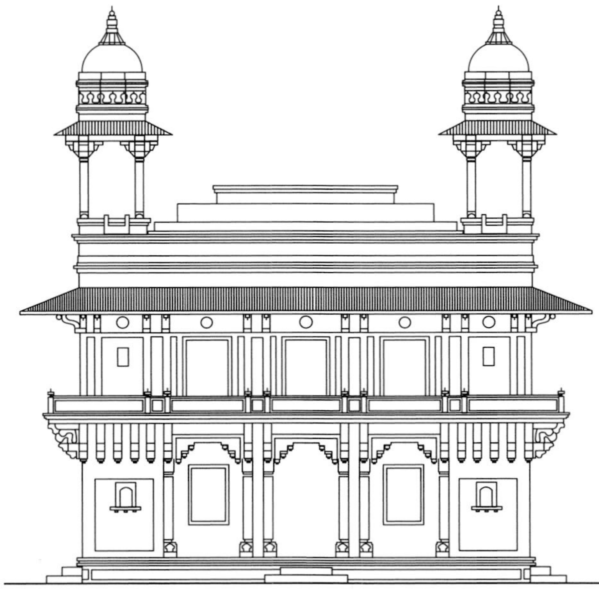

2

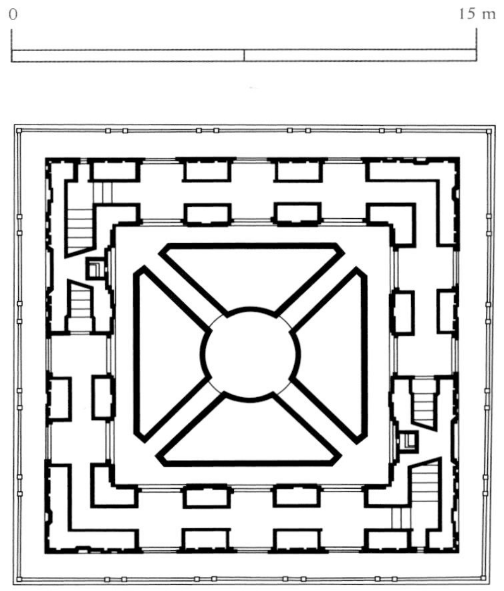

3

The key building in the cities created by the Turkish-Mongol conquerors in the territories over which they reigned was naturally the place of prayer, and the most important structure in Akbar's new capital was the great Friday Mosque, south-west of the palace complex, which was begun in 1571. Its vast courtyard is 132 metres wide and 155 metres deep and surrounded by arcades. The prayer hall is transverse, on the pattern of mosques built in India under the Lodi sultans and Sher Shah Suri, with a façade 87 metres wide. The central section has a fine dome some 12 metres in diameter over the space in front of the principal *mihrab*. In the middle is an *iwan* with a semi-octagonal vault; its *pishtaq*-like façade has coloured stone inlay in tones from white to dark red, and is topped by a row of five small *chhatris*. Other *chhatris* stand on the roofs of the porticoes surrounding the courtyard. The two wings have smaller domes over the *qiblas* of secondary *mihrabs*, and arcades on five columns at either end.

After 1575, the mosque was given a great entrance to the south, the Buland Darwaza ('Sublime Gate'). This commemorates a victory by Akbar in Gujarat, so it is a monument to a heroic feat of arms as well as an expression of piety. It is a majestic creation 41 metres tall, which projects beyond the southern wall of the mosque and stands on terraces that compensate

The Friday Mosque

The range on the west side of the court (*above*) contains the central prayer hall behind the *iwan* and further spaces for worship in the wings. Inside, the wings (*opposite, top*) display stilted Persian arches combined with carpentry techniques in stone. The main prayer hall (*opposite, below*) has a dome supported on wide squinches; rich carved decoration covers the area of the *mihrab* and *minbar*, at the left. The monumental Buland Darwaza (*opposite, centre*), surmounted by rows of *chhatris*, leads into the mosque from the south.

The tomb of Shaikh Salim Chishti

The tomb-shrine in the courtyard of the mosque, originally built by Akbar, became a place of pilgrimage and was rebuilt in white marble by Jahangir *c.* 1606.

opposite, top The funerary chamber is surrounded by a gallery for the rite of circumambulation, lit by marble *jalis*.

opposite, centre The funerary chamber, where the holy man's tomb is still the object of veneration by pilgrims.

opposite, below A coloured panel shows a vase of immortality, from which a bunch of flowers emerges, symbolizing life. The style is characteristic of the period of Jahangir.

for the fall of the land and make it seem taller still, an impression intensified by the immense stairway that leads up to it. The outer façade is a powerful *pishtaq* structure with chamfered corners, decorated with a frame of beige marble carved in relief with a Qur'anic inscription in naskhi script. The vast *iwan* is similar to that of the prayer hall, with a semi-octagonal vault, but larger. It too is crowned by a row of *chhatris*. The inner façade is lower, to fit in with the scale of the courtyard of the mosque.

There are two mausoleums on the north side of the courtyard. One is that of Islam Khan; the other is that of Shaikh Salim Chishti (1480–1572), the holy man who had predicted the birth of Akbar's son, the future Emperor Jahangir. The monument erected by Akbar was replaced by Jahangir around 1606 by the beautiful white marble tomb that we see today, probably because of the growing popularity of pilgrimages to the site. It consists of a square domed funerary chamber surrounded by a magnificent peripheral corridor designed for the rite of circumambulation. It is perhaps the first building to make exclusive use of glowing white marble, such as would characterize the work of Shah Jahan. Precious and refined, with walls consisting entirely of pierced marble panels of spider's-web-like fineness, it displays the extraordinary virtuosity of the Hindu craftsmen who made it. The delicacy of the patterns of these translucent *jalis*, based on hexagons, octagons and star-shaped polygons, makes the mausoleum a place of enchantment.

SIKANDRA: AKBAR'S COSMIC TOMB

Akbar had definite ideas about architecture, as about all things related to an omnipotent prince, and he determined to design his own mausoleum, on a vast site at Sikandra, half-way between Agra and Fatehpur Sikri. Work began several years before his death, but had to be finished by his son Jahangir.

The tomb is strictly oriented to the points of the compass, and stands at the centre of a square garden of *chahar bagh* type which measures 700 x 700 metres – four times larger than that of Humayun's Tomb, some forty years earlier (ill. p. 239). Apart from the garden with its two intersecting axes marked by

left, above The western pavilion, seen from outside. Akbar designed his own mausoleum, but it was not finished until 1613, by his son Jahangir. The style of the buildings, and especially the decoration, reflects this evolution: the western pavilion seems to belong to the last phase.

left, centre Detail of a panel on the gate.

left, below The main entrance to the gardens that surround the mausoleum. The corners of the pavilion bear four white marble minarets, while its façades are covered with luxuriant polychrome decoration combining floral and geometrical motifs.

above The eastern pavilion is linked by an axial path to the tomb in the centre, of which we see here one of the large marble *chhatris* on the top storey. Like Humayun's Tomb, Akbar's is set in the centre of a large square area with four gates, constituting a garden of Paradise.

gates to north, south, east and west, and the central position of the tomb, the two designs have absolutely nothing in common.

One is immediately struck by the curious appearance of the main entrance gate, to the south. It is two-storeyed, with a tall *pishtaq*, but then unexpectedly has white marble minarets rising from the corners; these are divided into three sections by balconies supported on brackets and have elegant *chhatris* at the top. Corner minarets were a popular feature in Timurid architecture; in India they were to undergo a series of changes. Here the vertical accents crown the entrance pavilion; on the Tomb of Jahangir at Lahore they adorn the main building (ill. p. 163); and at the Taj Mahal in Agra they become four freestanding towers, placed on the diagonal axes of the mausoleum (ill. pp. 274–75).

The monumental gate at Sikandra has elaborate decoration in which geometrical motifs – variations on the square, hexagon and octagon – are combined with vigorous arabesques of vine scrolls, branches and leaves alternating with large white flowers on a red ground. This luxuriant floral decoration is characteristic of the last phase of Jahangir's contributions to the ornamental programme begun by Akbar. The three other gates are also very richly ornamented, with both geometrical and floral motifs in a number of styles. The most striking feature throughout is the emphasis on abstract rhythms.

What are the most significant differences between Akbar's Mausoleum at Sikandra and that of Humayun in Delhi (ill. pp. 239–40)? At Sikandra the central building – which contains the sarcophagus, in a dark crypt, and the cenotaph on the topmost level – has no real façades, nor does it have a dome. It is a truncated pyramid, measuring 105 x 105 metres, consisting of five tiers of terraces, reaching a height of 22 metres.

The lowest level is surrounded by arcades filled with pierced stone screens; in the centre of each side is a magnificent *iwan* leading to the tomb at the heart of the building. These have half-octagon vaults supported on squinches incrusted with *muqarnas*; they are set as *pishtaqs* in frames covered with stone mosaic in geometrical patterns and finished off with a row of cruciform battlements; at the top, each has a rectangular pavilion made of white marble, in contrast to the red sandstone of which the rest of the structure is built.

Seen from the first terrace, the upper floors depart radically from the design of Humayun's Tomb. There are no solid walls: instead, we see a superimposition of finely articulated airy structures, in which Persian arcades are combined with delicate pavilions of red sandstone and little *chhatris* with white marble domes. Apart from the arches, the architectural system everywhere consists of lintels, brackets and corbelling that recall the carpentry-like stonework at Fatehpur Sikri.

Humayun's Tomb has a central dome of dazzling marble that mesmerically draws the eye; Akbar's Tomb, by contrast, has a space surrounded by a white marble portico, with eleven arches on each side filled with magnificent *jalis*. These screens, which play endless variations on geometrical themes, shelter a gallery intended for the rite of circumambulation. In the centre of the terrace, exposed to the sky, is an extremely simple white marble cenotaph, of the same design as the sarcophagus in the depths below. The corners of the terrace are marked by four *chhatris* that enhance the feeling of emptiness, and

above The tomb, seen from the first terrace. Akbar's tomb is a many-tiered structure: its design combines light arcades of red sandstone with an upper gallery of marble, whose openings are filled with *jalis*. All five levels bear airy pavilions in the form of *chhatris*.

opposite, top The main gate leading to the funerary chamber. Akbar's remains lie at the heart of an orthogonal system symbolizing the centre of the universe.

opposite, centre At the topmost level, on a terrace paved with coloured stone slabs, stands Akbar's cenotaph, with the vault of heaven for its dome. The surrounding gallery served for circumambulation.

intensify one's sense of connection to the sky.

Some reconstructions, supposedly based on an original design that no-one has ever seen, have the building crowned by a dome, but they are wrong. Akbar's body was covered by the vault of heaven, which was traversed by the stars, the sun and the moon, giving the building its cosmological significance. The same principle applied in the courts of Persian mosques, where the sky served as a dome. A text engraved on Akbar's cenotaph confirms this interpretation: 'May his soul shine like the rays of the sun and of the moon in the light of God.' Like most Mughal epigraphs, including those of the Taj Mahal, the inscription is by the calligrapher Abd al-Haq Shirazi, whose name indicates that he came from the city of Shiraz in Iran.

The garden and mausoleum exude an impression of serenity, which is increased by the luxuriant vegetation, the tall trees, the groups of tame monkeys, and the birdsong. The murmuring of fountains and cascades in the irrigation system transforms an enchanting setting into an atmosphere of Paradise. Akbar's Tomb at Sikandra has no parallels among other mausoleums; it is both the masterpiece of the architecture of his time and its swan song.

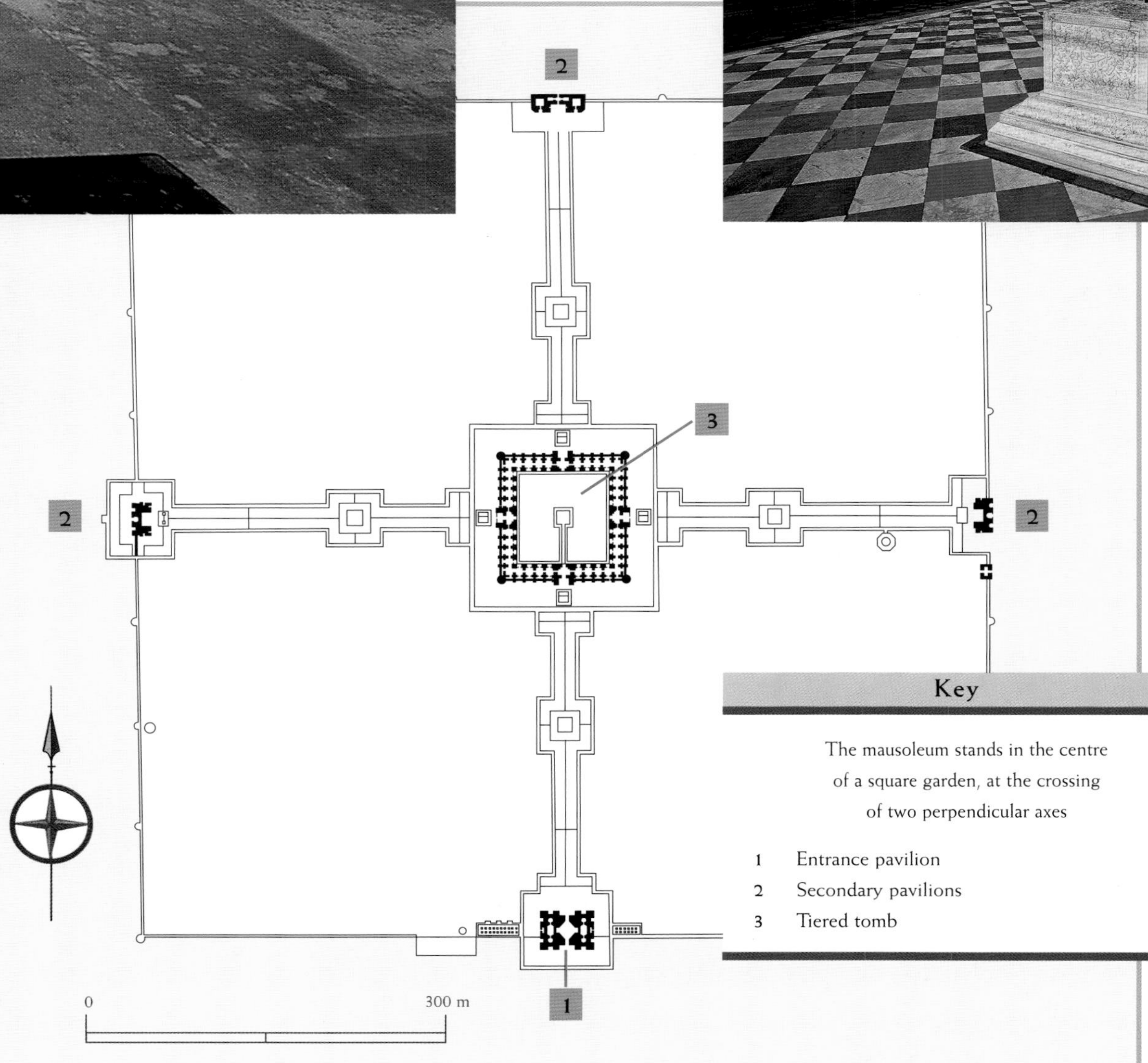

Key

The mausoleum stands in the centre of a square garden, at the crossing of two perpendicular axes

1 Entrance pavilion
2 Secondary pavilions
3 Tiered tomb

above Aerial view of the Maidan, the great royal square in Isfahan. Set back from its southern end is the Mosque of the Imam, built by Shah 'Abbas between 1612 and 1630. There is a marked shift in axes between the two: the square runs north-south, whereas the *qibla* of the mosque has to be oriented towards the Ka'ba in Mecca (see the plan of the city, p. 135).

right The vault of the *pishtaq* facing the square is lined with intricate *muqarnas* covered in magnificent tile mosaic, creating the effect of a blue grotto.

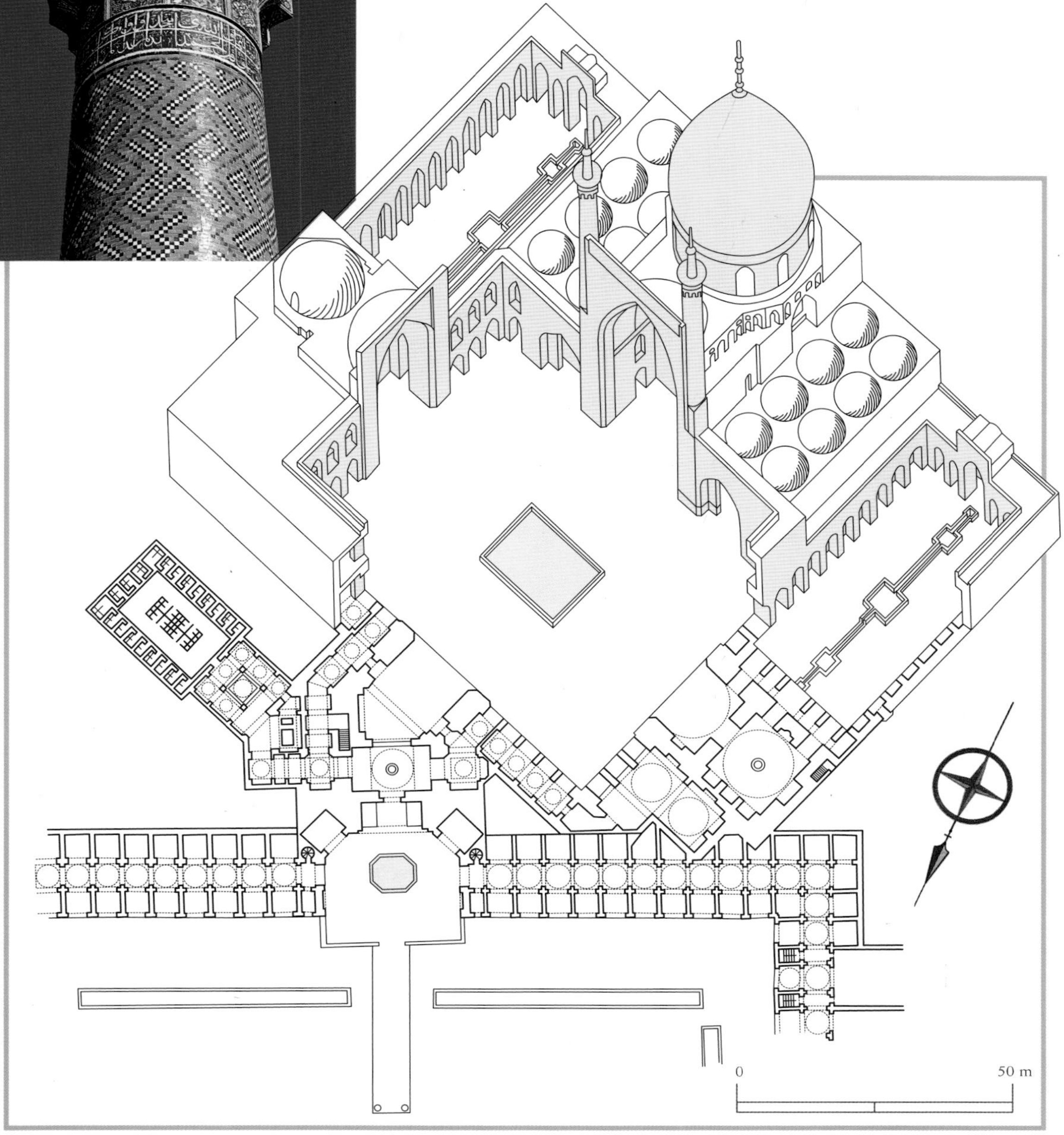

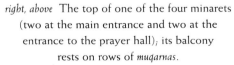

right, above The top of one of the four minarets (two at the main entrance and two at the entrance to the prayer hall); its balcony rests on rows of *muqarnas*.

right, centre Axonometric view of the mosque (the entrance area is shown in plan). The courtyard with its four *iwans* is an inward-looking space focused on the ablutions pool. The bulbous dome on a high drum forms the outer covering of the prayer hall. (Courtesy Klaus W. Herdeg)

right, below Detail of a decorative Safavid mosaic on the mosque.

Isfahan: The Mosque of the Imam or Mosque of the Shah

The Mosque of the Imam in Isfahan, formerly known as the Mosque of the Shah, is Shah 'Abbas's chief work of religious architecture. Built by a Persian architect called Ali Akbar Isfahani (Ali the Great of Isfahan), it was begun in 1612, when the shah was forty-three, and was not finished until 1630, a year after his death. It stands at the southern end of the great Maidan-i Shah, and forms a complex 130 metres wide and 150 metres deep. The prayer area is flanked by two *madrasas*, each with a courtyard measuring 60 x 30 metres down the centre of which flows a canal punctuated by rectangular pools.

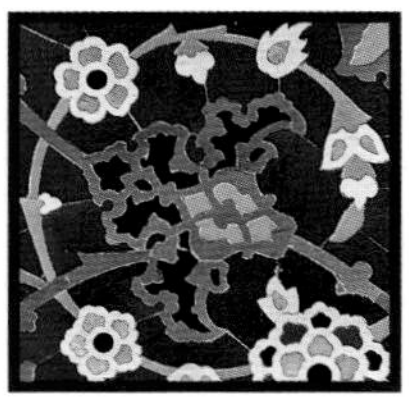

The 45-degree change of axis between the mosque and the Maidan, necessitated by the building's ritual orientation towards the Ka'ba at Mecca, has already been mentioned (p. 138). Let us now consider its spatial organization, and especially that of its central courtyard, 70 metres long and 50 metres wide, which has a beautiful pool for ablutions (measuring 19 x 14 metres) in the centre. In the middle of every façade is a monumental *iwan*, which interrupts the two storeys of arcades behind which lie the cells of the teachers and mullahs. On the prayer hall range, this regular pattern at the sides is

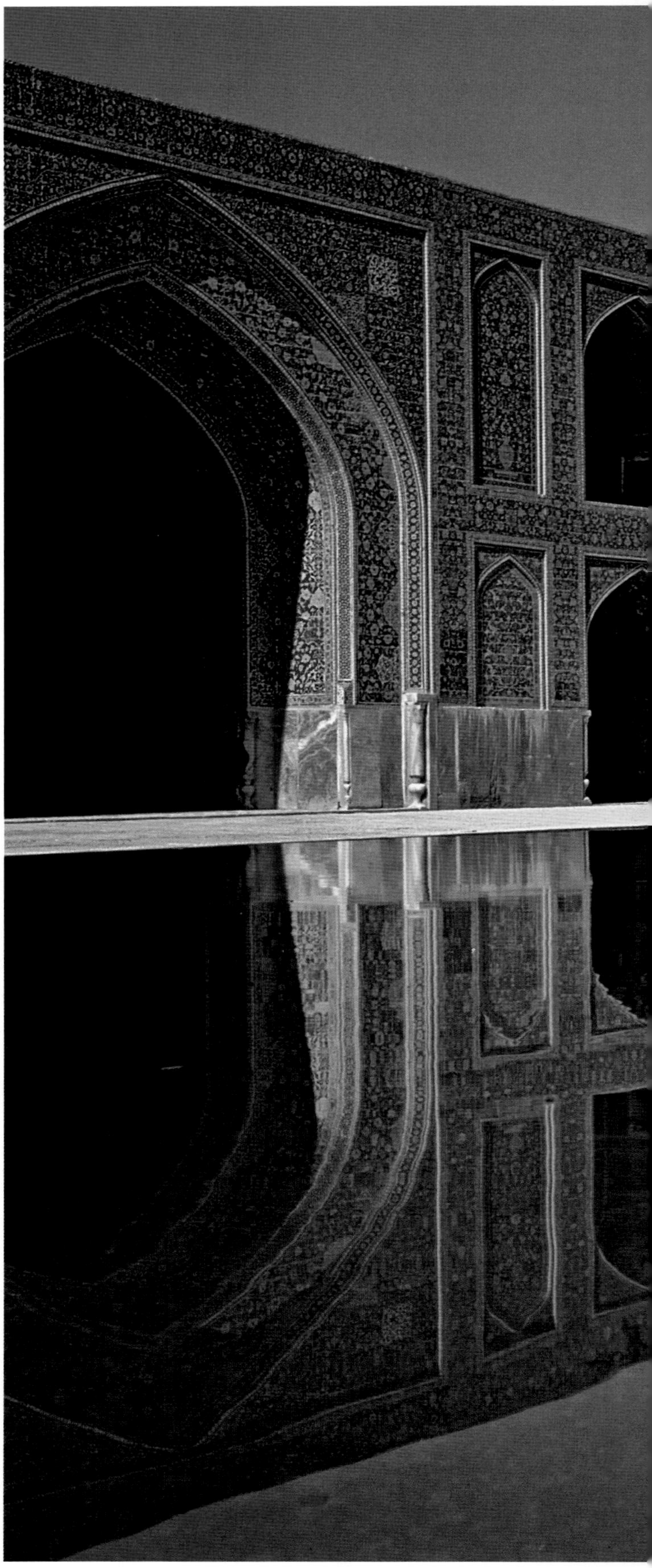

replaced by tall arches that lead into hypostyle halls.

The courtyard that is a distinctive feature of the Persian mosque (it comes from vernacular architecture – the traditional house) is based on a centripetal organization, with the frames of the *iwans* arranged in pairs face to face. The axes that govern them cross in the middle of the pool. The eastern, western and northern *iwans* are the same size, whereas the fourth, leading to the sanctuary and thus the most important, is much larger, with a diameter identical to that of the domed hall beyond.

top Detail of the *muqarnas* of the *iwan* leading into the prayer hall.

above At sunrise, the great western *iwan* is reflected in the central basin. The architect created an image whose real half blends with its virtual half – its reflection – to produce a sort of 'mandala' emblematic of Shi'ite mysticism (see p. 273).

right The two tiers of arcades evoke the superimposed galleries mentioned in the Qur'an (see p. 269). The courtyard is identified with the heavenly city, which Twelver Shi'ites call 'Hurqalya'.

overleaf The courtyard, with the entrance to the prayer hall on the left. This plate from Pascal Coste's great work, *Les Monuments modernes de la Perse* (1867), shows it in all its splendour, unaffected by the ravages of time (André Godard would be called upon to restore it between 1930 and 1960.)

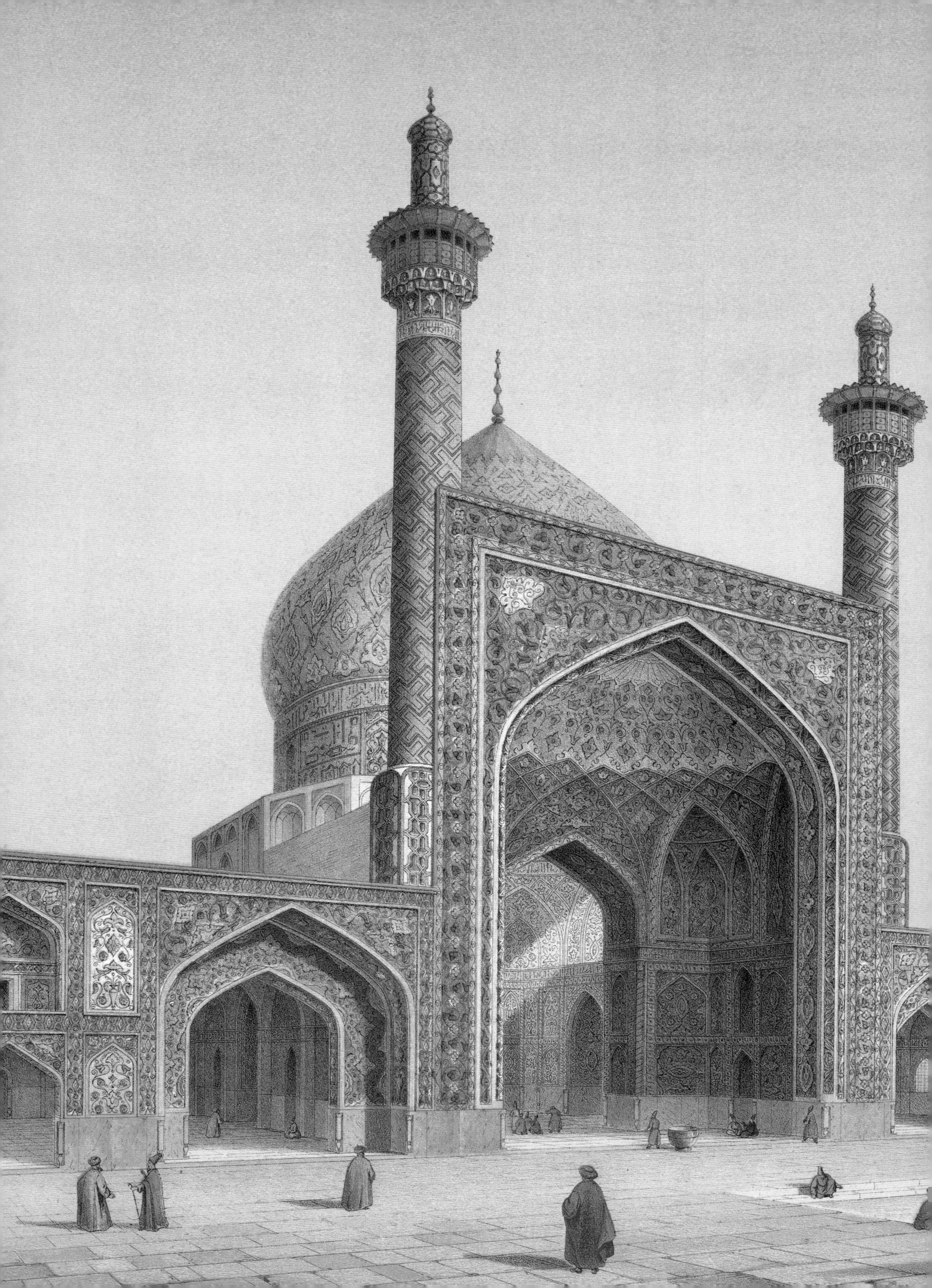

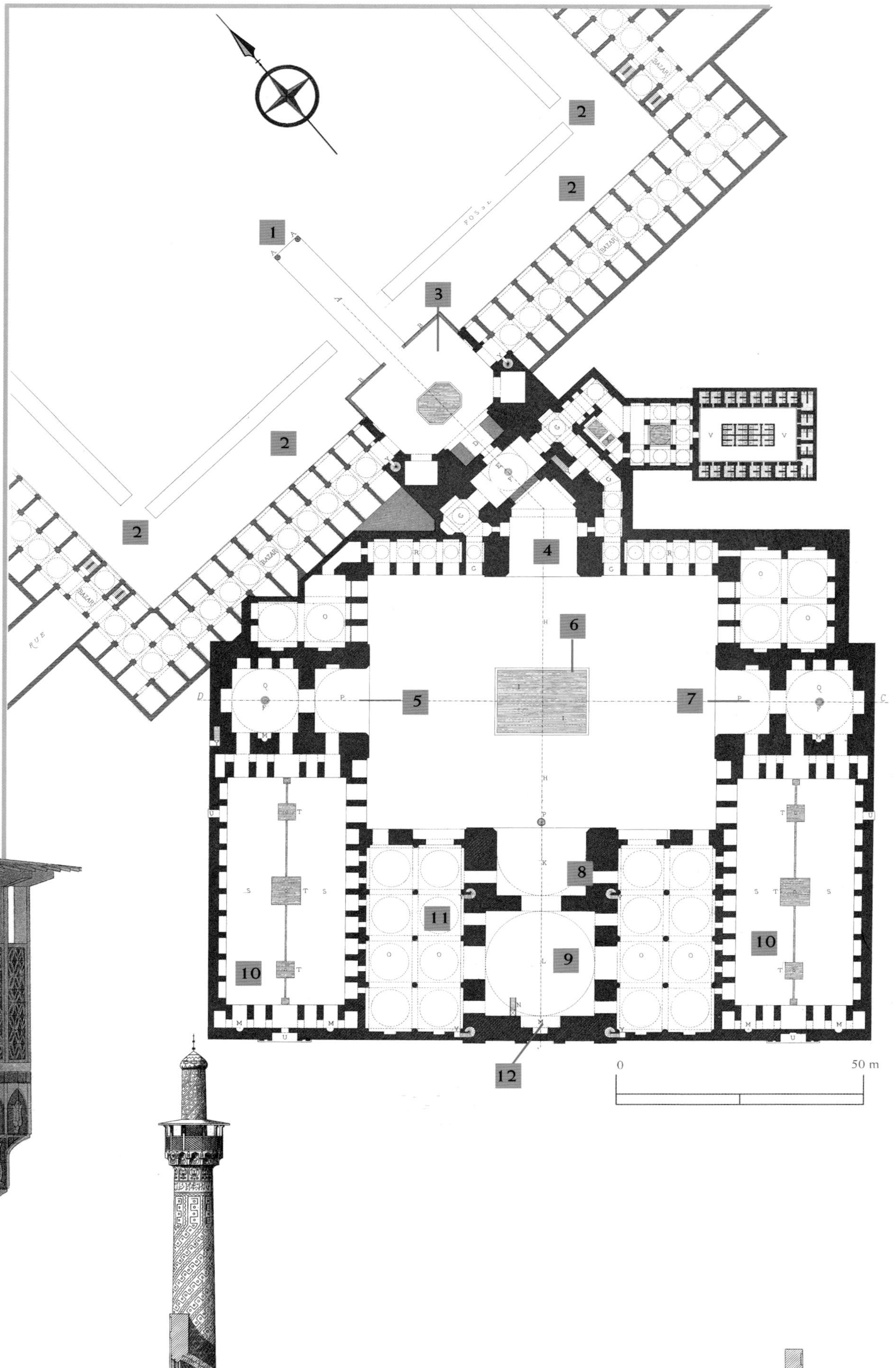

1
2
2
2
2
3
4
5
6
7
8
9
10
10
11
12
BAZAR
FOSSE
RUE
0
50 m

Echelle de
0 1 2 3 4 5 10 15 20 25 30 35 40

Key

Plan of the mosque showing its relationship to the axis of the Maidan, based on a measured drawing by Pascal Coste

1 Maidan-i Shah
2 Shops around the square
3 *Pishtaq*
4 Northern *iwan*
5 Western *iwan* and domed hall
6 Central ablutions pool
7 Eastern *iwan* and domed hall
8 Southern *iwan*
9 Large domed prayer hall
10 Eastern and western *madrasas*
11 Eastern and western hypostyle halls
12 Main *mihrab*

In plan the Mosque of the Imam is symmetrical, apart from the side next to the Maidan with its great *pishtaq* flanked by two minarets, which has its own symmetry. All else is inward-facing. The courtyard occupies the largest space, and above it the vault of heaven forms a cosmic dome.

All the visible surfaces are covered in coloured ceramic – the arcades, the *pishtaq*, the minarets, the *iwans* and their surrounds, the great bulbous dome on its drum, the domed halls, the hypostyle halls, and the arcades of the *madrasas* at the sides. The technique is not the same everywhere, however. Extremely fine tile mosaic, rather than tiles, is used on the *muqarnas* vault and handsome framing panels of the main entrance *pishtaq*. Tile mosaic is found here and there in various other places, such as the chamfered arch of the northern *iwan*.

After this, tile mosaic was given up as being too time-consuming. Use was made instead of glazed bricks and especially of tiles (*kashi*) which were much quicker to apply. It is said that Shah 'Abbas, frustrated by the slow pace of the work and anxious to see it finished, ordered that all coloured ornamentation was henceforth to be done with *kashi*s. The decorations on *kashis* were produced by passing the tile through the kiln again a second time after painting it with all the coloured glazes required. For tile mosaics the processes were quite different: large pieces in a single colour were fired separately and then cut up into the desired shapes, which were positioned next to each other according to the 'cartoon' of the design. In fact qualitatively the *kashi* technique was a step backward: colours fired separately could be fired at the optimum temperature for each one, whereas the firing of all colours simultaneously led to a slight reduction in the intensity of some pigments.

At various points in Persian mosques, one is struck by the presence of monumental inscriptions. These may be in kufic, thuluth or naskhi script, and they served different functions. They include quotations from the Qur'an: significant passages from the *suras* appear on borders and in friezes, notably on *iwans* and inside the sanctuary, so that the mosque becomes an open book. Other inscriptions are more lapidary, using graphic symbols for the sacred names of the Shi'ite trinity of Allah, Muhammad and Ali. Large geometrical characters cover the cylindrical surfaces of minarets with mysterious cryptograms that are so stylized as to be undecipherable; these also occur on gates and walls.

Other inscriptions are historical rather than devotional, and provide useful information. One

opposite, left The top of one of the minarets of the *pishtaq*, from a plate in Pascal Coste's *Les Monuments modernes de la Perse* (1867).

below Longitudinal section by Pascal Coste. From left to right, he shows: part of the Maidan; the *pishtaq* with one of its minarets; the vestibule; the northern *iwan*; the courtyard with two tiers of arcades flanking the eastern *iwan*; the southern *iwan* with one of its minarets; and the prayer hall with its double-shelled dome.

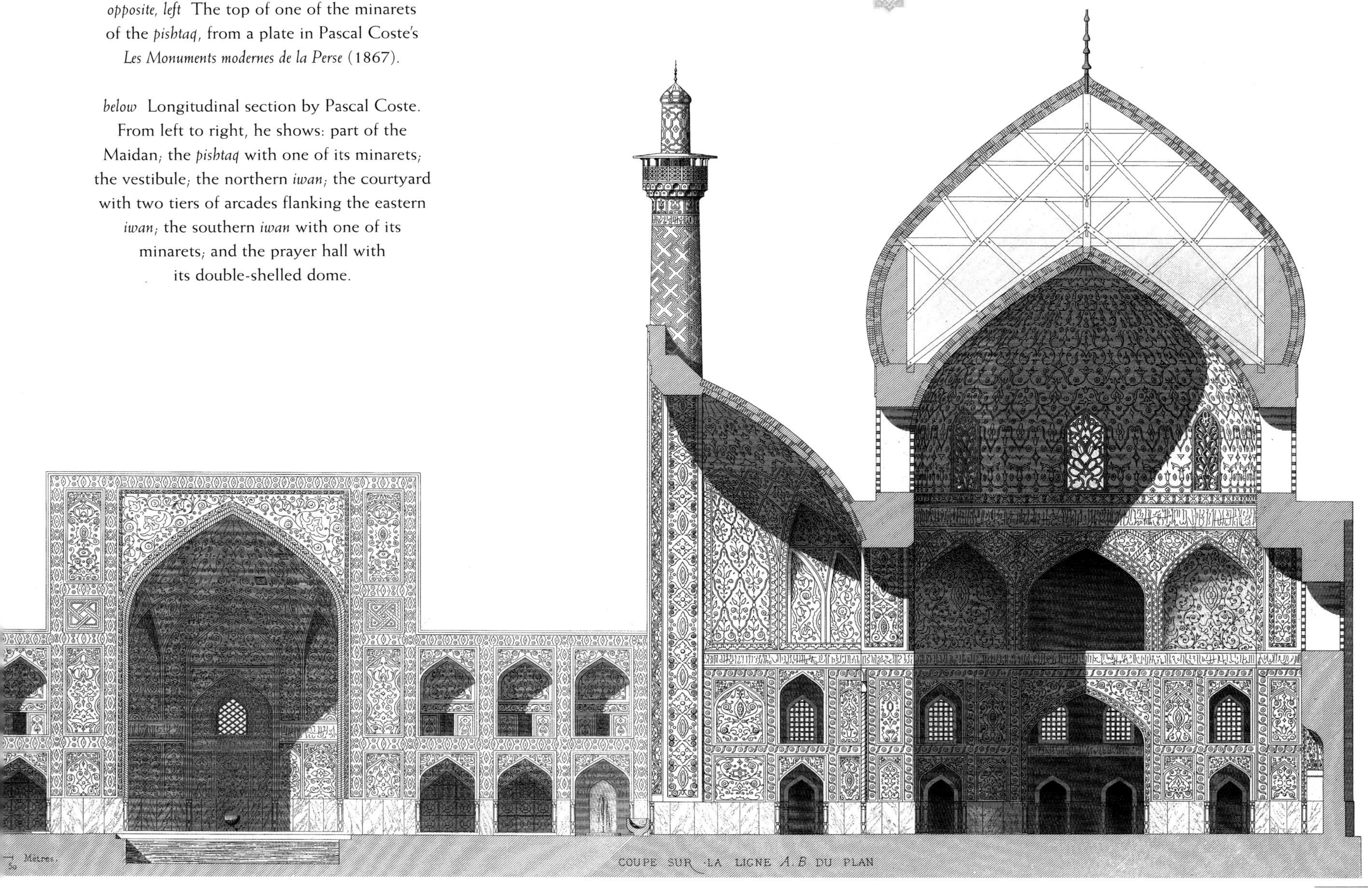

below Detail of a panel of *kashis* with a branching floral pattern. Shah 'Abbas ordered that tiles be used, rather than labour-intensive tile mosaic, to speed up work on the mosque.

right A measured drawing by Pascal Coste of the polychrome tile facing of the great *iwan*. Coste shows not only the decorative pattern but, meticulously, the individual tiles covering the building's brick structure.

on the great doorway of the Mosque of the Imam reads: 'The construction of this cathedral mosque was ordered, at his own expense, by the most noble of the rulers of the earth . . . Abu'l Muzaffar Abbas Husaini Musawi Safavi Bahadur Khan' (i.e. Shah 'Abbas I). The calligrapher left his own signature as well, from which we know the date work was completed on the *pishtaq*: 'Written by Ali Rida Abbasi, 1026' (1616). The signature indicates the calligrapher's high status, and his pride in his work.

Another inscription on the mosque is a sort of colophon, giving the architect's name: 'With the help of God and his generous assistance, construction of this mosque . . . was brought to completion. It is as holy as the al-Aqsa Mosque, whose attendance is blessed . . . The architect, who, in this work, has shown himself the equal of the best engineers is the remearkable Master Ali Akbar Isfahani. May God honour him with great dignity.'

It took millions of glazed bricks and 23-centimetre-square *kashis* to cover the visible surfaces of the mosque, but the result was more than worth the effort. On all sides there are bunches of flowers, garlands, branches, sprays, every conceivable shape and arrangement, and vases sprouting trunks and stems. This decoration adorns the exterior walls, niches and minarets, and the surfaces of the domes – the latter realized, for stability, not in tiles but in bricks cut to shape and glazed. And it also covers interior walls, the soffits of vaults and domes, etc. Colour is now

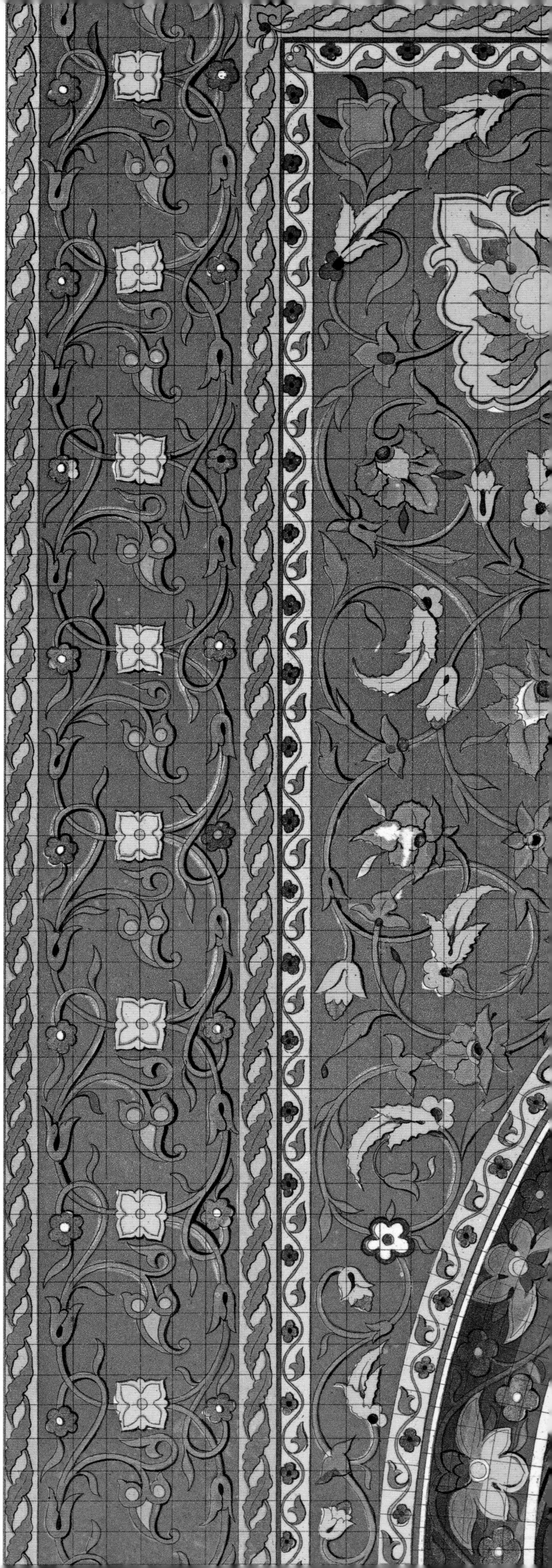

below The decoration of the dome over the *mihrab* area in the prayer hall is particularly splendid. Smooth squinches link the square plan to the circle of the dome, which has eight windows filled with pierced panels.

opposite, above Looking up in one of the side halls. The smooth squinches recur here, and the shimmering tile decoration is again very rich, but there are only four windows in the dome.

everywhere, and plants have invaded every corner of the building. These luxuriant motifs make the mosque into an enchanted space, and more: it is a garden of Paradise. The leaves and flowers with which the building is decorated suggest the eternal spring of Eden. In the mosque, this immortal, unchanging vegetation is a symbol of eternal life. I have been led to this interpretation through a study of the sources. It is based on passages in the Qur'an, such as the following:

Allah has promised to believers, men and women, gardens beneath which rivers flow, wherein they will abide, and delightful dwelling-places in Gardens of Eternity (9:72).

The similitude of the Heaven promised to the God-fearing is, that through it flow streams: its fruit is everlasting, and so is its shade. That is the reward of those who are righteous (13:36).

Then those who believed and did good works will be honoured and made happy in a garden (30:16).

The courtyard of the Mosque of the Imam has two levels of arcades that are reflected in the central pool, corresponding in a most arresting way to another passage in the Qur'an:

> But for them who fear their Lord there will be galleries in Paradise, above which there will be other galleries. Spring waters will run at their feet (39:21).

The theme of water is also present everywhere in these references to Paradise. The four *iwans* of Persian mosques suggest grottoes or fresh springs,

right, centre The two hypostyle halls that flank the central prayer hall are covered by shallow vaults springing from broad Persian arches that rest on octagonal stone columns. Each hall has two subsidiary *mihrabs* in the *qibla* wall, at the back.

with their *muqarnas* like water frozen in the act of splashing. Another text echoes this theme:

> Those who fear God's majesty will have two gardens, both adorned with groves of trees, both containing springs of fresh water. . . . In addition to these two gardens, there will be two more: two gardens covered with vegetation, where two springs will gush forth (55:46, 50; 62, 66).

This passage, which is so precise, seems to demand to be associated with the *chahar bagh*, the four-part Persian garden based on a cruciform plan related to the four Rivers of Paradise mentioned in the book of Genesis. The whole scheme of the four-*iwan* mosque is a transposition into architectural terms of the sacred texts of Islam.

Let us look further in the quest for meaning. The dome, with its enormous bulbous shape covered with spiralling branches, suggests a gigantic tree. It is the tree that Muhammad had seen at the edge of Paradise, described in the Qur'an: 'He had already seen it in a dream. It is the Tree of the boundary, where is the garden of eternal abode' (LIII, 14–15). Thus the great dome represents the frontier of the sacred world: it stands above the *mihrab*, which is the symbolic door to the world everlasting.

All of these symbols were explored in depth by Shi'ite mystics. One of the most important of them, as-Suhrawardi, lived in Isfahan in the 12th century; he was one of the group that Henry Corbin, the great Iranologist, called the 'Persian Platonists'. As-Suhrawardi mentions the Tuba tree that stands on the boundary between this world and the next. It is the Tree of Life, symbol

below Detail of a jamb, showing a spirally twisted shaft springing from a vase, symbolizing the Tree of Life. Flat walls, as here, are faced with floral *kashis*, whereas vaults with their complex shapes (*right*) required tile mosaic.

right The central section of the vigorously modelled *muqarnas* above the entrance to the mosque proper. Each of the cells is covered with the polychrome tile mosaic for which Iran was famous.

of resurrection and life everlasting, that grows on the road to Paradise, on the threshold of the 'Land of Souls'.

In Shi'ite Iran, according to Henry Corbin, the process of resurrection was seen as akin to passing through a mirror. That idea was developed by the philosopher Mohsen Fayz Kashani, who lived in the 17th century, at the very time when the Mosque of the Imam was being built: 'it is the world of archetypal images, in which spirits become flesh and flesh becomes spirit. The appearance of figures in mirrors, or in any reflective surface such as clear water, takes place in this in-between world, since all the figures reflected by mirrors also belong to that world.' Seen in this way, the central pool of the mosque becomes the place of passage from one universe to the other; it is the point at which transfiguration occurs, the transcendental entrance to the garden of Eden. The western *iwan* of the Mosque of the Imam seen at dawn (ill. p. 260) illustrates this symbolism: the real structure combines with the reflection to produce a revelatory vision – a cruciform image that embodies the transition from one world to the next, the union of zenith and nadir, like a symbol of the resurrection. This 'icon' in which there is no single right way up becomes a sort of hypnotic mandala, which endows the building with its full mystical and emblematic significance.

Not only texts but numbers play an important role in the symbolism of the mosque. The number 4, manifest in the four gardens of the Qur'anic Paradise, corresponding to the Persian *chahar bagh*, governs the courtyard with its four *iwans* – grottoes or springs that allude to the four Rivers of Paradise in Genesis. The entire building reflects this four-part system, based on two intersecting orthogonal axes that generate a double symmetry.

But another significant number is 12, which plays a key role in Twelver Shi'ism, based on veneration of the Twelve Imams. It is to the twelfth of these twelve, the Mahdi or 'hidden Imam', who will return at the end of time, on the day of Resurrection, that Shah 'Abbas's mosque is dedicated.

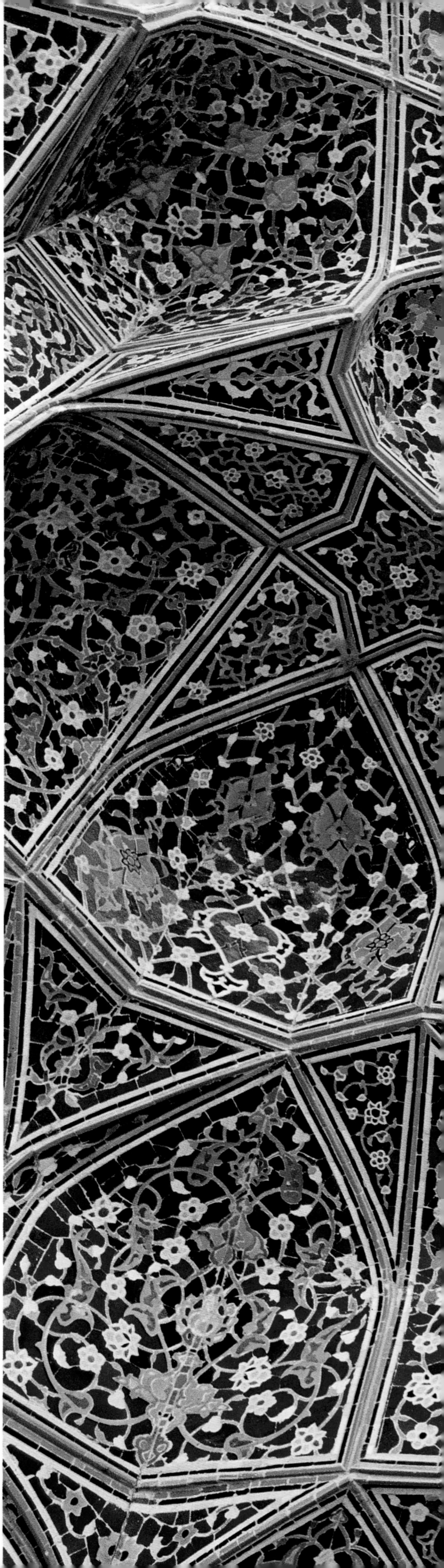

Examined in this light, the proportions of the courtyard, which is the heart of the building, are revealing, for they provide the key to Shi'ite symbolism: the rectangular plan is based on the proportions of the Pythagorean or right-angled triangle. Persian scholars knew Greek sources – witness the philosophy of the 'Persian Platonists' – and these placed great importance on numbers and mathematical proportions. This understanding of proportions allowed them to detect the special significance of a building.

The simplest way to construct a right-angled triangle is to give the sides the proportions of 3, 4 and 5: the short side is equal to 3 units, the side at a right angle to that is 4, and the hypotenuse (or diagonal) is5. These three numbers have the special property of producing the whole-number squares 9, 16 and 25. For the Shi'ites, however, they had another, more important, property: the sum of 3, 4 and 5 is 12, the number of Imams in Twelver Shi'ism.

By basing his plan for the courtyard of a mosque dedicated to the twelfth Imam on the proportions of the famous Pythagorean triangle, Ali Akbar Isfahani inscribed at the heart of the building both its intended use and its profound significance.

Tiles on the walls in the arcades surrounding the courtyard reveal a world peopled with goats, birds, flowers and trees, and strange Chinese-style clouds that are reminders of the influence of imported ceramics.

Agra: the Glorious Taj Mahal, Shah Jahan's Mausoleum

The Taj Mahal was built by the Mughal emperor Shah Jahan in the middle third of the 17th century. (For a discussion of the Taj in its historical setting, and the argument that Shah Jahan built it for himself, see pp. 178–81.) It stands more than a kilometre southeast of the Red Fort at Agra, on a rectangular site one narrow end of which borders the Jumna River. The site is strictly oriented north-south, and measures 565 x 305 metres (ill. p. 277 below). At the centre is a garden of *chahar bagh* type 300 metres square, which is divided into four by two orthogonal axes, formed by slightly raised marble water channels. These four waterways that meet in a large central pool represent the four Rivers of Paradise. Each quadrant of the *chahar bagh* is divided into four, and those squares are again divided into four, producing the sort of 'ordered and symmetrical' grid that was already admired by the emperor Babur.

opposite, above Detail of the *pietra dura* decoration on the holiest parts of the mausoleum.

opposite, below Looking down towards the entrance across the gardens, showing their axial water channel and fountain, their orthogonal organization, and the symmetrical planting.

above The glowing vision of the famous tomb known as the Taj Mahal, a Paradisal structure which the Mughal Emperor Shah Jahan intended for himself. It received his remains in 1666, having earlier received those of his wife Mumtaz Mahal, who died young in 1631.

The gardens of the Taj Mahal, and the mausoleum itself, are reached through an entrance on the south side of the garden, where a subsidiary area measuring 305 x 130 metres accommodates the great gateway and the service buildings. The monumental gate forms a grand prelude in red sandstone to the symphony of masses and volumes in radiant white marble of the mausoleum, which lies 350 metres away on the other side of the gardens. It has a large central *iwan* linked by two tiers of niches to octagonal corner turrets topped by *chhatris*. Fine white marble decoration sets off the lively red of the sandstone.

Seen from this gate early in the morning, in the pink mist of dawn, the Taj Mahal has an unreal appearance, as though the delicately modulated mass of marble supporting the great dome on a drum framed by *chhatris* was entirely translucent.

The tomb stands on a terrace overlooking the Jumna, supported on an artificial platform 95 metres square and 5.5 metres high which is made up of some 50,000 cubic metres, or 120,000 tons, of infill. This plinth, entirely faced in white marble, holds up the famous mausoleum like an offering. The tomb itself forms a taut unit, fitted into a square of 57 x 57 metres, with on each face a large *iwan* in a rectangular frame, behind which, with an irresistible thrust, the bulbous dome shoots up, reaching a height of 73 metres at the tip of the gilt bronze finial on its apex. The dome is buttressed by four masses on the diagonals which have chamfered corners and are themselves given rigidity

opposite Axonometric view of the Taj Mahal complex. At the near end are the monumental entrance and ancillary buildings; in the centre, a *chahar bagh* garden with central pool; at the far end, the main buildings, with the tomb flanked by a mosque on the left and guesthouse on the right. The Jumna River lies beyond. (Courtesy Klaus W. Herdeg)

opposite and above The entrance gate sets the scene for the mausoleum, perfectly framing its *iwan* 350 metres away. With octagonal corner turrets topped by *chhatris* and inset niches, it is built of red sandstone, whereas the tomb is entirely of white marble. Here marble is used only for the calligraphic and floral decorations.

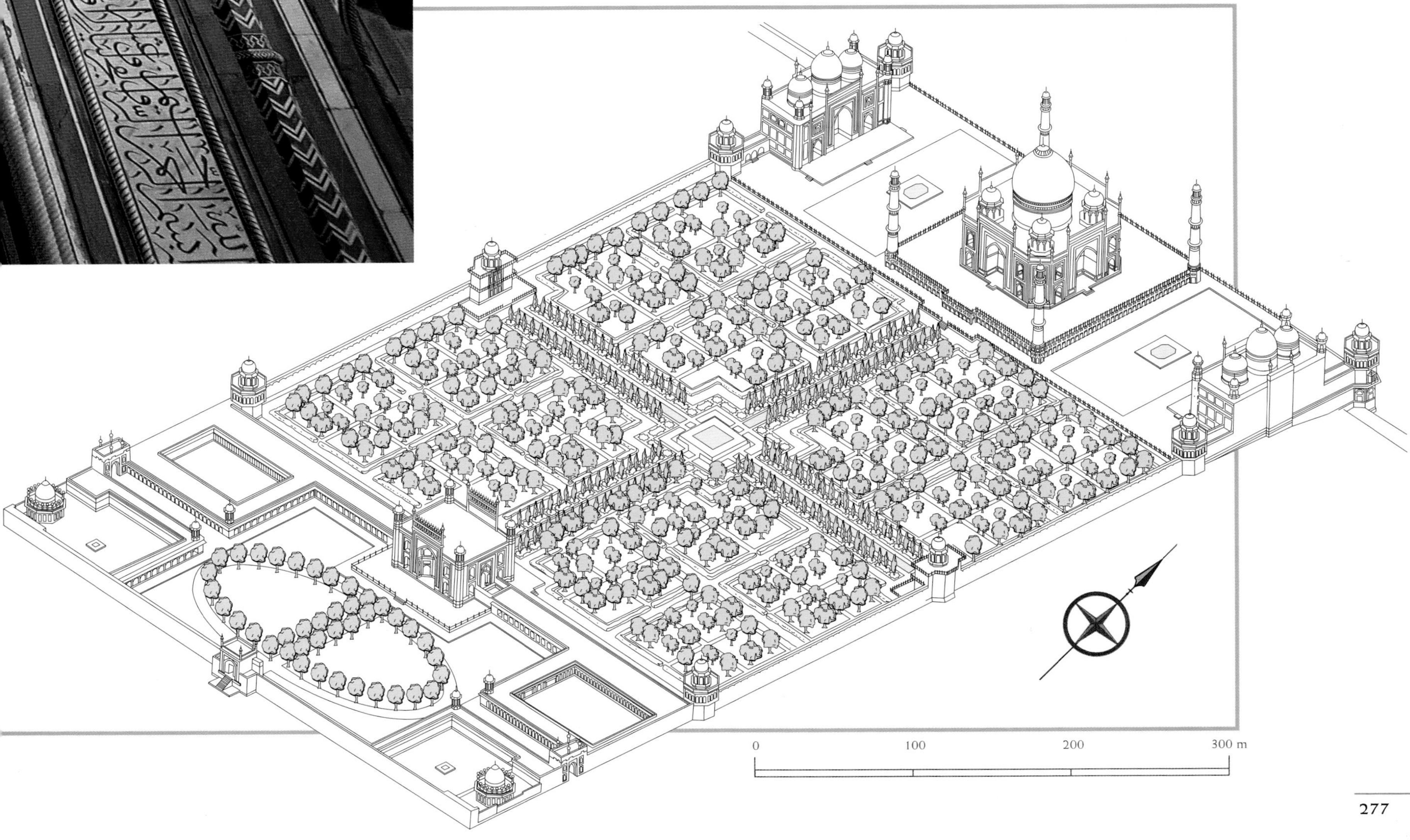

'The Taje Mahel, at Agra', from Thomas and William Daniell's *Oriental Scenery*, 1795.
The gate leading into the garden is in the foreground; the white silhouette of the tomb appears in the distance.

by two tiers of vaulted openings. These corner masses have four large *chhatris* on their roofs, which provide a visual link between them and the dome. Framing the building at the corners of the plinth, four handsome minarets 42 metres tall stand in isolation; they are divided into three stages that taper towards the top, and are crowned and roofed by small *chhatris*.

This play of elegant and harmonious masses produces a profound impression of balance and serenity. The juxtaposition of the soaring shafts of the minarets and the solid volume of the main body creates a welcome contrast between upward movement and static mass. The roofscape of the tomb reads like a pyramid of spherical surfaces, giving a final touch of lyrical perfection.

The Taj Mahal is axially framed to east and west by two buildings in red sandstone, both topped by three white domes. These ancillary structures are perfectly matched, although they do not serve the same function: the one to the east (right) was designed to accommodate important guests; the one to the west (left) is a funerary mosque dedicated to the memory of the departed. The two structures, guesthouse and mosque, were intended for the pilgrims who came to the tomb of Shah Jahan and his wife, Mumtaz Mahal.

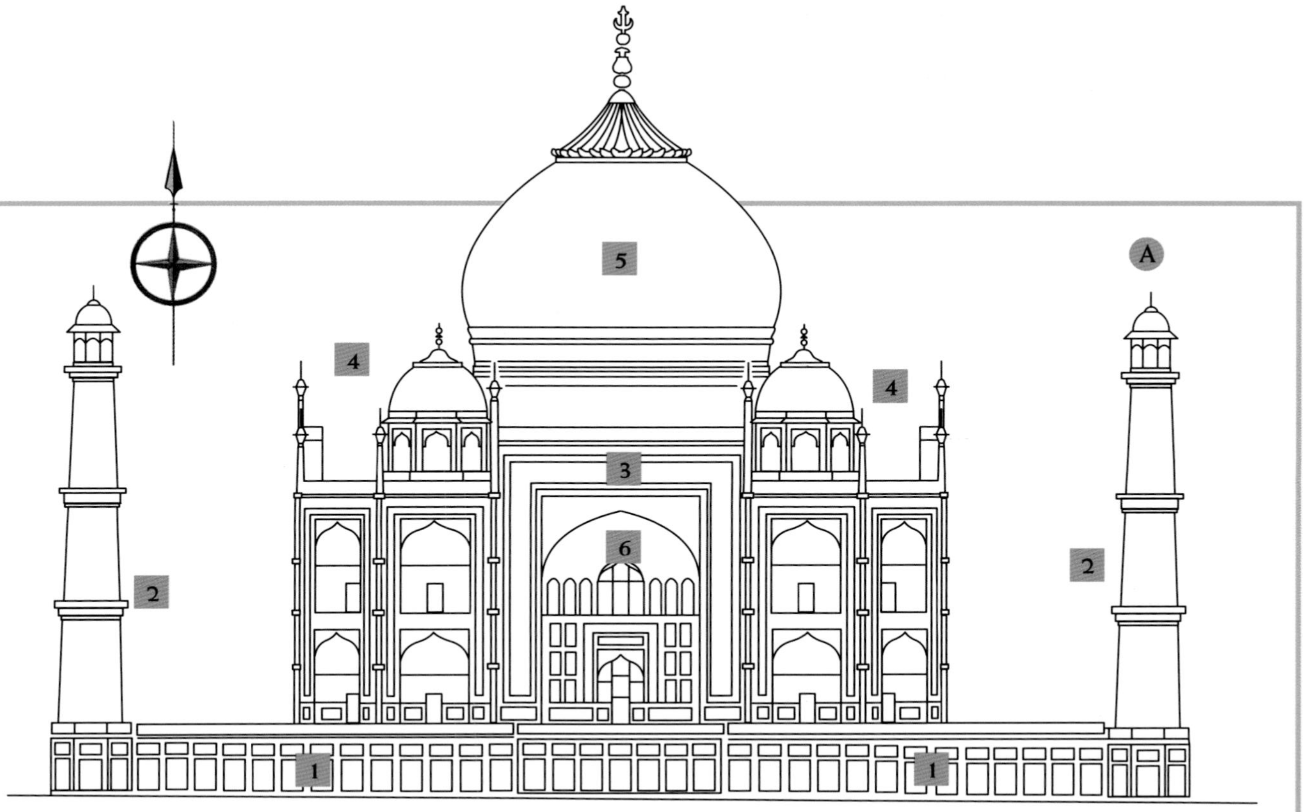

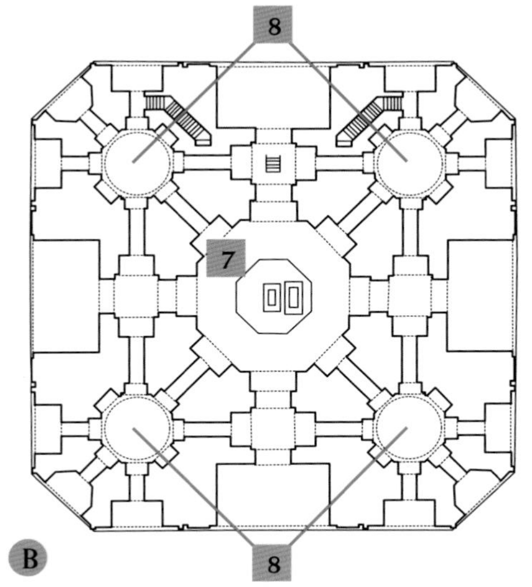

Key

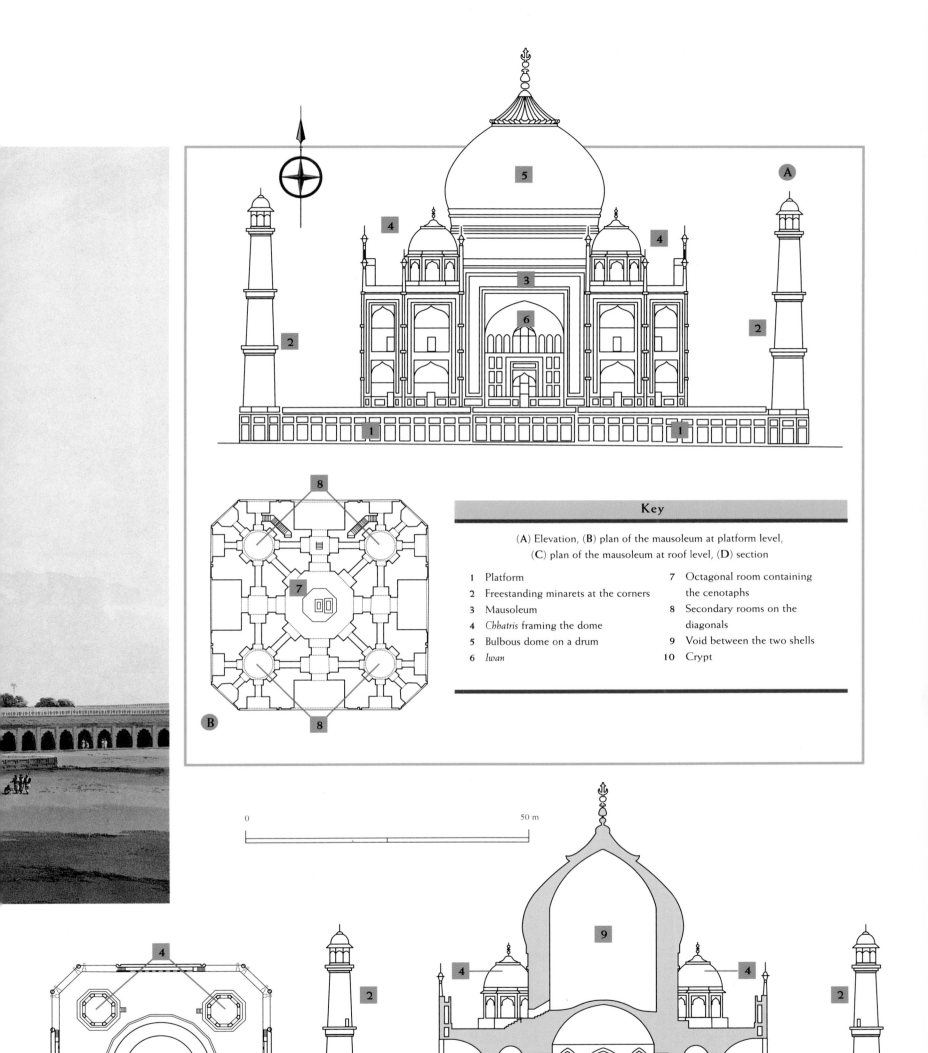

(**A**) Elevation, (**B**) plan of the mausoleum at platform level, (**C**) plan of the mausoleum at roof level, (**D**) section

1. Platform
2. Freestanding minarets at the corners
3. Mausoleum
4. *Chhatris* framing the dome
5. Bulbous dome on a drum
6. *Iwan*
7. Octagonal room containing the cenotaphs
8. Secondary rooms on the diagonals
9. Void between the two shells
10. Crypt

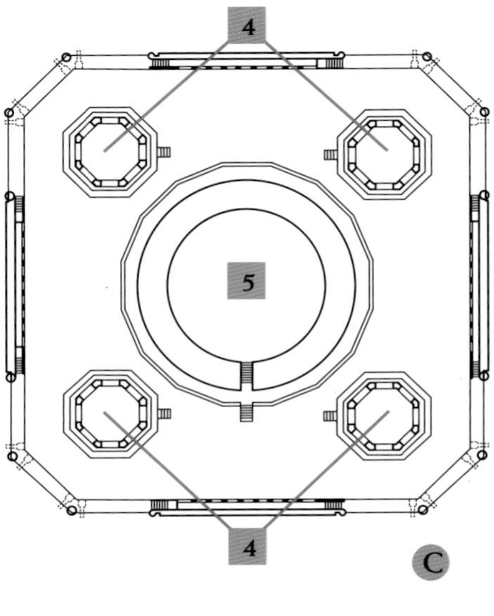

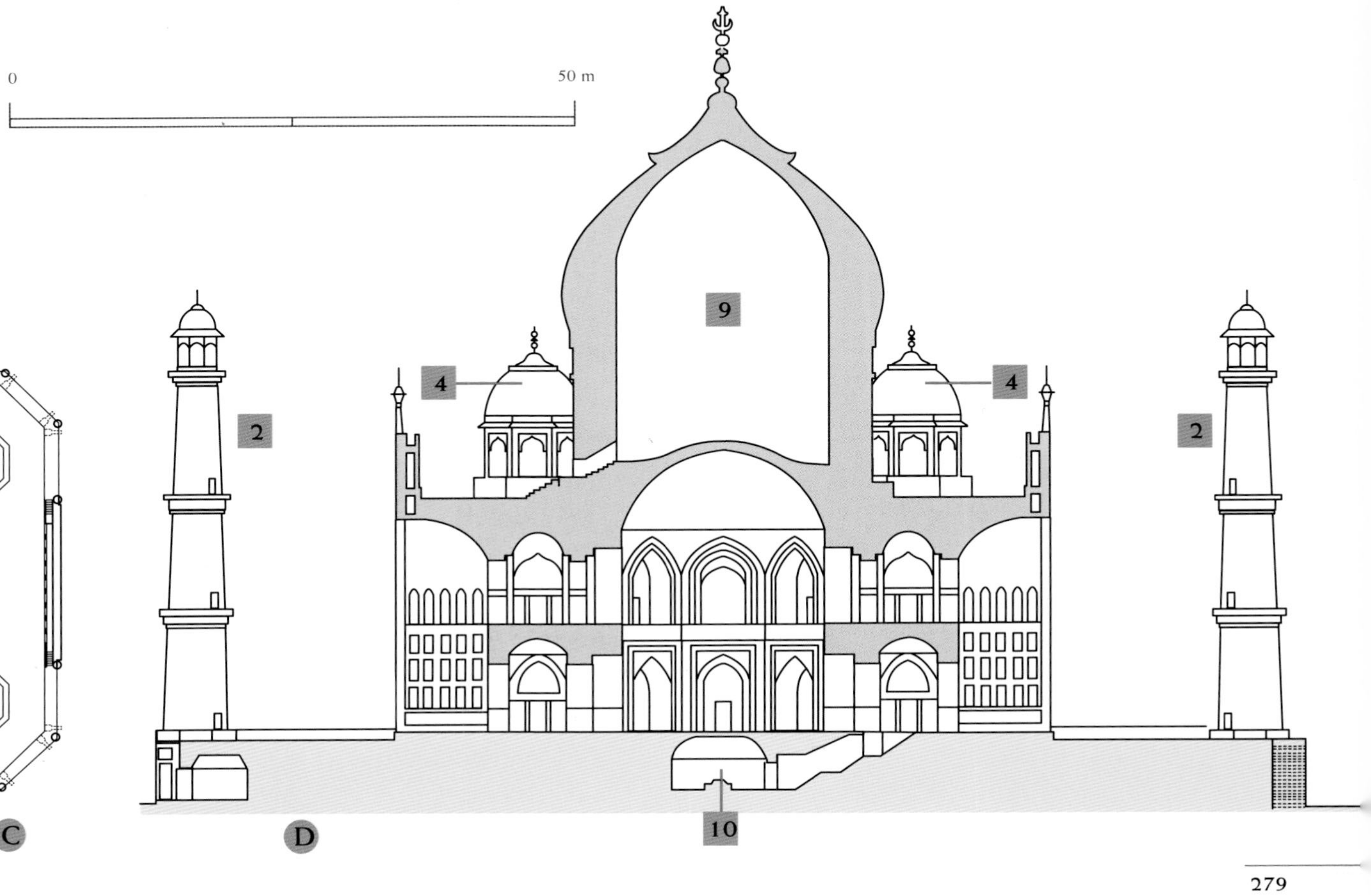

The white marble tomb, framed by minarets, is flanked by the red sandstone guesthouse on the left and mosque on the right. Seen from the north in the late afternoon, the complex is shimmeringly reflected in the waters of the Jumna.

When you enter the mausoleum through the axial *iwan* you come first to an antechamber which is linked at the sides to octagonal rooms in the corners of the building. These four secondary rooms are stages on an outer path suitable for the ritual of circumambulation. Moving on to the funerary chamber, which is also octagonal, the pilgrim reaches the most important space of all, which contains the cenotaphs of the emperor and empress. This chamber, which measures 18 metres in diameter and 25 metres to the top of the shallow inner dome, has two tiers of arcades filled with *jalis*. In the centre, a tall octagonal screen, also filled with pierced marble panels, encloses the sumptuous cenotaphs but allows the pilgrim to glimpse their white marble surfaces encrusted with *pietra dura* floral motifs. This central zone is a space of exquisite refinement, where the sacredness of the place is at its most intense. Around the octagonal screen, again, is a space for circumambulation.

The real tombs of Shah Jahan and Mumtaz Mahal are in a vaulted crypt immediately below the cenotaphs, in what had by then become the standard arrangement in Islamic India.

right, above and centre The cenotaphs of Shah Jahan and Mumtaz Mahal in the octagonal room at the heart of the Taj Mahal are protected by finely carved *jalis* of white marble. Pilgrims show their veneration by circumambulating this screen. The cenotaphs themselves are of white marble with delicate *pietra dura* inlay in the form of bunches of flowers, single blooms, or friezes.

right, below One of the galleries that link the secondary rooms in the corners of the mausoleum. Everywhere the light is softened by *jalis*.

An impressive early example of the practice occurs in the Gur-i Amir, the tomb of Shah Jahan's ancestor Timur, in Samarqand.

The funerary chamber is given a feeling of balance and harmony by the lower of the double shells of the dome. Between this and the great dome visible from outside there is a dark, inaccessible void, 19 metres in diameter and 27 metres high, which is paradoxically the largest space in the whole mausoleum, though it has no function other than to give the building a silhouette of unrivalled grace and elegance. This Timurid formula of the double-shelled dome was taken up very early in India: we have already come across it in Humayun's Tomb (ill. p. 238, below), begun in 1557, and even before the Mughals it had been used in the Mausoleum of Sikander Lodi in Delhi, built c. 1518.

The bulbous dome of the Taj Mahal stands on a drum 26 metres in diameter and some 12

metres high, and is topped by a 10-metre tall gilt bronze finial that incorporates the traditional crescent moon.

Coming closer to the Taj Mahal, one is struck by the richness and quality of the materials used, the glittering whiteness of the translucent marble, and the perfection of its precious surfaces – but what is striking above all is the extraordinary profusion of the decoration. All the surfaces are adorned with reliefs, with inlaid strips of black marble, with geometrical and other repetitive patterns, with inscriptions in elegant thuluth characters, with floral panels, with friezes and with borders, and with inlaid precious and semi-precious stones in the *pietra dura* technique, forming sparkling colourful bunches of flowers. Everywhere is a feast for the eyes – walls, *jalis*, panels, piers, arcades, tympanums, star-patterned floors, and the soffits of the great *iwans*, where counterfeit honeycomb and rib vaulting enlivens the concave surfaces.

As one would expect, the most sumptuous ornament is that on the cenotaphs, where *pietra dura* reaches perfection, and the Iranian-Timurid passion for the world of flowers was given free rein. Babur had written with enthusiasm about the splendours of nature and listed the varieties of flowers to be found in India, and that same interest in plants underlies the Mughal rulers' love of rose gardens, of beds with innumerable types of blooms, and of trees. It is reflected in manuscript paintings as well as in the delicate inlays of coloured stones that gleam from the polished surfaces of the finest Mughal tombs.

The quintessence of this floral ornament is seen at the Taj Mahal, adorned as it is with an extraordinary range of colours, achieved by means of different stones – agate, carnelian, lapis lazuli, onyx, turquoise, amethyst, alabaster, jasper, coral, and various marbles. The colours transform both exterior and, especially, interior surfaces

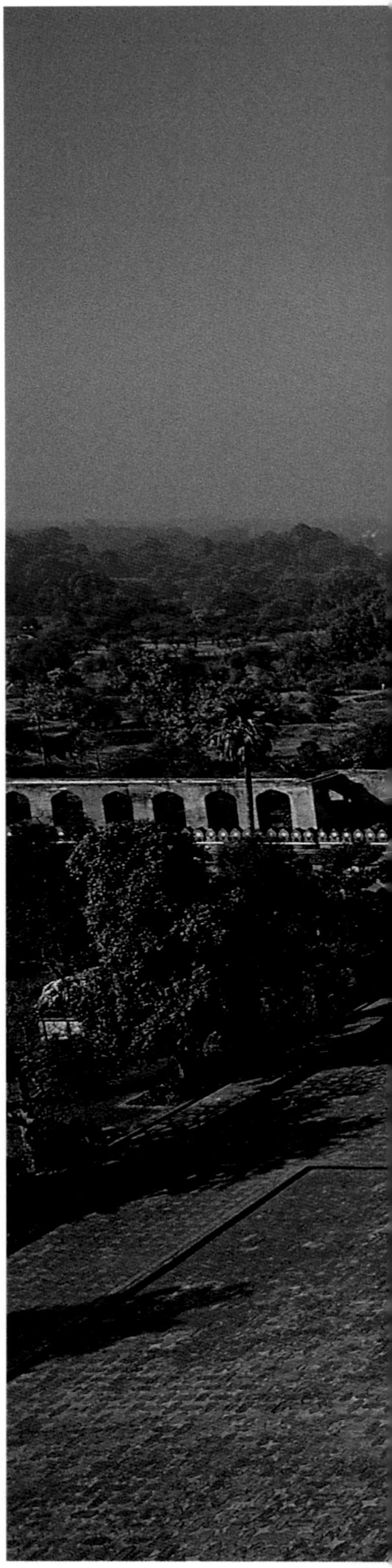

left The Tomb of Khan-i Khanan in Delh
built *c.* 1627, has lost its marble decoratio
but its form is interestingly close to
that of the Taj Mahal.

opposite, centre, and above The mosque that flanks the Taj Mahal to the west has three domes resting on drums with a black-and-white chequer pattern. In the oblong prayer hall (*opposite, centre*) the presence of the *mibrab* is emphasized by the use of white marble rather than red sandstone. In the distance to the right of the mosque, where the Jumna bends, is the Red Fort, from which Shah Jahan spent years contemplating the mausoleum he would one day occupy.

opposite The dome on its high drum, with its tall gilt bronze finial, seen from the upper level of the south-western minaret. In the foreground, an octagonal *chhatri* and two pinnacles form a transition between the dome and the chamfered corner.

below One of the chamfered corners, showing the articulation. The dazzlingly white marble is everywhere adorned with floral motifs and inscriptions.

bottom A flowering plant carved in white marble.

into a brilliant bouquet. Everything expresses joy and happiness: Islamic tombs are not places of sorrow.

What meticulous labour on the part of hundreds of craftsmen lies behind all this ornamentation – behind the ever-vital plant forms, like those on Timurid and Safavid monuments, behind the delicate arabesques, the repeated patterns that appear rhythmically in border and frames, the elegant calligraphy of the texts enclosed in friezes, the low relief of the false honeycomb ornament on the *iwans*, and above all what infinite patience was required to produce the *jalis*, whose skilful rhythms and geometrical patterning creates subtle barriers that invite one to peer through.

The Taj Mahal was also the setting for splendid entertainments hosted by the ruler: these were sumptuous and joyous celebrations, suggesting the ineffable joys which, the Prophet promised, await the devout in the Gardens of Paradise. Shah Jahan's guests moved down the paths of the park to the sound of fountains and birdsong, and enjoyed magnificent hospitality from the future inhabitant of the tomb. No funereal thoughts came to lessen the splendour and gaiety of the fireworks that lit up the night sky of Agra when he entertained the court. The fame of these festivities spread to far-off countries, and made the Great Mughal the paradigm of the all-powerful, magnificent ruler.

left, above The Madrasa Mader-i Shah, seen from the air. It was built in 1706–14 by the Safavid Shah Sultan Husain. As in the Mosque of the Imam (ill. pp. 258, 262), the beautiful dome is flanked by two minarets; but here the corners of the courtyard are canted.

left, centre A detail of the ornament of flowering branches on the dome. Bricks glazed on the outer face are assembled to form a magnificent decoration of intertwining fronds, emphasized by black arabesques.

left, below An ornamental motif in which a geometric frame encloses a naturalistic, 'romantic', bunch of flowers typical of the 18th century.

opposite Pascal Coste's view of the main *iwan*, with its two minarets that frame the dome; on either side are two arcaded tiers of rooms for teachers and students. Compare Coste's elevation, also from *Les Monuments modernes de la Perse* (1867), on pp. 186–87.

Isfahan: the Madrasa Mader-i Shah and the 'Baroquizing' of Shapes

The Madrasa of the Mother of the Shah was built by Shah Sultan Husain (1694–1722) only eight years before the catastrophic Afghan invasion that put an end to the Safavid dynasty. Looking at this magnificent ensemble, there is nothing to suggest imminent collapse; Isfahan was a flourishing capital, and European travellers such as Jean Chardin, a Huguenot jeweller who lived there for four years, considered it one of the largest cities of its time. It was said to have six hundred caravanserais and three hundred *hammams*

The complex of the *madrasa* was built between 1706 and 1714 on the east side of the great Chahar Bagh avenue as it descends towards the Zayandeh Rud (ill. p. 153 below). The site, which measures 114 x 220 metres (making a total area of some 25,000 square metres), accommodates a series of superb buildings: a *madrasa* with its mosque, a large caravanserai, stables, and an immense bazaar. The latter runs along the northern edge of the complex and consists of 84 shops on both sides of a covered passage. Parallel to the bazaar is an axial channel which links the three courtyard buildings. This 'river' starts at the public avenue and flows from west to east. It first runs under the entrance vestibule of the *madrasa*, then emerges in the *chahar bagh* garden, before going underground again below the *iwan* opposite; it reappears in the vast court of the caravanserai, where it is bridged by a central platform, then disappears under the eastern *iwan* of the caravanserai, and finally emerges in the centre of the stable courtyard. The conceit is a grand essay in urbanism.

The *madrasa* itself is centred on a courtyard planted with trees that measures 60 x 70 metres and is divided into two symmetrical parts by the central channel. It has the traditional plan with four *iwan*s; these lead into oblong halls with shallow vaults.

The north-south axis, perpendicular to the water, is focused on the mosque, whose *iwan* leads to a circular prayer hall. That hall is surmounted by a bulbous dome framed by two minarets, as at Shah 'Abbas's Mosque of the Imam, which it fully equals in the elegance of the dome's profile and the perfection of its vegetal decorations on a turquoise background. The general impression is very different, however, because of the large trees – planes, poplars and pines – that grow among the flowers in the courtyard. Here, natural vegetation has in a sense taken the place of *kashis*, and instead of bouquets on the walls we often find geometrical motifs.

Key

1 Entrance to the bazaar from the Chahar Bagh
2 Covered gallery of the bazaar
3 Main entrance to the *madrasa*
4 Western vestibule
5 Traditional four-part garden
6 Water channel
7 Northern vestibule opening off the bazaar
8 Northern *iwan*
9 Southern *iwan*
10 Prayer hall of the mosque
11 Eastern vestibule
12 Hypostyle winter hall
13 Garden of the caravanserai
14 Northern *iwan* of the caravanserai
15 Water channel in the garden of the caravanserai
16 Stables

left The top of one of the minarets. Pascal Coste's measured drawing minutely records the *muqarnas* that support the balcony from which the muezzin calls the faithful to prayer.

below The *madrasa*, seen in a mid-19th-century engraving. It presents a façade with a double tier of arcades to the prestigious Chahar Bagh avenue, laid out by Shah 'Abbas a century earlier, which is planted with trees and has a central water-channel. The dome and minarets appear at the right, seen from the side.

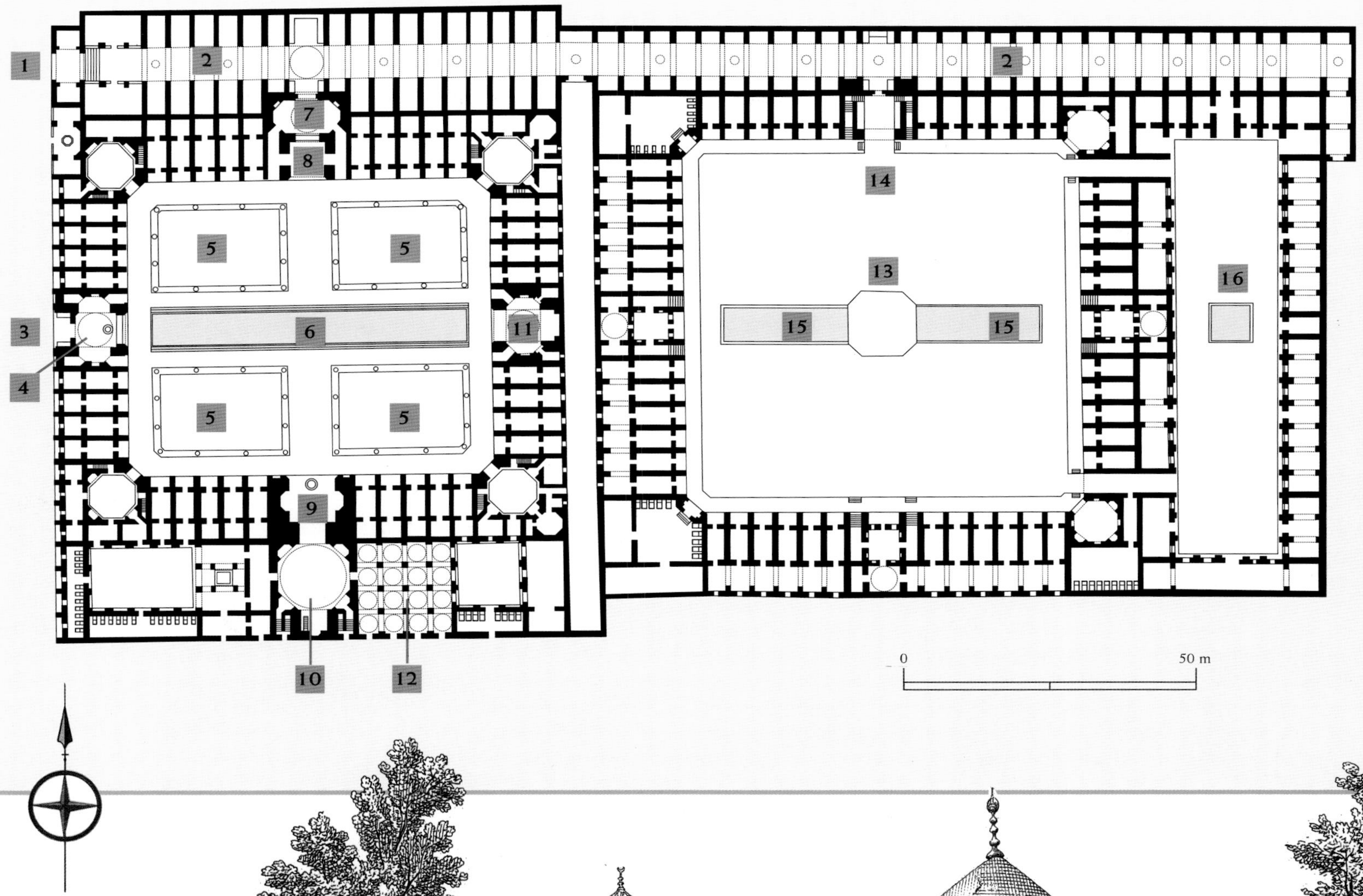
1
2
2
7
8
14
5
5
13
16
3
6
11
15
15
4
5
5
9
10
12
0
50 m

The northern *iwan* of the *madrasa*, with to left and right two levels of cells for teachers and students. In this shady courtyard, the green-toned decoration harmonizes with the green of the great trees.

right, above The sunny, buttercup-yellow tiled vault of the entrance vestibule on the west side offers a complex pattern of intersecting ribs above the polygonal apse.

right, centre In the eastern vestibule, the apses have honeycomb vaults of infinite complexity, which take the Safavid style to a 'baroque' extreme.

The courtyard façades have two tiers of arcaded openings between the *iwans* that front 80 cells for teachers and students. On both storeys these openings have what appear to be masonry vaults covered with honeycombs emphasized by lines painted on a white background. But all is not what it seems: the 'vaults' are made of plaster on a wooden structure.

The main *iwan* that leads to the prayer hall demonstrates the principle of the fragmentation of surfaces that characterizes the late Safavid style. Instead of smooth, gleaming surfaces, what we see now is something far more complex: each face of the *iwan* and of the vestibule is given apse-like features, each of which in turn has little apses, with the effect of producing a space that is almost baroque. Instead of smooth walls, there are designs that are infinitely subdivided, and topped by faceted vaults. The corners dissolve into ever smaller honeycombs, into networks of ribs, pendentives, and hollows. Passing over all these surfaces, light is fragmented.

right The elegant pair of minarets that flank the dome of the mosque.

Similarly, the vaults of the halls mostly have a shallow profile, on which the decoration appears to seethe. Hundreds of coloured glazed bricks play formal geometrical games in which yellow and blue-green are dominant. This mosaic of a new type, larger in scale than before, covers every surface with patterns made up from square, triangular, hexagonal or octagonal elements. Plant motifs survive only in a few floral panels and in the great branching trails on the dome.

Another change in outlook reflected in architecture can be seen in the vaults of the vestibules and halls: these are reduced to two-thirds of their previous height, and instead of squinches they have networks of

ribs that extend down into pendentives. The smoothness of the springing enhances the unity between walls and ceilings.

The features noted in the *madrasa* recur in the great caravanserai (now a hotel), which had 94 rooms on two floors to accommodate travellers. Here too the composition is based on four axial *iwans*.

It is clear that late Safavid architecture was moving in directions that were profoundly new, in the matter both of three-dimensional composition and of ornament, just as the dynasty was about to succumb to Afghan aggression.

opposite, above A sacred inscription so stylized as to seem a cryptogram.

opposite, below Each of the rooms of the school has a balcony covered by a honeycomb vault with painted ribbing. These *muqarnas* are realized in plaster.

above Water fills the ablutions pool to the brim, creating a perfect reflection of the surrounding façades. The corners are canted, and have bridging arches that open into small courtyards with a baroque octagonal shape.

overleaf The southern *iwan* that leads into the prayer hall of the mosque is based on a 16-sided polygon. It is covered with a subtle pattern of ribbing and, at the corners, honeycomb-filled squinches covered in ornate 'pointillist' patterns that contrast with the floral scrolls on the vault.

The Origins of Muslim Iran: History and Culture 622–900

The pages that follow are designed to situate the Persian world in history and in the realm of artistic creation. A look at the main facts leading up to the Persian renaissance should illuminate the origin of cultural traits that underlie the works considered in this study.

p. 296, above The Prophet Muhammad in Paradise, from a Safavid manuscript.

p. 296, below A classic motif of Umayyad art, seen in a mosaic in the Great Mosque at Damascus dating from 707–714: heavenly dwellings beside flowing water, under the branches of a great tree.

p. 297 A gold-ground mosaic in the courtyard of the Great Mosque at Damascus shows palaces under shady trees beside a River of Paradise, alluding to the afterlife promised to believers in the Qur'an.

above The great arch of the Sasanian palace of Ctesiphon in Mesopotamia dates from the reign of Chosroes I in the 6th century. This extraordinary brick vault 36 metres high was that of the royal hall. Muslim architects saw it as a paradigm to be surpassed.

The ancient civilization of Iran first came into contact with Europe when Cyrus moved into Anatolia and conquered the Greek cities of Ionia. After that there were Greeks in the service of the Achaemenid rulers, and they were involved in the construction of the palaces of Pasargadae, Susa and Persepolis. This is known from foundation inscriptions, written in cuneiform characters, on heavy 'pages' of gold.

Alexander for a brief time assumed the Achaemenid throne, and then under the Seleucids the East was Hellenized and permanent links were forged between Asia and the West; in this state of symbiosis Greek kingdoms flourished not only from the Mediterranean coast to Iran, but as far as Bactria and the Indus delta. Roman imperialism was felt in the East before the empire was proclaimed in Rome: it led to constant fighting, first with the Parthians (who came into contact with Rome under Sulla in the 1st century BCE) and then with the Sasanians (224–651), until the early 7th century. By then, Iran had been the most fearsome adversary of the Hellenic world, the Roman Empire and finally Byzantium for more than half a millennium.

Milestones on the road to this profound antagonism include the defeat of Crassus's legions at Carrhae in 54 BCE, Trajan's campaigns against the Parthians in 114–117, those of Verus in 162–166, the expedition of Septimius Severus in 195, and the annexation of Mesopotamia in 199, before the advent of the Sasanians. The Persian wars resumed in 231, and again in 241, when the Sasanians invaded the Near East during a great period of crisis for the Roman Empire. Valerian was taken prisoner near Edessa in 260; the Emperor Carus resumed fighting in 282, invaded Mesopotamia, and signed a treaty in 287; but conflict resumed in 297, and again in 338–350, after the death of Constantine. Yet another Persian war broke out in 363, under Julian the Apostate, and Theodosius concluded a new treaty in 387. During the Byzantine period things seemed to settle down after the war against Bahram V around 420: a 'hundred-year peace' was concluded at the time when Attila and the Huns were attacking the empire. But in 476 Anastasius I, the emperor in the East, broke off relations with Iran, rekindling conflict in 502. Neither side emerged victorious, but fighting temporarily stopped.

The struggle between the two great powers now reached a decisive phase, and over the course of a century (527–629) the entire region witnessed the most extraordinary feats of arms. Under Justinian, conflict with the Sasanians intensified: the Persians were defeated by Belisarius in 530, but in 540 hostilities resumed when Chosroes I captured Antioch. A truce was declared in 555, followed by the signing of a treaty in 562. But Justinian II refused to pay tribute to the Persians, and fighting

top Floral carving in the Sasanian cave at Takh-i Bostan, 4th century.

above A relief at Naqsh-i Rustam depicts the triumph of the Sasanian ruler Shapur I (241–272) – who wears a turreted crown surmounted by a globe – over the Roman emperors Philip the Arabian (244–249) and Valerian (253–260).

started again in 572. Chosroes took Apamea, but was defeated at Melitene in 575.

This constant fighting, and the exhaustion of the two warring powers, favoured the first movements of the turbulent tribes in Arabia. In 578, Chosroes had to do battle with the neighbouring Arab princes as well: there were the Lakhmids, who were his vassals, and also the Ghassanids, who were allies of the Byzantine Christians. Their attempt to throw off the yoke was crushed by Tiberius II. In 581, the Emperor Maurice defeated the Persians and placed Chosroes II on the Sasanian throne. A great ruler, Chosroes succeeded in occupying Syria in 605, and in 609 he took Chalcedon and threatened Constantinople.

This was just the time, around 610, when in Arabia, according to tradition, Muhammad was called by God through the intermediary of the Archangel Gabriel, and ordered to spread the Word. Muhammad's 'recitation' went on until his death in 632. The transcription of his message by the faithful resulted in the Qur'an, which was completed by the *hadith*. Thus was born the third religion of the Book. What is important here is to recall that the expansion of Islam coincided with the antagonism between Byzantines and Sasanians at the beginning of the 7th century. Distracted by their struggle, the two opponents were unaware of the mounting threat from Arabia. Between 611 and 614 the Persians invaded the eastern provinces of the Byzantine Empire. Sasanian troops took Jerusalem, where they stole the famous relic of the True Cross and took it off to Ctesiphon, and occupied Egypt in 618. In a move to take them by surprise, Heraclius entered Armenia and defeated the Persian general Shahrbaraz in 622. The Persians quit Pontus and Cappadocia, and in the confusion Heraclius pushed on, taking possession of Media Atropatene and entering Ctesiphon in 627. In 629 the Sasanians withdrew from Byzantine territory, returned the True Cross, and fell into a state of anarchy.

The Arab tribes, aflame with the desire to spread their new faith, took advantage of the situation, and Abu Bakr, the Prophet's successor, launched his horsemen against Syria and Babylonia. This was the beginning of the expansion of Islam. Ctesiphon fell in 637, after the Arab victory at the battle of al-Qadisiyya, where their forces annihilated the Sasanians. Soon afterwards, in 638, Omar took possession of Jerusalem, the Holy City.

My aim in chronicling all these dates and feats of arms is to show how events accelerated, and to bring out the desire for absolute power of the Sasanians and Byzantines: the former were destroyed, and the latter were greatly weakened by a contest to which both sacrificed everything.

Muhammad, Prophet and Founder

left Angels appear around the Ka'ba in Mecca at the birth of the Prophet Muhammad: an Ottoman miniature of 1594, from the *Siyer i-Nebi* or *Life of Muhammad* by Sufti Abdullah, court painter to Murad III. (Topkapi Library, Istanbul)

opposite, above left The Archangel Gabriel announces to Muhammad his prophetic mission; the Prophet, surrounded by a golden halo, wears a veil as a sign of respect. From the *Siyer i-Nebi*, late 16th century. (Topkapi Library, Istanbul)

opposite, above right The people of Mecca surrounding the Ka'ba, a cubic monument which contains the Black Stone venerated by Muslims. Circumambulation of this sacred object is the high point of any pilgrimage.

opposite, below A page from a 9th-century Qur'an in large kufic script. The words of this holy book, which contains God's revelation to Muhammad, form the basis of the Muslim faith.

Muhammad was born in Mecca in 570 to a wealthy family that had fallen on hard times. He lost his father when he was two and his mother when he was eight. He was raised by his uncle, a merchant, who made him a caravan driver on the stretch from the Red Sea to the Mediterranean in the great commercial route linking East and West. It seems that in Arabia Muhammad got to know members of the Jewish community, who taught him the writings of the Torah. Then, in Syria, the future prophet met a Christian priest who introduced him to the Gospels. At the age of twenty-five he married a rich widow, fifteen years his senior, with whom he had several children. Of them all only a daughter, Fatima, survived; she married Alì, Muhammad's first cousin.

Muhammad was forty when he heard God's call for the first time: the Archangel Gabriel exhorted him to 'recite in the name of Allah' – hence the name *Qur'an*, or 'recitation', given to his message. Muhammad was now more than a prophet: he was the messenger of God, and he proclaimed a new religion – *Islam*, or 'submission to the will of God'. His words and deeds were noted by his early followers, and collated up to the time of the third caliph, 'Uthman (644–656). After that, further oral accounts of Muhammad were collected up to the 9th century; known as the *hadith*, these constitute the second basis of Islamic dogma and law, the *sunna*.

Muhammad began to preach in Mecca, and persisted for a dozen years, although his message was greeted with sarcasm and ridicule by the wealthy merchants: they refused to believe the revelations of a self-proclaimed prophet in the lineage of the Jewish men of God, one who referred to Abraham, Ishmael, Adam, Noah, Moses, Lot, Elijah and Elisha as well as to Joseph, Jesus and Mary. Feeling himself misunderstood and threatened, Muhammad decided to move with his followers to the oasis of Yathrib, which was renamed Medinat al-Nebi, 'the Prophet's city' (now Medina). This migration – the *hijra* or Hegira – took place in 622, and from it the Muslim calendar is reckoned. The Muslim calendar is based on the lunar year of 354 or 355 days, so it has become progressively more and more out of step with the solar calendars (first Julian, then Gregorian) of antiquity and Christendom.

In Medina Muhammad founded the first Muslim 'state', and over the course of the ten years there he continued his revelation. His powerfully lyrical language is based on the usage of pre-Islamic Arabia, and his role as the vehicle of the word of God was to lead to Arabic becoming the language of a large proportion of humanity. In his capacity as head of the community of the faithful, Muhammad showed himself to be a fine strategist and able negotiator; he even launched raids to cut off caravan traffic with Mecca, prefiguring the *jihad* or holy war that was to be an essential force in the spread of the Muslim religion.

Muhammad still felt himself an exile in the oasis of Medina, however. Wishing to put an end to the antagonism with Mecca, in the sixth year of the Hegira he decided to make a pilgrimage there with his followers; a truce was agreed for the following year. In 629 he marched on Mecca and entered as a conqueror. He smashed the idols of the old pre-Islamic sanctuary, sparing only the Black Stone, because it had been venerated by Abraham and his son Ishmael.

In his own house in Medina, Muhammad established a place of meeting and prayer for his small community – effectively the first mosque. His house was oriented north-south, and consisted of an enclosure surrounding a roughly square courtyard some

50 x 50 metres (roughly 100 cubits), with rooms on the west side made of mud brick. Against the north wall of the courtyard he built a lean-to structure with a roof of palm leaves resting on two rows of supports made of palm tree trunks. This was the first prayer hall; here, sheltered from the sun and infrequent rain, the faithful could hear the words of the Prophet and perform the ritual gestures and prostration that he prescribed. The back wall of this rough construction was perpendicular to the direction of Jerusalem, so those prostrating themselves before it were facing towards the city: this was the first *qibla*.

In the orientation to Jerusalem Muhammad was paying homage to the Holy City and placing himself in the tradition of the great revealed religions that had gone before. He wanted to show that Islam was a continuation of Judaism, and he also attempted to have himself recognized as a successor to Christ; but neither the Jews nor the Christian community of Najran accepted his claims. A decisive break with the Jewish community occurred in 630, and then the split became definitive: Muhammad expelled or ordered the massacre of all adherents of the religions that preceded his own. When he returned from his pilgrimage to Mecca he decided to give up the orientation of the mosque that he had built. Medina is situated roughly on a line between Jerusalem and Mecca: thus if the orientation were reversed, the faithful would face the Ka'ba. The south wall of the courtyard of his house became the new *qibla*, and a new structure covered with leaves supported on rows of palm tree trunks was erected there. Islam was given an axis of its own. Henceforth, the orientation of this first mosque would be followed by all mosques throughout the Islamic world, forming an immense concentric crown around Mecca.

A niche in the wall of the *qibla* marked the precise direction for prayer: this was the *mihrab*. Next to it was a pulpit shaped like a straight staircase, the *minbar*, from the top of which the preacher addressed the faithful. Many studies have attempted to establish the origin of these two elements, but their conclusions have been contradictory.

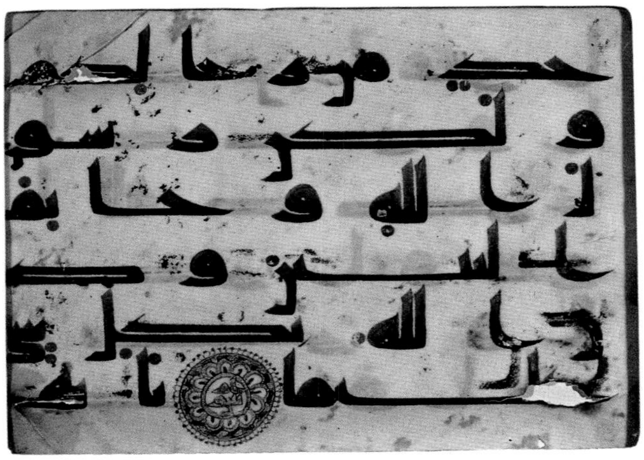

PRECEDENTS AND ISLAMIC LAW

That first mosque in Medina did not spring fully formed out of nothing: it grew out of a particular historical context, and reflected various influences of which the sources need to be considered. Its characteristics are: a hypostyle hall, whose roof is supported by columns or piers; and an oblong space wider than it is deep, of which the end wall is the *qibla*, which has an emblematic niche, the *mihrab*. Within this space, the faithful position themselves in transverse rows. The *mihrab* is accompanied by the preacher's pulpit, or *minbar*. In front of the prayer hall is a courtyard surrounded by porticoes. Later the group came to include a tower, or minaret, from the top of which the muezzin called the faithful to prayer.

Most of these elements were already in existence when the Prophet founded the first mosque in his house. The temple of Huqqa in southern Arabia, dating from the 2nd century BCE and attributed to the ancient Himyarites, long before the advent of Islam, has a transverse oblong hall preceded by a square courtyard surrounded by porticoes. The second synagogue of Dura Europus, on the Euphrates, in the middle of the Syrian desert, dating from the 3rd century CE, has an interesting plan: at the end of a small courtyard, surrounded on three sides by masonry columns, is a transverse oblong prayer hall (measuring 13 x 8 metres); and in that is a niche framed by two small engaged columns without capitals; covered by an apse decorated with a large shell. This niche clearly anticipates the first *mihrab*; and it is flanked on the right by some steps that suggest a *minbar*. And finally, the Christian churches of Syria and Palestine also have an apse, often framed by small columns, and sometimes a tower from which the call to prayer is sounded by blows on wooden beams, the ancestors of bells.

The first mosque thus fits into a coherent pre-existing pattern. And while the *mihrab* suggests the apse of a church, that apse itself derives from the canopied niche that held the image of the deified ruler in a secular Roman basilica. But the *mihrab* contains neither a statue – for the second Commandment, against the making of images, is strictly obeyed in Islam – nor an abstract symbol like the tabernacle that holds the Eucharist in a Christian church. The *mihrab* may perhaps have been intended to suggest the presence of the Prophet; but what it suggests most of all is a door opening onto the beyond, to the world of the divine, giving a physical image of the direction of prayer.

The Qur'an, completed by the *hadith*, is the basic text of the third revealed religion. It provides a complete system of law, both divine and human, which includes both ritual instructions concerning prayer and legal, cosmological and eschatological prescriptions. Fundamentally, Islamic law – the Divine Law, or *sharia* – which regulates man's behaviour 'makes no distinction between spiritual and temporal, between sacred and profane' (S. H. Nasr). Islam is a strictly monotheistic religion which exalts unity, in particular the unity of the divine principle ("There is no god but God'). And just as God is one, so Nature is one. Thus in Islamic countries the Law regulates all conduct – religious, social, political and economic. The Qur'an contains both a doctrinal message and instructions for living; further, it is a work concerned with history and cosmology, a metaphysical exposition, and a lesson in eschatology. It is concerned both with the past and with humanity's ultimate future. Since the Law provides norms for human behaviour, the Qur'an regulates prayer, ritual, purificatory gestures and fasts, as well as pilgrimage and *jihad*. In the *suras* Muhammad brought a

opposite, above One of the helpers building the first mosque in Medina.

opposite, below Muhammad, after his flight from Mecca in 622, directs the building of the first mosque in the Islamic world in his own house in Medina. The Prophet is shown on the right, veiled and with a halo of fire. From a manuscript of the *Siyer-i Nebi*, late 16th century. (The New York Public Library, New York)

below The Archangel Gabriel guiding the Prophet Muhammad in heaven. In this 16th-century Persian miniature Muhammad is shown in the sky on his mount Buraq – half-mare and half-woman – surrounded by angels, in an extraordinary depiction of mystical exaltation. (British Library, London)

message to his people that endowed the faithful with a quasi-irresistible faith and dynamism. Out of a few Arab tribes, hitherto absorbed in anarchic internal squabbles, the Prophet forged the spearhead of a movement of conquest which in the course of a single century was to create one of the greatest empires humanity has ever known.

The Sasanians and Byzantines were exhausted after their repeated clashes, and this explains how they could be defeated by a swarm of Arab horsemen, moved by a new faith. The energy devoted to tribal warfare was now channelled into wars of conquest. The expansion began with Abu Bakr – one of the Prophet's nine fathers-in-law – who was caliph from 632 to 634, and continued with Omar, his successor from 634 to 644. Palestine and Syria were wrenched from the Byzantines, then the army of Heraclius was defeated on the Yarmuk in 636. Jerusalem and Damascus initially escaped because the Arabs had no siege weapons, but fell in 638. The capture of the Holy City was a decisive moment: according to the Qur'an, it was from the Temple Mount that the Prophet made his famous nocturnal ascent to heaven astride his mythical steed Buraq, half mare and half woman, and was granted a vision of the face of Allah.

The Islamic forces had begun by launching an assault on the Sasanian Empire: they crossed the Euphrates in 635 and, after the battle of al-Qadisiyya, sacked Ctesiphon in 637. The last Persian ruler, Yazdigird, took refuge in Merv, and was assassinated there in 651. In Mesopotamia, the Arabs founded the cities of Basra and Kufa. With the victory of Nahavand in 642 the plateaux of Iran were open to them, and from there they continued east as far as Khorasan and Afghanistan, where they took Kabul and Kandahar, and finally reached Seistan, on the border of India, in 654.

Their triumphant progress westward took place at the same time, and encountered little resistance. In 640, Egypt was conquered by 'Amr ibn al-'As, who founded Fustat on the site where Cairo later grew up. A Byzantine counter-offensive ended in defeat in 642 with the sacking of Alexandria. Further west still, Arab forces reached Tripolitania and launched raids on Barbary in 647.

This moment saw the establishment of the first Arab 'empire', with its capital at Medina and the Caliph 'Uthman (644–656) as its ruler. The victors then split up into a number of factions, and 'Uthman was assassinated. He was succeeded by the leader of the opposition – Ali, the Prophet's son-in-law and cousin. 'Aishah, the widow of Muhammad, allied herself with the party of Mu'awiya, who had fled Medina and eventually settled in Damascus as its governor. In 656 Ali was forced to wage war against Mu'awiya, but arms failed to settle the conflict between the two, each of whom was convinced that he was the legitimate caliph. Ali was assassinated outside the door of the mosque at Kufa in 661. Further conquest ceased during these troubles.

The Arab Empire under the Umayyads

Mu'awiya (660–680) succeeded in getting himself recognized as the legitimate caliph by the 'community' and founded the Umayyad dynasty, which lasted from 660 to 750. Most importantly, his title was recognized by Ali's heirs, Hasan and Husayn. Soon afterward, however, in 671, this harmony was shattered, and Mu'awiya was forced to confront the claims of the Alids to legitimacy. His response was a public curse on Ali. Husayn was killed at Kerbala in 680; for some of the faithful, his death as a martyr strengthened their determination to see the Prophet's family as the sole source of legitimacy.

From 680 to 683, Mu'awiya's son Yazid I, who succeeded his father as caliph, reigned in Damascus, where he developed a court based on the Byzantine model. His authority was threatened by the presence of an 'anti-caliph' in Mecca, in the person of 'Abd Allah ibn az-Zubayr: he sent troops to besiege the city, but its inhabitants received support from tribes opposed to the dynastic principle, and Mecca held out until 693. In the meantime, the brief reign of Marwan I (683–685) was followed by that of 'Abd al-Malik (685–705). He restored order to the empire, and placed the administration, which had been under the control of an elite of Byzantine origin, in Arab hands. His reign saw the construction of the first great Umayyad building in Jerusalem, the Dome of the Rock (687–692), which we shall consider in detail later.

In 705, the Caliph al-Walid I, 'Abd al-Malik's son, demonstrated the grandeur and artistic vision of the time by building the splendid Great Mosque of the Umayyads in Damascus (706–715). Muslim power was now demonstrating its ability to create masterpieces comparable to those of Graeco-Roman antiquity and the Byzantine world. Arab expansion resumed under the Umayyads, and went on to reach its greatest extent. In 705 Samarkand and Bukhara became the seats of Arab governorships. Islamic troops penetrated Chinese Turkestan, and to the southeast they invaded the Indus delta and entered Multan. In 751, they defeated the Chinese at Talas, on the Syr Darya (Jaxartes).

At the other end of the empire, the Arabs gained a toehold in Spain, after having conquered Barbary: in 711 Tariq disembarked at Gibraltar, and by 714 the entire country was subdued. Raids pushed into Gaul, where the Arab armies took Narbonne and advanced as far as Carcassonne; following the Rhone Valley, they reached Burgundy. They were not stopped until 732, when their army, under the command of a prefect of Spain, the Emir 'Abd ar-Rahman, was defeated by the forces of Charles Martel at Poitiers.

Byzantium was now the only major adversary still capable of resisting the Muslim advance, and the Umayyads made a new attempt to attack Constantinople in 717–718; but though the Caliph Suleyman had a fleet of more than a thousand ships under the command of a son of 'Abd al-Malik, he was forced to abandon his plan. Suleyman and Omar II both reigned only two years, but after them unrest came to an end with the reign of Hisham, fourth son of 'Abd al-Malik, who held power for twenty years (724–743). His policies were well-advised, and he enforced the payment of taxes needed to maintain the army. Khalid, governor of the eastern provinces, stimulated great development in his region, but his wise rule came to an end when rumours led to him being arraigned in court. During the caliphate of Yazid III, beginning in 744, the Umayyad Empire was shaken by revolts in the east which ultimately led to the fall of the dynasty. It was replaced by the 'Abbasids in 750.

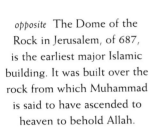

opposite The Dome of the Rock in Jerusalem, of 687, is the earliest major Islamic building. It was built over the rock from which Muhammad is said to have ascended to heaven to behold Allah.

right Looking across the prayer hall in the Umayyad Great Mosque in Damascus, begun in 707 by 'Abd al-Malik on the site of the Christian basilica of St John the Baptist, which had itself replaced the Temple of Jupiter in the 4th century.

UMAYYAD ARCHITECTURE

It will be useful to pause here in our historical overview and consider the architectural flowering that took place under the Umayyads, since it was to influence subsequent development. The Arabs emerged from the desert in the mid-7th century with no architectural tradition comparable to that of their Byzantine and Sasanian neighbours. Their only buildings were crude structures of mud brick or earth, sometimes incorporating rough stone. Floors were made of palm tree trunks, and palm leaves might be used instead of flat roofs.

In the lands that they occupied during the first century of their conquest of the ancient world, the Arabs discovered an art and a technique of construction which they took up and exploited, especially with the help of native architects drafted into their service . A prodigious amount of building activity had taken place throughout the Romano-Byzantine Empire – one need only think of Baalbek, Palmyra and Gerash in the Near East, and Alexandria, Leptis Magna and Sabratha in North Africa. There were hundreds of ancient buildings, some adapted for Christian worship, for the Arab conquerors to admire. Byzantine architecture had reached its high point in 532, a century before the Hegira, with the construction of the great basilica of Santa Sofia in Constantinople; Muslim armies did not see that until 1453, but they could see many other churches, such as that of St Catherine on Mount Sinai, of 548, and other buildings erected in the brilliant reign of Justinian.

Earlier buildings known to the Muslims are the Church of the Nativity in Bethlehem and the Holy Sepulchre in Jerusalem, dating from the time of Constantine (335), the late 5th-century church of St Simeon at Qal'at as-Sim'an, and other Christian architecture of northern Syria.

The ancient buildings were of the most varied types: there were basilican halls with several aisles covered by timber roofs or vaults, centrally planned buildings covered by domes, churches, forums, thermal baths, nymphaea, theatres, circuses, markets, cryptoporticus and mausoleums, all expressions of the brilliant art of the late antique and early Christian worlds. Everywhere, wide paved streets, colonnades, aqueducts, statues and mosaics were evidence of a luxurious and grand style of urban life.

The Dome of the Rock in Jerusalem

below View within the double ambulatory, where pilgrims could perform the rite of circumambulation The style is that of Imperial Byzantine architecture, with re-used ancient columns of coloured marble, gilded capitals, and mosaics.

opposite The octagonal building is crowned by a cupola (originally made of wood) covered with gilded sheets of copper. The blue tile decoration above the high marble dado dates from the Ottoman period.

THE DOME OF THE ROCK IN JERUSALEM

Islam's earliest religious structures, apart from the rough enclosures that constituted the first mosques during the period of expansion, were built under the Umayyads, and inspired by the technical and aesthetic legacy of late antiquity and early Christianity. Among these creations is a major work which fortunately has survived unaltered to the present day, and which shows the magnificence that Umayyad architecture had achieved at such an early date. The Dome of the Rock in Jerusalem was commissioned by the Caliph 'Abd al-Malik and begun in 687 on the Temple Mount. It is neither a mosque nor a mausoleum, but a commemorative building, honouring the holy rock from which, according to the brief mention of the Prophet's nocturnal voyage in the Qur'an, Muhammad ascended to heaven. He had come from Mecca borne across the skies on the back of the legendary Buraq all the way to Jerusalem, and then rose, guided by the Archangel Gabriel, up to the throne of God, where he contemplated the majesty of Allah.

In Jerusalem, as in Mecca with the Black Stone of the Ka'ba, it is a rock that is the object of veneration. The Dome of the Rock was built when the 'anti-caliph' 'Abd Allah ibn az-Zubayr had seized power in Mecca, and pilgrimage to the Black Stone was interrupted by the siege of the city by troops from Damascus. 'Abd al-Malik determined to make Jerusalem as important a place of pilgrimage as Mecca, and employed Byzantine architects in his service to construct a memorial in the form of a centrally planned building on the model of a Christian martyrium intended for the worship of relics. Its plan suited the ancient ritual of circumambulation, which was a practice known in Christianity as well as in Islam.

Outside, the building appears as an octagon with four axial entrances. Inside, two concentric colonnades articulate the space around the holy rock: the outer one is octagonal, with triple arcades between the eight corner piers; the inner one is circular, with arcades grouped in fours between four piers placed on the diagonals of the building. A dome rises in the centre, raised on a drum with sixteen openings for illumination. In this double-ring structure, covered by flat ceilings, the faithful circle the sacred rock as they circle the Ka'ba in Mecca, although there they do it in the open air.

The whole building is conceived in the Byzantine style, with mosaic decorations of leaves and vine scrolls on a gold background, a tall external plinth faced in marble with geometrical motifs, antique monolithic columns made of various precious marbles resting on cubic bases, Corinthian capitals crowned with impost blocks, and carved lintels.

The dome, 22 metres in diameter, is built of wood on the principle of two shells set one into the other, like that which must have surmounted the octagon of St Simeon at Qal'at as-Sim'an in Syria. Its slightly bulbous curve was covered with sheets of copper gilded with pure gold. In the richness of its mosaic decorations, the Dome of the Rock can compete with the best Byzantine schemes. Thus the earliest Islamic building, while following in the tradition of such Christian structures as the octagon of St Simeon and that of St Philip at Hierapolis, was a dazzling success. It provided the faithful with a jewel-like setting for their devotions.

The Caliph al-Walid then determined to complete the site and to provide a true mosque. At the southern boundary of the Haram ash-Sharif (the *temenos* of the Temple built by Herod the Great and destroyed by Titus), on the north-south axis of the rotunda and thus oriented towards the Ka'ba, in 705–709 he built the al-Aqsa Mosque. This has been much altered, but it retains its original T plan with seven aisles perpendicular to the *qibla*. The *mihrab* is preceded by a dome placed over a crossing, of which the main (south-facing) arch and the squinches have mosaics in Byzantine style.

At the same time, in Medina, al-Walid replaced the first mosque in the courtyard of the house of the Prophet by a vast new building four times larger than the old. Hypostyle spaces surround an almost square courtyard, bordered with porticoes; there were now 233 columns and a *qibla* 100 metres wide.

left The central element of the Great Mosque. The façade is crowned by a classical pediment and covered with sumptuous gold-ground mosaic. The imagery includes palaces under luxuriant trees, as in the mosaics around the courtyard (ill. pp. 296, 297).

THE GREAT MOSQUE OF THE UMAYYADS IN DAMASCUS

The Caliph al-Walid reserved the most important sacred building of his reign for his capital, Damascus. The Damascus mosque long constituted the prototype for mosques throughout classical Islam, so it is important for us to look at the circumstances of its construction. It was built on the *temenos* of an early 2nd-century Roman temple dedicated to the Damascene Jupiter (the Syrian god Hadad), which stood in the middle of the ancient city on a site that measured 175 x 100 metres, and was oriented east-west, with the main entrance facing the rising sun. We know little about this great temple beyond the fact that it was remarkably large (probably similar to the Temple of Bacchus at Baalbek), and that it was demolished around 390, in the reign of Theodosius, to make way for a Byzantine basilica dedicated to St John the Baptist.

As was common practice at the time, the Christians re-used the columns of the peristyle of the Temple of Jupiter – in all some forty shafts, with their fine Corinthian capitals. The venerable basilica of St John was in use for two and a half centuries. When the Arabs captured Damascus in 636, they at first coexisted with the Christians, and shared the ancient *temenos* with them, each religion praying in its own way. Around 664, however, the Muslims, who had made Damascus the capital of the Umayyad Empire, demanded exclusive use of the entire ancient site. The Arab chroniclers of al-Walid's reign are unanimous in recording that he demolished the basilica of St John the Baptist to build his mosque.

The building that we see today (which has undergone radical restoration, especially after a disastrous fire in 1893) presents a surprising arrangement. The prayer hall is not in the centre of the site, as were the Roman temple and, later, the Byzantine basilica: instead, it is shifted to the south, pressing up against the entire southern boundary; and this southern wall is that of the *qibla*. The direction of Mecca required that the building's orientation be shifted by 90 degrees compared with that of both the Roman temple and the Byzantine basilica. The prayer hall covers an area of 136 x 38 metres. A short axial nave emphasizes the presence of the principal *mihrab*; on either side, two wings of 56 metres each are divided transversely into three bays by two rows of columns supporting arches. Above these transverse colonnades (of 10 shafts each) is a row of smaller arches on colonnettes. Covering the structure is an open timber roof.

Faced with this shallow space, which extends entirely in width, one cannot help seeing the two arcades as if they

right, above In the courtyard, eight re-used antique columns support an octagonal aedicule that served as a treasury under the Umayyads. Its walls are covered by rich ornamental motifs in gold-ground mosaic.

right, centre The three transverse arcades of the prayer hall: two levels of arches – two in the upper tier for each single arch below – resting on tall granite columns support an open timber ceiling.

right, below Detail of the mosaics on the façade. The subject is a triumphal arch or city gate, with a vault seen in sharp perspective.

were separating a very long central nave from two flanking aisles, as in a church with a non-projecting transept. Closer examination shows that all the components – columns, capitals and arcades – are Romano-Byzantine in style. The character of the Great Mosque of Damascus is explained by a wholesale re-use of materials: the Temple of Jupiter had been dismantled to build the basilica of St John; then the Byzantine basilica, which probably had a nave and double aisles, was dismantled by al-Walid's craftsmen, and the beautiful Roman columns and great Byzantine arches were re-assembled in the new arrangement. The space now extended laterally, rather than longitudinally; it conformed to the new orientation towards the Ka'ba, but it also had a distinctive new character that was long to be felt in classical Islamic art.

The courtyard that precedes the prayer hall is enclosed on three sides by high walls lined with arcades. Marvellous mosaics in Byzantine style show landscapes with luxuriant green trees and columned pavilions reflected in the flowing waters of paradisiacal rivers.

Further evidence of Umayyads' respect for the past appears in an aedicule in the left-hand range of the Great Mosque: this is said to contain a holy relic, the head of St John (Yahya in Arabic), still venerated today.

From Umayyads to 'Abbasids

The Umayyad caliphs sought the pleasure of shady countryside, water, and estates where the desert was made to bloom – witness the mosaics of the Great Mosque. In the 8th century they built splendid palaces in the centre of vast agricultural estates, and used the surrounding land for hunting. The remains of these palaces, such as Qasr 'Amra, Qasr al-Kharana, Khirbat al-Mafjar and Mshatta, show the extent to which Umayyad art was influenced by the techniques and forms of imperial Rome. They are built around courtyards, are often square like a Roman fort, and have vaulted or domed rooms, nymphaea and pools, providing a setting for luxurious living. These walled complexes recall the Roman *limes* and give an austere impression; but one soon realizes that their towers and wall-walks are make-believe, and their fortifications symbolic: Arab power was such that there were no enemies to fear.

The same disposition is found in the small Umayyad city of Anjar, on the edge of the Biqa' valley in Lebanon. Built in 714, it follows the Roman formula of the *urbs quadrata*, with two main streets meeting at right angles corresponding to the ancient *cardo* and *decumanus*, and enclosed within curtain walls reinforced by semicircular towers. The grid plan of the streets, lined with porticoes and shops, governs the orthogonal disposition of the houses and public buildings.

Just as they had taken up their predecessors' building techniques, using arches, vaults and domes in their mosques and palaces, so the Arabs made Greek and Roman thought their own. What is most astonishing about the development of Arab civilization in the Umayyad period is the rapidity with which the Muslims, so soon after leaving the Arabian peninsula and giving up inter-tribal fighting, adapted to the high culture of the Romano-Byzantine world. The process of acculturation took only one or two generations. Guided by the elite among the conquered people, the victors quickly assimilated the knowledge, literature, philosophy, and also the highly developed scientific and technical thought of late Antiquity, steeping themselves in it all and making their own contributions. Starting from the texts of Ptolemy and Galen, Arab scholars pushed physics, mathematics, astronomy, geography and medicine beyond the knowledge of the ancient world.

The ritual of the caliph's court was as formal and splendid as that of Byzantium, because it had assimilated the etiquette and customs of its predecessors. An entire new administration was set up that perpetuated the forms of government introduced under Justinian and Heraclius. Thus in all respects, not just in the field of architecture, the caliphate was marked by continuity. Eventually the Muslim world would affirm its own identity, chiefly through the contributions of the 'Abbasids from the mid-8th century onward.

It is difficult to summarize the chain of events that led to the replacement of the caliphs of Damascus by those of Baghdad when the 'Abbasids came to power, but the result was that the eastern part of the empire became more important, as the centre of power was shifted to the east. The martyrdom of Husayn had provoked a march of 'penitents' at Kufa in 685, which ended in the massacre of the protesters. A Shi'ite revolt led the authorities to appoint al-Hadjadj governor of the provinces of the old Sasanian empire and to concentrate Syrian troops at Wasit in Iraq.

In 700, the 'nobles' rose up against al-Hadjadj, and at the same time an egalitarian movement known as the Kharijis began to spread in Iran and Iraq. In 716 an impulse favouring the 'Abbasids, as supporters of the line of imams of the Prophet's family, began to gain ground. In 736 it took root in Khorasan, in eastern Iraq, between Nishapur and Balkh. Then followed the revolt of Zayd, an Alid (adherent of the cause of Ali), at Kufa in 740, and from then on events accelerated: Abu Salama took the lead of the pro-'Abbasid movement in 744, and Abu Muslim, military chief of Khorasan, proclaimed himself 'Commander for the Family'. In 747, Khorasan rebelled and declared its faith in

the 'Imam to come'. The revolt spread to Kufa, where Abu al-'Abbas, later known as as-Saffah, was appointed caliph. At the Battle of the Great Zab River, Marwan II – who had moved to Harran in Mesopotamia to be closer to the centre of operations – met his death, and in Damascus the other Umayyads were massacred. The only one to escape, 'Abd ar-Rahman, from 755 ruled the independent emirate of al-Andalus in Spain, which in 929 became the Umayyad caliphate of Cordoba.

An Umayyad mosaic from the throne room in the palace of Khirbat al-Mafjar, made in the first quarter of the 8th century in an 'antique' style. The scene shows a lion hunting a gazelle under a large tree with thick leaves, loaded with fruit.

THE 'ABBASIDS

The second Arab dynasty, the 'Abbasids, ruled over an empire centered on Mesopotamia. They took their name from their founder, Abu al-'Abbas, who was descended from one of Muhammad's uncles. Their accession was helped by support from the Alids and by the actions of Abu Muslim in Khorasan. Abu al-'Abbas had himself proclaimed caliph in Kufa; after the assassination of the Umayyads he became known as as-Saffah, 'the Bloodthirsty'. Henceforth Western influence, based on Romano-Byzantine sources, gave way before new ideas derived from Sasanian Iran. The Sasanian capital was Ctesiphon, near Baghdad in Iraq, where the remains of the magnificent 36-metre-high brick *iwan* of the king's throne room survive (ill. p. 298). Iran had been humiliated by the Muslim victory, followed by the Arab occupation: it gradually regained its importance in the 'Abbasid Empire.

The territorial holdings of the 'Abbasids did not have the unity of the Umayyad Empire. 'Abbasid preeminence endured in theory for half a millennium, but only the first two centuries, from 750 to 932, were the age of the Great 'Abbasids, and after that the empire began a long process of retrenchment. Spain had broken away from the old empire when 'Abd ar-Rahman I assumed power in Cordoba in 755; then Ifriqiyah, under the Aghlabids of Qairawan, proclaimed its independence around the year 800; around 820–830 the Tahirids of Khorasan broke away, followed in 867 by the Saffarids of Iran, and in 868 by the Tulunids of Egypt. Finally the Buyid emirs, of Persian origin, effectively seized power in Baghdad, and held the caliphate in guardianship from 932 to 1055, reviving Sasanian court protocol and customs. The situation was further complicated by the presence of a Turkish 'praetorian guard', which was a constant source of tension in the palace and whose authority grew beyond all bounds. The Turks took over from the troops of Khorasan and proclaimed their Sunnite faith, leading to serious incidents between the Arab and Persian communities.

In the Mesopotamian plain, the 'Abbasid period was a time of high culture based on two capitals: the Round City of Baghdad, founded by al-Mansur (754–775), and the immense agglomeration of Samarra, begun in 836 by al-Mu'tasim. The 'Abbasids presided over a magnificent period: all the arts, learning, power and glory of the Islamic world converged on these great cities, which had populations of more than half a million at a time when Paris had fewer than 30,000 inhabitants.

Ephemeral Magnificence: The Architecture of the 'Abbasids

Heirs to Sasanian knowledge and techniques, the 'Abbasid caliphs promoted a civilization whose splendour is attested to by its architecture, despite the loss of hundreds of buildings erected too quickly and often in perishable materials. Outstanding is the immense fortified palace of Ukhaidir, built in 778 in the tradition of the Umayyad palaces of the Palestinian desert, in the middle of the once-fertile Iraqi steppe, 120 kilometres southeast of Baghdad. 'Isa ibn Musa, nephew of the Caliph al-Mansur, ousted by Harun al-Rashid, feared for his life and retired to this vast fortress that covered an area of 635 x 531 metres. From this castle he ruled over a vast agricultural estate, which was then productive thanks to an irrigation system fed by the Tigris river. It was surrounded by a curtain wall with 72 semicircular towers, machicoulis and a wall-walk: at Ukhaidir the defenses were no longer merely for show.

Inside, within a second perimeter wall, the prince built the palace proper, measuring 112 x 82 metres. A vestibule covered with a pointed tunnel vault opens on to a central courtyard surrounded by identical apartments, each with its own small courtyard. Next to the main entrance is a little mosque with a courtyard, bordered on three sides by porticoes with vaults supported on brick columns.

Ukhaidir stands on the edge of the plain between the Tigris and Euphrates, where the local stone is poor: the palace is built of rubble set in clay mortar and, for the vaults and more elaborate structures, of fired brick covered with stucco. A good knowledge of statics is indicated by the use of pointed arches and a pointed tunnel vault to make up for the structural weakness of the building material.

The lack of good building materials is even more marked in the Mesopotamian plain. Here the complete absence of stone led to the use of mud brick or stucco for the main structure as well as for the decoration, reserving fired brick for more elaborate details and for load-bearing structures. Any stone had to be imported from the distant Zagros Mountains, so it was used very parsimoniously.

Fifteen years before Ukhaidir was built, in 762, the Caliph al-Mansur – 'the Victorious' – had founded the new 'Abbasid capital, Baghdad, or Medinet es-Salam ('the City of Peace'), on the left bank of the Tigris, upstream from the ancient Sasanian capital of Ctesiphon. It stood on a flood plain and was built entirely of cob or brick, so that within a few centuries nothing was left of it but its fame. Like the Sumerian and Babylonian settlements, al-Mansur's city literally melted away, as much from the river's flooding and winter rains as from the destruction wrought by conquerors. What it looked like, however, can be imagined thanks to the very precise descriptions given by Arab authors.

The originality of Baghdad lay in its plan: it was round. Measuring 2,600 metres across at its outermost edge, it was protected by three concentric walls: the first had 112 towers, while the second, preceded by a steep *glacis*, had strong fortified gates; the city itself was reached through four gates in the third wall, situated on the diagonals of the cardinal points. It had a radial plan: radiating streets divided it into 45 quarters of various sizes containing houses, markets, bazaars and shops. In the centre was a circular park, 1,500 metres in diameter, which contained the palace and mosque of the caliph; the palace buildings themselves were enclosed in a square of 200 x 200 metres. The Great Mosque of Baghdad had a plan with a courtyard and four *iwans*; above the *mihrab* was a large dome some 40 metres high, entirely clad in brick with a green glaze, the Prophet's colour. The size of these buildings – even if the Arab historians were exaggerating a little – indicates the builders' skill. The impressive remains of Ctesiphon were there as a challenge to the Islamic rulers, who could not rest until they had equalled or surpassed them.

The presence of the caliph's personal Turkish guard in the heart of the Round City led to frequent clashes with the inhabitants, and even to attempts to overthrow the government. As a solution, the Caliph al-Mu'tasim (833–842), al-Mansur's successor, decided to found Samarra, 150 kilometres further upstream along the Tigris. The new capital, which housed both the court and the administration, soon spread its grid plan out for 35 kilometres along the river, with immense palaces, mosques and gardens. Unlike Baghdad, Samarra has left remarkable remains, especially the two great mosques, among the largest in the Muslim world, which have curious spiral minarets that recall Babylonian ziggurats.

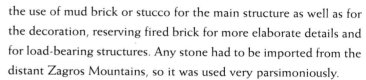

opposite An icon of 'Abbasid architecture: the 9th-century minaret of the Great Mosque at Samarra, known as al-Malawiya. Its spiral form was inspired by the ancient Babylonian ziggurats of Mesopotamia.

The Great Mosque of Samarra, built in 848–852 by the Caliph al-Mutawakkil (847–861), is an extraordinary creation. It is surrounded by high walls punctuated by 44 semicircular towers, on the model of a fortified palace or city, and measures 240 x 156 metres. Inside, the hypostyle hall and three porticoes surrounding the courtyard had a total of 216 octagonal pilasters supporting flat timber roofs. The perimeter wall survives and, to the north, the strange brick minaret known as al-Malawiya, with a solid core wrapped by a five-turn spiral ramp, 55 metres tall.

The idea is echoed in the district of Abu Dulaf, where another Great Mosque, built twelve years later, in 859, has a similar but slightly smaller minaret, and a perimeter wall measuring 213 x 135 metres. The prayer hall here has 17 7-bay aisles perpendicular to the *qibla*: instead of piers supporting flat roofs, these are composed of pointed arches made of fired brick, a significant architectural advance.

The palaces of Samarra reached a great size. With its parks and gardens, the Jawsaq al-Khaqani, constructed by al-Mu'tasim, covered an area of some 150 hectares along the Tigris with a symmetrical grid plan. All that survives is a monumental triple arcade of pointed arches, which stands by itself 1.5 kilometres away, in a field of ruins that can scarcely be made out except from an aeroplane.

The same principles, applied every more rigorously, appear in the immense complex of the Balkuwara palace, built in 850–860 by al-Mutawakkil, which has a surrounding wall with 160 towers. It is laid out within an enfilade of gardens in the Persian *chahar bagh* manner, in such a way as to require a progress of 300 metres before the throne room is reached. Beyond that, you emerge on a vast terrace overlooking the Tigris. The palace building has an unusual arrangement designed for court ritual, with the royal hall in the middle of a central cruciform structure, which has a dome buttressed by four *iwans*. It was sumptuously decorated: the walls were covered with carved and painted stucco and panelled with exotic wood, and further ornamented with frescoes, mirrors and marble – all plundered by the conquerors who subsequently occupied this famous capital of the Arab world.

Samarra is also the site of the first Islamic mausoleum, that of al-Muntasir, who died in 862. The Qubbat al-Sulaybiyya is octagonal, like the Dome of the Rock, and similarly lent itself to circumambulation around the central space. Islam in its early days had strongly egalitarian principles, but the caliph's mother (who was an Orthodox Christian) managed to bury her son in a commemorative monument, in the antique tradition. Later, both al-Mutazz (d. 869) and al-Muhtadi (d. 870) were buried in this 'pantheon' of caliphs, which became an archetypal model for much Islamic funerary architecture.

Samarra was an enormous city with splendid monuments, but it was abandoned after only fifty years. Under the Caliph al-Mu'tamid (870–892) the court returned to Baghdad, despite the inconvenience of the palace there. The city soon outgrew the narrow limits of the Round City, and began to extend along the north bank of the Tigris.

The 'Abbasid dynasty grew up on the foundations of Sasanian culture. The 'Persian' spirit had fed the art and architecture, institutions and administrative system of the rulers of ancient Iran, and it went on to inspire the 'Abbasid court at both Baghdad and Samarra. The pre-Islamic influence can be seen especially in the architectural motif of the *iwan*, which grew out of the great arch of Ctesiphon (there is also the *iwan*-like 6th-century 'grotto' of Takh-i Bostan). The courtyard with four *iwans*, that characteristic feature of Persian mosques, seems to go back to the cruciform hall of the palace of Bishapur, through the intermediary of the palace of Lashkari Bazar, built by Mahmud of Ghazna (998–1030).

Evidence thus shows that Persian architecture derives from the fired brick tradition of Ctesiphon, with the use on a grand scale of arches and vaults. And the parks and pools of 'Abbasid palaces follow the *chahar bagh* plan that goes back to Achaemenid and Hellenistic prototypes (an arrangement also found in Umayyad Andalusia, at Medinet az-Zahara).

From the 10th century onward, the Persian influence that had been detectable in the creations of the 'Abbasids became ever stronger, with the renaissance of Persian thought and culture that began at this time.

GLOSSARY

dikka Platform from which prayers are led in large mosques, to ensure that prostration is synchronized.

diwan Persian term that originally meant official registers, then came to mean administrative offices, and finally denoted the ruler's council and the structures in which this met. The *diwan-i amm* is the hall of public audience, the *diwan-i khass* the hall of private audience.

hadith The precepts of Muhammad, collected up to the 9th century. For Shi'ites, the *hadith* also includes the sayings of the twelve Imams.

haftrangi Literally 'seven colours'; a technique used in the decoration of ceramics.

hammam Public or private baths, based on the model of Roman baths.

haram Consecrated area; especially the area in a mosque in front of the *mihrab* where prayers are said.

Hegira The flight of Muhammad to Yathrib (Medina), from the date of which (16 July 622) the Islamic era is calculated.

Hurqalya One of the three cities of the next world mentioned by Persian Islamic mystics.

Husayn Son of Ali and Fatima. Assassinated in 680 in Kerbala, and venerated by Shi'ites as a direct descendant of the Prophet.

imam Literally, 'he who stands in front' during prayers. In general, an Islamic religious dignitary. For Shi'ites, an heir of the teaching of the Prophet.

Imamism Shi'ite school that regards the Imams and their descendants, the 'Imamzadeh', as spiritual guides.

Isma'ili Shi'ite sect venerating seven Imams, in the belief that the line ended with Isma'il. Also known as 'Sevener', by contrast with 'Twelver'. Associated with the Fatimids, who traced their descent from Fatima and ruled Egypt and north Africa 909–1171.

iwan Vaulted space, open at the front, usually facing a court or a square. A characteristic feature of Persian architecture popular from the time of the Seljuqs on.

jali Indian term for a pierced screen allowing air and light to pass, typically carved out of stone or marble. Similar screens elsewhere in the Islamic world may be made of stone, marble, wood, or even ceramic.

jami Arabic term denoting a communal meeting place for prayer, i.e. the Great Mosque or Friday Mosque.

jihad Arabic term signifying holy war against the infidel. According to the Qur'an, *jihad* is a religious duty on a par with prayer and pilgrimage to Mecca.

Ka'ba The most sacred site of Islam, in Mecca, containing the Black Stone. The sanctuary, believed to have been founded by Abraham, is the object of pilgrimage and ritual circumambulation.

kashi Contraction of 'kashani' (from Kashan, the Iranian city famous for the production of ceramics), denoting a polychrome tile used in Persian architecture.

Kharijites A strict and egalitarian sect formed by supporters of Ali who gathered round the caliph Mu'awiya in the 7th century.

kufic Stylized, angular form of Arabic writing, which originated in Kufa. It appeared in the 8th century in inscriptions and in manuscripts of the Qur'an.

madrasa Qur'anic school, diffused through the Islamic world by Sunni orthodoxy. Its typology is often confused with that of the four-*iwan* courtyard building. *Madrasas* were actively promoted by the Seljuq Turks, and came to be adopted by the Shi'ites.

Mahdi The 'hidden Imam' of the Shi'ites, who will reappear at the end of the world.

maidan Persian term denoting a large city square. It may be used for horse-racing, for playing polo, or for military parades.

mihrab Niche in the *qibla* (q.v.) in a mosque that indicates the direction of prayer, towards the Ka'ba in Mecca.

minaret Tall tower from which the muezzin calls the faithful to prayer.

minbar Pulpit at the top of a flight of steps in a mosque, from where the preacher speaks to the assembled congregation.

muezzin Man who calls the faithful to prayer. According to tradition, the first muezzin was a black companion of the Prophet, called Bilal.

mullah A judicial or religious functionary.

noria A Persian wheel: a large wooden wheel used to raise water to irrigate a field or garden. The water is raised in buckets, as the wheel is powered by paddles in the water. Oxen or camels may also be used to turn the wheel.

pilgrimage One of the duties of all practising Muslims is to visit Mecca at least once and to circumambulate the Ka'ba.

pishtaq Persian term for a large portal in the form of an *iwan* that leads into a mosque, a *madrasa* or a mausoleum.

qadi Islamic judge and lawyer, responsible for applying the Law in accordance with the Qur'an and tradition.

qasr Arabic term for a castle, a fort or a stronghold in the Syrian-Jordanian desert.

qibla Wall at the end of a mosque containing the *mihrab* niche. The *qibla* stands at right angles to the direction of Mecca.

Qur'an Text 'recited' by Muhammad to spread his teaching, consisting of 114 *suras*, compiled after his death. The Prophet's message is also contained in the *hadith*, written down by the 9th century. Together, Qur'an and *hadith* make up the *Sunna*, or tradition.

Sasanians Pre-Islamic dynasty in Iran who ruled 224–651 over an empire that stretched from Mesopotamia to the Indus.

Seljuqs Dynasty of sultans of Turkish origin and Sunni orthodoxy, who reigned over Iran and Iraq in the 11th and 12th centuries. A branch of the Seljuqs defeated the Byzantines in Anatolia at the battle of Manzikert (1071) and founded the Sultanate of Rum.

Sevener *see* Isma'ili

Shi'ism The smaller of the two great divisions of Islam, for whom religious legitimacy is based on descendance from the Prophet, in the tradition of Ali, Fatima and Husayn. It is distinct from the Sunni majority in rejecting the authority of the caliph.

Sunna Religious theory and practice based on the Qur'an and *hadith*; the foundation of Sunni orthodoxy.

Sunnism The larger of the two great divisions of Islam, committed to the legitimacy of the caliph. Its beliefs are based on the *Sunna*.

thuluth Refined, elegant cursive script with high ascenders.

tiraz Arabic term for an official weaving shop; a state manufactory producing the fine textiles used for court dress.

tuba Tree of Paradise or Tree of Life in Shi'ite mystical theology.

Twelver Denotes the Shi'ite sect venerating the twelve Imams (Ali and his descendants), seen as the repositories of Muslim doctrine and law. The twelfth Imam, the Mahdi or 'hidden Imam', will return at the end of time.

Umayyads First Islamic dynasty of Arab rulers, who reigned in Damascus, succeeding the caliphs of Medina. Founded by Mu'awiya in 660 and overthrown in 750 by the 'Abbasids in a bloody *coup d'état*.

vizir First minister in a Muslim monarchy, often the real holder of power.

SELECT BIBLIOGRAPHY

Archaeological Survey of India, Annual Reports, Calcutta/New Delhi, 1902–1938.

Ardalan, Nader, and Laleh Bakhtiar, *The Sense of Unity, The Sufi Tradition in Persian Architecture,* London/Chicago, 1973.

Arts de l'Asie centrale, gen. ed. Pierre Chuvin, Paris, 1999.

Ascher, Catherine B., *Architecture of Mughal India,* Cambridge, 1992.

Atasoy, Nurhan, Afif Bahnasi and Michael Rogers, *The Art of Islam,* Paris, 1990.

Bammate, H., *Apports des Musulmans à la Civilisation,* Geneva, 1962.

Babur, *Babur-nama. Memoirs of Babur,* trans. Annette Susannah Beveridge, 1922/repr. New Delhi, 1979

Bianca, Stefano, *Hofbau und Paradiesgarten, Architektur und Lebensformen in der Islamischen Welt,* Munich, 1991.

Brandenburg, Dietrich, *Der Taj Mahâl in Agra,* Berlin, 1969.

Brown, Percy, *Indian Architecture (Islamic Period),* Bombay, 1942.

Cahen, C., *L'Islam des origines au début de l'Empire ottoman,* in *Histoire universelle,* vol. 14, Paris, 1970.

*Cambridge History of India,*vol. 4, *The Mughal Period,* ed. Sir Richard Burn, Cambridge, 1937.

Cambridge History of Iran, vol. 6, *The Timurid and Safavid Periods,* ed. Peter Jackson, Cambridge, 1986.

——, vol.7, *From Nadir Shah to the Islamic Republic,* ed. Peter Avery, Gavin Hambly and Charles Melville, Cambridge, 1991.

Canfield, Robert l., ed., *Turko-Persian Historical Perspective,* Cambridge. 1991.

Corbin, Henry, *En Islam iranien,* Paris, 1971–73.

—— *Philosophie iranienne et philosophie comparée,* Paris,1985.

—— *Spiritual body and celestial earth. from Mazdean Iran to Shi'ite Iran,* trans. Nancy Pearson, Princeton, 1977.

Creswell, K. A. C., *Early Muslim Architecture,* Oxford, 1932–40.

Ecochard, M., *Filiation des monuments grecs, byzantins et islamiques,* Paris, 1977.

Ettinghausen, Richard, and Oleg Grabar, *The Art and Architecture of Islam, 650–1250,* Harmondsworth, 1987.

Fourniau, Vincent, ed., *Samarcande 1400–1500, La Cité-oasis de Tamerlan,* Paris, 1995.

Frishman, Martin, and Hasan-Uddin Khan, eds, *The Mosque,* London/New York, 1994

Gabriel, André, *Le Masjid-é Djuma,* Ars Islamica, Michigan, 1935.

Galdieri, E. *Isfahan, Masgid-i Gum'a,* Rome, 1972.

Godard, André, articles in *Athar-é Iran,* Tehran, 1936, 1937, 1949.

—— *The Art of Iran,* London, 1965.

Goldenstein, Youri, *Samarcande – Boukhara – Chakhrisabz – Khiva,* Courbevoie, 1995.

Golombek, Lisa, and Donald N. Wilber, *The Timurid Architecture of Iran and Turan,* Princeton, 1988.

Golvin, L., *Essai sur l'Architecture religieuse musulmane,* Paris, 1970–73.

Grabar, O., *Islamic Architecture and its Decoration A.D. 800–1500,* London, 1964.

Gray, Basil, *Persian Painting,* Geneva/London, 1961/1977.

Hattstein, Markus, and Peter Delius, eds, *Islam, Kunst und Architektur,* Cologne, 2000.

Herdeg, Klaus, *Formal Structure in Islamic Architecture of Iran and Turkistan,* New York, 1990.

Hillenbrand, Robert, *Islamic Art and Architecture,* London/New York, 1999

Koch, Ebba, *Mughal Architecture,* Munich, 1991.

Kuhnel, Ernst, *Islamische Schriftkunst,* Graz, 1972.

Lall, John, *Taj Mahal & The Glory of Mughal Agra,* New Delhi, 1982.

Magowan, Robin, *Fabled Cities of Central Asia. Samarkand, Bukhara, Khiva,* London, 1990.

Maisons d'Ispahan, ed. Darab Diba, Philippe Revault and Serge Santelli, preface by Henri Stierlin, Paris, 2001.

Melville, Charles, ed., *Safavid Persia, The History and Politics of an Islamic Society,* London/New York/Cambridge, 1996.

Michell, George, *The Royal Palaces of India,* London/New York, 1994.

——, ed., *Architecture of the Islamic World, Its History and Social Meaning,* London, 1978.

Mouliérac, Jeanne, *Céramiques du monde musulman,* Paris, 1999.

Nasr, Sayyed Hossein, *Islam, Perspectives et réalités,* Paris, 1975.

Neugebauer, Otto, *The Exact Sciences in Antiquity,* Copenhagen, 1951.

Okada, Amina, *The Taj Mahal,* photographs by J.-L. Nou, New York/London, 1993.

Pope, Arthur Upham, *Persian Architecture, The Triumph of Form and Colour, London/*New York 1965.

Sarre, Friedrich, *Denkmäler persischer Baukunst,* Berlin, 1910.

Schimmel, Annelise, *The Celestial Garden in Islam,* Washington, 1976.

Schlumberger, Daniel, *Le Palais ghaznévide de Lashkari Bazar,* in *Syria,* 1952.

Siraju-'l-Islam, Muhammad, *The Lodi Phase of Indo-Islamic Architecture,* thesis, Berlin, 1960.

Sohravardi, *Le Livre de la Sagesse orientale,* trans. Henry Corbin, 1986.

Sourdel-Thomine, D. and J., *La Civilisation de l'Islam classique,* Paris, 1968.

Soustiel, Jean, *La Céramique islamique,* Fribourg/Paris, 1985.

Stierlin, Henri, *Architecture de l'Islam, de l'Atlantique au Gange,* Fribourg, 1979.

—— *Inde, des Moghols aux Maharajas,* Paris, 1985.

—— *Iran des bâtisseurs,* Geneva, 1971.

——- *Islam, les origines, de Bagdad à Cordoue,* Cologne, 1996.

—— *Ispahan, Image du Paradis,* preface by Henry Corbin, Geneva/Paris, 1976.

—— *Le Monde arabe,* Paris/Geneva, 1981.

—— *Le Monde de la Perse,* Paris/Geneva, 1980.

Tadgell, Christopher, *The History of Architecture in India,* London, 1990.

Volwahsen, Andreas, *Living Architecture: Islamic Indian,* trans. Ann E. Keep, London, 1970.

Voyageurs arabes, trans. Paule Charles-Dominique, Paris, 1995.

Wetzel, Friedrich, *Islamische Grabbauten in Indien aus der Zeit der Soldatenkaiser – 1320–1540,* Leipzig, 1919.

Wilber, Donald N., *The Architecture of Islamic Iran: The Il-Khanid Period,* Princeton, 1955.

—— *Persian Gardens and Garden Pavilions,* Rutland, 1962

Würfel, Kurt, *Isfahan, das ist die Hälfte der Welt,* Zurich, 1974.

Zander, Giuseppe, *Travaux de restauration de Monuments historiques en Iran,* Rome, 1968.

INDEX

Page numbers in *italic* type refer to pages on which illustrations appear

ACKNOWLEDGMENTS FOR ILLUSTRATIONS

All photographs are by Henri and Annie Stierlin, with the following exceptions:

22 Giovanni Dagli Orti
23 Giovanni Dagli Orti
24 Barney Burstein/Corbis/Grazia Neri
40 *below* Fototeca Storica Nazionale
42 *above* Fototeca Storica Nazionale
42 *below* Annabal Mit
48 Fototeca Storica Nazionale
49 Fototeca Storica Nazionale
50 Roger Wood/Corbis/Grazia Neri
51 Roger Wood/Corbis/Grazia Neri
53 Photographic Service, Howard University Art Museum, President and Fellows of Howard College
54 *below* Ann & Bury Peerless
54–55 Ann & Bury Peerless
58 *above* Fototeca Storica Nazionale
58 *below* The Bridgeman Art Library
59 The Artarchive
60 The Bridgeman Library
61 The Bridgeman Library
72 *above* Barnabas Bosshart/Corbis/Grazia Neri
72 *below* AP Photo/Vahid Salemì
73 Thomas Abercrombie/National Geographic
81 Fundacao Calouste Gulbenkian, Museu
82 Georg Gester
85 *above left* Giovanni Dagli Orti
90 *above* Massimo Borchi/Archivio White Star
92–93 Ann & Bury Peerless
92 *left, centre* Aga Khan Visual Archives/Massachusetts Institute of Technology
92 *below* Aga Khan Visual Archives/Massachusetts Institute of Technology
100 The British Library
100–101 Massimo Borchi/Archivio White Star
103 Freer Gallery of Art & Arthur M. Sackler Gallery
106 *top* Massimo Borchi/Archivio White Star
106–7 Massimo Borchi/Archivio White Star
120 Bibliothèque Nationale de France, Paris
121 The British Library
122 *below* Archivio Scala
126 Giovanni Dagli Orti
127 Archivio Scala
134–35 *below* Archivio White Star
135 *top* Archivio White Star
135 *right* Archivio White Star
138–39 Archivio White Star
146–47 Archivio White Star
Technology 148 *below* Archivio White Star
149 Archivio White Star
151 Archivio White Star
152–53 *above* Archivio White Star
152–53 *below* Archivio White Star
168 *above* Flavio Pagani
170 *below* Massimo Borchi/Archivio White Star
171 *above* Massimo Borchi/Archivio White Star
171 *centre* Tibor Bognar
172 *centre* Thomas Dix
176 *above* Massimo Borchi/Archivio White Star
178 *below* Massimo Borchi/Archivio White Star
178–79 *below* Luciano Romano
181 Massimo Borchi/Archivio White Star
184–85 The Bridgeman Library
185 *above left* The Bridgeman Library
185 *above right* Victoria & Albert Picture Library
186–87 *below* Archivio White Star
200 *above right* Thomas Dix
201 Thomas Dix
204 *centre* Thomas Dix
204 *below* Tibor Bognar
204–5 Thomas Dix
206 *above* Thomas Dix
206 *below* Stockshooter/Marka
206–7 Flavio Pagani
215 *below* Archivio White Star
222 Massimo Borchi/Archivio White Star
223 *centre* Massimo Borchi/Archivio White Star
224 *above right* Thomas Dix
224 *below* Thomas Dix
226 *above* Massimo Borchi/Archivio White Star
226 *below* Massimo Borchi/Archivio White Star
228 Thomas Dix
229 Thomas Dix
229 *above* Massimo Borchi/Archivio White Star
240–41 Thomas Dix
244 *below* Massimo Borchi/Archivio White Star
244–45 Massimo Borchi/Archivio White Star
248 *above* Massimo Borchi/Archivio White Star
250 *above* Massimo Borchi/Archivio White Star
250 *centre* Massimo Borchi/Archivio White Star
250 *below* Massimo Borchi/Archivio White Star
250–51 Massimo Borchi/Archivio White Star
253 *above* Massimo Borchi/Archivio White Star
253 *centre* Massimo Borchi/Archivio White Star
253 *below* Massimo Borchi/Archivio White Star
262–63 Archivio White Star
264 *left* Archivio White Star
264 *right* Archivio White Star
264–65 *below* Archivio White Star
266–67 Archivio White Star
274 *above* Massimo Borchi/Archivio White Star
278 Archivio White Star
279 Archivio White Star
282 *above* Massimo Borchi/Archivio White Star
282 *centre* Massimo Borchi/Archivio White Star
285 *below* Massimo Borchi/Archivio White Star
287 Archivio White Star
288 *left* Archivio White Star
288–89 *below* Archivio White Star
302 Fototeca Storica Nazionale
303 Aisa
304 Marcello Bertinetti
309 *centre* Aisa
310–11 Archivio Scala

The drawings on pp. 112, 136, 230, 259 and 277 were supplied by Klaus W. Herdeg
Line drawings: Angelo Colombo/Archivio White Star
Map (pp. 14–15): Elisabetta Ferrero/Archivio White Star